MY MARQUETTE

Marquette Forever!

Tyler R. Tichelaar

MY MARQUETTE

Explore the Queen City of the North, Its History, People, and Places With Native Son

Tyler R. Tichelaar
Author of *The Marquette Trilogy*

My Marquette

Explore the Queen City of the North,
Its History, People, and Places
With Native Son
Tyler R. Tichelaar
Author of *The Marquette Trilogy*

Copyright 2011 Marquette Fiction

Marquette Fiction
1202 Pine Street
Marquette, MI 49855
www.MarquetteFiction.com

ISBN: 9780979179051

Print coordination:
Globe Printing, Inc. Ishpeming, MI
www.globeprinting.net

Interior layout & design: Larry Alexander
Cover Design: Victor Volkman
Front Cover photographs: Ann Gonyea and Sonny Longtine
Back cover photograph: Evelyn Bendick

To the Great-Aunts and Great-Uncles
Kit, Jack, Jolly, Vi, Barb, Sadie, Ione, and Frank
&
To All Those Who Love Marquette

"Wasn't I lucky to be born in my favorite city?"

— Tootie in the film *Meet Me in St. Louis* (1944)

TABLE OF CONTENTS

WHY I WROTE THIS BOOK

This book is written for the visitor who wants to know more about Marquette, for the longtime Marquette resident who loves its history, for people who want a tour guide as they walk around Marquette, for readers of my novels who want to know more about the people and places that inspired my characters and stories, and finally, to preserve some oral history and memories of myself and others before they are lost.

I first decided to write *My Marquette* for two reasons—because I have repeatedly been asked to give walking tours of Marquette to book clubs and other groups interested in the city's history and my novels, and because my readers constantly ask me about what parts of my novels are true and what parts fiction. The short answer is that all the events in my novels that affect the city at large are true, as are all the historical people listed in the front of each book, but all the main characters and their personal stories are fictional. To make the distinction clearer, I felt a book about Marquette, specifically a tour of different places around the city would be insightful to readers while allowing me to discuss how growing up and living in Marquette inspired me to write my novels. I hope that by sharing my personal connections to Marquette, its history and the people and places that have made it so well-loved for me, the reader will equally come to feel that special connection I have for my favorite city, The Queen City of the North.

Many books have already been written about Marquette, and I list several of them at the end of this book for further reference. *My Marquette* contains a great deal of history, but it is not intended to be a thorough or chronological history of Marquette. Nor is it a complete depiction of every important place in the city or a full source of biographical information for the city's important pioneers—to create such a book would have been overwhelming. Instead, I discussed "my" Marquette—the Marquette I grew up in and knew well, the stories that have inspired my writing, and the history that I think will entertain and inform my readers.

I have arranged the book by different areas of Marquette, which allows readers, if they so choose, to tour Marquette by car or on foot while reading the book. The maps at the beginning of each section of the book should assist in the process. I have included a few places outside of Marquette, notably Big Bay and the Huron Mountain Club, which are frequently mentioned in my novels, as well as the Crossroads where I actually grew up. I have also included genealogy charts of my family for easy reference as well as genealogy charts of many of Marquette's pioneer and prominent families, so readers can keep track of who's who since so many of Marquette's most distinguished families intermarried and were related in ways that can make a person's head spin. For those readers not familiar with my novels, I have included short descriptions of them at the back of this book, and on the genealogy charts, some of my family members are notated as being the inspiration for different characters in my novels. Finally, a complete Marquette timeline is included.

This book could easily have been three or four times as long, so I had to make difficult decisions about leaving out some things in the interest of space. I apologize for any serious oversights or errors. Marquette has far more history and places of interest than I could ever fully discuss. In some cases, I cover ground other authors have covered before; in other places I believe I have written the most extensive history to date, especially in relation to the historical residential section of Marquette. I hope this book will give the reader a greater appreciation of Marquette and inspire further exploration. I thank my readers for their many suggestions over the years to write a Marquette history book, and I hope this work will meet with their approval.

Tyler R. Tichelaar
Marquette, Michigan
August 31, 2010

ACKNOWLEDGMENTS

Writing a book like this one is far from a solitary experience and more difficult in its own way than a novel that does not require all the additional layout, photographs, and even research. I have many people to thank for their words of encouragement and support who said, "I'd like to read that book" when I discussed my ideas with them. They are too numerous to thank individually, but I appreciate all their ideas. I equally thank all the readers of my previous novels whose constant questions about the true stories behind my novels made me think such a book would be enjoyable. Among those who most deserve thanks are:

Lee Laforge, manager of Book World, who first told me I should write a history of Marquette.

The many past writers and historians of Marquette, most notably, Fred Rydholm, whose *Superior Heartland* kept me up late at night reading with fascination as I researched my novels, and Sonny Longtine, not only the co-author of the marvelous *Marquette Then & Now* but also my neighbor who generously shared his photographs, many of which are included in this book and on the cover, as well as his suggestions with me.

Larry Alexander, the designer and layout person for this book. We have been friends since graduate school at Northern Michigan University. Not only has he put up with me all this time, but he has designed my websites and come to my aid in computer crises. I appreciate his patience as I continually asked to change where a picture was located or the way a page looked.

Ann Gonyea for the cover photography and getting the right angle for a picture.

John and Nancy Grossman at Back Channel Press have managed the printing and layout of all my previous books, and they were more than understanding and willing to answer my many questions as I embarked on writing a new kind of book.

Victor Volkman did a superb job in designing the cover for me and offering additional advice on layout to make the pages more easily readable.

Rosemary Michelin, librarian of the John M. Longyear Research Library at the Marquette County History Museum, not only tirelessly pulled files for me but led me to some new directions I would not otherwise have considered. Thanks also to assistance from Meridith Ruppert and Jennifer Lammi at the Museum. Thank you to Jim Koski for information about South Marquette during an informative walking tour. The Marquette County History Museum is also thanked for its permission to use many of the photographs in this book.

Jack Deo of Superior View also provided me with numerous photographs of Marquette, past and present, as well as the cover photos for most of my previous novels.

Debbie Glade, for reading drafts of different sections of this book and offering encouraging words.

My second cousin, Nanette Rushton, who provided her memories of life on Ridge Street and of the Rankin family and read early drafts of the residential section.

Lynn and Lon Emerick, fellow writers who have become like family over the years. I so appreciate their sharing their memories of Dorothy Maywood Bird with me, and all their advice over the years on publishing books.

Fred Stonehouse, the expert on all things maritime, who helped me sort out the Frink family's roles as lighthouse keepers along Lake Superior.

Holly Barra and Jim Mansfield, descendants of Marquette architect Hampson Gregory, for sharing information about their ancestor.

Emily Betinis, for sharing information about the Reverend Bates Burt family.

Anne Outhwaite Maurer and James Pickands Cass for their information about their Outhwaite and Pickands ancestors.

John Frederickson, great-grandson of Carroll Watson Rankin, for his memories of the family.

Pat Ryan O'Day for her many stories of Marquette's past and for putting me in touch with people who would have information I needed.

Babette Welch and her husband Gregg Seiple, who own the Swineford Home at 424 Cedar Street, for allowing me to see the inside of that Marquette landmark.

Dennis McCowen, owner of the Merritt Home, for giving me a tour inside, including allowing me to go up in its tower on a blizzardy spring day.

Lorana Jinkerson for sharing information on her underground home.

Rachel Goldsmith for information and a photo of her father, David Goldsmith.

Joyce L. Mayer, director of the Moss Mansion in Montana, for sharing the history of that Lake Superior Sandstone home.

Many thanks to everyone over the years who has made me more aware of my family's history, including my late cousins, Jerry McCombie, Jean Martel, and Robert Bishop. Thank you to my great-aunt, Sadie White Johnson Merchant, who was always willing to share family stories, and saved the day by having a photo of the Bavarian Inn when no others could be found. A special thanks to my late grandfather, Lester White, whose stories of his childhood first made me interested in Marquette's past. Thank you to my cousin, Lynn Hiti, who has sent me numerous files and documents and shared genealogy discoveries with me for many, many years, especially about the Bishop family, and to my cousins, Shirley Herbert and her son Paul who provided me with our Civil War ancestors' military records. Thank you to cousins Ben and Pat Hassenger for their information on our Zryd ancestors. Also to my distant cousin Kori Carothers, who sent me information about her ancestor Francis Marion Bishop. And thank you, especially, to my mother who allowed me to raid the family photograph albums for memorable moments captured on film. I have been in touch with so many relatives over the years who have given me information that if I forget any of their names here, know that your contributions have been greatly appreciated.

Finally, thank you to all of my readers who have been integral to my fulfilling my dream since childhood to write books people would love to read and which would help make their lives happier.

WHY I WRITE ABOUT MARQUETTE

Where do you come up with your ideas? What made you decide to write about Marquette? Ever since *Iron Pioneers* was first published, my readers continually ask me these questions.

My answer is that having been born and raised in Marquette, and being so encul-turated into the city's history and its people, as an author I simply cannot *not* write about it. The best advice a writer is given is "Write what you know" and if I know any place, it is my hometown, where I and generations of my ancestors have lived. I am unable to remember the first time I saw St. Peter's Cathedral, the Old Savings Bank, or Presque Isle Park. They have always been there, always been a part of my conscious world—always actively influenced my imagination.

My earliest memories include my grandfather telling me about Marquette's past, stories I never forgot that made me wonder what it was like to grow up in this town in the early twentieth century, when automobiles were still a novelty, long before television, in days when my grandpa would get a quarter to scrub the kitchen floor, and he would use that quarter to treat himself and a friend to a silent movie at the Delft Theatre and still have change left over for snacks.

Since I was eight years old, I knew I wanted to write stories, and growing up in a town where my family had lived so long, hearing story after story about the past, I wanted to write down those stories and make the past come alive for people. While in college, I became interested in family history. I learned then that the earliest branch of my family came to Marquette in 1849, the year the village was founded, and my family has lived in Marquette ever since. As I learned more about my ancestors and Marquette's history, I could not help but imagine what it would have been like for a person to come by schooner across Lake Superior in 1849, to see only a wilderness where a village was to be built, and what it was like after two decades of struggling to build that town, to see it destroyed by fire in 1868, only to spring up again, grander than before. And what of the winters? Feet and feet of snow, and no snowblowers or modern snowplows. What an amazing courage and determination the pioneers had to carry on each day in the nineteenth century. In my novels, I tried to recreate the early settlers' experiences so readers would understand and appreciate their cour-age and draw their own strength from the examples of those mighty pioneers.

The scene in *Iron Pioneers* that I feel best demonstrates *The Marquette Trilogy*'s themes of courage and survival is when Molly and Patrick talk about why they left Ireland to come to America. Their discussion reflects the tales of many immigrants who came to Marquette—some like Patrick to escape religious or political oppression—some like Molly, to avoid poverty and suffering. Molly's daughter, Kathy, after overhearing her mother relate how her ancestors had starved during the Irish potato famine, and knowing that others around the world are far from as fortunate as her, asks her future husband what the past and her ancestors should mean to her.

"How can we live in America, knowing that others are suffering?" Kathy asked.

"By appreciating our good fortune and being happy."

"Happy?" she asked, feeling it impossible after years of living under her stepfather's oppression, after the suffering her mother had known. She feared to be happy from fear it would not last.

"Yes, happy," said Patrick. "All those people who suffered would want us to be happy, to live and marry and have children who will not know such pain. We are the extensions of our parents and grandparents and all those brave people; we're a continuation of their spirits, and our happiness helps to validate their struggles, to give meaning to their lives."

He only understood this truth as he spoke it, as he suddenly believed the world could be a wonderful place; that everything could work out for the best. He felt like an old Celtic bard who foresaw a hopeful future capable of washing away past grief.

I wrote my trilogy as a tribute to those pioneers who built Marquette, and those like them in every community who built this nation despite the difficulties they faced. Whether a person has ever visited Marquette should not determine whether they find enjoyment or inspiration from the history of this fine city. The story of Marquette is the story of the American Dream, of dreams for a better future and the struggles to achieve that dream, the hopes and fears of countless American generations of immigrants seeking a better world, and how some achieved it, some failed, and some persevered without giving up. Based on the pioneers' examples, my novels have hopefully inspired readers with the courage to endure their own trials and overcome them. To give people that courage, and to hear how much my novels have resonated with them, has made the many lonely hours of writing all worthwhile.

In writing about Marquette, I knew I wanted to capture the magic of one particular place and allow readers to travel there and come to know it as well as I did. I have lived in Marquette all my life except six years when I foolishly thought I would find a better life elsewhere, only to feel exiled. While I was away, Marquette celebrated its sesquicentennial in 1999, and that same year, I, homesick, decided to write about its history.

I had written other novels, but never satisfied with them, I had left them unpublished. When I began writing *Iron Pioneers* and its sequels, although I knew the task would be monumental, I finally felt I had found my voice, the books I was actually born to write.

I wrote about the outdoors—the wild, thick forests, the temperate, green-leaved splendid summers of blueberry picking and daring to enter Lake Superior's cool waters, the roar of the winter wind, the blizzards that leave behind snowbanks that must be shoveled, and ultimately, the sense of peace one feels among so much natural beauty. I wrote about Marquette's history, for I could not imagine a more inspiring story than the American Dream played out in a quest to build an industrial empire along Lake Superior, of an iron discovery that produced more wealth than the California Gold Rush, of a mined product that helped to win major wars and change the world. And I wrote about the change and decline of that iron industry, how it affected the people who lived in Marquette, sometimes fulfilling, often destroying their dreams.

Mostly, however, I wrote about life in a small town, of the relationships between people in a community. Many people think small towns are quiet and dull because they lack the fast-paced lifestyle of metropolitan areas. But small towns have a greater and more personal drama. Willa Cather, author of *O Pioneers* and one of my greatest influences—my title *Iron Pioneers* is partly a tribute to her—best described the relationships in small towns in a passage I used as the front quote for *Narrow Lives*:

> *In little towns, lives roll along so close to one another; loves and hates beat about, their wings almost touching. On the sidewalks along which everybody comes and goes, you must, if you walk abroad at all, at some time pass within a few inches of the man who cheated and betrayed you, or the woman you desire more than anything else in the world. Her skirt brushes against you. You say good-morning and go on. It is a close shave. Out in the world the escapes are not so narrow.*

> — Lucy Gayheart

Relationships are complex in small towns, the layers of social networks dizzying; in the intertwining family trees and the friendships of my characters, I tried to capture this reality. A love affair or a conflict between friends can be of mammoth proportions in the history of a small town—as important to its inhabitants as a world war is on a national or international scale. It was that personal connection to each person and place that one feels living in a small town that I wanted to capture in my fiction.

I have felt lonely in large cities, walking down streets where not a face is familiar, where no one notices you. In Marquette, although it has grown to where I can go into a store without seeing a familiar face, I know if I stop to speak to any stranger for a minute and name a few friends or acquaintances, the stranger and I will know someone in common. We are only separated by a degree or two in our little city of twenty thousand people.

Living your entire life in the same place breeds familiarity. Even if I see no one I know when I walk about Marquette, the city is rich with memories and history for me. It is an indescribable comfort to enter the downtown post office and recall that my grandfather helped to build it during the Great Depression. I can walk down Washington Street and see the stone in the sidewalk marking where the Marquette Opera House once stood, where my grandfather proposed to my grandmother before it burned down in the great fire and blizzard of 1938. The First Methodist Church has a stained glass memorial window to honor my ancestral aunt and uncle, Delivan and Pamelia Bishop, who were among its founders in the 1850s. I look out onto Iron Bay and imagine what my ancestors must have felt when they first arrived on its shore. My readers tell me, because of my novels, they now walk about Marquette, equally imagining what life was like here for the generations before them—to me, that is the ultimate compliment to my work—that it has made my readers imaginative and interested in history and especially their own family stories.

A timelessness settles over a person who grows older while living in the same place. You talk about Cliffs Ridge, the ski hill whose name was changed to Marquette Mountain twenty years ago, yet your old friends know exactly where you mean and do not correct you—it is still Cliffs Ridge in their memories too. As you drive into South Marquette on County Road 553, you turn your head out of habit to look at the old red brick house of the Brookridge estate, which you have always admired, only to realize it is 2010 now, not 1982, and the house was torn down nearly twenty years ago to build the new assisted living facility, Brookridge Heights.

Moments of joy from your past keep you connected to people. Thirty years ago, the Marquette Mall had a fountain with colored lights—so many people have told me they had forgotten about it, and they were glad when I reminded them of its beauty in *Superior Heritage*. Every place I step, I remember a dozen moments from my own past—I stop to get gas at a station where once stood the Bavarian Inn where I had breakfast dozens of time. I go to the remodeled Delft Theatre and can still remember the first movie I saw there when I was three years old—memories layer themselves on top of each other. The past never dies—we can travel back to it in our minds, and reading a book is the opportunity to enter another world or an author's mind and experience another person's experiences.

I imagine such nostalgia and family connections are why people enjoy my books, why some of my readers stay in Marquette despite the possibility of better lives elsewhere, or why many of my readers, exiled from Upper Michigan, find comfort for their homesickness by revisiting Marquette through my words. Books and memories allow you to go home again.

This deep abiding connection, this sense of place, of belonging, of knowing I am home and knowing how much that is to be valued—that is why I write about Marquette.

WRITING THE MARQUETTE TRILOGY: FICTIONALIZING MY FAMILY

Before beginning our tour of Marquette, readers may like to know about my family and roots in the area, especially readers of my novels. Those not interested in genealogy or who have not yet read my novels may choose to skip ahead to Part One.

I am frequently asked whether any of the characters in my novels are based on real people. While all the characters are fictional, they were inspired by my family's long connection to Marquette, yet no character is intended as an accurate portrayal of any real person. It would be impossible, however, to understand my love for Marquette and my inspiration without knowing something about the history of Marquette and my family's long residence in my hometown.

The story of my family in Marquette is that of my mother's family. I am the seventh generation on my maternal side to live in Marquette, and other branches of the family—my distant cousins, now have as many as nine generations in Marquette. I must have well over a hundred distant cousins in this town, many of whom I have never met. I am descended from several of Marquette's early families, many of whom intermarried, much as the early families in my novels intermarried with one another, for Marquette was a small world in the nineteenth century. Because I have so many family branches, I have broken them up into four groups below to make them easier to follow. The family tree charts at the back of the book will also help in following the successive generations. I will refer to various family members throughout the rest of the book in telling the history of Marquette.

THE REMINGTON, BISHOP, & WHITE FAMILIES

Marquette, or rather, the settlement of Worcester which would later have its name changed to Marquette, was established in 1849. The first census taken was in 1850. On that census are listed Edmond and Jemima Remington and their children, including their oldest daughter Adda, who was born in 1845. Edmond and Jemima are my great-great-great grandparents, six generations back. They came to Marquette from Vermont according to the census. Edmond was born about 1821 and Jemima about 1820. Although best guesses exist about Edmond and Jemima's ancestors which include American Revolutionary War soldiers

Edmond & Jemima Remington

for grandfathers and *Mayflower* Pilgrim ancestors, we know few details about their lives before they came to Marquette. They were the first of my ancestors to arrive on Lake Superior's shores.

My next ancestors to arrive in Marquette were my four greats-grandparents, Basil and Eliza Bishop. From one of Basil's letters, we know he arrived on May 1, 1850. The 1850 census was taken on July 22, 1850, so Basil and Eliza should have appeared on it. Instead, the only Bishop listed has the first name of Beelzebub and he is thirty-five years old. Since no other record exists of a Beelzebub in Marquette history, it is fair to guess Basil was joking with the census taker, providing one of the Devil's biblical names; the census taker apparently failed to get the joke. Basil also lied about his age—he would have been sixty-one at the time. However, Beelzebub is listed as a bloomer from New York, a job description and former residence that matches Basil Bishop's true background.

Basil & Eliza Bishop

Basil Bishop was born in Vermont in 1789. His Bishop family ancestors were Puritans who first settled in Connecticut in the seventeenth century—other branches of the family include colonial governors of Connecticut and Massachusetts Bay. Basil was the son and grandson of American Revolutionary War soldiers, and during the War of 1812, he served at the Battle of Plattsburg. In 1812, he also built a famous forge at Split Rock Falls in New York. His family prospered along with his business; his wife Elizabeth "Betsey" Brittell would bear him eighteen children. Then as the prosperous couple entered their golden years, they decided to move to the new settlement of Marquette, founded in 1849 by Amos Harlow.

The journey was arduous; the Bishops travelled through Ohio, where they contracted the ague, from which they would suffer the rest of their lives. Far from disappointed by the journey, Basil wrote to a friend of his arrival in Marquette (note, his original spelling, far from standard, has been retained):

> *I heard of the iron Mountains on Lake Superior & that a Forge was going & I was wholly bent to Sea it & in April I Started & Reached hear the 1 day of May 1850 the next day I was on the Iron Mountains & Sea to Sea Millions upon Millions of the Richest ore I ever Saw piled up 200ft above*

the Laurel Maple timber land below it was the most delightfull Seane I ever experienced.

Basil believed the iron ore of Michigan's Upper Peninsula was the finest he had ever seen in forty years of working with iron. Although his original intention was to build his own forge, he ended up instead working in the one owned by Amos Harlow, the village's founder.

The early years of Marquette were difficult ones of near starvation in winter, and little contact with the outside world due to no railroads and the short shipping season. Nevertheless, Basil continually wrote letters to praise Marquette. He convinced four of his adult children, Delivan, Lucia, Omelia, and Rosalia and his wife's nephew, Daniel Brittell, to move to the new settlement. He proudly watched the little village grow, and in 1852, he wrote to a friend, "it is but 2 years last july that the first blow was Struck hear & now it is quite a viledge 15 large uprite houses 95 numerous log & Small ones a forge 130 ft long a machine Shop Shingle Mill Lath Mill & grist mill all under one Roof." Today's Marquette residents who grumble about short growing seasons will marvel when Basil declares the area has the best growing soil ever, and that visitors to Marquette find it a "great wonder" to see Basil's "Beets Carrots Cabbage Cucumbers onions corn pumpkin squash sugar cane 9 ft hy and beans…narrow fat peas 2 roes 6 rods long that were 9 feet hy & loaded down with pods." His visitors "expressed much astonishment to sea such crops heare where all thought this was a frozen reagion as I once did." The visitors indeed would have been astonished were all this true—certainly, the sugarcane was an exaggeration.

Basil wrote of how rich everyone in Marquette was growing, and he was pleased to see his children prospering beyond their dreams. Writing to his other children back East, he remarks:

> *I suppose you thought I was a visionary & too much taken up with this contry but experience now shows I was right in all my prodictions as far more has come to pass than I ever named in so short a time & now there is every indication of there being double of the business done hear next season than was done hear before in one year.*

Basil foresaw a great industrial metropolis arising in Marquette, and his letters speak of early Upper Peninsula dreams of statehood. In a letter of December 1858, Basil notes, "a voat was passed in the legislature of this state last winter to let all of the Upper Peninsula for a new state & the first voat gave us a new state lacking but one & all believe we shall soon be set of & heare will be the capitol." Perhaps Basil was too visionary in this respect, but his letters speak to the optimism and determination of Marquette's first settlers, a spirit of survival that continues with today's residents. When he passed away in 1865, Basil could feel proud of his contributions to the new community.

In 2001, a plaque was placed at Basil Bishop's grave in Park Cemetery to commemorate him as a War of 1812 veteran. His letters are available at the Marquette County History Museum. He was indeed, a great iron pioneer, perhaps not remembered in the history books, but one who intimately knew the early Marquette residents and their experiences.

While iron ore attracted the Bishops to Marquette, religious reasons inspired them once they arrived. Delivan, Basil's son, was a founder of Marquette's First Methodist Church and many of the family would be involved in church activities including the Methodists' two primary social causes: temperance and the abolition of slavery.

Two members of the third generation of the Bishop family would serve in the Civil War. One of them would be Delivan and Pamelia Bishop's son, Francis Marion Bishop. Francis was my great-great grandfather's first cousin, and important to my family history because more than fifty of his letters he wrote home during the Civil War have survived. The letters allow the modern reader to understand what it was like to be twenty, brave, homesick, and frightened. His parents' return letters have not survived, but his responses to them give insight into Marquette's early years. He comments in 1863, after hearing of the burning down of the nearby village of Chocolay, that he had warned people the fire would happen, and next time maybe they will be more careful. He constantly names relatives, friends, and church members, asking to be remembered to them. He asks his grandfather to write if he can, and he tells his father to thank Mr. Everett, presumably businessman Philo M. Everett, for the loan of thirty dollars.

Francis continually comments on the war, the marches, army food, and his fellow soldiers. The dramatic climax of the letters occurs when an army chaplain writes to Francis' parents: "your son Marion still lives. He is in Washington, badly wounded, but will recover, so says his surgeon. The ball lodged in his shoulder blade has been extracted and he is doing nicely." A few weeks later, Francis describes in near-epic prose how he fell at the Battle of Fredericksburg:

At the time I received my wound we were advancing on the enemies works in double-quick time at charge bayonet. When within about 20 paces of our line I saw my Company were somewhat scattered by getting over a fence we had to pass and turning for a moment to my men I waved my sword over my head shouted "Come on Boys" Mind you I was not behind them but no sooner had I turned again to face the foe than I felt a stinging sensation pass through my left breast near the heart and I fell powerless to the Earth, turning as I fell striking on my back. I uttered a low groan and offered a prayer to God. [I fell] with sword unsheathed for the protection of our glorious starry Banner, whose gallent folds waved o'er my head as I fell, for you must know mine was a post of honor, as commander of the 1st Company I stood beside the good old flag of freedom [and I now have] an honorable scar and one received in the best cause for which ever man fought and died.

Despite his wounds, Francis wanted to continue his service so he was transferred to be Adjutant at Rock Island, Illinois, a prison for Confederate soldiers in the Mississippi River. Here his duties were less rigorous, although he does mention a break-out when the prisoners dug a tunnel. Six rebels escaped and one drowned trying to get across the river, while an officer of the guard was also killed.

When the war ended, Francis remained in Illinois to study zoology at Illinois Wesleyan University. His interest in Marquette continued, and prior to an 1866 visit he remarks, "I expect I will scarcely know Marquette when I see it. It has grown so much if I am to judge from the [Lake Superior] Journal."

In May 1871, Francis joined Major Powell's second expedition down the Colorado and Green Rivers and through the Grand Canyon; today, the expedition is considered the last great exploration of the American West. Powell's first voyage had been a disaster that included shipwreck and the murder of crew members by the Shivwits Indians. Francis, known by his fellow travellers as "Cap" for achieving the rank of captain during the Civil War, was ready for adventure and fame as the expedition's zoologist and cartographer.

The journey was the adventure of a lifetime, marked by difficult work, rough rapids, and placid moments of floating down river while Major Powell read aloud from the Bible or Tennyson's poetry. While the first expedition had been a travel into the unknown, this journey would be more scientific, as surveys were conducted and specimens gathered. Moments of excitement included Francis being attacked

Francis Marion Bishop

by a deer he had to wrestle by grabbing its antlers. The Fourth of July was celebrated by a simple shooting off of guns. At times, the men had to carry their gear overland when the river was too wild to be navigated. Most of the travelers kept diaries, including Francis, and hundreds of photographs were taken. Francis' maps of the river and canyons would become the first official government surveys of the area. However, in the spring of the expedition's second year, Francis' war wounds became too painful for him to continue the journey; reluctantly, he left the party before the final stretch through the Grand Canyon. His companions sadly parted from him, and they named Bishop Creek in the Uintas Mountains in his honor.

Francis then settled in Utah, befriending the local Mormons. He converted to the new religion and married the daughter of Orson Pratt, one of the original twelve apostles of the Mormon Church; one wonders what his staunch Methodist parents thought of his religious conversion and marriage. If only their letters to him had survived! Francis became Chair of the Natural Science Department at Deseret University, today's University of Utah, where the originals of his letters currently reside. In later years, his companions from the expedition visited him and presented him with Major Powell's special chair from the expedition. Francis would long remember his famous journey, and in his later years, he published an article on Major Powell's life and his own journal from the expedition. He died in Utah in 1933, at the age of ninety.

Francis Marion Bishop is today one of Marquette's famous, although forgotten sons, a pioneer of national importance.

Francis' cousin, Jerome, also fought in the Civil War, but he was content later to return to Marquette to raise a family. Jerome Nehemiah White, my great-

great-grandfather, came to Marquette in 1853 as a child of twelve. He was the son of Basil Bishop's daughter, Rosalia, and her husband Cyrus Beardsley White. Jerome was one of several Marquette men to join the Michigan 27th. By the end of the war, his company had marched across the South, from Mississippi and Kentucky to Tennessee and Virginia. They fought at such significant battles as Cold Harbor, Petersburg, and the Battle of the Wilderness. The strenuous

Jerome White

marching and Southern climate caused Jerome to suffer from sunstroke. At Petersburg, he was wounded by a ball entering his left and exiting through his right side. He was sent to a hospital in Washington where he recovered, although he would suffer partial paralysis the remainder of his life. He was released from the hospital as the war was ending, and family tradition states he was in the Ford Theatre the night of Abraham Lincoln's assassination, a possibility since he was in Washington D.C. at the time.

Cyrus & Rosalia White

After the war, Jerome returned to Marquette and raised a family. He continued his Methodist association by serving as the Superintendent of the Chocolay branch of the Sunday School. He also farmed in Cherry Creek, where his house still stands today. In 1900, he died of wounds received from a runaway carriage accident at the Carp River Bridge.

Jerome's wife was Adda, the daughter of Edmond and Jemima Remington. Jerome and Adda married in 1861, before he went away to the war. He was nineteen and a half, she a few months shy of sixteen at the time of the marriage. Adda's mother, Jemima, had died two months before at the young age of forty. Her father, Edmond, remarried in less than four months to Hannah, an Irish immigrant. Edmond

Adda Remington White

then joined the Michigan 27th with his son-in-law Jerome. Like Jerome, Edmond was wounded in battle and survived. After the war, he and his new wife and children left Marquette and moved to South Dakota. In 1882, Edmond would commit suicide by drinking strychnine, apparently because he could no longer tolerate the pain from his war wounds. His daughter, Adda, would remain in Marquette with her husband, Jerome; she would die in 1891 at the young age of forty-six. Jerome and Adda would have twelve children, the tenth of whom, Jay Earle White, would be my great-grandfather.

Jay & Barbara White

Readers of my novels will find that in the history of my Bishop, Remington, and White ancestors are sources for some of the characters in *Iron Pioneers*. The Bishop family influenced the Brookfields and the Whites influenced creation of the Whitmans. Lucius Brookfield is largely based on Basil Bishop from the information I have about Basil from his letters. Lucius' wife, Rebecca, the staunch old Methodist, however, is completely based in my imagination. Nothing has been left to tell me anything about Elizabeth Bishop's character other than Basil's words of praise for her after her death. Rosalia Bishop was a source for both of Lucius' daughters, Sophia and Cordelia. Like Cordelia, Rosalia owned a boarding house, and like Sophia, Rosalia was said not always to be a pleasant woman. She does not look terribly pleasant in the one photograph surviving of her. But that statement is based on what her grandson, Jay Earle White, told his children about her and it may or may not be true. Everything about Sophia's social-climbing aspirations is completely my imagination. The Hennings in my novels are also completely made up. I knew so little about the Remington family that other than Edmond Remington remarrying and moving away from the area, nothing is based in fact there—the Remingtons certainly were far from being as wealthy as the Hennings. In *Iron Pioneers*, Gerald Henning marries Sophia after his first wife Clara dies. I have had many complaints from my readers about Clara's early death, but please note Jemima Remington died at forty, a fairly young death as well. Jacob Whitman is loosely based on Jerome White, but I borrowed from Francis Marion Bishop's Civil War letters to create the letters in *Iron Pioneers* that Jacob writes home to his family.

THE MCCOMBIE, ZRYD, & STEWART FAMILIES

My great-grandfather, Jay Earle White, married Barbara Margaret McCombie, whose family inspired the Scottish Dalrymple family in *Iron Pioneers*. Barbara's grandfather, William John McCombie, my great-great-great-grandfather, was born in Nova Scotia in 1819—his parents had migrated to Nova Scotia from Scotland. William John McCombie came to Marquette around 1870 with two of his sons, one of whom, William Forrest McCombie, was Barbara's father. In my novel, these family members were a very loose basis for Arthur Dalrymple and his son Charles Dalrymple. In writing about Arthur Dalrymple's tales of Scotland's glory, I simply enjoyed imagining what my ancestors might have thought and how they might have felt about their mother countries as well as their new one. The only facts about William For-

William John McCombie

rest McCombie's life used to create Charles Dalrymple are the mention that he had helped to rebuild Chicago after the great fire in *Iron Pioneers*, and that he helped to dismantle the Longyear Mansion as told in *The Queen City*.

William Forrest McCombie's wife was Elizabeth May Zryd. She is the source for Christina Dalrymple in the novels, although she did not come to Marquette with her husband in real life. In just a few places, references are made in my novels to Christina Dalrymple's maiden name being Zurbrugg—there is even a piece of china inherited by the Whitmans from Great-Grandma Zurbrugg. I borrowed the surname from among the Zryd ancestors back in Switzerland.

The Zryd family founder in the United States was Elizabeth's father, Joseph Zryd, who was born in Frutigen, Switzerland and whose parents and siblings migrated to Canada. He married Barbara Stewart in Canada, where their daughter Elizabeth was born. They came to Marquette sometime between

Joseph & Barbara Zryd

1870 and 1882, the latter being the year Elizabeth married William Forrest Mc-Combie in Marquette. Barbara Stewart's siblings, Mary, William, and Elizabeth also came to Marquette. Elizabeth married Peter Dolf, who was a prominent policeman in the city. Mary's daughter Helen Rutherford would end up marrying William Forrest McCombie's brother, Daniel Bently McCombie. William Stewart would own the Pioneer Livery Stable in Marquette.

While the Zryds and Stewarts were largely left out of my novels, Joseph Zryd was well-known in Marquette in its early days as a violin player. He apparently had been well-taught to play the violin back in Switzerland, and he was often the entertainment at many gatherings in Marquette's early days, as testified by Carroll Watson Rankin, author of *Dandelion Cottage*, who wrote a paper about Marquette's past and in describing Marquette entertainment in the 1800s, said, "Then came Zryd with his wonderful violin." In a letter about her family, Joseph Zryd's granddaughter Barbara McCombie stated, "My Mother's father was a fine violinist. He could play like the wind whistling thro the trees. He could make you laugh and make you cry" and in her diary, Barbara recalls in 1903 when her grandfather Zryd and his friend, Captain Kruger, both played the violin at her wedding. I wish I could have been there to hear Joseph Zryd play that day and to meet all the other family members who attended—I am fortunate to have inherited my great-grandmother's collection of calling cards she kept from her wedding guests, and I have pondered over the names of these friends and relatives, wondering what their lives must have been like.

William Forrest McCombie deserves mention for one other reason. He was a writer of short stories. A couple of them have been preserved, and while they are very rough, when I discovered them, as well as some short stories his daughter, Barbara, wrote, I felt like crying over the joy of knowing my ancestors had also aspired to telling stories. Barbara was also a diarist, and I adapted some of her diary passages for the diary passages of Margaret Dalrymple Whitman in *Superior Heritage*.

Jay Earle White and Barbara Margaret McCombie are the sources for Will Whitman and Margaret Dalrymple in the novels, and being my great-grand-

William Forrest & Elizabeth McCombie

parents, I knew more about them than my earlier Marquette ancestors, but I exaggerated their characters and made up many of the stories in the novels. Jay Earle White was a carpenter who built numerous homes around Marquette, many now a century old and still standing. He died in 1963, eight years before I was born, and Barbara McCombie White died in 1976 when I was only five.

Born in 1885, Great-Grandma White is the only person born in the nineteenth century I consciously remember ever having met, and I only have two memories of her, one in her wheelchair, the other in her bed, both not long before she died. But somehow what family members said about her—her love of clothes, that she should have been a career woman or an opera singer—made her seem to me one of the most fascinating people in the family, and when people ask me whether I have a favorite character, it is undoubtedly, Margaret Dalrymple, loosely based on my great-grand-mother, although Margaret is highly exaggerated for dramatic and plot purposes. My great-grandmother liked to brag about how many dresses she had, and she always claimed we were related to royalty, although she had no proof of it. I took this bit of family history and exaggerated it to create Margaret's childish dreams of being rich one day. My great-grandmother was also opposed to my grandparents' marriage because my grandpa was a Baptist and my grandmother a Catholic, but what my great-grandmother's actual words and thoughts were, I don't know. It is completely made up. I was afraid someone in the family would object to Margaret's depiction in the novels, but she is a fictional character, and I think she is my most fully developed character at least in my trilogy. She is the character who ties all the novels together—the only one who appears in all three books, and she is dynamic, maturing, and softening as the books go on, coming to terms with the dreams that never manifested for her, her jealousy over her sister Sarah's easier life, and her frustration over her nagging sister-in-law Harriett. Margaret represents to me that life of quiet desperation Thoreau wrote about, and she lives that life desperately but with courage; in the end, I believe the reader comes to identify and empathize with her.

Jay Earle White and Barbara Margaret McCombie were the parents of nine children, who were my greatest source of information in writing my novels. The eldest of these children was my grandfather, Lester Earle White, who married Grace Elizabeth Molby. They became the inspiration for Henry Whitman and Beth McCarey in *The Queen* City and *Superior Heritage.* I will talk more about my grandparents and my great-aunts and uncles later as I discuss specific places in Marquette.

THE BUSCHELL & MOLBY FAMILIES

My grandmother's family settled in South Marquette, and they were among Marquette's earliest residents. My great-great grandparents John and Elizabeth Buschell were married in Marquette in 1858. Neither John nor Elizabeth are listed on the first Marquette census of 1850 and no relatives appear to have been in Marquette with them.

John was born in 1820 in Saxony, then one of the many little kingdoms and principalities that made up greater Germany, while Elizabeth was born in Massachusetts of Irish parents. No information has been found about their parents or families. John and Elizabeth were to become my inspiration for Fritz and Molly Bergmann in *Iron Pioneers*. Since John was clearly German, I decided to make Fritz part of the group of German immigrants who arrived in Marquette that first year of 1849 and be among those who came down with typhoid and for whom, Peter White, perhaps Marquette's most famous pioneer, cared, bathing them in the makeshift hospital. These Germans later started to walk to Milwaukee in December to prevent the rest of the village from having to starve until word was sent after them that the supply ship had finally arrived.

In the novel, Fritz is frequently ill, never having quite recovered from the typhoid. Since I know so little about John Buschell, I used my imagination to fill in the holes. I can find no death record for John. I only know he and Elizabeth had their last child, Thomas Buschell, in 1876 and then on the 1880 census, Elizabeth is remarried to a Jeremiah O'Leary. Perhaps John's death was not reported and I can find no listing for him in a cemetery. In any case, I assume since Elizabeth remarried and since divorce was not common in those days, especially among Catholics, that John died, and since Fritz therefore would also die young, the typhoid and a lingering weakness as a result was a good way to explain his untimely death.

When I first became interested in genealogy and tried to find information about my Grandma Grace Molby White's family, I heard stories that we were supposedly related to Mrs. O'Leary, whose cow started the great Chicago Fire. I assume this story comes from Elizabeth's second husband being an O'Leary. I have not been able to locate much information about Jeremiah O'Leary other than that he was Irish and came to Marquette through Canada—his naturalization and immigration records exist in the Marquette County records. I have not been able to locate any relatives for him, but in Elizabeth's obituary, it does state that she lived in Chicago for some time, so it is possible that Jeremiah had relatives in Chicago whom they went to visit, but for now a blood connection has not been confirmed between Jeremiah or the Mrs.O'Leary who had the infamous cow.

In *Iron Pioneers*, I also had Molly remarry, but I deviated from the family history, feeling I had already attested to the presence of Irish immigrants in Marquette, so I married her instead to an Italian, the brutish saloonkeeper, Joseph Montoni. I felt I wanted the novels to represent the wide number of immigrants who came to Upper Michigan, and the Italian population was significant, although that Montoni beats his wife and dies in a saloon brawl would not make his nation proud.

I also wanted motivation for Molly's character to transform over the course of the novel from an outspoken, sharp-tongued young woman to a rather saintly one by the end, and an abusive husband served this purpose because her marriage thereby taught her about survival, love, forgiveness, and how to strengthen her faith in God. I was inspired to depict Molly as becoming kind and faith-filled by Elizabeth Buschell O'Leary's obituary in *The Mining Journal* in 1897 which said, "Among her neighbors and friends Mrs. O'Leary will long be remembered for her many acts of kindness."

John and Elizabeth Buschell had several children, two of whom particularly have lived on in family stories, notably their son Frank and their daughter Lily, the inspirations for Karl and Kathy Bergmann in *Iron Pioneers*. Frank Buschell, like Karl, was a logger and he did end up in the Keweenaw Peninsula. Rather than marrying a Finnish wife who died in childbirth, the real Frank Buschell's wife, Mary, gave birth to several children, most notably for my fiction, Valma Buschell, the inspiration for Thelma Bergmann. Valma was my grandmother's cousin and like Thelma, she came to live in Marquette. She was a wonderful pianist but she also suffered from epilepsy, which I changed in the novel to multiple sclerosis. I am sure she was much brighter than I depict Thelma as being, but one other aspect of her story is true. As far as I knew, she never married, but one day while looking through the Marquette County marriage records, I stumbled upon a listing for her in the marriage index. Surprised, I went to find the actual marriage record, only to find there was none. The clerk at the courthouse explained to me that the license must have been applied for, but that the couple had never married, and therefore, had not returned the document. What happened to Valma's prospective marriage, I don't know, but she never did marry. In writing fiction, however, I could always make up stories to fill in the blanks as I did here, having Thelma Bergmann elope with Vincent Smiley to Mackinac Island, only to find out he was a bigamist and her marriage not legal.

Valma never adopted children, but I decided in *The Queen City* that Thelma would adopt Jessie Hopewell. I was inspired by this plot twist after visiting the historical Honolulu House in Marshall, Michigan. In the house was a photo of a girl who had been adopted by the female owner of the house—only the owners had been white, and the girl was black. Interracial adoptions in the early nineteenth century must not have been common, so again, I thought it would make a great story. Only, Marshall, Michigan was more likely to have black residents—it being near the route of the Underground Railroad that aided escaped slaves. Upper Michigan has very few black residents, and I had given little treatment to the large Finnish population in Upper Michigan, so I decided to make the adopted child Finnish and her adoption explainable since Thelma was herself half-Finnish although her mother had died before she really knew her. It also allowed me, in the person of Jesse's father, to tell the fascinating true story of how many American Finns had left during the Great Depression to go to Karelia, in Russia.

One last interesting piece about the Buschell Family is that Buschell Lake, just south of Marquette, is named for them. No one seems to know exactly how the lake came to be named for the family—I would assume it was named for John or for Frank and that one of them owned property on it, although I have been unable to find a property record to confirm this.

As for Frank's sister, Lily Buschell, she married John Molby (originally Mulvey), who came to Marquette in 1882. John and Lily would be my grandmother's parents. Like her counterpart, Kathy, in the novel, Lily would end up becoming nearly deaf from the measles. I don't know when this happened, but I decided to place it during World War I for dramatic purposes. Also, as in the novel, my great-grandparents' sons went off to fight in World War I. My grandmother, Grace Molby White, said she remembered as a child going down to the train station to see her brothers leave for the

William Molby (Front Center)

war. Both Daniel and William would fight in the war, William going to Camp Custer in September 1917 for training and Daniel to Camp Gordon, Georgia in June 1918. After my grandmother died, we found among her belongings a handkerchief that had "Paris 1918" stitched on it which she had preserved—doubtless the gift of one of her brothers. She would have only been thirteen the year the war ended, although I chose to make her counterpart, Beth McCarey, five years younger so she would be all the more confused in trying to make sense out of the war.

My grandmother said very little about her family whenever anyone asked her questions. She told me her father was from New York, but other records say he was from Canada, and one family story said the Molby family left Ireland because they were rebels. I have found no direct connection to Ireland, but because Great-Grandpa Molby's past was such a mystery—after nearly twenty years of searching, I still haven't found out where he was born or who his parents were—I decided to make up information and depict Patrick McCarey as a rebel who did have to flee Ireland. This decision also allowed for the dramatic scenes in *The Queen City* when he is old and senile, and while hallucinating, he runs from the house, believing British soldiers are after him. John Molby was himself a bit senile and ended up running down the street in his nightclothes at the end of his life, and my grandparents would have to chase after him to bring him home when he was living with them, although what he was thinking during this time remains a mystery. I also made Patrick an atheist in the novel because John Molby apparently did not go to church or at least was not Catholic, while his wife attended St. Peter's Cathedral and made sure all the children were baptized there. John Molby's funeral was held at the First Presbyterian Church, although he was not a member there, and he was buried in the Protestant Park Cemetery while his wife and several children are buried in the Catholic Holy Cross Cemetery.

According to my other family members, the older Molby generations never talked about the family. Part of the reason I'm sure is because of the tragedies they experienced. My grandmother was one of ten children, yet none of her eight brothers lived beyond their early fifties. My mother never knew any of her Molby uncles as a result and my grandmother almost never talked about them. Only after we found her brother's obituaries among my grandmother's belongings after she died did we know my grandmother's brother Charles was accidentally electrocuted at his job in his early twenties, leaving behind a wife and daughter with whom the rest of the family lost contact. Other brothers died of heart attacks, or what today sounds like an aneurism, and one brother died of alcoholism. I imagine all these early deaths were painful for

Molby Home

my grandmother, who by age thirty-six, only had her sister Mary still alive, and Mary would die in 1958 at only sixty-two of cancer. My grandmother was convinced she would die young like the rest of her family, but surprisingly, she lived until 1992, passing away at the ripe old age of eighty-seven.

In writing *The Marquette Trilogy*, I found it necessary to reduce Beth McCarey's siblings down to three brothers—eight brothers and a sister would have been too many for a reader. I had one brother die in World War I, one die in the Barnes-Hecker mining disaster for its historical significance, and the third brother, Michael, become a priest. None of my grandmother's brothers became priests, but I had my reasons for Michael to become a priest in the novels as I'll explain later when I discuss St. Michael's Parish.

My Great-Grandpa and Grandma Molby lived at 609 Division Street (today 1509 Division) in Marquette—their house is still standing today although it was sold out of the family in the 1930s when John, then a widower, went to live with his adult children. In the novels, I had the Bergmann and McCarey families live within only a block or so of St. Peter's Cathedral because of the importance of Catholicism in their lives, and especially, partially to explain how the nearby cathedral's influence would have inspired Michael's desire to become a priest—along with the influence of his saintly grandmother, Molly, whose obituary as given in *The Queen City* closely resembles that of her real-life basis, Elizabeth Buschell O'Leary.

Today, the Molby name still exists in Marquette in the descendants of my grandmother's brothers. The Buschell name is not found in Marquette, but Frank Buschell's descendants populate the Keweenaw Peninsula, carrying on his name.

THE BERTRAND & TICHELAAR FAMILIES

One other family is mentioned in *Iron Pioneers*, the French-Canadian Varin family. The influence of French-Canadians in Upper Michigan could not be overlooked, and while my father's family is not from Marquette, they are French-Canadian long-term residents of Upper Michigan. In *Iron Pioneers*, the first fictional character to appear is Pierre Varin, a voyageur traveling with Father Marquette. He is later the ancestor of Jean Varin, husband of Suzanne Varin, who comes to Marquette in the 1850s.

My paternal grandmother was Harriet Bertrand, and her French-Canadian ancestors had been in Montreal since the 1600s and in Menominee, Michigan since the 1880s. In fact, the name Varin is among my ancestral surnames, but a few generations earlier than my grandmother. While my mother's family has the long history with Marquette, my father's family has a far longer history in the Great Lakes region. My most notable paternal ancestor was the famous explorer and Governor of the Wisconsin Territories, Nicolas Perrot (1644-1717). Consequently, I created an early voyageur character in Pierre Varin, and then reintroduced the Varin family to Marquette. I chose to have Jean Varin die in the Civil War so Suzanne could marry Lucius Brookfield, as my ancestor Basil Bishop had remarried a younger woman after his wife's death, although Basil's second wife was in her early sixties at the time, not a young twenty-something. Suzanne's family moves away from Marquette to Wisconsin, but over time her descendants move back to Michigan, and one descendant, Marie Varin, marries a Dutch immigrant named Vandelaare. My grandpa, Bernard Tichelaar, was a Dutch immigrant, and so consequently, I connected a fictional version of my father's family into *The Marquette Trilogy* when Tom Vandelaare, son of Marie Varin and her Dutch husband, marries Ellen Whitman, daughter of Henry and Beth Whitman.

Such are the fragments of family stories from which I created fiction. I will include more family stories where appropriate throughout the book, emphasizing events that happened in different places in Marquette.

I find great satisfaction in my readers telling me their own family stories, and I believe my books have been largely successful because they have made people realize how closely they are connected to history. Not one of our ancestors is unimportant. If just one ancestor had not lived, I would not be here today. Family history is human history. DNA has shown that anyone of European descent today can claim to be descended from anyone who lived in Europe and had descendants prior to the twelfth century, so we are all the descendants of Charlemagne, of Alfred the Great, William the Conqueror and so many other famous names, and having such knowledge makes us realize how close we are as a human family, and how ridiculous are prejudice and racism. I have traced my family back to the first century and can claim ancestors in every country in Europe and most countries in Asia. I am sure people of African and Asian descent can make similar claims. The lives of all these ancestors are to be marveled over and appreciated, and I hope my books have inspired people to understand that. By telling the story of a place and the people who lived there—basically a family story—I hope it bring my readers a little closer to understanding their own family histories and to understanding how the history of a place is still alive and of value.

And now, onto the tour of Marquette, the Queen City of the North.

PART I:
IN THE BEGINNING
ON IRON BAY

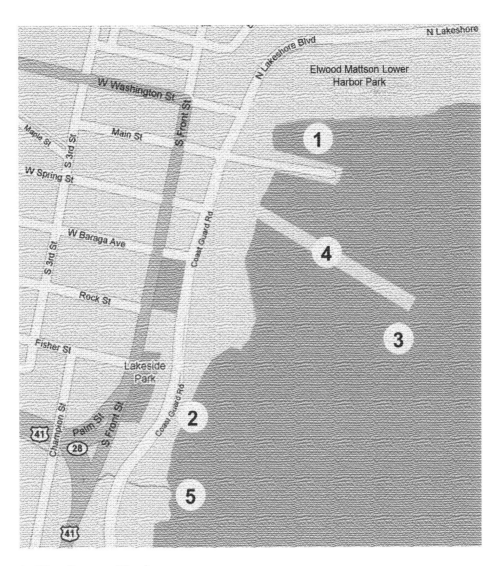

1. The Lower Harbor
2. Founders Landing
3. Ripley's Rock
4. Ore Docks
5. Gaines Rock & The Northwestern Hotel

THE LOWER HARBOR

"Clara, there it is!" Gerald exclaimed. She turned in the direction he pointed as he came and linked his arm in hers. She dimly made out a few logs floating in the water; in another minute, they were discernible as a small dock. Then between the trees a couple wooden structures became visible.

"There's Worcester," said Mr. Harlow, joining them on deck.

— Iron Pioneers

My first published novel, *Iron Pioneers*, begins with the arrival in Marquette—then known as the village of Worcester—of Clara and Gerald Henning. We first see the rugged wilderness settlement through Clara's eyes as she approaches the harbor on a schooner in the summer of 1849.

The town had been established as a harbor where iron ore could be shipped out of Upper

Marquette from Mattson Park ~ Lower Harbor

Michigan on the Great Lakes to such industrial centers as Buffalo and Pittsburgh and even to Canada. Iron ore had been discovered in 1844, just west in the area that would become the cities of Negaunee and Ishpeming, so the ore was carried from the mines to Marquette to be shipped. During those early years, the ships that came in and out of the harbor were Marquette's only link to civilization, and during winter, with Lake Superior mostly frozen and travel on it impossible, Marquette was isolated, no hope of contact with the outside world existing unless one wished to snowshoe or take a dogsled hundreds of miles to Green Bay or Milwaukee.

In the years that followed, the harbor would grow into a major shipping port for iron ore, lumber, and fish. By the early twentieth century, the harbor would contain five large docks. (The productivity and demand for iron ore even resulted in another dock being built in North Marquette near Presque Isle Park, resulting in it being known as the Upper Harbor, while Iron Bay's harbor became the Lower Harbor.) The shipping season from the Lower Harbor was usually mid-April to late November, although in mild winters, ships ran until late December. By the start of the twentieth century, ships from across the Great Lakes would fill the Lower Harbor. Even passenger ships arrived, carrying tourists who came to enjoy Marquette's reputedly healthy climate and cool summer temperatures.

From 1925 to 1976, the Spear's Coal Dock flourished at the harbor's north end where coal was delivered by ship and then delivered to the city's power plants to keep Marquette's homes warm during long winters. Then once the Presque Isle Power Plant at the harbor's south end was built, the Spear's dock went out of business.

As the twentieth century waned and many of the old mines closed, the ore docks became less needed and eventually were torn down. Today, only one dock remains, no longer connected to the railroad, almost all traces of which are gone. Instead, the harbor has transformed itself into a recreational center for Marquette.

In the 1980s, Mattson Park was created after the Spear's Coal Dock was removed and the area cleaned up. Today, the park is central to Marquette's summer activities, being host to many festivals including the International Food Fest, the Seafood Fest, and the Blues Fest. It includes a large children's playground and a marina. At its far end is the Lake Superior Theatre, a boathouse belonging to the Frazier family that is annually turned into a summer theatre; several plays are performed there every season and at least one always in some way commemorates Upper Michigan history and the proud heritage derived from the early settlers.

Clara and Gerald Henning would scarcely recognize the harbor today. No bands play to greet incoming ships as they once did. Few sea vessels other than yachts and the occasional tourist cruise ship enter the harbor. While Iron Bay's appearance has changed, it remains a central part of Marquette residents' lives, and the recent establishment of "Founders Landing" shows that the city's early settlers are far from forgotten.

FOUNDERS LANDING

As she stepped out of the wooden hut, she scanned the other log cabins under construction. A few wigwams and a lodge house were in the distance; she wondered whether Indians resided in them or had white men taken possession. Scarcely enough buildings existed to qualify as a village. She looked down to the lake where the lone dock stood. The schooner had already disappeared from sight, leaving no chance to escape. Lake Superior stood before her—the only source of communication with the outside world—so large she could not see Canada across it. How long before another ship would come, before ships would come regularly?

— Iron Pioneers

Today, the area known as Founders Landing along the south end of Iron Bay is being reclaimed by Marquette's residents to honor the city's heritage. For years, this area was industrialized and belonged to the railroads, but in recent years, it was purchased with the intention to turn it into a historic park. Various ethnic and historical monuments as well as condominiums and a hotel are slated to be erected in the area.

The name, Founders Landing, was chosen because at this spot on May 18, 1849, Robert Graveraet and Peter White first arrived by rowboat with a few hired workers to establish the town. They were greeted by Charles Kawbawgam, last Chief of the

**Reenactment of Peter White & Robert Graveraet Landing
on May 18, 1849**

Chippewa Indians, and they were even invited to live in his lodgehouse while they built their own homes. Soon after, the Harlow family arrived—Amos Harlow having technically been commissioned to establish the community, and hence, he became known as the founder of Marquette.

In 2009, on the 160th anniversary of White and Graveraet's arrival, the first event was held at the new Founders Landing. I was among the forty or so hardy people who gathered there at six in the morning to see a rowboat appear in the harbor just after sunrise with local citizens playing the roles of Peter White, Robert Graveraet, and the Native Americans who greeted them. The event was organized by Frida Waara and former Marquette mayor, Jerry Irby. A proclamation from Michigan Governor Jennifer Granholm was read which officially established May 18th as Founders Day for Marquette.

Those who have left Marquette and now return years later are impressed by how the lakeshore has been reclaimed from its industrial past and transformed into a new waterfront park. Founders Landing stands as a testament to good planning in Marquette and the community's appreciation for the lake and a desire to keep the waterfront accessible to everyone.

Peter White and Robert Graveraet would doubtless be happy to see the spot where they first landed so appreciated still today.

RIPLEY'S ROCK

Then on Christmas Day, on the distant horizon, a sail was spotted by a Worcester man. A holler went up. People gathered to look. Cheers rang out. Every man, woman and child in the village rushed to the shore, the ship clearly in view. In came the Siscowit, *in it came to Iron Bay! Safe again were the courageous mariners; saved was the settlement of Worcester! The schooner docked at Ripley's Rock, its brave men, their bodies frozen, forgot the cold as they were warmly hailed as heroes. The village burst with good will as each person helped to unload the supplies and praise the men who had saved them all. This Christmas was the finest any of them had ever known. This Christmas was the one they would remember when all others were forgotten. This moment had been the most vital in the village's history. Not a single heart failed to give thanks that day. Worcester would survive through this winter, to face many more winters to come.*

— Iron Pioneers

In the middle of Iron Bay is Ripley's Rock, a rocky little island named for Calvin Ripley, captain of the *Fur Trader*. In the fall of 1848, nearly a year before Marquette was founded, Captain Ripley came into Iron Bay with a heavy cargo as a terrible storm raged. Rather than let the *Fur Trader* crash against the rock, Ripley managed to come around the lee of the little island and hook his schooner to it. He then staunchly waited out the storm for three days. The rock has been known as Ripley's Rock ever since.

The above passage from *Iron Pioneers* describes the first winter in Marquette when the settlers waited for a supply ship to arrive that was so late

Ripley's Rock

in coming, they feared starvation. The ship, the *Siscowit*, was stranded in the ice in the harbor of the little village of L'Anse, some seventy miles away by land, but once the residents of Marquette (then named Worcester) learned where it was, they bravely found men to sail it across Lake Superior to Marquette. After forcing their way through a terrible blizzard of ice and snow that made the schooner's deck into a skating rink, the *Siscowit* arrived in Iron Bay and moored at Ripley's Rock—there being no dock at the time.

It was not uncommon in Marquette's early years for schooners to dock at Ripley's Rock, and then for smaller boats to go out to bring in the supplies. Livestock was usually unloaded directly into the water and made to swim to shore.

In the late 1860s, a band shell was built on Ripley's Rock, and the Marquette Union Band played concerts for the townspeople from there. Later, a dance pavilion was built and a small narrow dock constructed in 1888 from the shore out to the rock. A Civil War cannon was also installed to celebrate the Fourth of July, but it is believed vandals pushed it into the lake where it apparently remains today.

Today the rock is vacant save for the seagulls, but it is a familiar sight to all Marquette residents.

ORE DOCKS

Industry is the future of this country. I tell you, these are marvelous times we live in. As a child, I never would have dreamt of such a thing as a locomotive, or that the United States would grow as it has—I remember back when

Lower Harbor Ore Docks ~ c. 1880

President Jefferson made the Louisiana Purchase, how astounded we were by the new size of the country, and yet look how the nation has expanded since then. Look at the trains we have, and the locks, and now this new pocket dock. The ship captain who came up with that idea was a true genius.

— Iron Pioneers

The history of the Lower Harbor is largely the history of shipping iron ore. Today, however, only the LS&I (Lake Superior and Ishpeming Railroad) ore dock remains, silent, unused, a giant monument to the harbor and city's industrial past.

From its founding, Marquette's purpose was to be a harbor town. Wasting no time, in the summer of 1849, Captain Samuel Moody erected the first dock, an ill-fated venture as I have Peter White describe in *Iron Pioneers*:

> *"Peter is one of the youngest and most active members of our settlement," said Mrs. Wheelock. "In fact, he helped to build the first dock. Peter, why don't you tell Mrs. Henning about it?"*
>
> *Peter laughed as Clara prepared herself for a humorous tale.*
>
> *"Well, any city needs a good dock," began Peter, "and we were determined ours would be one of the best. Captain Moody was in charge, and in no time at all, he had us hauling entire trees into the water and piling them crossways until we had built two tiers from the lake bottom up level with*

the water. Then we covered it all with sand and rocks. In just two days, we had the dock finished. We believed we had accomplished the first step in transforming Worcester into a future industrial metropolis. We imagined a hundred years from now our descendants would look upon the dock and praise us for our ingenuity."

Clara smiled at Peter's self-mocking tone.

"Next morning, imagine our surprise when we discovered one of Lake Superior's calmest days had been enough to wash the dock away. Not a single rock or log was left behind to mark where it had been. The sand was so smooth you never would have known the dock existed. How easily man's grandest schemes succumb to Nature's power."

There was a moment's pause while Peter smirked. Then Mrs. Wheelock scolded, "Peter, be fair. Finish the story."

Peter grinned but obeyed.

"The entire episode was so comically tragic I could not help but feel some record of it should remain for the city's future annals. I took a stick and wrote on the sand, 'This is the spot where Capt. Moody built his dock.' Well, Captain Moody took one look at that and wiped it away with his feet. He was apparently not as amused as I was, and he told me I would be discharged from his service at the end of the month."

Clara had been smiling, but the story's conclusion saddened her.

"What a shame. You didn't mean any harm by it, and it was as much your work as his that failed."

"I was sorry to offend him," Peter confessed, "but he hasn't dismissed me yet. Either he quickly got over his temper or he's forgotten about it. I'm certainly not going to remind him."

Despite this disastrous beginning, another dock was soon built, although Ripley's Rock also remained in use for some time.

The earliest docks were low and built so that ore cars could be rolled out onto them. In those first years before railroads were built, a wagon road, and then later a wooden plank road, was built from the infant mines in what are now the towns of Negaunee and Ishpeming. The ore was carried in ore cars or by wagon to the docks; the ore was then deposited onto the dock and shoveled onto the decks of schooners. The process could take several days from the time the ore left the mine until it was loaded onto a ship.

1855 is probably the most important year in the history of the iron industry in Marquette. In that year, the Jackson Iron Company built the first dock designed specifically for loading iron ore. That same year, the railroad came to Marquette. A steam engine would be able to transport the ore from the mines by railroad in a much more efficient manner. When the new *Sebastopol* steam engine arrived on the dock in Marquette's harbor, the ore cars' mule-drivers, afraid they would be out of work, threatened to riot and destroy the steam engine, but they were soon made to see reason at the point of a shotgun. Also in 1855, the locks were built at Sault Sainte Marie, which allowed for easier passage for ships from Lake Superior into the lower Great Lakes. In *Iron Pioneers*, Gerald Henning comments upon these improvements to Lucius Brookfield:

> *"With the plank road, we could only transport thirty-five tons of iron ore a day, but with the steam locomotives, there's twelve hundred tons being shipped daily to Marquette's docks."*
>
> *"It's unbelievable," said Lucius, shaking his head. "I never would have imagined it could be done so quickly and efficiently."*
>
> *"Same with the Soo Locks making things easier," said Gerald. "And now we have that new pocket dock so we can dump the ore right into the hold of a ship rather than shoveling it on top from the dock—it's amazing. We live in a time of true industry, and Marquette will be great because of it."*

The first pocket dock was built in Marquette in 1857 by the Lake Superior Iron Company, and soon all the other docks built would follow the pocket dock model. Pocket docks towered above the ships, and they were built so ore could be transported up onto them by railroad, then be dumped into a dock's pockets, which were giant chutes that would then lower into a ship. The new pocket dock design also meant a new design for ore boats. The first schooner to try to carry ore from a pocket dock found that the weight of the ore sliding into it came so fast and heavily that it nearly made the schooner sink. Soon great ore boats with metal hulls were built to carry the ore. The increased efficiency of railroads, pocket docks, and larger, stronger ships allowed for the mines, railroads, and ships to meet the growing demand for iron ore by an industrial America, especially as the Civil War approached.

Traffic in the Marquette harbor grew quickly. As early as 1859, Peter White, in a letter to the Secretary of the Light House Board, stated, "There are nine steamers coming into this harbor about twice a week each—and upward of twenty sail vessels in the iron ore trade lying in this port—constantly arriving and departing."

The traffic continued to increase so that by the end of the Civil War in 1865, the Bay de Nocquet and Marquette Railroad's dock was built with a capacity for 8,000 tons. The building of enormous ore docks had only just begun.

During the Civil War, Caleb Rockford, in *Iron Pioneers*, unable to enlist in the Union army with his cousin, Jacob Whitman, takes a job on one of the ore docks because he is aware of the importance of shipping the iron ore to support the war effort. The following passage describes Caleb's initial attempt to be employed on the ore docks.

The cousins walked across town to the Lake Superior Iron Company's dock. There men were busy loading iron ore from railroad cars onto ships. The cousins climbed to the top of the dock, twenty-five feet above the lake. Built in 1857, it was the world's first pocket dock. The dock's chutes released iron ore from its pockets into the hull of the ship. Several men with long poles poked at ore caught in the pockets to push it through the chutes. The cousins watched this innovative process until a foreman was free to talk with them.

"Do you think you can handle this kind of work?" asked the boss after Caleb explained why he was there.

"It doesn't look easy," said Caleb, "but I'm willing to give it a try."

"What kind of work have you done?"

"Just office work, but I'd rather work outdoors like this."

"Where'd you do office work?"

Caleb told him. The man put two and two together and realized Caleb was Gerald Henning's stepson. He had great respect for Mr. Henning, most of the town did, but he did not respect sons, much less stepsons, of rich men. He assessed Caleb's size, build, and air of capability; he found them all lacking, but he was shorthanded, and he did not want Mr. Henning as an enemy.

"All right, I'll give you a chance, but you make sure you're here on time each morning and ready to work hard all day."

"Yes, sir," Caleb replied.

The boss walked off. A man who had overheard the conversation said, "Don't worry; 'tain't hard as it looks. Your muscles'll be sore the first few days, but then you'll get used ta it. I've been workin' these docks nearly ten years now, and I tell ya the work is easy compared ta when I started."

"You must have been here before the railroad and the pocket dock were built," Jacob said.

"Yup. Those days it was a downright primitive procedure. Why these last five years or so have been marvels of ingenuity."

"How's it different?" asked Caleb. As a boy, he had watched the pocket dock and the railroad being built, yet he hardly understood their significance.

"Why, before the railroad, we had ta haul that ore in carts with mules down the plank road. Then, since there weren't no pocket docks for the ore ta pour inta the ship from, and no ships yet built just ta carry ore, we had ta unload the cars and shovel the ore onta the dock. Then we shoveled it inta wheelbarrows and pushed those up the gangplank, strugglin' and strainin' all the way. From them wheelbarrows, we shoveled the ore onta the ship's deck or hold, depending on the ship's size. It used ta take nearly thirty men and several days ta load a ship with just a few hunderd tons. Now we can do it easy in a day."

"I guess I won't complain about the work then," said Caleb.

"You'll do jus' fine," replied the dockhand, patting Caleb on the shoulder. "I'll keep an eye on ya."

Caleb thanked the man. Then the cousins returned down the twenty-five feet of stairs.

"Congratulations," Jacob said at the bottom. "You've got a new job."

Caleb does do just fine, and although he regrets he does not go to war, he realizes the importance of his new job.

For those who remained at home, bravery was equally needed. Caleb Rockford dutifully went to work everyday, finding the labor less exhausting and more stimulating as the weeks passed. His back grew stronger, his stamina greater, and soon he could climb the twenty-five feet of stairs to the top of the dock without feeling out of breath. He diligently worked while constantly concerned for his cousin. He and Jacob had never gone more than a day without seeing each other; it was strange now not to talk with Jacob, not to know what he was doing or where he was. He wished he had gone to the war if only to look out for his cousin, but he also knew that working on the ore dock provided a vital service to the nation. The iron ore he loaded onto ships made its way to Cleveland and Toledo, then was trans-ported overland to the furnaces of Pittsburgh. That iron ore would win the war—it would be made into Union Ironclad ships, into swords and bayonets, rifles and cannons, cannon balls and iron slugs to fill canisters for shrapnel; it would empower the railroads that brought the men to the front line; it would create the bullet that shot the rebel soldier who otherwise might shoot Jacob. Caleb was helping to win the war, to bring Jacob and thousands of other soldiers home all the sooner. He was proud to be a part of something greater than himself, and proud to do it without his mother or stepfather's help.

By 1868, the Lower Harbor contained five wooden docks. Then the disastrous fire of June 11, 1868 left Marquette in shambles, and only one of the five wooden docks, the Cleveland Iron Mining Company Dock, survived because the crew of one ship sprayed it with water.

Despite the fire, the people of Marquette rallied, raised their city from the ashes to be grander than before, and quickly rebuilt their harbor, the life-blood of their existence. By the advent of the twentieth century, six new wooden docks greeted incoming ships.

Today, the only dock in the harbor is dock #6, built in 1931. It is 3,546 feet long, 85 feet high above the water and can hold up to 52,000 tons of ore in its pockets. The dock has sat vacant since 1971. For many years, the railroad trestle still ran out to the dock, and in 1988, the skeletal remains of a teenage boy were found in one of the pocket chutes—most likely from playing on the dock and falling inside, never to be found until it was too late.

Talks of tearing down dock #6 have

Lower Habor Ore Dock ~ c. 1998

largely been dismissed, both because the locals wish to keep it for its distinctive look, and because the cost to destroy it would be expensive. Various plans have been discussed about renovating the dock as a restaurant, turning it into condominiums, or incorporating it into Founders Landing's attractions, but no firm developments have yet happened.

The old dock is now the last monument to the Lower Harbor's active past. North of Marquette, in Presque Isle's Harbor, is its older sister, the LS&I dock, which still unloads iron ore onto ships, the last dock functioning in Marquette.

But one cannot imagine the old Lower Harbor dock is lonely. On the Fourth of July, fireworks are shot off which illuminate it in a spectacular manner. The dock gives distinction and character to the Lower Harbor, and for anyone who is driving home to Marquette along US 41, it is the first beacon of welcome. Especially at night, when Marquette's lights sparkle against it, the dock is the most familiar and welcome sight one can imagine, a clear sign one is home again. Hopefully the great dock will be preserved. Hardly a person alive today can remember the harbor before the dock was there. It has witnessed half the city's history, and is a constant reminder of the iron industry that built Marquette and continues to be part of its lifeblood today.

GAINES ROCK & THE NORTHWESTERN HOTEL

When dusk approached, the newlyweds departed in the Hennings' carriage for Marquette's finest hotel, the Northwestern, with its three floors and one hundred rooms. Here the happy couple would spend their wedding night before embarking by ship tomorrow for Chicago.

— Iron Pioneers

William Gaines

The area around Gaines Rock was inhabited by the Chippewa when Peter White and Robert Graveraet first arrived in Iron Bay. Not many years later, William Gaines took up residence there. The Gaines family would remain at the rock from 1855-1917. William Gaines, born a slave, was the natural son of a white Virginia shipbuilder, who freed him and then sent him to Houghton, Michigan to work in the copper mines. Before Gaines left Virginia, he purchased his wife from his father and took her with him to Upper Michigan. Then in 1855, after being injured in the mines,

Gaines Rock

Gaines came to Marquette to work for Heman Ely as a groundskeeper and gardener. Ely owned a two and a half acre estate complete with streams and little footbridges—a property so substantial that it would host Marquette's first official Fourth of July celebrations, including a giant picnic and a cannon to fire.

William and Mary Gaines would build their home near the rock that bears their name, and there they would raise their three children while William worked for Heman Ely and also did gardening and landscaping for the Amos Harlow home on Fourth Street when it was built in the 1870s. William would become a particular favorite with Marquette's children because he always carried pennies in one pocket and candy in another, both of which he liberally passed out. After his death in 1903, William's descendants would remain in the area until 1917.

Near Gaines Rock in 1851 was built the Barney Exchange Hotel, followed about a dozen years later by the Jackson Hotel, which would later be renamed the Northwestern Hotel. The Northwestern was a commodious three story structure with 100 rooms and additional cottages. Its amenities included a dining room that could hold 125 guests, a billiard room, croquet and tennis courts, a private dock, a bandstand, a

Northwestern Hotel ~ c. 1870

fountain, and a pool with brook trout. In fact, its owner reputedly took special guests fishing in the basement by opening a trap door in the floor above a stream that flowed into the pool. The cook could easily prepare dinner from the trout caught. Many wealthy people, including Andrew Carnegie, would stay at the Northwestern, often spending entire summers there to enjoy the cool lake breezes and the excellent fishing. An 1870 newspaper article referred to the hotel as the heart of Marquette's social activity.

In *Iron Pioneers*, Jacob and Agnes Whitman spend their honeymoon at the Northwestern, only to be disturbed that night by cries of fire—it was 1868, and Marquette would burn down, but the Northwestern was far enough from downtown to escape being scorched. Ironically, fifteen years later, fire would catch up with the hotel, reducing it to ashes.

During much of the twentieth century, primarily due to its close location to the railroad yard, Gaines Rock became a place for hobos to stowaway or disembark from trains, and soon a small community of them was living near Gaines Rock. Children were warned by their parents not to go near this "Bum's Jungle," which remained until the 1960s when passenger trains declined and the city cleaned up the area. Today, Gaines Rock is part of Founders Landing and a new hotel is being raised nearby.

As the home first of Native Americans and then an African American family, Gaines Rock is an early sign of multiculturalism in Marquette. While the Gaines family is perhaps the best known African American family in Marquette's history, its location at Marquette's point of founding raises questions of what life was like for all the immigrants and people of various backgrounds who came to Marquette. Even today, Marquette has only a small African American population. Their stories have yet to be told fully—in my own fiction, only in *The Only Thing That Lasts* do I include African American characters in Jones and Jenny, servants to Carolina Smith. What the African American experience and those of all Marquette's residents has been remains fascinating and invaluable history. As Founders Landing seeks to embrace all the cultures that came to Marquette, it is serendipitous that Gaines Rock is at its center.

PART II:
SOUTH MARQUETTE

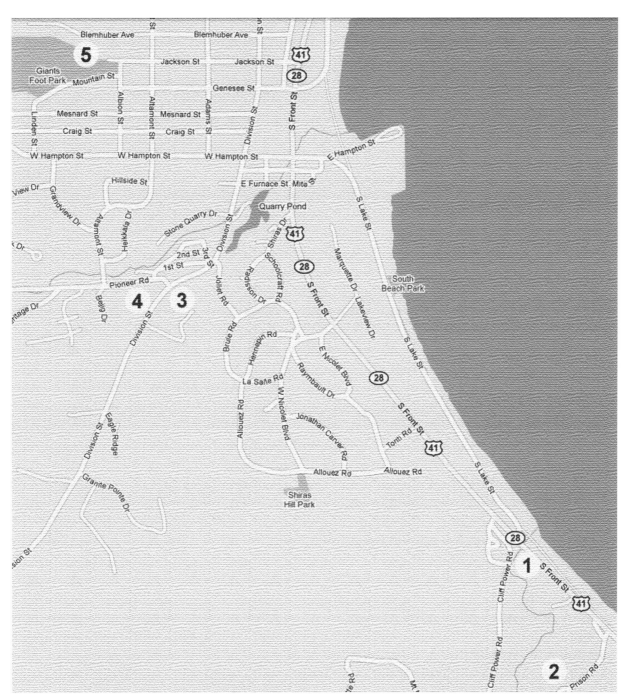

1. Carp River & Charcoal Kilns
2. Marquette Branch Prison
3. Brookridge
4. Old Catholic Cemetery
5. Hotel Superior

CARP RIVER & CHARCOAL KILNS

Gerald immediately took Lucius to the river bank where the forge was to be built. The old man heartily approved, and he made several suggestions until Gerald was thoroughly impressed with his knowledge and experience. As they walked back to town, Lucius keeping up with Gerald's swift gait, Gerald described the hardships to be expected from a life in this wilderness.

"They can't be any worse than when I was a boy," Lucius replied. "My father uprooted us from Vermont to go into upstate New York, which was all wilderness at the turn of the century, but now it's so built up my father wouldn't recognize it if he were alive."

Gerald felt the true pioneer spirit in this man, and Lucius had an incredible knowledge of iron ore; he had made blooms out of ore shipped from all over the world, even as far away as Russia. Then as Gerald and Lucius passed the little blacksmith building, Lucius suggested they peek inside. They watched the blacksmith for a minute; then Lucius started to ask the man questions. Gerald stood silently, knowing nothing about the work, while Lucius rolled up his shirt sleeves, picked up a hammer and tongs and struck some blows, showing the blacksmith himself a trick or two. Gerald watched the veins of Lucius's arms bulge as he swung the hammer with the strength and dexterity

Charcoal Kiln

of a man half his age. Gerald knew he personally lacked such physical power. Lucius appeared a veritable Vulcan come to bring civilization to the pioneers. Yet what most impressed Gerald was the man's eagerness and his apparent enjoyment in getting his hands dirty; such earthiness would prove the foundation of his shrewd business mind. Gerald's father was brilliant at bookkeeping and business deals, but the actual labor itself—never would he have stooped to such work. But Lucius did not stoop; in labor, he manifested his mastery of Vulcan's art. Lucius would be a strength to Gerald's business ventures and to the entire community...

— Iron Pioneers

Just south of Marquette and Iron Bay is the Carp River. Here in *Iron Pioneers*, I imagined Gerald Henning and Lucius Brookfield building their first forge. Forges were generally built along rivers and streams so the moving water could be used to power them. One of the first forges, the Jackson forge, was built farther up the Carp River just south of present-day Negaunee; today its location is part of the Michigan Iron Industry Museum on Forge Road.

Several forges were built around Marquette in those early days, so I decided to invent a fictional one for Lucius and Gerald to operate. My ancestor, Basil Bishop, whom Lucius is loosely based upon, never did build the forge he initially intended when he decided to come to Marquette, but rather he worked with the city's founder, Amos Harlow, at the one he established.

Forges ultimately proved to be ineffective because of the cost to refine the ore prior to shipping it. By the late 1850s, the local forges were already shutting down, and the ore began to be shipped raw to Pittsburgh, Buffalo, Cleveland and other industrial centers where greater resources were available to refine the ore before turning it into steel.

Today, the only remnant of the early iron ore industry along the Carp River are two charcoal kilns that stand beside US 41 as you head south out of Marquette. These charcoal kilns were not connected to a forge, but rather used as part of a blast furnace to produce pig iron. In 1852, John Burt started a sawmill on the Carp River, and later, in 1872, he built the Carp River Blast Furnace. Thirty-six charcoal kilns were built for the furnace where hardwood was burned to supply fuel for the furnace. The kilns functioned from 1874 to 1916. The remaining two kilns have been preserved with timber inserts to keep them from crumbling down, and they are protected from vandals by a cyclone fence.

The Carp River is also notable in my own family's history because my great-great grandfather, Jerome White, died from serious injuries in a runaway carriage accident at the Carp River Bridge in 1900. Jerome, the source for Jacob Whitman in *Iron Pioneers*, lived on what is today Ford Road in Cherry Creek. I decided his fictional counterpart would also die fairly young, but when I realized what I originally conceived as one historical novel was going to become a trilogy, I had to decide where to divide the books. I thought it would be more dramatic if Jacob Whitman died at the end of the first book, thus leaving suspense about what would become of his two young sons. Consequently, I changed his death to 1897 to coincide with celebrations surrounding the unveiling that year of the Father Marquette statue, which I felt a fitting place to end my first novel about Marquette's history. A sudden death

The Jerome White House in Cherry Creek

for Jacob was also more dramatic than letting him linger for weeks as did Jerome White, following his accident. And so, the Carp River got written out of the scene, but nevertheless, Jerome's runaway carriage accident did inspire a dramatic death for Jacob even if the deaths happened differently.

MARQUETTE BRANCH PRISON &
THE SUNKEN GARDENS

"Patrick's a good husband to Kathy; he's got a good, steady job at the prison."

"The prison? Where's that?"

"Oh, it's a state branch prison. It was built just south of town maybe half a dozen years ago. It's a large sandstone building, quite impressive. You should drive past it before you leave."

Gerald shook his head in wonder. "A state prison here in Marquette. I can't believe it."

"They built it here because we're so remote from the rest of the state. Most of the prisoners come from Lower Michigan, and if they break out, they only get lost in the woods, especially in winter, so they're soon caught. Even if the prisoners got out of the Upper Peninsula, they'd have to travel through Wisconsin to get back downstate."

— Iron Pioneers

Marquette Branch Prison's Sunken Garden & Frog Fountain ~ 1998

Where should you go on your Sunday drive? To Marquette Branch Prison of course. People used to do it all the time to see the sunken gardens, which were quite beautiful in their day, although they have not been kept up as well in recent years. In *Superior Heritage*, John Vandelaare first learns about his great-grandfather, Patrick McCarey, when as a young boy, his grandparents take him for a drive through the prison grounds and his grandmother mentions that her father used to be a guard at the prison.

Marquette Branch Prison was built in 1889 because prisons in Lower Michigan were becoming overcrowded and because the Marquette Business Association, and Peter White in particular, lobbied to get a prison in Marquette to provide jobs in the area. Since the prison's construction, thousands of inmates have been incarcerated there.

It's almost a shame the prison is not viewable from US 41. The main administration building is built of sandstone like many other Marquette buildings. Its turrets and high towers make it look like a foreboding castle.

The prison is one of the few Marquette landmarks to have an entire book written about it, *One Hundred Years at Hard Labor: A History of Marquette State Prison* by Ike Wood. The book goes into great detail about many of the wardens, guards, and prisoners, and also the prison breaks that occurred during the prison's first century.

Not mentioned in *One Hundred Years at Hard Labor*, was my great-grandfather, John Molby. However, Mr. Wood rectified this oversight by signing a special book to my cousin, Ted Molby, and mentioning my great-grandfather as a prison guard in it. My great-grandfather's role as a prison guard inspired me to have Patrick McCarey work as a prison guard in *Iron Pioneers* and *The Queen City*. While I do not know precisely what years my great-grandfather served there, for dramatic reasons, I made Patrick a guard during the 1921 Prison Riot, when a prisoner nearly kills him, but he is rescued by another prisoner, Harry Cumming, because he had been kind to Harry earlier.

The 1921 Prison Riot was the worst prison riot, but other riots have occurred over the years, and not a few prison breaks have taken place. Escapes seem few and far between today but several happened during my childhood. Prisoners who do escape usually try to get through the woods since the only other option is Lake Superior. The woods behind the prison ultimately will lead the prisoner into Marquette or to County Road 480 or County Road 553. I grew up by the Crossroads where County

Road 480 and Country Road 553 meet. At least twice, prisoners have been caught in this vicinity. Once a prisoner was caught at a gas station by the Crossroads, five miles from the prison and a half mile from my house. Another prisoner was actually caught in my next door neighbor's backyard. He was ready to give himself up at that point. Five miles of forest were enough for him.

Most of the escaped prisoners have no idea what to do once they get outside the prison's walls. The Upper Peninsula is such an isolated place it is hard to get out of it without being caught—an escapee would either have to make it to the Wisconsin border, at least eighty miles away, over the International Bridge into Canada—unlikely to be successful and 150 miles from Marquette—or over the Mackinac Bridge to Lower Michigan, 165 miles from Marquette. But even to reach these safe havens, first the escapee has to get through the woods, and since many of the prison inmates come from Lower Michigan and metropolitan areas, they do not have the skills to survive in the woods, especially in winter when the temperature is commonly around zero and the snow several feet deep or in summer when the humidity and the mosquitoes can drive a person nearly mad. Couple those conditions with fear of being lost and starving and it is not surprising that a prisoner will turn himself in when he reaches civilization. To my knowledge, no prisoner has ever successfully gotten out of Upper Michigan without being captured.

In 2004, local author and Northern Michigan University professor John Smolens wrote the novel, *Cold*, about a convict who escapes from Marquette Branch Prison in the dead of winter. He encounters a widow in her cabin. What ensues between them, once she realizes he's an escaped prisoner, is wonderfully suspenseful.

But what about those popular gardens that inspired Sunday drives? In the 1920s, the sunken gardens were built and dedicated to Warden Corgan and his wife after Mrs. Corgan had first suggested laying out the gardens to beautify the prison and provide activity for the prisoners. Although the gardens have not always been kept up, they are still available to be viewed whenever the prison gates are open, which is most days. Many people squirm at the thought of riding through the prison to see the gardens, but no one has ever had a problem, although photos are no longer allowed. Be sure not to miss the spitting frog fountain.

Spitting Frog Fountain

BROOKRIDGE

Because of my memory, I can always be back in the past again—like when I drive along County Road 553, and I come around the curve into Marquette, still expecting to see the old Brookridge Estate standing there, momentarily forgetting it's been torn down. As long as I remember, the past is still part of the present for me, and I'll always be able to live in Old Marquette. As I get older, I imagine I'll live even more in the past, but maybe that's what it means to get older.

— Superior Heritage

I grew up by the Crossroads south of town, so whenever I came into Marquette with my parents on County Road 553, I would pass by the old Brookridge estate. I was always a bookworm, always reading in the backseat of the car, but when we approached the curve where the road came into Marquette, I would reverently look up from my book and turn my head to the right where the Brookridge estate stood proudly like some old English estate, the home of a country squire, a carriage house in the back, an apple orchard to the side, and with a lane lined with Lombardy Poplars that led up to the front door. In those days, I felt if I could have lived in any house in Marquette, the Brookridge estate would have been the one. The entire property spoke of a time past, a simpler time that created within me a sort of "Good Old Days" nostalgia. Although it was by then abandoned and a couple of its windows broken, the house's stately presence could still be felt. I dreamed of the day when I would purchase it and rename it Plumfield after the boys' school in Louisa May Alcott's *Little Men*, one of my favorite books at the time—the ideal place for a boy to grow up.

Even when I found out the Brookridge estate had originally been the Marquette County Poor Farm, I thought no less of it. If anything, I probably thought that made it all the better—it had been a charitable place, and a farm, and so had Plumfield been as the Bhaers took in boys to their school and turned their lives around.

Brookridge Estate ~ c. 1905

The first poor farm in Marquette began on this site in 1873. In 1900, Marquette residents decided an improved structure was necessary and the new facility, the one I would so grow to love, was built at a cost of $15,000 in 1901. The staunch new building of red brick, sandstone, and yellow trim looked like a giant, solid home, a safe haven. Twenty-seven rooms sat on forty-seven acres of pastures, orchards, and woods surrounded by a brook. The farm produced vegetables and potatoes and even had some cows to produce dairy products.

While officially named the Marquette County Citizens' Home, everyone in Marquette commonly knew it as "the Poor Farm." Its residents were self-sustaining, taking care of the house and property. Fred Rydholm, local Marquette historian, noted in a 1986 *Mining Journal* article that his mother worked there as a nurse about 1912 at which time it also served as Marquette's earliest nursing home, primarily for older people including lumberjacks in their sunset years. At its peak, as many as thirty-five people lived in the house, but by the mid-twentieth century, the population declined. When the building finally closed its doors in 1965, it had only a dozen residents remaining.

Four years later the house became a teaching facility, operated by the Marquette Alger Intermediate School District, for emotionally impaired children, and was renamed Brookridge. Funds to sustain the facility were scarce and after twelve years the house was closed. It was during the years it was closed that I remember it.

Various attempts were made to save the property as a historical landmark and it was even listed on the National and State Registers of Historic Places for its distinctive early twentieth century architecture. Talk of turning the property into a country inn or a holistic healthcare center fell through in the 1980s. Then in 1994, the property was sold to Marquette General Hospital and the grand old house razed.

I was devastated by the tearing down of my dream home. I still have all the articles from *The Mining Journal* about the debate over what to do with the property and its eventual demolition. I am no poet, but I was moved enough at the time to write a mournful poem over the loss of my imaginary home, which I'll spare the reader from perusing.

Like John Vandelaare in the quotation above, every once in a while I still catch myself in a time warp, turning my head as I drive by to look at the old Brookridge estate. Since 1998, the modern Brookridge Heights assisted living facility has stood in its place, but in my mind's eye, the grand old house is still there, waiting for me to ride up to it on my horse and announce I am home like any good English country squire would do.

CATHOLIC CEMETERIES: PIONEER ROAD & HOLY CROSS CEMETERY

The family got through the funeral. Grandpa had not gone to church in fifty years, but the funeral must be religious. Grandma wanted him buried in Holy Cross Cemetery, not in Park Cemetery with his Protestant relatives.

— Superior Heritage

OLD CATHOLIC CEMETERY

ON THESE GROUNDS LIE THE BODIES OF CATHOLIC PIONEERS WHO WERE BURIED HERE DURING THE YEARS 1850-1900.

ALTHOUGH THE GRAVE MARKERS HAVE BEEN RELOCATED TO HOLY CROSS CEMETERY, MARQUETTE, THE REMAINS ARE STILL ON THESE HALLOWED GROUNDS.

Requiescant in pace!

Old Catholic Cemetery Marker

Holy Cross Cemetery Marker

Across the street from the former Brookridge estate, on the corner of County Road 553 and Pioneer Road, is a patch of woods where once the Old Catholic Cemetery existed. It became the burial place for Marquette's Catholics in 1861. Prior to that, Catholics had been buried on the property where the cathedral now stands. The new cemetery would within fifty years become the Old Catholic Cemetery. By the early 1900s, the new Holy Cross Cemetery off Wright Street opened, and between 1912 and 1925, the remains of some 165

Relocated Grave Markers

Catholics were transferred from the old cemetery to the new one, although not all the bodies were removed.

While I do not know for certain where they rest, my best guess is that my great-great-grandparents, John Buschell, his wife Elizabeth, and maybe her second husband Jeremiah O'Leary are all buried in the Old Catholic Cemetery.

Today, the forest has reclaimed the old cemetery property off Pioneer Road. Gradually, while some of the bodies were left behind, all the gravestones were removed—some for a time in the 1980s I remember being in the front yard of the John Burt Pioneer home when it was still a museum, but eventually all the stones that remained intact were transferred to Holy Cross Cemetery where they lie in the grass, most of them scarcely readable.

Today, all Catholics are buried at Holy Cross Cemetery in Marquette. In the cemetery's early years, Catholics were strict that only Catholics could be buried there. As a result, my great-grandmother, Lily Buschell Molby, lies in Holy Cross while her husband, John Molby, not being Catholic, is buried in Park Cemetery, which accepted all denominations.

By the 1980s, burial laws were less strict. John and Lily's daughter, my grandmother, Grace Molby White, also married outside the Catholic Church, but she wanted to be buried in the Catholic cemetery, so my grandpa, raised a Baptist, also agreed to be buried there. Today my grandparents rest in Holy Cross Cemetery with my grandma's family while my grandpa's family rests in Park Cemetery.

A few years after my grandparents passed away, my parents bought plots near them in Holy Cross Cemetery, including plots for my brother and me. At only thirty years old, I wasn't too crazy about having a grave plot waiting for me, but I guess it doesn't hurt to plan ahead.

Grace & Lester White Grave

HOTEL SUPERIOR

"There's the Hotel Superior!" shouted Clarence.

"That's a hotel?" asked Gerald as Will turned the wagon up its driveway.

"Yes," said Will. "It was built to be a fashionable health resort. Marquette is considered to have the healthiest climate in the world because of its fresh air and clean water, so people come from all over the country to spend summers here."

"I can see why," said Gerald, straining his head to see the top of the Hotel Superior. "It looks like you could fit the entire population of Marquette into this hotel—probably all the livestock from the surrounding farms as well."

"Only the richest people can stay or eat here," said Clarence.

"Well," said Gerald, raising his eyebrows, "I hope they'll let us in then."

— Iron Pioneers

Hotel Superior

Today, all that remains of the Hotel Superior are a few foundation pieces at the terminal points of Blemhuber and Jackson Streets. There is little point in going to the site and trying to locate these—they are not easy to find. Better to look at a photograph of the grandest hotel Marquette has ever known.

The Hotel Superior was built with the belief that Marquette could be celebrated as a health spa environment full of fresh air, clean water, and refreshing lake breezes that would invigorate people. It was the northern answer to the doctor's urging a sick person to spend the summer at the seashore. A visit to Marquette was touted as able to relieve hay fever sufferers, and also as the perfect place to summer if you were wealthy and traveling on the Great Lakes. The intention was for the Hotel Superior to outrival all other hotels on the lakes, including the recently built Grand Hotel on Mackinac Island.

The Hotel Superior's enormous tower rose up two hundred feet, while its pointed arches resembled a Bavarian castle. Inside, visitors were treated to the latest innovations in plumbing and electric lighting. Even Turkish baths were available. The spacious porch was sixteen feet wide, and the porch and rooms provided a view of scenic Lake Superior as well as South Marquette. Lush gardens filled the grounds. Nothing like the Hotel Superior had ever been seen, or ever again would be seen, in Marquette.

But right from its opening in 1891, the Hotel Superior would have its troubles. When I wrote the original draft of *Iron Pioneers*, I set in 1894 the scene where Gerald Henning takes his grandsons to lunch at the Hotel Superior and they are pleasantly surprised to be joined by Peter White. Later, in double checking my facts, I discovered that as early as the summer of 1894, the hotel had closed because of financial troubles. Fortunately, it reopened in 1895, so I moved the scene to that year.

Considering how few years the Hotel Superior actually operated, I set as many scenes as possible there—two. The second scene is in 1897, when a ball was held in the hotel following the unveiling of the Father Marquette Statue—at this grand ball, thirteen year old Margaret Dalrymple is annoyed that handsome seventeen year old Will Whitman is dancing with a "hussy" (Lorna Sheldon, who would eventually be the mother of Eliza Graham in *The Only Thing That Lasts*). By the time of *The Queen City*'s opening in 1902, the Hotel Superior was already closed. Neither the hay fever sufferers, nor the rich and famous came frequently enough to keep the magnificent summer resort in business.

From 1902 onward, the Hotel Superior stood vacant. As long as it remained standing, Marquette residents dreamed of it someday reopening, of its two hundred rooms filled, of people once more strolling along its five hundred foot veranda. But as the years passed, twenty-seven acres of gardens became grown over and the orchestra music could no longer be heard.

The Hotel Superior became the stuff of mystery in its last years. Boys would reputedly break in to roller skate in the hallways and have pillow fights which resulted in feathers flying out of the high windows and covering South Marquette. Then after it was torn down in 1929, a task Will and Henry Whitman assist with in *The Queen City*, it became the stuff of legend. Local English professor and author, James Cloyd Bowman, whose book *Pecos Bill: The Greatest Cowboy of All Time* was a Newberry Honor book in 1938, used the Hotel Superior as the subject of his 1940 children's novel, *Mystery Mountain*.

The glory of the Hotel Superior lingered long in the memories of Marquette's residents. My great-aunts and uncles who remembered it from their youth frequently mentioned it to me, although it would have already been long closed by the time they were all born.

Anyone who sees a picture of the Hotel Superior today marvels that it ever stood in Marquette. We can only now imagine what it was like to stroll its veranda or to sit in its dining room and have lunch with Peter White.

PART III:
DOWNTOWN MARQUETTE

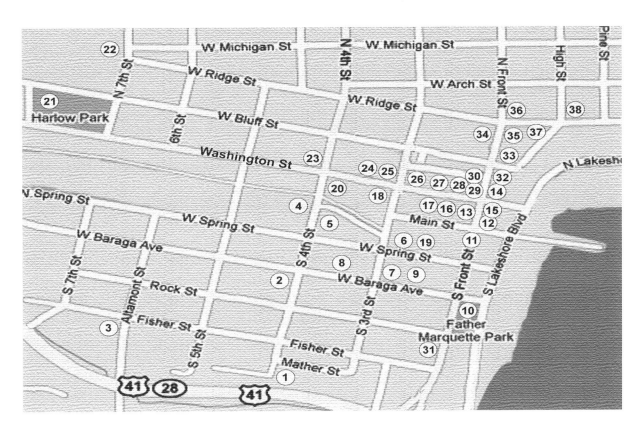

1. Bishop Baraga Home
2. St. Peter's Cathedral
3. Holy Family Orphanage
4. The Harlow House
5. The Red Owl & IGA
6. Janzen Hotel
7. Marquette County History Museum
8. Marquette County Courthouse
9. Early Marquette Boarding
    Houses & Livery Stables
10. Father Marquette Statue
11. Front Street
12. The Shamrock Bar (Elizabeth's Chop House)
13. First National Bank (Wells Fargo)
14. Union National Bank (Peninsula Bank)
15. Savings Bank
16. Donckers
17. The Delft Theatre
18. The Coffee Cup (Washington St.)
19. The Coffee Cup (Spring St.)

20. The Mining Journal
21. Harlow Park & Veterans Memorial
22. Park Cemetery
23. St. John the Baptist Catholic Church
24. Old City Hall
25. The Post Office
26. Superior View
27. The Marquette Opera House
28. The Nordic Theatre (Book World)
29. The First Clifton Hotel
30. The Second Clifton Hotel
31. Hotel Marquette
32. First Presbyterian Church
33. Landmark Inn
34. Peter White Public Library
35. The First Baptist Church (Front St.)
36. First Methodist Church
37. First Church of Christ, Scientist
    (Marquette Citadel)
38. St. Paul's Episcopal Church

BISHOP BARAGA HOME

Bishop Frederic Baraga

Bishop Baraga had been born in 1797 to a wealthy family in Slovenia, part of the Austrian empire. When Baraga entered the priesthood, he could have received a comfortable livelihood for the remainder of his days. Instead, at the age of thirty-three, he followed the Lord's call to go to America. After four months in Cincinnati where he worked as a missionary and learned English, he traveled to Arbre Croche in Michigan's Lower Peninsula to serve the Ottawa Indians. Lower Michigan had many missionaries, so Baraga soon felt called to spread the Word of God to the Chippewa of the Upper Peninsula. In 1837, he traveled to La Pointe, the first missionary to visit there since Father Marquette nearly two centuries before. Then he traveled on in 1843 to Keweenaw Bay to found another mission in L'Anse. After that, he never failed as a true missionary, constantly moving from one community to another; he preached and established congregations throughout the peninsula, often helping to build birchbark churches with his own hands; he converted the locals and said Masses for them, then moved on to find new converts, but always he returned to help each congregation grow in its faith. When he made a trip to Europe, he found himself a celebrity; he held audiences with the pope, dined with royalty, and became the most talked about man on the continent, but his visit and all the attention it gave him only made him homesick for the natives of Michigan who needed him. He loved the Chippewa so much, he learned their language and wrote their first dictionary and a large collection of religious and

Baraga Home

moral instructions for them. After years of self-sacrificing dedication, he humbly accepted the title of Bishop in 1853 in Sault Sainte Marie. The title did not alter his determination; he continued to preach, to walk or snowshoe through all types of weather from one parish to the next, to spread God's love to His people, now both the Chippewa and the white settlers who had arrived because of the iron ore. Upper Michigan's fierce weather had worn his face until he came to resemble the natives; some said this change was a mark of his saintliness. Now this great man had decided to honor Marquette, centrally located and named for Baraga's missionary predecessor, by building his cathedral there.

— Iron Pioneers

Bishop Frederic Baraga visited Marquette many times following the city's founding in 1849. Then in 1864, with his laying of the cornerstone in Marquette for St. Peter's Cathedral, the center of the new Upper Michigan Diocese was transferred from Sault Sainte Marie to Marquette as a more central location. Bishop Baraga soon after moved to Marquette and settled in this brick home just a couple of blocks south from the new cathedral, where he would live until his death in 1868.

One can imagine Bishop Baraga standing in the house's little tower, looking out over the lake in winter or watching the residents bustle about the streets of Marquette. One wonders whether he ever felt like Moses seeing the Promised Land—marveling at how the Upper Peninsula had changed in the more than thirty years since he first arrived, long before iron ore and copper led to the influx of settlers, and whether he felt satisfaction in all the good he had done for so many for so long.

Today, Bishop Baraga's home is the headquarters of the Bishop Baraga Association which has several thousand members worldwide. The association's main purpose is to further the cause for the canonization of Bishop Baraga, an effort that has been in progress since the 1950s and which my cousin, Monsignor Joseph Zryd, played a major role in promoting as president of the association in 1955 when Bishop Noa set up the historical commission to begin the canonization process. Members of the diocese have fervently worked since then to achieve Bishop Baraga's canonization based on his years of dedication to the natives and settlers of Upper Michigan as well as the miracles ascribed to him, including healings of different ailments and his intercession through prayer. The house is open by appointment for research into the association's archives about Bishop Baraga and the Catholic Church's presence in Upper Michigan.

ST. PETER'S CATHEDRAL

Ellen had never been in the cathedral before. She knew it was the church her mother had been raised in, but because the Whitmans lived in North Marquette, they attended nearby St. Michael's. Her mother had often told her how beautiful the cathedral was and that someday they would go there, but Ellen had never dreamt her first visit would include her own uncle saying the Mass. She was always quiet and attentive during church, fearful of doing anything that would increase her years in Pur-

St. Peter's Cathedral

gatory. But today it was hard to be attentive because St. Peter's Cathedral was the most splendid building she had ever seen. She tried hard to concentrate on the homily, but her mind soon wandered into marveling over the pillars and stained glass windows. Paying attention was even more difficult when she noticed her brother's eyes were closed.

Ellen tried to focus on the giant mosaic above the altar where Christ was depicted as ascending toward Heaven. An angel on Christ's right held St. Peter's Basilica in Rome, while an angel on Christ's left held St. Peter's Cathedral in Marquette; both buildings bore the namesake of the first pope of the Catholic Church. Kneeling before Christ was St. Peter himself, while

St. Peter's - Interior

looking on were the other eleven apostles holding various books, crosses, and swords. Below the apostles were several sheep, but Ellen was not sure why. She leaned over and whispered to Jessie, who was twenty-four and a teacher, "What does that Latin mean below the picture?"

"You are Peter, the Rock," said Jessie, while Beth and Thelma frowned at her, "and upon this Rock I will build my Church, and the powers of Hell will not prevail against it, and I will give to you the keys to the Kingdom of Heaven. Alleluia."

Ellen nodded in understanding. Christ was holding keys in his hand and giving them to St. Peter to designate him as head of the church. That must be why the cathedral was named for St. Peter, because it was the seat of the bishop, the head of all the other Catholic churches in Upper Michigan. Ellen loved that the mosaic was so symbolic, elevating it beyond being a pretty picture into a true piece of art. She hoped one day she could create such magnificent art.

Stained Glass Windows & Statues of Mary & St. Anne

Then Ellen realized her uncle's homily was over, and she felt guilty that she had not listened. Now the Eucharistic prayers began. She knelt, listening to the rhythmic Latin and staring at Monsignor McCarey's back as he prayed, but she was also daydreaming of someday painting pictures as beautiful as the cathedral's stained glass windows; she loved the windows, but she thought it unclear which saints were depicted other than St. Patrick because of the snakes in his window. Ellen thought people would like the windows more if they understood the windows told stories. She wanted to paint pictures that told stories; perhaps she would be an illustrator, like N.C. Wyeth, who had wonderfully illustrated so many of her favorite books.

When Communion came, Ellen walked down the aisle with her family. Monsignor presented her with the body and blood of Christ. As she received it into her mouth, she wished it would make her feel different, better; she believed it could if she were good enough and learned to pay attention in church. As she knelt after Communion, she prayed the Eucharist would transform her so she would always be good, or at least quit losing her temper with Jimmy. But she felt God must understand when she lost her temper since her brother would purposely irritate her when he knew she was trying extra hard to be good.

— Superior Heritage

St. Peter's Cathedral is probably the building that stands out the most to visitors in Marquette. Its high towers and red roof can be seen two miles away due to its size and Marquette's many hills. Not surprisingly, in 1996, the *Chicago Tribune* praised it as "the most beautiful sandstone building in the world." Its Romanesque architecture, marked by its giant round pillars and rounded interior roof, and its large Gothic stained glass windows leave a person in awe and feeling reverent.

Bishop Baraga first chose the site of the current cathedral for a church in 1853. Then in 1864, a new church was built with the intention it would become the new cathedral of the diocese since Marquette was more centrally located than Sault Sainte Marie. Bishop Baraga himself laid the new cathedral's cornerstone.

The original cathedral was much smaller than the current structure, but for the time, it was sizeable and cost a considerable $12,000 to build. It would serve the parish until 1879 when it burnt down. What caused the fire is open to speculation, but rumor has it that some parishioners purposely set the fire because they were angry at Bishop Vertin for transferring their priest to another parish. In *Iron Pioneers*, Molly fears her husband, Joseph Montoni, might be responsible for the fire.

The new cathedral began construction in 1880 under the supervision of local builder and architect Hampson Gregory. Readers of *Iron Pioneers* will recall that during this time, Molly had to attend services at the French Catholic Church on Washington Street. However, the French church was not large enough to accommodate two parishes for long, and so on Christmas Eve, 1883, while the cathedral was still being built, the basement was covered over so services could be held there. The construction would not be completed until 1890.

When finished, the cathedral at the time looked similar to how it does today but without its current high towers, or its chapel which were added during its reconstruction following the 1935 fire.

In 1930, a tunnel was constructed between the cathedral and the rectory. During this time, many coffins were found that had been buried in the cathedral grounds in the nineteenth century. An undertaker was called in to move the coffins to Holy Cross Cemetery. Ghost stories are told that people still see apparitions of the coffins in the tunnels.

In 1935, the cathedral was destroyed by yet another fire. During the fire, the parish priest decided he had to rescue the Blessed Sacrament. With the help of the custodian, he managed to accomplish this feat just before the roof fell in.

Again, the cathedral was rebuilt. The original sandstone walls had largely survived, but the towers and interior were rebuilt and refurbished. The new cathedral rose up more splendid than before. In 1947, it was again completely remodeled, at which time was added the mosaic in the front, depicting Christ and his apostles and two angels, one holding St. Peter's in Rome and one St. Peter's in Marquette.

Among the cathedral's many other aesthetic highlights are the numerous stained

Chapel of the Blessed Sacrament

glass windows, the Chapel of the Blessed Sacrament—where perpetual adoration of the Eucharistic host, the Body of Christ, is held, meaning someone is always present praying before the sacrament both day and night—and of course, the crypt where rests Bishop Baraga and several of the Marquette Diocese's former bishops.

In 1981, some remodeling of the cathedral was done, but it is basically the same building as then. A parish center was later added to the side of the building.

Behind the cathedral is the Bishop Baraga School, actually the second school. The original school stood across the street where today the new city hall stands. Originally, the school was kindergarten through twelfth grade, but today it is the elementary school for the Father Marquette Schools, while St. Michael's Parish is host to the Middle School. No Catholic high school exists any longer in Marquette.

My grandmother's family—the Buschells and Molbys—being Catholic, attended the cathedral during many of its early years. I have found baptismal records from the cathedral for many of my Molby great-uncles dating back to the 1890s and early 1900s. My grandmother and her siblings attended Bishop Baraga School, and my grandmother's 1923 high school diploma remains in our family's possession.

None of my grandmother's family became priests or nuns, but in writing *The Queen City*, I imagined young Michael McCarey being overwhelmed with desire to serve God after growing up in the cathedral's shadow, which leads to his decision to become a priest.

The cathedral's long, historic role in Marquette history is too great to detail fully, but some of the highlights include the funeral of Bishop Baraga in the first cathedral in 1868. Out of great respect for him, Catholics and Protestants alike flooded the cathedral during a January blizzard, a crowd even standing outdoors for the service. Charles Kawbawgam, last chief of the local Chippewa, had his funeral in the current cathedral in 1902, and again the crowd was enormous. More recently, the cathedral has been featured in televised masses on EWTN, the Catholic Eternal Word Television Network.

Bishop Baraga's Tomb

In my novels, Kathy Bergmann and Patrick McCarey are wed in the cathedral in 1884 during the time of its reconstruction. The passage from *Superior Heritage* quoted at the beginning of this section takes place in 1952 when eleven year old Ellen Whitman attends Mass at the cathedral for the first time. Her thoughts are similar to what mine were when I was young—thoughts of awe over the cathedral's beauty, which I still feel as an adult.

Mary Dwyer

One person I always associate with the cathedral, as I'm sure many older Marquette residents do, is Mary Dwyer. As a layperson, Mary was devoted to caring for the cathedral, mostly simply cleaning it and making sure everything was in proper order. Often at night the lights in the cathedral would be on late as she cleaned inside. Her house stood at the end of what is today the cathedral's parking lot. She left the house to the diocese and in her later years resided at Snowberry Heights, the nearby Senior Citizen home.

Mary was a frequent visitor to my grandparents' home. She was initially friends with my grandma's sister, Mary, but my grandmother and she also became close friends and she always attended family parties. I remember her constantly coming in her long red coat with her fur collar and her white hair braided into a bun, and at Christmas, she would always give my brother and me each a dollar in a money holder. She never married, but her legacy goes on in her constant willingness to serve the church and the kind words she always had for people. She was always a woman of great faith.

Bishop's Throne

Another person it is impossible not to think about when talking about St. Peter's Cathedral is the late Monsignor Louis Cappo, who was rector of the cathedral for nearly thirty years and a priest in the diocese for over sixty years, besides helping to found the Lake Superior Community Partnership and being involved in numerous ways in community undertakings. Even when it was not his turn to say Mass, Monsignor Cappo would be seen in the church greeting people or giving the announcements before the final blessing. He was so attached to the church I often thought he would end up haunting it someday. When he died in 2007, it was actually rumored that people saw him walking down the aisle during his own funeral as if letting his parishioners know he was still with them in spirit. He remains greatly missed by the congregation.

Bishop Baraga would be pleased today to see the cathedral that rose up from the cornerstone he initially laid. Nearly two centuries later, the mission he began in Upper Michigan continues.

St. Peter's Cathedral has a wonderful website at www.stpetercathedral.org which details and explains all the interior artwork from statues to mosaics, including the biblical figures and stories of saints featured in the stained glass windows. It is the perfect tour of one of Marquette's most remarkable buildings.

Shrine of the Little Flower

CATHOLICISM IN THE MARQUETTE TRILOGY

The following article was originally published in the *UP Catholic* on June 16, 2006, following the publication of my first novel, *Iron Pioneers*:

Historical Novel Depicts Early Catholic Church in Marquette

Have you ever wished you could meet Father Marquette or Bishop Baraga? Have you ever wondered what it was like to be a Catholic when Upper Michigan was first settled? Read the new historical novel *Iron Pioneers* and see life through the eyes of early Marquette Catholics.

Iron Pioneers is the first novel in a trilogy about Marquette's history and people from 1849-1999. The author, Tyler R. Tichelaar, is a seventh generation Marquette resident and a member of St. Michael's Parish.

"In writing the history of Marquette, it is impossible not to discuss the Catholic Church," says Tichelaar. "Throughout the last century and a half, approximately fifty percent of Upper Michigan's population has been Catholic, and Bishop Baraga and Father Marquette are internationally famous."

The first white people in Upper Michigan included many Catholic missionaries. The Prologue to *Iron Pioneers* depicts Father Marquette's visit to the area in 1671 when he said a Mass and converted many of the Ojibwa. Father Marquette is depicted as pleased with the people's faith and their beautiful land, never imagining someday a city will be built there that bears his name.

In *Iron Pioneers*, the Catholic Church is a constant presence in the early settlers' lives. The pioneers are a mix of Catholics and Protestants from New England, Quebec, and Europe. These characters experience each other's religious differences and prejudices, yet work together to survive in a rugged new land.

Religious tensions arise among the characters. Rebecca

Brookfield, a staunch Methodist, promotes temperance and is alarmed that the Catholics drink wine at Communion. Other characters fear family conflicts if they marry outside of their religion.

Historical Catholic moments abound in *Iron Pioneers*. Bishop Baraga lays the cornerstone of St. Peter's Cathedral in 1864. Baraga's 1868 funeral is depicted, with the cathedral packed to overflowing, and a crowd standing outside in a raging blizzard to pay its final respects.

While canonization efforts for Bishop Baraga did not begin until the twentieth century, in *Iron Pioneers*, the characters recognize their bishop's saintliness. Molly Bergmann brings her baby to Bishop Baraga when the child is burning up with a fever. She credits Baraga with healing the child when he lays his hand on its forehead. "Miracles were attested to at the end of Bishop Baraga's life," says Tichelaar. "I wished to create a fictional miracle that could very easily occur, yet be explained rationally as just a turn in the fever. That Molly chooses to believe the event is a miracle reflects her own faith and the power of the Church in her life."

The novel also tells of a scandal in the diocese. Bishop Vertin made himself unpopular by transferring the pastor of St. Peter's Cathedral to Mackinac Island in 1879. Shortly after the transfer, the cathedral mysteriously burnt. Rumor was that angry parishioners burnt down the cathedral. "No one knows if parishioners were responsible for the fire," says Tichelaar, "but the possibility makes a great story." In *Iron Pioneers*, Molly Bergmann suspects her husband, an Italian Catholic saloonkeeper, was involved in the cathedral's destruction.

Most importantly, *Iron Pioneers* explores religious faith. The characters pray, go to confession, and struggle to know and follow God's will. Patrick, an Irish immigrant, expresses concern that the Catholic Church in Ireland is rigid and does not help the oppressed Irish. He also questions the purpose of the vision at Knock which did not relieve the people from their poverty. Other characters trust in God despite their obstacles. Molly Bergmann finds strength in her marital trials; after going to confession, she is inspired to be charitable rather than consider her own unhappiness.

"Religion played a vital role in early Marquette's history," says Tichelaar. "I strove to create characters deeply concerned with their spiritual lives. I don't think the novel could be realistic without characters who question God and struggle with their faith. This search for faith and meaning is what made those pioneers' lives of value; it is the same quest for faith and meaning we pursue today. Lessons learned from those early pioneers, both Catholic and Protestant, can strengthen our faith in the twenty-first century."

HOLY FAMILY ORPHANAGE

She went and adopted Jessie, but she stuck me in the orphanage with a bunch of nuns...if the old woman didn't want me, what right did she have to stick me in a Catholic orphanage? We were good Finnish Lutherans until she stuck her nose in our business.

— Narrow Lives

In *The Queen City*, Thelma Bergmann adopts Jessie Hopewell, but no one wants to adopt Jessie's sister, Lyla. Consequently, Lyla is sent to the Holy Family Orphanage. Years later, as an adult, Lyla remains bitter over the situation as obvious from her complaint above.

Former Holy Family Orphanage

Whether or not Thelma Bergmann made the right decision in not adopting Lyla—based on Lyla's personality readers are bound to differ in their opinions—Lyla does end up going to the orphanage. She does not view her experience there as very pleasant, but then, Lyla is not a very pleasant person from the way she is depicted in my novels. Nevertheless, as an author, my heart goes out to her and I have every intention of letting her tell her own full story in a future book.

What was it like to be a child in the Holy Family Orphanage, or even one of the sisters who cared for the children? Whenever I drive past the abandoned building on Altamont and Fisher Streets, I can only wonder what stories it would tell if its walls could talk.

Built in 1915, the Holy Family Orphanage was the dream of Bishop Frederick Eis of the Marquette Diocese. Bishop Eis wished to have a place that would provide a shelter to the children, as well as be a school to prepare them to enter the adult world. The cost to build the orphanage ranged between $90,000 to $120,000, an astronomical sum a century ago, but Bishop Eis knew the welfare and care of the children was priceless.

Doubtless, life in the orphanage was far from perfect, but it did provide a buffer between the children and life on the streets. The building was built to be sturdy, made of concrete and brick with sandstone arched porches for decoration. The Sisters of Saint Agnes came to instruct, feed, clothe, discipline, and love sometimes as many as 200 children at a time.

The orphanage would stay open for more than fifty years. Its final inhabitants were a group of Cuban children, refugees from Fidel Castro's Revolution. Imagine the thoughts of those boys, fleeing their warm native tropical land to experience their first winter in Marquette.

No one can speak for all the children who passed through the orphanage's doors. Many of them probably felt bitter, abandoned by their parents, or grieving over parents' deaths. Others may have longed to be adopted, or simply longed for the day they could leave to be on their own. The orphanage was far from a life on Park Avenue, but it was a home, an in-between place, for many children, doubtless a place that gave hope to go out and find a better life when they were old enough.

Today, the orphanage is in a dilapidated and abandoned state. It remains, looming on the hill as people drive by on US 41, scarcely noticing it is there. It should be noticed. It was the home to thousands over the course of its lifetime. A million dreams were dreamt by its children. Today, perhaps the orphanage has its own dreams for a brighter future. It has passed through about a dozen owners' hands in the last twenty years, awaiting development or destruction. After providing a home to thousands, it is now itself an abandoned orphan.

The Holy Family Orphanage's future is less important than the story of all those who passed through it. These are the real life stories which are greater than fiction, the stories that bear remembering, the truth about what life was like in Marquette nearly a century ago. Who can count how many people's lives today would be different if they, their parents, or grandparents had not found at the Holy Family Orphanage a family when they had none?

THE HARLOW HOUSE

Harlow House

"Were you just visiting the Harlows?" asked Cordelia.

"Yes," Sophia replied. "Since Gerald has business dealings with Mr. Harlow, I try to stay friendly with them."

"They have been good friends," Gerald said. "Especially when Clara and I first came here, they were very helpful to us in purchasing land to build a house."

Sophia frowned as she unpinned her hat. References to Clara still annoyed her after all these years.

"What is the inside of their new house like?" Cordelia asked. "It looks so grand, especially with that large park surrounding it."

"I personally don't know why they built there," Sophia replied. "Not when all the fashionable people are building on Ridge Street."

"It's convenient to the main part of town," Gerald replied, "and Mr. Harlow believes it will be on the edge of the city square."

"I suppose since Mr. Harlow is so involved in city politics, he thinks he has to be closer to the courthouse," said Sophia. "Well, it is a fine house. I'm not saying it isn't, but our house is far more comfortable and stylish."

"Is it nice inside?" Cordelia asked again.

"Oh, it's grand enough. The porticoes have Corinthian columns and the entire building is rather Italianate with high windows. There are high ceilings inside and the fireplaces have Tudor arch styles. The floors are pine, and Mrs. Harlow copied us in making hardwood window and door moldings. I don't care at all for the spiral staircase; I think a central staircase *like ours is much more grand in appearance."*

"I bet it would suit me fine," said Cordelia, "though I think the Calls' house looks more charming."

— Iron Pioneers

Amos Harlow

Amos Harlow was commissioned with founding the Marquette Iron Company which included establishing the village that would become Marquette. He partnered with Waterman A. Fisher, who remained back East but was the primary financial backer in the enterprise, as well as Edward Clarke who came to Marquette and Robert J. Graveraet of Mackinac Island, who arrived at Gaines Rock on May 18, 1849 with Peter White.

Amos Harlow left Massachusetts in 1849 with his wife Olive, their daughter, three year old Ellen, and Olive's mother, Martha Bacon. According to their descendant, Ruth Alden Clark Lill, in her book *Twenties That Didn't Roar: Growing Up in Marquette*, Olive, whose teeth were bothering her, knew there would be no dentists in their new village, so she had all her teeth pulled before leaving Massachusetts—she was only twenty-six years old. The Har-lows travelled by train and then by ship to reach Sault Sainte Marie. Amos left the women in the Sault while he went on to the new settlement to erect living quarters for his family. After finding an old fishing hut to serve as a temporary home, Amos returned to the Sault to collect his family and bring them to the new village where the other men had started to arrive.

My novel *Iron Pioneers* opens when Mr. Harlow is again returning with supplies from the Sault. He is companion to Gerald and Clara Henning on their trip across Lake Superior. Upon arrival in the new village, he soon introduces Clara to his wife and mother-in-law who tell Clara about their adventures upon arrival, a scene I based upon Lill's retelling of Olive's diary.

Olive Harlow

"Olive, tell her about your first meeting with a Chippewa," laughed Mrs. Bacon.

"Oh," Olive laughed. "My first morning here, I was determined to see everything I possibly could about my new home. I stepped out my front door and practically the first thing I saw was a wigwam. I'd never seen one before, and I was just so curious it never suggested itself to my brain that it might be someone's home. So I went over and opened up the blanket door, and to my amazement saw two squaws. At first I was surprised, and a little frightened, but they smiled and giggled, and then I giggled back and retreated."

"I would have been terrified!" Clara gasped. "You're lucky they weren't male Indians."

"Oh, the male Indians are just as kind as the women," replied Mrs. Harlow. "They've already assisted us a great deal. Chief Marji Gesick has been very kind by stopping to inquire how we are all coming along, and Charley Kawbawgam has an Indian village not far away on the Carp River. He's been showing the men the best hunting and fishing grounds, and some white men are even staying in his lodge house. Granted, we've only been here about a month, but so far, there's been no need to worry, and our hearts are strong. Now that my husband has brought us some more supplies, we should have little trouble getting by for several months. I don't think it's going to be easy, but I feel this little settlement will grow and prosper faster than one might suspect."

"Yes," said Mrs. Bacon, "the men had the dock built in just three days, and the sawmill and forge should be finished before winter arrives. It may not be until next year that we really become a businesslike town, but it will happen soon enough."

The Marquette House

By 1850, Amos Harlow had a forge in use to make blooms from the iron ore. That same year, my ancestor, Basil Bishop, arrived in Marquette, and although he initially intended to start his own forge, he began working with Mr. Harlow in his.

The Harlows prospered in Marquette, working their way up from living in an abandoned fishing hut to building a large house near the lake. Mrs. Harlow opened her home up to be part boarding house to make room for all the newcomers to the town. She often had as many as forty mouths to feed including German laborers, local Indians, visitors, and hospital patients. The building had one large open room on the top floor which served as a place for community meetings, an emergency hospital when needed, and the meeting space for the First Presbyterian Church, a congregation that still flourishes today. This large house was eventually sold and became one of Marquette's first hotels, the Marquette House.

In the early 1870s, Amos Harlow built his fine brick Victorian home on Fourth Street, the house that in *Iron Pioneers* Sophia Henning tries to downplay as not as grand as her own. Harlow reputedly built the house at this location because he believed the town would be centered where he lived—as Marquette rebuilt after the 1868 fire it was not yet determined that the downtown would grow up Front Street's hill and then turn down Washington Street.

Soon after building his home, Amos Harlow also constructed his famous "Harlow's Wooden Man." Fifteen feet tall and constructed from tree components, the Wooden Man had a coat of cedar bark, a collar, white birch bark shirt cuffs and hat, and a beard made of untwined rope. The Wooden Man instantly became a hit around Marquette and in 1891 participated in a mock marriage ceremony. Later, it would be featured in "Ripley's Believe It or Not." Today, residents still peek at the Harlow property to catch a glimpse of it.

Harlow's Wooden Man

On the other end of the Harlow property is the Clark house, built by the Harlows' grandson, Harlow Alden Clark, to provide room for his growing family separate from his parents' home. The two homes have remained in the Harlow family until recently, and many of the Harlows' descendants still live in Marquette and are members of the First Presbyterian church.

In October 2009, the Harlow home was open to the public for an antique sale pending the sale of the house. I went to the sale, not for antiques, but to see the home of Marquette's founder. Once inside, I admired the rounded staircase and large windows, but then I couldn't resist looking at the books. I thought it might be nice to own one Amos wrote his name in if I could find one. The second book I picked up was an old hymnal printed in 1857 and sure enough Amos Harlow's signature claimed it as his own—but I found this less remarkable than the first book I picked up, also a hymnal printed in 1848, and signed by my great-great-great-great aunt Omelia F. Bishop, daughter of Basil Bishop, with the date Marquette July 6, 1851 in it. I was amused to see her future sister-in-law Ellen Eddy had also written her name in the book followed by the statement "This is not your book, Omelia." Since the Bishops knew the Harlows, I am not surprised one of their books ended up in the Harlow home. Today, both books are part of my personal library—if only those hymnals could talk, what family stories they might tell.

One can only imagine what Amos and Olive Harlow would feel about how Marquette has grown and changed since they first arrived, but I think they would be proud to know they are far from forgotten and that their industrious pioneer spirit and love of Marquette are carried on by today's residents.

THE RED OWL & IGA

Most grocery store customers walk past the stock boys in their aprons, ignoring them as if they were part of the shelving or the freezers. Occasionally, you might get a smile out of someone, and there's always the crabby old woman who thinks you're just there so she can rant at you about the price of milk, or the old geezer who thinks you're interested to know what he paid for much redder, tastier grapes when he was stationed in Italy during the First World War.

But Mrs. Marshall was different. She didn't say anything more about my father, and of course, I was afraid to ask anything more. But from that day on, whenever she came into the Red Owl, she always spoke to me, and not just to ask where we had moved the cereal or when we were going to get an angel food cake mix, but to ask how I was, and not in that fake way of being polite, but with her eyes, showing she cared about my answer.

— Narrow Lives

When I was a boy, where Amos Harlow had once envisioned Marquette's city square would exist was instead the Red Owl grocery store, which later would be

Red Owl Grocery Store ~ c. 1960

an IGA. In the 1970s and 1980s, it was one of the largest grocery stores in Marquette, although small compared to Marquette's current Super One, Econo Foods, and Walmart Food Center. Today, the Geraldine DeFant Building has replaced the old Red Owl. A later Red Owl store existed for a short time in the building today occupied by Office Max next to Shopko.

In *Narrow Lives* and *Superior Heritage*, Scofield Blackmore gets a job at the Red Owl so he can support his family. Since grocery stores are places where people tend to bump into each other, it served as a perfect place for people to share information with one another in a novel. Scofield meets Danielle Marshall at the Red Owl; she will later help him to change his life. Beth Whitman learns Scofield has a baby when she sees his wife at the grocery store with their child. Later, Scofield learns about his mysterious father by a chance encounter with a stranger there.

As a boy, I found the grocery store a fun place to go to get candy bars, sugared cereal, and trading cards from the latest movies like *E.T.* or *The Empire Strikes Back*. Other small Marquette grocery stores I remember were Dick's Family Foods on Washington Street (today Northern Stationers), and Angeli's Grocery in the Marquette Mall (where Riverside Auto is now). The former IGA store on Third Street still exists today as Valle's—it is there John Vandelaare's mother, Ellen, bumps into the novelist Robert O'Neill, resulting in a chain of events that will change John's life.

With the opening of the larger grocery stores, the small family grocery stores closed. Even so, people still tend to bump into people they might otherwise not meet in the aisles of Econo Foods or Super One. Sometimes you get more than just groceries at a grocery store.

JANZEN HOTEL

"Hello, Roy," said Beth, coming into the room. "I thought I heard a voice."

"Henry and Bill didn't come home," Will told her, knowing she had hoped it was her husband. He explained to Roy, "Your brothers couldn't get the truck up the hill from downtown so they stayed at the Janzen last night. We can't hear from them now that the telephone lines are down. We suspect they're helping fight the fire."

— The Queen City

The Janzen Hotel on Spring Street stands on the site where first the European Hotel was built in 1856. That building was bought by William Janzen and renamed the Peninsula House in 1886, but in 1892, Janzen tore it down to build a new hotel named for himself. The Janzen Hotel would continue as a hotel until 1983. Although built for middle class travelers and not as plush as some of the other hotels in the downtown area, its convenience to the nearby railroad depot gave

Janzen Hotel

it plenty of business, so that it long outlasted many of Marquette's more superior hotels. Even the mayor is said to have eaten Sunday dinner there.

In *The Queen City*, Henry and Bill Whitman, during the city's worst blizzard on January 23, 1938, cannot get their truck up the hills on Front, Third, or Fourth Streets to reach their home in North Marquette, so they check into the Janzen Hotel. Having them stay at the Janzen was a convenient way for me to have them aid in fighting the 1938 fire that ravaged Marquette. They are awakened in the early morning to cries of fire and soon rush to Washington Street to find the downtown engulfed in flames despite the raging blizzard.

The Janzen Hotel itself would catch on fire in 1983. Although only the third floor was damaged, the city determined that the old hotel violated numerous codes and should be demolished; however, the cost to demolish it was double its value, and the people of Marquette, always nostalgic although not always successful in their efforts, rallied to save the building. The result transformed the Janzen Hotel into the Janzen House, a non-profit organization that provides a home to those who need a helping hand to get their lives back on track. Residents are allowed to stay up to two years and must go to counseling, back to school, or commit to some other activity to improve their lives. The building now provides a second chance for many residents in the community who might otherwise be homeless. The Janzen House stands as a testimony to a community that cares—both about its past and about its residents' futures.

MARQUETTE COUNTY HISTORY MUSEUM

The telephone broke his happy musings. When the genius burned and his fingers flew over the keyboard, scarcely fast enough to capture his thoughts, John would leave the answering machine on. But today, since he was only daydreaming, he picked up the phone.

"Hello."

"Is John Vandelaare there, please?"

"This is he."

Imagining it was a telemarketer, he prepared to hang up the minute the female voice mentioned she was with a credit card or long distance phone company.

"Hi, this is Wendy Dawson. I'm researching my family tree, and I think we may be related. I'm doing some research this morning at the Marquette Historical Society, and the librarian here told me you're researching the Brookfield and Henning families. Are you related to them?"

"Yes, I'm descended from them," John replied.

"Oh, good. I'm related to them as well, but I don't have a lot of information. I'm only in Marquette for a few days, but would you be interested in meeting to share notes?"

"Sure," said John.

— Superior Heritage

The scene above of distant relatives connecting is more likely to happen today through the Internet, but I actually have had distant cousins visit the history museum's John M. Longyear research library and as a result be connected with me so we could share information.

As I write these words, the Marquette County History Museum is preparing to relocate to a new home, the old Marq-Tran bus depot on Spring Street, which will be renovated and

New Museum Construction ~ June 2010

Front of Old History Museum

expanded to display far more of its current large collection. The new museum has been designed by local architect Barry Polzin. Groundbreaking for the project began on October 26, 2009, and I and many Marquette residents eagerly await the grand opening of the new building.

The Marquette County History Museum and historical society was founded in 1918 by local residents. A bequest from Mary Beecher Longyear allowed for the museum to purchase the building on Front Street beside the Peter White Public Library in 1937 and it opened its doors to the public in 1949. For sixty years the building held numerous special exhibits ranging from "The Lake Effect" to an "Anatomy of a Yooper" and my all time favorite, the Marquette Sesquicentennial Exhibit of 1999.

Regular exhibits include numerous pieces of Marquette history from dioramas of an Ojibwa family to the William Austin Burt Survey Party that discovered the region's iron ore.

More than just a museum, the historical society keeps history alive in the area with numerous events every year including historical home tours, walking tours of the downtown and residential areas, cemetery tours, an antiques auction, and numerous fundraising events. The society also publishes the journal *Harlow's Wooden Man*.

Among the many pieces in the museum's collection, one that has always interested me is the program from Buffalo Bill's visit to Marquette in 1902. I depicted that visit in the opening pages of *The Queen City*. My great-

Old History Museum Side Porch

grandparents, Jay and Barbara White, attended the event together, apparently while they were courting. I wonder whether their stories of the event interested their son, my grandfather, whose favorite book was *The Autobiography of Buffalo Bill*, a book he read numerous times and which stayed in his mind so vividly he was always telling me about Buffalo Bill's escapades. Today, the book is in my collection.

I have also appreciated the carved Victorian porch at the entrance to the research library in the old building. The porch came from the Brotherton pioneer home —the Brotherton family married into a branch of my Bishop family.

Buffalo Bill Play Bill ~ 1902 Marquette Visit

The museum staff has always been wonderfully supportive of historical efforts in the community. I am pleased to have my books at their gift shop, and I thank all the staff members, especially research librarian Rosemary Michelin, for their help while I was researching this book.

MARQUETTE COUNTY COURTHOUSE

Courthouse in Winter

Patrick referred to the famous lawsuit former President Theodore Roosevelt had filed in 1913 against an Upper Peninsula newspaper, the Iron Ore. *Roosevelt had visited Marquette by train in October 1912 to campaign for the presidency. His speech was well received in Marquette, but his voice was raspy, causing some people to speculate whether he had been intoxicated. Rumor spread until the* Iron Ore *ran an editorial that slandered the former president as a drunk. When Roosevelt heard the accusation, he had the newspaper investigated, then ordered his attorneys to start a libel suit. The trial began May 26th, 1913 at the Marquette County Courthouse. Roosevelt had arrived early that morning on the Chicago and Northwestern Railroad to be greeted by a cheering crowd. He joked with reporters and appeared completely fearless.*

When the trial began, Roosevelt painstakingly listed every drink he could recall having in his life, and with forty witnesses on his side, many of them holding high political office in Washington, his opponent scarcely had a chance. After five days of trial, the newspaper editor finally read a prepared statement admitting he was mistaken in his accusations against the former president. Theodore Roosevelt could have been awarded $10,000 under Michigan law, but instead, he requested only six cents for compensation because "That's about the price of a GOOD paper." The Iron Ore *cost only three cents.*

— The Queen City

One of the difficulties of writing historical novels is finding a logical way to make the characters witness major historical events. In the case of the famous Theodore Roosevelt trial above, I realized I could not include every piece of Marquette history in my novels, so I avoided creating a scene around the trial—I didn't have any characters I felt were in a position to be friends with Roosevelt or get close enough to him to attend the trial, but I still wanted to tell the story—so I had to summarize it. Had I created into a scene every story in Marquette's history, I'd have had at least six novels instead of three.

As described above, the Roosevelt Trial is one of the two most famous events that happened at the Marquette County Courthouse.

The other event was the filming of *Anatomy of a Murder* based on the trial of Lieutenant Coleman Peterson for the murder of Mike Chenoweth in Big Bay. Peterson's lawyer, John Voelker, wrote his novel *Anatomy of a Murder* based on the trial, publishing it under his pseudonym,

Theodore Roosevelt Campaigning in Marquette ~ 1912

Robert Traver. The novel became such a bestseller that Hollywood producer Otto Preminger decided to film it. He could have easily chosen to make the movie in Hollywood, but he thought he would visit Marquette County to get a few shots for the picture. Charmed with the area, Preminger decided to film the entire movie in Marquette County, most notably in Ishpeming, Big Bay, at Mount Shasta Restaurant in Michigamme, and in the Marquette County Courthouse in the very room where the actual trial had been held. The film would star Jimmy Stewart as defense attorney Paul Biegler, a character based on Voelker himself, while Ben Gazzara would play Lieutenant Manion (based on Lieutenant Peterson), Lee Remick would play Mrs. Manion, and George C. Scott would be the assistant state attorney general. Other stars included Kathryn Lee Crosby, Eve Arden, Arthur O'Connell, and Orson Bean.

The filming began in early spring—hardly spring in Upper Michigan. In one shot, Preminger had paper leaves taped to trees. In another, he had to have the snow hosed off the courthouse lawn. Inside the courthouse itself, a paint job was done so the building would look better on black and white film. Only the best for Hollywood.

Judge Joseph Welch, John Voelker, Otto Preminger

In 2009, Marquette County celebrated the fiftieth anniversary of the film, and although no movie stars were walking the streets of Marquette, the excitement over the film remained high. Many locals got to be extras in the film, including Joan Hansen, who was friends with Voelker's daughter and would later write *Anatomy of "Anatomy": The Making of a Movie.*

Numerous stories are still told about how kind and friendly all the movie stars were to the local people. Jimmy Stewart reportedly loved it here, saying it reminded him of his small hometown in Pennsylvania. Kathryn Lee Crosby was considered the most friendly movie star—she even let some local star struck girls come up to her room while she did her laundry so she could sign autographs for them, and she told them to come visit her if they were ever in California. And local author Sonny Longtine still recalls fifty years later, how he was too shy to ask Lee Remick to dance when he saw her at the Roosevelt Bar in Ishpeming. "I blew my only chance for fifteen minutes of fame and shattered my ego with ineptness," Longtine said. "At the time, my testosterone level far exceeded my social skills. I still regret it."

Of course, I had to build a scene around the filming of the movie, so in *Superior Heritage*, Thelma, who is crazy about movie stars throughout her life, manages to get permission for her, her adopted daughter Jessie, and cousin Beth to watch the filming one afternoon. Besides the thrill of seeing the movie stars, Beth gets to talk with director Otto Preminger:

> *Lee Remick stepped down from the witness stand while Jimmy Stewart stepped up to speak to her. Otto Preminger came down the aisle toward the door, but he paused when he saw Beth sitting beside Thelma.*
>
> *"Ladies," he said, nodding his head, "do you have parts as extras?"*
>
> *"No," said Thelma, to Beth's alarm. They would be thrown out now for certain. "We just came to gawk at all the talent."*

Preminger smiled. "My dear," he said, looking straight at Beth, "you are vonderfully plump. I think you would make a perfect extra. Vould you like to be in my movie?"

Beth was startled. She had always been self-conscious about her weight, especially now that she had gained an extra twenty pounds since Jim moved away.

"No thank you," she said.

"Ah, you are a beautiful voman. It is too bad. I know a scene that vould be perfect for you."

"No, I couldn't, really," said Beth.

"All right, vell enjoy yourselves, ladies," he smiled before passing out the door.

"Beth, what a compliment, to be called beautiful by Otto Preminger."

"Well, he did say she was fat, Mother," said Jessie.

"Yes, but he thought my being plump added to my beauty," Beth smiled. She was deeply pleased.

While the Marquette County Courthouse may be a movie star in its own right, more important to me is that it is the great record keeper of the county's history—here are the birth and death records, the marriage certificates, the property records, the details of court cases. My cousin, Betty Johnson, worked for many years in the Register of Deeds office. When I was researching my family tree, I relied on the courthouse records to find names of parents of great-great-grandparents and their places of birth. And here I discovered my grandma's cousin Valma Buschell's secret that she had almost gotten married—a secret that inspired the scene in *The Queen City* where Thelma elopes.

My grandparents were married in the courthouse after years of being engaged but not marrying because of their family's religious differences over Grandpa being Baptist and Grandma being Catholic. Grandma finally gave in and agreed to be wed at the courthouse by the Baptist minister. That wouldn't be the end, however, of the religious controversy in the family as I'll explain later when discussing St. Michael's Parish.

Marquette's original courthouse was built on the same property where the current one stands. First in 1855 was built the town jail, and two years later, a wooden courthouse, typical for the time with two floors, shuttered windows, and a pillar-supported portico. In an 1858 letter, my ancestor Basil Bishop (remember he was not much of a speller) referred to the building as "our eligant cort hous."

By 1902, a new courthouse was deemed necessary and the city issued bonds to raise the money. The old courthouse was first moved to the edge of the property until the new one was completed and then sold to the Catholic Diocese, which dismantled it and used the timbers to build the Bishop Baraga School.

Marquette's Original Courthouse & Jail

In 1904, the new courthouse had its grand dedication the same day as the Peter White Public Library, a day of great civic pride in Marquette. Well over a century later, these sister buildings have served generations of Marquette residents.

Today, the courthouse remains not only a place of trials and records, but has been used as a historical monument to celebrate its past, including showings of *Anatomy of a Murder* in the courtroom where the film was first shot, and reenactments of the famous Theodore Roosevelt trial. The courthouse will continue to serve the residents of Marquette County and provide justice for many years to come.

EARLY MARQUETTE BOARDING HOUSES & LIVERY STABLES

In the heart of the fire, only the Tremont house on Superior Street was saved by people throwing wet carpets at the roof, and the Chicago and Northwestern Railroad office was equally spared. The wideness of Superior Street as the main thoroughfare in the village prevented the flames from spreading to the street's south side where the cathedral stood. All the city's other businesses were lost except a drugstore and a meat market where Superior and Front Streets met.

— Iron Pioneers

Among Marquette's earliest establishments were its boarding houses which catered to the growing population, including single men, lumberjacks, sailors, and families. My ancestor Rosalia Bishop White and her sister Lucia Bishop Bignall would both operate boarding houses in Marquette's early years. While I do not know the name of Rosalia's boarding house, if it had one, Lucia and her husband Joseph established the Filmore House. Joseph Bignall purchased the property for $100, a great price at the time considering the lot encompassed a quarter block between Third and Front Street. Later city maps however show that it was not that large and several other buildings were located in that portion of the block. The Filmore House was located at 156 W. Baraga Avenue, directly on the corner across from the courthouse and where today the new history museum is located. Perhaps the boarding house was named for then U.S President Millard Fillmore. Although this cannot be confirmed and the name was spelled differently, the Bishops did have a connection to President Fillmore. Back east, Lucia's first cousin, the early American artist Annette Bishop, lived for a time with President Fillmore's family and painted a portrait of the president's wife, Abigail.

While the Bignalls lived in Marquette, their daughters attended the first Marquette school with Amos Harlow's children. Their son, Elbert Joseph Bignall, was the first white child born in the village of Marquette in 1851.

In 1865, Joseph Bignall deeded the boarding house to Tim Hurley, and the family moved to Minnesota. They would later move to Colorado, although Joseph and Lucia's son, Elbert Joseph, would return to live in Marquette in 1877 and marry

Rosalia Corlista King, the daughter of his cousin Eugenia Sylvia White. (Marriages between cousins were not uncommon in the nineteenth century, so it was not out of line in *Iron Pioneers* when I had cousins Edna Whitman and Esau Brookfield marry). Many of the Bignall descendants still reside in the Marquette area today.

The Filmore House would change hands over the years before finally being torn down in 1952. The site remained empty then until 1963 when the A&P supermarket was built on the property. Later the Marq-Tran bus depot was in that place before the history museum came to occupy the property.

Basil Bishop attributed the success of both Rosalia and Lucia's boarding houses to his daughters rather than to their husbands. In an 1858 letter, he writes:

> *Bignal has a larg hous well furnished he keeps a boarding hous & is doing well he is worth over $2000 but as one man said who knew it all answer his wife Cyrus White came heare poor I sent him $100 cash to get him heare he has paid me that & now is worth over one thousand clear & has good furniture rooms carpeted and papered & one sette that cost $20 below & he bought & paid for 5 acres of land adjoining me The question is who erned all this is answered the same as Bignall Rosalia erns a washing $12 pr weak for months together Lutia done that and more for years.*

In *Iron Pioneers,* I merged Rosalia and Lucia to create Cordelia Whitman (Basil Bishop actually had a daughter named Cordelia who remained in New York). To make matters more interesting, I had Cordelia's boarding house destroyed in the 1868 fire where it lies in approximately the same area as the Filmore House. Following the fire, Cordelia is stoic about the loss of her home:

> *"Oh Jacob," said Edna, burying her face in his sleeve, so glad he was safe, "the library is completely gone. Fifteen hundred volumes, and the boarding house—"*
>
> *Mention of the boarding house made Jacob think of his mother. He found her in the west parlor. Cordelia's entire domestic world was upset by the loss of her boarding house, but she smiled when she saw her son. "I'm fine now that you're safe," she said, thankful to hug him. "I won't have to cook and clean for a while. I needed a little break anyway."*
>
> *Jacob smiled at her courage.*

Cordelia rebuilds her boarding house north of Washington Street—I imagine on Bluff Street most likely. It is here that her son, Jacob, tries to get her to take in an unlikely boarder, who turns out to be her long lost brother, Darius Brookfield. Darius, who dresses like some mountain man or character from the Wild West, was also inspired by a family story. Basil and Eliza Bishop had a son, Darwin, who went out West as an Indian scout and was never heard from again. I was always curious about what happened to him, and while the family must have mourned him as dead, I thought I would remedy their grief a bit by having Darius track his family down in Marquette. It is Darius' son, Esau, who marries his cousin, Edna Whitman.

I don't know how long Rosalia White operated her boarding house. After her husband died in 1896, she decided to move to Tacoma, Washington to live near her daughter. (Her fictional counterpart, Cordelia, later moves West to live near Edna, Esau, and Darius). Rosalia Bishop White would not die until 1918 at age 96. During her lifetime, she saw the entire westward expansion and she herself moved from the East to the West Coast, stopping in Marquette for nearly half a century to run a boarding house.

In the 1890s, just down the street at 111 W. Superior Street (today's Baraga Avenue) was William Stewart's Pioneer Livery and Boarding Stables, advertised in Polk's 1895-6 directory as having "The best single and double rigs in the City. Commercial travelers, Hunters, and Hotels attended to on short notice" so if you needed a ride to your board-

Pioneer Livery Ad ~ 1895 Polk's Directory

ing house Stewart's operation could help you. I mention William Stewart because he was the brother to my great-great-great-grandmother Barbara Stewart who married Joseph Zryd. Ironically, in the same directory, George F. Reed's Palace Livery and Boarding Stable advertised that it had "the best rigs in the City" and also "the finest Hack in the City for Parties and Funerals." Who really had the best rigs in Marquette is lost to history.

FATHER MARQUETTE STATUE

In another second, the figure of Father Marquette was clearly revealed to all the residents of his namesake city. The crowd applauded and the people murmured with delight that the statue faced the town. The figure of the Jesuit priest stood atop a pedestal of sandstone, and on its base was a relief of Father Marquette preaching to the Indians at Lighthouse

Father Marquette Statue Unveiling ~ 1897

Point. But most striking was the statue itself. Father Marquette stood looking about him with wonder, as though admiring the beauty of the land he had visited; his brow spoke of determination to carry out his Christian mission to the Indians. His bearded face and large forehead suggested wisdom beyond his years. History had lost all record of the Jesuit missionary's appearance, only knowing he had died at the young age of thirty-eight, but here he was portrayed as a figure of indestructible and eternal force. His left hand clutched his robe, as if he had just stepped out of a canoe and was steeling himself against a harsh northern wind; in one hand he held a piece of paper, perhaps Marquette's city charter.

Margaret looked at the statue and saw a romantic hero, but the older residents of Marquette, saw a pioneer like themselves; someone with a harsh, grim look who had known years of hardship; Father Marquette was one of them, the very first to experience the rigors of this land. Molly Montoni looked at the statue and remembered her first husband who like Father Marquette had also died young, but who would be proud of the community's survival. Charles Kawbawgam saw in the statue a symbol of how much his world had changed, and that change had begun with the coming of this black robe. Jacob Whitman looked at the statue and saw the immigrant spirit of all those pioneers, his parents and grandparents, his in-laws, cousins, aunt and uncle, his precious Agnes, and even himself, when he had come as a boy to a village of a few wooden buildings on the shores of Lake Superior. That moment of the statue's unveiling seemed a little eternity as everyone contemplated the changes of Marquette's half century.

— Iron Pioneers

Father Marquette first arrived on the shores of Marquette in 1671, where in 1849 a city would be founded in his honor. By the 1890s, Marquette was a prosperous town with several prominent city buildings and a significant role in the nation's industry. Out of civic pride, the time had come to erect a statue to its namesake. Marquette's citizens were aware that Wisconsin had just commissioned a statue of Father Marquette for Statuary Hall in Washington D.C., so they wanted a similar statue for themselves. Peter White was opposed at first to the statue because of the financial panic of 1893 and initially did not donate money to the cause, but later, he did support the cause, and when the statue was unveiled, rumors would surface that the statue looked like Peter White.

At the time, no one knew what Father Marquette looked like. Not until the 1960s did a portrait surface, which the Marquette County History Museum received from a museum in Paris. The portrait was supposedly drawn just before Father Marquette left France in 1666. He would have been in his late twenties at the time, although the portrait makes him look like a balding middle-aged man.

The statue was placed near the new waterworks building across from the foot of Ridge Street. It was a beautiful part of town at the time, with the Longyear Mansion overlooking it and the lakeshore nearby.

Relief ~ Father Marquette Statue

Controversy ensued as to whether Father Marquette should face the lake or the city, so not until the unveiling in 1897 was it revealed he would face the town.

The day of the unveiling, as described in *Iron Pioneers,* was a day of great civic pride in Marquette. Peter White was so proud of the statue he raised money to have a similar one placed in Marquette Park on Mackinac Island.

In 1912, the statue was moved to its current location in Father Marquette Park near the current Chamber of Commerce building. The move occurred after railroad tracks laid near the Waterworks building ended plans for a park along the lakeshore. The giant cast iron flowerpot by the new City Waterworks building is the only sign remaining of the statue's original foundation.

In her 1906 children's novel *The Girls of Gardenville*, local author Carroll Watson Rankin depicts a young lady first learning how to drive an automobile. Losing control of her vehicle as she comes down a large hill, she smashes into a statue. Rankin must have imagined a car bolting down Ridge Street's hill into the Father Marquette statue. History has not preserved any actual automobile assaults to the statue but that same year, discussion about moving the statue began. Hopefully, Father Marquette feels safe today on a small hill, far from the reach of any out-of-control vehicles.

FRONT STREET

She had found San Francisco to be amazing. The high hills remind-
ed her of several of Marquette's streets, and peeking between the city's tall
buildings was the ocean, just as back home, Lake Superior was visible be-
tween banks and stores on Front Street. She had always loved streetcars
and mourned the recent dissolution of them in Marquette.

— The Queen City

Among my earliest memories is riding in the car up Front Street. It is a distinctive street with historic old buildings and most notably the Old Savings Bank's clock
tower, which to my young imagination seemed equal to London's Big Ben as I had
seen it depicted in the Disney cartoon *Peter Pan*. The street's high hill gives Marquette the air of a smaller San Francisco, especially in photographs that depict the
old streetcars running up it. I know few city streets with more character.

In my childhood, the
Soo Line railroad trestle
ran over the downtown
buildings—it had been
built so trains could
carry ore to the docks
without interrupting
the traffic. When the
Lower Harbor ore docks
quit being used, the
trestle was no longer
needed, and although
many people wanted to
preserve it, in 2000 it
was removed.

Railroad Trestle Being Removed

I cannot mention every place in Marquette, but among Front Street's notable
businesses is Getz's, in operation since 1900; it has outlived other downtown
department stores by becoming the major supplier of Carhart clothing, and it does
more business online than locally. In my childhood, the Chinese Palace stood at the
bottom of the street—as kids, my friends and I were convinced it served cat and

Getz's Department Store

rat—typical Chinese restaurant horror stories I'm afraid. The Rosewood Inn, for many years threatened with demolition and its awning hanging down, is now beautifully restored and includes several stores and businesses. The Vierling Restaurant has been famous for over a century for its whitefish, brewery, and French onion soup. Across the street from it on Main is Upfront & Co., a premiere restaurant and nightclub, worth a visit just for

its architectural look—a fine example of how old buildings can be reused with a little imagination.

The changes made to Front Street during my lifetime have all been for the better, which reflects how much the people of Marquette care about their past and the beauty of their city.

But I do miss the old railroad trestle.

Restored Rosewood Block

THE SHAMROCK BAR (ELIZABETH'S CHOP HOUSE)

John forgot about Dickens once he and Derek were at the movie and then at the Shamrock Bar. He enjoyed talking to Derek, but he felt odd at the Shamrock, suddenly realizing how much younger than him were most of the students; it was a college hangout, while he was now a Ph.D. student. He felt like an outsider now, but he dismissed the feeling as simply being tired from his long drive.

— Superior Heritage

The younger generation always has its favorite hangout, and the place seems to change every few years. When I first started college and before I was too young really to go out to the bars, the Alibi on Wright Street was the place to go. When it was later turned into The Beach Club, its popularity was short-lived. The Westwood Lanes and My Place at the Holiday Inn were also popular, but by the time I was in college, their popularity had started to wane. In the early

Elizabeth's Chop House ~ Former Shamrock Bar

2000s, everyone seemed to be going to Flanigan's Bar for karaoke night, and more recently the Mattrix has been Marquette's hot spot for the younger crowd, but for a few short years in the early to mid-1990s when I was in college, the favorite place was definitely the Shamrock.

The Shamrock dubbed itself as an Irish bar although there wasn't much that was noticeably Irish about it. I wasn't one to go out to the bars often—it was too noisy and hard to talk to people—but I had a few close friends I would join at the Shamrock a couple of times a month on a Friday or Saturday night. There was never a night I went there when I didn't see the bar lined with college students you had to push through to get to the main room where the dance floor and tables were located. The dance floor was always packed with people, and behind it were several tables and then the doors out onto the porch. Somehow, my friends and I always managed to find a table, and then we would order drinks—favorites were Long Island ice tea, snake nuts, and screwdrivers, and you could never go wrong with just plain beer. The bands were always local and we enjoyed dancing the night away.

College goes by much too quickly and now all my friends from my undergraduate days have moved away. While I stay in touch with most of them, like John in *Superior Heritage*, you quickly realize you have grown past the age of the college crowd. So did the Shamrock. In 2007, its doors closed and it was sold to Tom Wahlstrom who transformed into Elizabeth's Chop House. Rumor has it that the building is haunted, particularly the basement, and that a funeral home once existed there. In any case, I am sure many former college students are haunted by memories of drooling over the opposite sex, too many drinks, as well as the good times they once had at the Shamrock bar.

MARQUETTE'S FIRST NATIONAL, UNION NATIONAL, & SAVINGS BANKS

First National Bank Interior ~ c. 1940

"I still can't get over this building," said Thelma. "Louis Kaufman gave us a masterpiece when he had this bank built." Since the 1920s, Marquette's First National Bank had been housed in a giant structure of Indiana limestone resembling a Greek Temple; its bronze doors were elaborately carved; the human eye was dazzled by its Corinthian columns and its interior gilded walls and ceiling. "They say it was the most expensive building per square foot in the country at the time it was built. Did you know Louis Kaufman also headed the finance committee to build the Empire State Building?"

"Yes, Mother," said Jessie, used to her mother's constant ramblings. She pushed the chair through the door and into the bank lobby.

"Look at those chandeliers," said Thelma. "Each cost over a thousand dollars; that's still big money now, but think what it was forty years ago."

They went up to the teller's window. In her wheelchair, Thelma could barely reach the counter, but she insisted on making her transactions without Jessie's help.

As the teller processed Thelma's withdrawal and tried to find crisp five dollar bills for her, Thelma chattered, "You're so lucky to work in this beautiful building. I love coming here. I bet Peter White would have been pleased to see his bank housed in this beautiful place. You know, I met Peter White once when I was a little girl—he was a jokester—he told me he knew Paul Bunyan personally. Isn't that funny? Oh, those are beautiful crisp bills for my Easter cards. Thank you. Happy Easter."

The teller smiled politely. She was twenty, and ignorant that Peter White had founded the bank where she worked; as for Paul Bunyan, she had never heard of him.

— Superior Heritage

Since Marquette's earliest days, the corner of Washington and Front Streets has been the banking center of the city. Initially, the Union National Bank, the Savings Bank, and the First National Bank all stood here. Today the Union National Bank has been replaced by the Peninsula Bank. The Savings Bank has been turned into business offices, and the First National Bank is the main local branch of the Wells Fargo banking empire.

FIRST NATIONAL BANK (WELLS FARGO)

Peter White started the First National Bank, Marquette's first bank, in 1864. The initial bank had some temporary offices until it moved into the Burt Building farther down Front Street.

First National Bank

While in its temporary location, one of the bank's most interesting connections to U.S. history occurred as the Civil War approached its end. In *Iron Pioneers,* Gerald Henning relates what happened to his family:

"I was talking to Peter White yesterday, and he told me the Secretary of War for the Confederacy came into his bank."

"The Secretary of the Confederacy!" exclaimed Sophia.

"Who's that?" asked Agnes, who was always afraid to read the war reports.

"John C. Breckinridge," Molly told her.

"Here in Marquette?" said Sophia. "Whatever for?"

"He was on his way to join a hunting party in Canada, but his ship docked in Marquette," Gerald replied. "I was surprised he's allowed in the North, but he was granted parole here upon his honor."

"Honor!" scoffed Caleb. "Those rebels have no honor."

"Hush, Caleb," said Sophia as if he were a child meant to be seen and not heard. "Let your stepfather finish."

"Breckinridge wanted to exchange his paper currency for gold, but it was

a Sunday so he was directed to Peter White's house for help. When Peter understood the situation, he said he would open up the bank for Breckinridge, but when they reached the bank, they found the teller who lives upstairs sitting in the bank and reading. When Peter asked the teller to open the vault, he refused."

"Good," said Caleb. "We shouldn't do those rebels any favors."

"He refused because it was a Sunday," said Gerald. "The teller said he would not transact any business on the Sabbath, even when Mr. Breckinridge explained he could not wait until Monday because his steamer was about to leave. But the teller could not be persuaded, so Peter asked him for the safe combination so he could get the money himself. The teller refused this as well, saying that writing down the combination numbers would be the same as opening the safe."

"How silly," said Agnes. "He's like those people in the Bible who wouldn't help their cow out of a hole on the Sabbath."

"So what did Peter do?" asked Sophia, naturally siding with the wealthy banker, despite her strict religious upbringing.

"Peter went to borrow the money from a friend who lives nearby and then he sent Mr. Breckinridge on his way. The teller, fearing Peter White's anger, then offered to resign, but Peter would not let him. He said he respected the teller for his principles, but not for his judgment."

Another interesting moment in the First National Bank's history occurred during the 1868 fire. With the downtown engulfed in flames, Peter White managed to rush into the bank, open the safe, and rescue the money and bank records. He had them carried to the harbor and placed on a barge that floated out into the bay so the bank property could not be burnt. The next day, Peter White held bank office hours amid the city's ruins.

Following the fire, a new bank was built on the southwest corner of Front and Spring Streets. At the turn into the twentieth century, Louis Kaufman, member of the Marquette banking family that owned the Savings Bank, gained majority control of the bank's stock, although Peter White remained president until his death.

In 1927, Louis Kaufman, then president of the bank, had

First National Doors

the current building erected at the corner of Front and Washington Streets. The building, still magnificent today, was said to be the most expensive building ever built per square foot at the time of its construction. Built of Indiana limestone and pink granite with its staunch Corinthian columns, it still inspires the confidence a bank desires and may have helped especially as the Great Depression approached. The Front Street entrance is notable for its bronze door, designed by John Polacheck of New York, who said it was the finest door his firm ever produced; when he learned the door would be in Marquette, Michigan rather than a larger metropolitan area, he was disappointed that more people would not be able to admire it. The bank's interior is equally exquisite with six elaborate chandeliers, a twenty-five foot high ceiling, and several types of imported Italian marble. Few places in Marquette make a person stop and stare at the ceiling like the First National Bank.

I'm sure I was not alone in my feeling of loss in 2000 when it was announced that the First National Bank was merging with Wells Fargo. After one hundred thirty-six years, Marquette's first bank no longer existed. Considering my parents had opened an account at First National Bank for me soon after I was born, I felt loyalty to First National Bank—a feeling I doubt anyone has toward a bank any longer, considering all the ups and downs in the banking industry in the last decade. But Wells Fargo has proven itself stable, and I am glad Louis Kaufman's magnificent bank building remains open for business.

UNION NATIONAL BANK (PENINSULA BANK)

Unlike the First National Bank, the Union National Bank was not so fortunate after years of bank mergers. On the northeast corner of Front and Washington, the Peninsula Bank stands where first was the Wilkinson Bank, a building built in 1889 out of Portage Entry sandstone and Chicago pressed brick. In 1901, the bank was reorganized and became the Marquette National Bank. Then in the early 1920s it was again

Union National Bank ~ c. 1930

reorganized as the Union National Bank—the name it would be known by for the longest period. During its first few years, John M. Longyear would be its president.

In 1971, the original 1889 structure was destroyed and replaced with the current building, most notable for its thermo-barrier windows that repel the hot summer sun and keep winter's cold blasts at bay, while also preventing people outside from looking in and giving employees a good view of Washington and Front Streets. In 1987, the Union National Bank merged and became a First of America branch. In 1998, another merger made it a National City bank. Today, it is once again locally owned as part of the Marquette County based Peninsula Bank, which has been in business since 1887.

SAVINGS BANK

The success of the iron industry was manifested in the buildings Gerald saw spread throughout downtown. The Savings Bank building on the corner of Front and Washington Streets was Marquette's first true skyscraper, five stories high on Front Street, six stories on Washington, and seven stories at its back facing the lake. Its crowning jewel was the ornate clock tower the residents of Marquette swore could rival London's Big Ben.

— Iron Pioneers

Savings Bank

While the First National Bank building may be more elaborate, no building in downtown Marquette catches the eye as quickly as the Savings Bank. Its tall clock tower is perhaps Marquette's best-known landmark. As a child, I equated it with Big Ben in London, and although I have since seen Big Ben in person, I still think the Savings Bank impressive. As Marquette's first skyscraper, it remains one of the tallest buildings in downtown Marquette well over a century after it was built.

The Savings Bank was organized by Nathan Kaufman and other Marquette businessmen in

1890, and in 1892, they built the current sandstone and red pressed brick structure with its crowning jewel—the first city clock in the Upper Peninsula. The clock still operates today although it has not chimed since 1979 when a wooden pin was accidentally broken while it was being cleaned.

In the early twentieth century, the Savings Bank merged with the First National Bank, at which time the Kaufmans had taken over control of the First National Bank as well.

In 1976, when the building's services were no longer needed for banking, three dentists, Robert Berube, James Jackson, and Peter Kelly, acquired the building and remodeled it as well as restoring much of the original oak interior. Today the building serves as offices for dentists and lawyers among others. As a child in the 1970s, I often went with one of my parents to pick up a wristwatch being repaired by Mr. Keskimaki, who had a shop in the downstairs for forty-seven years until 2004.

For the past several years, the clock tower has been central to Marquette's New Year's Eve celebrations. A miniature version of New York's Times Square ball drop is enacted with a lit up ball dropping from the clock tower. Washington and Front Streets are notoriously packed with people who will turn out to welcome the New Year even when the wind chill is subzero.

Readers of my novels will perhaps best remember Marquette's banks because of my most villainous character, the bank vice-president, Lysander Blackmore. Known for cheating people as well as cheating on his wife, Lysander's bad reputation made me unwilling to name which bank employed him, although it is clear it is a bank on the corner of Washington and Front Streets. In *The Queen City*, Margaret Whitman has a memorable showdown with Lysander when the bank threatens to foreclose on the Whitman farm. She refuses to leave the bank until she can see Mr. Blackmore, and he finally gives in rather than create a scene in the lobby. In the end, Margaret saves her farm, although she has to stoop to blackmail to accomplish it. Fortunately, Margaret knows a secret Mr. Blackmore would prefer his wife did not know. Since Lysander Blackmore ends up blowing out his brains the day after the 1929 stock market crash, I doubt any of Marquette's banks would lay claim to him.

While Marquette now has numerous banks and credit unions, the corner of Washington and Front Streets remains the visual symbol of Marquette's banking history.

DONCKERS

"I was going to offer to buy us cokes at Donckers," Beth replied.

"All right," said Thelma. "All this shopping has made me thirsty."

The girls were soon seated in Donckers. Thelma had her back to the door. Beth was the only one to see the two young men in their work clothes come inside.

"I can at least buy you something for your trip," Henry Whitman told his younger brother. "If you're going to travel across country, you'll need some chocolate."

Roy did not want any candy, but he let Henry buy it so his brother would feel better. He would miss Henry just as much as Henry would miss him.

As the soda jerk filled a bag with chocolates, Henry spotted Beth. An awkward moment followed. Neither had told their families about the other. Should they, in a public place, with family members present, acknowledge each other? Henry recognized Thelma from Beth's descriptions. He did not know whether they could trust Thelma to be silent, but he figured Roy could keep the secret for one day until he left town.

— The Queen City

Donckers is one of the oldest businesses in Marquette, established in 1896. Until 2007, it remained in the Donckers family, and fortunately, its new owner has appreciated the Donckers legacy not only enough to continue its operation as it was but to bring back the old soda fountain and provide a lunch counter upstairs.

From its early days, Donckers had a soda fountain, and in the 1950s when milk shakes and cherry cokes were popular, it was the place to hang out for the teenage crowd. In the 1980s, my brother and I would often spend a

Donckers

summer day at my grandparents' house in North Marquette and spend our afternoon walking downtown—Donckers was usually the destination—although I made sure we stopped at Snowbound Books on the way back.

The recent return of Donckers' soda fountain and its new lunch counter reflect once again that Marquette is ever nostalgic. In 2009, part of my mother's 50th class reunion for John D. Pierce School was held here; the Bishop Baraga class of 1959 also wanted the location for the same evening, so the two classes agreed to share and remember their high school days together.

The downstairs continues to be packed with every kind of candy imaginable from a variety of chocolate confections and truffles to jujubes, gummy butterflies, candy flying saucers, fudge, and hard candies of every flavor. It is not uncommon when I visit friends in other parts of the country that they ask I bring them candy from Donckers. Having served Marquette in three different centuries, Donckers is not likely to leave its place in the heart of downtown Marquette or the hearts of its residents any time soon.

THE DELFT THEATRE

On Saturdays, John and Chad often went to matinees at the Delft The-atre. The movies were not always spectacular, often children's shows they had outgrown. Robinson Crusoe, The Journey of Natty Gann, The Watcher in the Woods *were films soon forgotten, but that hardly mattered; the true glamor was being at a movie theatre, especially the fabulous old Delft. This theatre, perhaps more than any place in Marquette, evoked history to them. When the boys saw* Annie, *they were impressed by the glamorous scene when the characters from the 1930s go to the movies at Radio City Music Hall, and the ushers danced down the aisle with flashlights to show them to their seats. The boys could just imagine that in its heyday, the Delft had been a similarly magical movie showplace. For seventy years, the theatre had stood along Washington Street, the most notable building on the block. During its long life, the theatre had shown films and been the sight of pub-lic performances. Now, as the theatre fell into neglect, its former grandeur made it all the more enticing. It was the only theatre in town with a round lit-tle ticket window inside the front door. From there rose a long hallway that led to double doors where the usher collected your ticket so you could enter a splendid fantasy world. Then you went down a tall flight of stairs until you came to the concession stand where a cluster of peo-ple competed for the cashiers' attention to buy popcorn, raisinettes, coca-colas, and sometimes, even ice cream! The con-cession stand was against the left wall while the right wall had a giant window that looked into the theatre itself so even the concession workers could watch the film when they were not busy serving customers.*

The theatre walls were covered with

Delft Theatre ~ 1998

winter scenes of children sledding. Protruding from the ceiling was the magnificent big round metal thing no one could define—it was not a chandelier because it had nothing to do with lighting; it had giant rings, one inside another, like a spaceship hovering over the audience, which only added to the atmosphere when watching Return of the Jedi, The Last Starfighter, *or* 2010.

Most impressive of all, the Delft boasted the largest screen in the Upper Peninsula—they did not make movie theaters with such big screens anymore. Drive-ins were now all but extinct and most old movie theaters had been replaced by multiplex cinemas. John had heard tales of such theaters from friends who had seen them downstate; he had heard that if you did not like a movie, you could sneak into another one, so you could see parts of three or four films on the same night. John thought this silly since you would never get to see a full film. He did not imagine Marquette would ever be big enough for a multiplex cinema. Three theaters, each showing one movie, was enough variety for Marquette.

— Superior Heritage

The Delft Theatre was actually part of a chain. Iron River, Munising, and Escanaba also had their own Delft theatres, built to look like Dutch buildings—hence the name Delft. Marquette's Delft Theatre has survived the others.

The theatre was built in 1914 and initially, besides showing silent films, had a stage for vaudeville and other performances. The Marquette Opera House across the street would have provided more "cultural" forms of entertainment.

About 1950, the stage was closed off and the movie screen—the largest ever in Upper Michigan—was permanently put into place. Then in 1985, it was divided into two separate rooms and screens, thus breaking up the U.P.'s largest screen. In the next decade, it was divided again, this time into five screens. Considerable remodeling was done at that point, including having the main entrance transferred from Washington Street—where the lighted marquee still hangs, to Main Street. As children, my brother and I always thought it a mystery how one could enter on Washington Street and exit on Main Street; we could not believe the metal shaft that crossed Hogan's Alley was really all of the Delft Theatre.

The original entrance to the Delft Theatre was on Washington Street where from the ticket booth you walked up a long sloping floor to another door where your tickets were collected. This large room is now the top floor theatre. When this section was remodeled, a Chinese painting was discovered from the theatre's early days. It has now been preserved and graces this individual room. The stairs to reach this top room were initially the stairs down to the concession stands on the left wall, and the giant theatre was on the left. In the back of the main theatre was a low wall, so if you got up from your seat to go to the bathroom, you could still watch the movie as you walked past the concession stand, or if you waited for your popcorn.

Despite the magic of going to the Delft Theatre, the bathrooms were another story. You had to go down into the basement, where a sort of lobby existed which had off it the dirty smelly bathrooms with old looking plumbing. The lobby always seemed to be filled with high school and college students who were smoking, a scary experience for little kids—especially in those days when parents thought nothing of sending their children to the bathroom on their own—but despite scary smoking college students, children were safe in the Delft Theatre. Today the main lobby and concession stands are where the restrooms once were located.

The interior of the main theatre room in the old days is accurate as described in *Superior Heritage.* I could not even begin to list all the movies I watched there, but I do remember the very first one. It was a few days before Christmas 1974 and I was three years old. My family had just moved into our new house in Stonegate by the Crossroads, and my dad took me to the movie so my mom could focus on unpacking. The movie was terrible—it was a Christmas film with Santa Claus being chased by the Devil who was out to stop him from delivering presents; in one scene, the Devil moved a chimney so Santa could not get inside a house and in another Santa had to climb a tree to escape an angry, barking dog. I've never been able to find out the name of this movie—nor am I surprised it's never been released on video. It wasn't fit viewing for a three year old.

Other early films I remember seeing at the Delft were the Disney cartoons—*Pinocchio, Peter Pan*, and *Snow White.* By middle school, my brother and I could go on our own—my mom would drop us off at the Saturday matinees to attend the same films Chad and John attend in *Superior Heritage.*

I miss the Delft's giant screen and reasonable prices for candy at the concession stand, but I think Marquette residents will agree with me that even with five screens, we are happy the Delft is still there with its marquee brightly lit to make Washington Street distinct. Long may the movie magic live on.

THE COFFEE CUP

Meet the Author of "The Queen City"

Tyler R. Tichelaar, a Marquette native with roots seven generations deep, will be at the Coffee Cup on **Saturday, October 28, 10am to 2pm** to meet readers and sign copies of "The Queen City", the second of a trilogy of novels inspired by Marquette's role in American history. Learn more and read an excerpt at www.marquettefiction.com

the Coffee Cup

Spring St. between Front & Third
Downtown Marquette · 228-6196
Mon-Fri · 6am-8pm, Sat & Sun 7am-7pm

"Where do we get coffee?" he asked as a form of apology.

When he had snapped at her, she had felt like crying, but now she felt a tingling sensation of pleasure because he had accepted her offer.

"Just down the street," she said, leading him west toward the Post Office. They crossed the street and entered The Coffee Cup. They easily found a seat, the morning rush being over, and it being too early for lunch.

— Superior Heritage

The original Coffee Cup restaurant was on Washington Street. When I wrote *Superior Heritage,* I had Theo and Jessie go there because it was convenient to the plot—not because I had any memories of it. Little did I know when I wrote the novel that by the time my books were published, another Coffee Cup restaurant would open on Spring Street in Marquette. It would be short-lived, but from 2005-2008, it was a popular place for many people, including my parents, to go and have coffee or breakfast. *The Mining Journal* dubbed it "the living room of Marquette" because of its friendly atmosphere, its bookshelves, couches, knick-knacks, and antique refrigerator that made it comfortable and cozy.

Owner Peggy Schwemin was responsible for its welcoming atmosphere. Not only did she welcome the patrons and keep a good rapport with them, but she supported aspiring

Former Coffee Cup

artists by letting them display and sell their paintings or crafts. When my parents told Peggy I had published a book, she agreed to carry it, and I had a book signing there for each of my first four novels.

Although the Coffee Cup has since closed, it is not forgotten. Its patrons have found new places to go for coffee and breakfast, but it's unlikely they will find such a homey, comfortable atmosphere again.

MY FIRST BOOK SIGNING—GRANDPA WOULD BE PROUD

The following article I wrote on my MySpace blog following my first book signing at the Coffee Cup on Saturday, May 6, 2006:

This past Saturday I had my first book signing for my first published novel *Iron Pioneers*. The book signing was held at the Coffee Cup in Marquette. I was excited to have my first signing at a coffee shop because it would attract a crowd even if people did not know about the book signing. In addition, I was fortunate to receive a great deal of publicity through the radio, TV, and local newspapers as well as by word of mouth.

And yet, I was nervous. Would anyone come? Would I spend the day sitting behind the table with a stack of books while people passed in and out of the coffee shop, avoiding me, making me feel pathetic. I had thought of asking a friend or family member to come and sit with me through the day, but I knew when my book was published that my motto had to be "Feel the Fear and Do It Anyway," and so far not one of my fears has manifested. So I told myself everything would go fine.

Then on the morning

First Book Signing ~ The Coffee Cup

of the book signing, I remembered that today was not the first time I had sat behind a table while selling something. When I was a boy, my grandpa went to many craft sales and flea markets to sell his woodworking, and I was always his helper. My grandpa was a retired carpenter, although he never really retired. In his later years, he made tables and cutting boards, mirrors, lazy susans, and footstools, and he sold them everywhere from church bazaars to craft sales at the Marquette Mall. Grandpa and I did everything together—unload the car, set up the tables, screw legs on the tables Grandpa had made, and talk to the customers.

People loved Grandpa's work—he was as much an artist in his woodworking as I am in my wordsmithing. Even now, nearly twenty years after his death, restaurants still have his mirrors; kitchens still have his cabinets. I remember during the slow moments at these sales, I would sit and read, but we rarely had slow moments—Grandpa usually outsold all the other artisans.

And Grandpa would introduce me to everyone who came up to the table, and proudly tell them how much I liked to read and how many books I owned. Neither of us knew then that all the stories he would tell me of local history and his own childhood would inspire me to write my novel trilogy about Marquette. When Grandpa passed away, going to the craft sales with him was one of the things I missed most. Remembering him the morning of my book signing made me feel if he could do it, so could I.

It turned out my book signing was a hit! I was ready to face everyone alone but several friends came to support me, and better yet, many people I did not know. Everyone was enthusiastic about my book, and people who had already read it, came and bought more copies to give as gifts. As I later packed the few books I had left into the car, I knew Grandpa would have been proud.

THE MINING JOURNAL

Will had often thought that to buy The Mining Journal *was a waste of money when the family could barely afford food for the table. Margaret, however, insisted the newspaper be purchased whenever she went into town. She would have bought* Harper's Bazaar, *the fashion magazines, or those rags about the movie stars if she could afford them. Deprived of such simple entertainments,* The Mining Journal *had to fulfill Margaret's longings for gossip. In the "City Brevities" column, she discovered who was visiting Marquette, who had gone on vacation, who was recently engaged, and who had married. She perused it with avid interest.*

Today Henry had brought The Mining Journal *home from town, but scarcely glancing at it, he had completely missed the headline about the wild car chase that resulted in the arrest of a moonshine dealer. Margaret believed alcohol consumption one of mankind's greatest sins; she would have passed over the article without interest if her eye had not caught Harry Cumming Jr.'s name. Then she read with fascinated alarm. Those Cummings had shamed the family again.*

— The Queen City

The Mining Journal more than any other publication has chronicled the history and culture of Marquette. It was always in our house when I was growing up, and although I probably referenced it most often for its TV Guide, in the early 1980s I became interested in reading it for its historical articles about Marquette. When people ask me how I did the research for my novels, the number one source is doubtless *The Mining Journal*. Other sources included numerous family stories handed down from my grandparents, parents, great-aunts and great-uncles, and numerous books, but *The Mining Journal* was a major source. For years I collected every article of historical interest the newspaper published, cutting them out and stuffing them in a drawer, not

The Mining Journal

knowing for what purpose. Then in 1999, when I started writing *The Marquette Trilogy*, I had stacks of articles I went through to organize, file, re-read, and find sources for my stories. Today I have a file cabinet overflowing with clippings—occasionally from other papers such as *The U.P. Catholic* and plenty from *Marquette Monthly*, but *The Mining Journal* remains predominant.

More than just a source of information, in my novels *The Mining Journal* is a source of family history and city gossip. It is where Lyla finds out about the death of Thelma Bergmann which leads to her showdown with her adopted sister, told from two different viewpoints in *Superior Heritage* and *Narrow Lives*. In *The Queen City*, *The Mining Journal* announces the birth of Scofield Blackmore, illegitimate child to the well-to-do banker, which becomes a source of scandal in the small town. In the early twentieth century, a "City Brevities" column—not quite a gossip column—noted who was visiting from out of town or who was going on a trip as Margaret Whitman notes in the passage above.

The Mining Journal's origins date back to 1846. According to its 1996 sesquicentennial special edition, *The Mining Journal*'s predecessor was the *Lake Superior News and Miner's Journal* begun by John N. Ingersoll, located in Copper Harbor, Michigan and printed weekly in summer and monthly in winter. By comparison, in 1996 *The Mining Journal*, with a daily circulation, would have 22,000 Sunday subscribers. In 1850, Ingersoll's paper was purchased by several Sault Sainte Marie businessmen and renamed the *Lake Superior Journal*. The paper moved to Marquette in 1855 when it was purchased by John Burt. Many of the *Lake Superior Journal*'s original issues are preserved on microfilm at Peter White Public Library, as are most issues of *The Mining Journal* since then.

In 1862, the *Lake Superior Journal* merged with the *Lake Superior News at Marquette* to be named *Lake Superior News and Journal*. Both my ancestor Basil Bishop and his grandson Francis Marion Bishop refer to this version in letters they wrote. Then the 1868 Marquette fire put the paper out of print from June 11 to July 25th. It recovered quickly when Alfred Swineford purchased it, and the following year, he renamed it *The Mining Journal*. Swineford ran the journal for the next twenty years while also twice serving as mayor of Marquette.

In 1889, Swineford sold the paper to the Russell family, who operated it through most of the twentieth century. The first Russell to operate *The Mining Journal* was James Russell, who was also warden at the Marquette Branch Prison from 1902-1917. His son Frank Russell Sr. operated the paper and then passed it on to his son, Frank Russell Jr., who would also begin WDMJ-TV, today known as WLUC TV6.

Besides the occasional mentions of events in *The Mining Journal*'s pages—obviously the ones mentioned in my novels are fictional—the paper is notable because its employees first noticed that Washington Street was on fire during the Great Blizzard of 1938 and sounded the alarm.

Today, *The Mining Journal* remains the primary source of information in Marquette from who is getting married, to who has been born or died, which businesses have opened, what city politicians are planning, and for historical articles. More than any other publication, *The Mining Journal* has been Marquette's daily chronicle.

HARLOW PARK & VETERANS MEMORIAL

The number of Marquette's sons who went to the war are too numerous to mention in full. Each one gave Marquette reason to be proud of its steadfast residents. David McClintock became a submarine commander at the Battle of Leyte Gulf. Otto Hultgren would be wounded three times, yet live to be Marquette's most decorated hero. Many families made multiple sacrifices: William White would serve with the air force in England, while his brother Roland served in France and Germany, and his brother Frank was stationed in the Pacific. The U.S. Naval Air Base in Illinois was flooded with soldiers from Northern State Teachers College who became known as the "U.P. Wildcats," after the college's team name; several accomplished pilots would spring from this group. Michigan's long winters forged the talents of many in the 10th Mountain Infantry Division, a skiing combat unit sent to the Italian Alps where it would achieve victories at Riva Ridge and Mount Belvedere. So many heroic exploits, too many to tell, but each a reason for gratitude.

— The Queen City

Marquette Area Veterans Memorial ~ Peace Globe

Harlow Park, named for city founder Amos Harlow, is at the edge of what can be considered the downtown area. It has long been a popular playground for children, and for several years, in the 1980s and 1990s, it was the site of the city Christmas tree. In the early twenty-first century, a Veterans memorial was also placed in the park, including a giant lit up peace globe. Since the Veterans memorial only includes the names of people whose family members donated to it, many veterans' names are missing, but included are bricks for many of my relatives.

Members of my family have fought in almost every war in United States history, and most of them lived in Marquette. My five-greats-grandfather, Elijah Bishop—father of Marquette pioneer Basil Bishop, fought in the American Revolution as did his father, brothers, and father-in-law. Basil Bishop fought in the War of 1812—he is believed to be the only War of 1812 veteran buried in Marquette. My great-great-great-grandfather, Edmond Remington, his son-in-law, Jerome White, and Jerome's cousin, Francis Marion Bishop, all served in the Civil War. Just shortly after the Spanish-American War, my great-great-uncle, Clement White, served in the Philippines. My great-great-uncle Byron McCombie and another relative, Robert S. Zryd, enlisted in World War I, as did my Grandma White's brothers William and Daniel Molby. My grandfather's brothers—Roland, William, and Frank White all fought in World War II. Numerous

cousins fought in the later twentieth century wars—Korea, Vietnam, and the Persian Gulf, as well as in Iraq in the twenty-first century.

Many veterans, my family members included, rest just above Harlow Park in Park Cemetery. Harlow Park is an appropriate place for a memorial to the veterans since it is in the center of Marquette where everyone who drives by can remember the sacrifice these brave souls made that Marquette might be free.

Veteran Bricks

PARK CEMETERY

One Saturday afternoon, he talked Chad into going with him to Park Cemetery.

"What were Grandpa's grandparents' names?" Chad asked as they got out of the car.

"Whitman I imagine," said John.

"Are you sure those are the grandparents he meant?"

"I don't know," said John. "His other grandparents were named Dalrymple."

They found Uncle Roy's stone beside the grave of their Great-Grandpa and Great-Grandma Whitman. Then they walked downhill in the direction Grandpa had pointed, carefully looking at the name on each stone.

After ten minutes, Chad said, "Here's a Whitman. Jacob Whitman and wife Agnes. Maybe they're great-grandpa's parents. Jacob was born in 1843 and died in 1897 and Agnes was born in 1851 and died in 1884."

"Yes, those were Great-Grandpa Whitman's parents' names according to his obituary," said John. "They died so young."

John scribbled down the names and dates. Then they wandered about, looking at other stones, searching for familiar names.

"Hey," said Chad. "Remember in Grandma's stuff we found that picture of Uncle Roy and Great-Grandma standing next to a gravestone. There were some trees near it. Maybe those are Great-Grandma's parents' graves."

"Were the trees big in the picture?" asked John, who could not remember.

"No," said Chad, "they were little, but it was a black and white picture, so the trees are probably grown now."

Twenty minutes later, they found the stone beside the trees. There lay Charles and Christina Dalrymple, and beside them was a smaller stone for Arthur Dalrymple. All three stones had birth and death dates on them, and below Arthur's name was written, "who was born in Pictou, Pictou, Nova Scotia."

"Great-Grandma had a brother named Charles,"

Basil Bishop Grave

Chad reminded John. "Remember he was married to that Aunt Harriet everyone says was really mean."

"But this Charles is too old to be Great-Grandma's brother. It must be her father."

"Then Arthur must have been her grandfather."

John thought for a minute. "That would make Arthur our great-great-great-grandfather."

John wrote down their names and dates. He doubted many people knew the names of their great-great-great grandfathers. He felt he had made a successful start.

— Superior Heritage

The above scene reflects my early interests in genealogy and my first efforts to learn about my ancestors.

My earliest memory of being in Park Cemetery was not until I was fifteen and attended my mother's cousin Robert Specker's funeral—I remember standing on the hill where he was buried near his father, my great-grandparents, and other family members. After the service, my grandfather said to me, "My grandparents are buried over there" and pointed toward Jerome White's grave. I little suspected in another year my grandfather would also be in a cemetery—although Holy Cross instead of Park Cemetery because my grandmother was Catholic and he wanted to be buried with her.

Jerome White Grave

That memory later led me to the rest of the White family's graves. From photographs I had seen, I was able to find the McCombie graves, and then later, the Remingtons and the Bishops' graves. Six generations of ancestors and relatives are buried in Park Cemetery.

The stones of my family members themselves tell stories. Jemima Remington's sad grave tells us "my daughter Alice lies by my side." William John McCombie's stone states he came from "Pictou, Pictou, Nova Scotia." Other stones are decorative—children's

Cyrus White Grave

graves are commonly marked with little lambs on top of them. Other graves have sculptured stones in various shapes—trees were popular, their limbs cut off to symbolize lives cut short.

The cemetery was initially the Episcopalian burying ground and then expanded to become Park Cemetery. Readers of *Iron Pioneers* will remember that Clara is buried here—one of the first Marquette pioneers in my novels. Later, people came to have picnics in the park, as Sophia Henning insists upon doing after her son Caleb Rockford drowns and is buried. Although the family thinks Sophia's grief excessive to want to picnic by her son's grave, Victorians frequently thought of cemeteries as parks where their loved ones would rest in serene beauty.

Park Cemetery's design is largely due to Peter White. In Marquette's early years, graves were dug randomly, but starting in 1872 Peter White initi-

Peter White Grave

ated a plan that included dredging the ponds, fencing the cemetery, and building the walking bridges to the little islands that are so quaint and charming. Improvements to the cemetery were ongoing for the next several decades. In 1926, Rolina Morrison,

Kaufman Mausoleum

whose father was the caretaker, brought a single water lily bulb from Portland, Oregon which her father planted. That single bulb resulted in the hundreds in the ponds today. In 1946, a section of the cemetery was set aside for Jewish burials, and in 2000, the cemetery sexton, William Malandrone designed a memorial for those resting in the Potter's Field, which until then was marked by a single white cross. Today, the cemetery remains a favorite place for people to go walking.

Most of Marquette's notable citizens rest here. Peter White is here as are the Kaufmans in their enormous mausoleum. The Harlow family and Robert Graveraet have less august stones.

Annabella Stonegate

My readers often ask me about Annabella Stonegate, the young girl who dies in a blizzard in *Iron Pioneers* and whom Will Whitman says became a ghost in *The Queen City*. Although the city records are curiously silent about her, I affix here a picture of her gravestone. To this day, she watches over those lost in blizzards as well as visiting her dead friends. More will be revealed about Annabella in my upcoming novel *Spirit of the North*.

Park Cemetery Lily Pond

ST. JOHN THE BAPTIST CATHOLIC CHURCH

After hastily dressing, I met Grandma and my aunt downstairs. We walked to the corner of Fourth Street, then proceeded down the hill to St. John the Baptist's Catholic Church, a large, dull colored brown brick church, with a bell tower in the back. We walked along its side, and only when we came around to its front door did I notice its aesthetic grandeur. Built in the Spanish Romanesque style, it was unique among Upper Peninsula churches, looking as if it belonged in Texas or Mexico. Stained glass windows ran along both its sides. The front doors were arched with a few steps leading up to them. Above the doors was a gorgeous rose window. But what I liked best were the statues of saints on top of the columns and apex of the evangelists and St. John the Baptist. The saints looked down with pensive faces upon all the church's visitors, blessing them as they passed inside.

I was not a very religious boy, only thinking to pray when I wanted or needed something, such as when my mother had died. My parents had dutifully taken me to a little stone church in our town, but they had scarcely ever said a word about religion to

St. John the Baptist Catholic Church

me. I had had no Catholic friends in South Carolina. All our neighbors were Baptists, and my parents had told me never to discuss religion with other people, probably because they feared prejudice against us as Catholics. But Upper Michigan had been settled largely by French Canadians and Irish and German immigrants, so the Catholic Church flourished here. And between going to school at Bishop Baraga and sitting in St. John the Baptist's, my heart would slowly fill with devotion to God. I loved the church's beautiful stained glass windows, the grand old hymns we sang, the ritual and the tradition, even the glorious sound of the ancient Latin tongue. St. John the Baptist had been opened in 1908, so it was quite a modern church at the time, although today it would seem very old fashioned. When it was torn down in 1986, I felt devastated, as if I had lost a family member, for I had worshipped within its walls nearly seventy years and always found peace there.

— The Only Thing That Lasts

My readers may remember in *Iron Pioneers* that when Molly goes to confession, it is to the French Catholic Church on Washington Street since those scenes take place in the early 1880s when St. Peter's Cathedral was being rebuilt. A French Catholic Church had been at the corner of Fourth and Washington Streets since 1872. Initially, the French Catholics were part of the cathedral's parish, but that year they organized as St. Jean Baptiste parish and bought the old Methodist church—the Methodists were busy erecting a new church on Ridge Street. All the services at this newly turned French Catholic Church were said in Latin and French (Catholic Masses were said in Latin until Vatican Council II decreed in the 1960s that the Mass could be said in the people's native tongue).

The French Catholic population continued to grow until a new, larger church was needed. The new church began construction in 1906 and opened its doors for Mass in 1908. The new St. John the Baptist Catholic Church was then probably, at least from its exterior, the most noticeable and impressive church in Marquette after the cathedral.

Although a church for French Catholics, St. John's style was Spanish Renaissance with a large rose window in the front and a façade that curved upward with four Corinthian pilasters, each with a statue on top of one of the four gospel writers. Another statue was in a shadow box window, and more statues on the very top of the church.

The church's interior was quite impressive with three aisles that led up to the altar, and the walls were imbedded with sixteen stained glass windows as well as the large rose window.

I regret that I was only inside the church once. My strongest memories are of its parking lot where my grandfather attended its craft shows for a few years. I remember he made $200 there once, the most he ever earned at a sale for his carpentry work—a sizeable amount of money nearly thirty years ago.

In *Superior Heritage*, I have recaptured one of those craft sales when John Vandelaare helps his grandfather, Henry Whitman, at one. While the ensuing meeting with author Robert O'Neill is completely fictional, the scene where Henry gives John

My Infant of Prague Statue

money to buy an Infant of Prague statue is based on my grandpa giving me money to do the same. Back then, I was quite a religious boy who read my Bible and thought about becoming a priest. Of all the vendors at that craft sale, I was only interested in the two nuns selling prayer cards, rosaries, and statues. I think I was their best customer that day, and they told me I should go to the seminary. I considered it at the time, but later, my love of writing overcame my religious aspirations, although many of my early spiritual interests are depicted in *Superior Heritage*.

When I was much older and I better understood how difficult the religious conflict in the family must have been for my grandparents to overcome, I thought how wonderful it was that my Baptist-raised grandfather had not thought twice about buying his grandson a Catholic statue. While honoring the Infant of Prague is supposed to bring blessings, today I treasure that statue for the memories it brings me of a generous, open-minded grandfather.

Not long after in 1986, St. John the Baptist was torn down. The parishioners were furious with the bishop's decision to sell the property. The claim was that the structure was weak and unsafe and even that the front wall might eventually fall into Washington Street. The repairs would cost a quarter million dollars. Parish efforts to raise enough money for the repairs were unsuccessful, and the money that was raised eventually went to fund scholarships and Catholic programs in Marquette. The parish closed in June, and what seemed cruel at the time, just a few days before Christmas, St. John's was torn down. Parishioners who watched the demolition have told me how difficult it was to pull down the front wall, making them doubt claims that the building was really unstable. Many hurt feelings resulted from the destruction as expressed in *Superior Heritage* by the O'Neill family.

Where St. John the Baptist stood is now a parking lot. The lone sign of the church's long presence there is its remaining bell tower and the parish offices which are now business suites.

St. John's Bell Tower

But St. John's lives on in the memories of its parishioners, and many of its artifacts were preserved. The stained glass windows were sold and several today grace people's homes. The antique pipe organ was sent to St. Mary-St. Joseph Church in Iron Mountain, and the bells from the tower were sent to St. Francis de Sales Church in Manistique. And every time I go to Mass at St. Michael's, I can see St. John's rose window suspended from the ceiling, recalling the earlier parish. St. John's spirit lives on in other congregations.

OLD CITY HALL

Farther down the street was the towering Post Office, and beside it, a robust new domed city hall built of Lake Superior Sandstone.

"These city buildings are as fine as any in New York," Gerald praised. He looked about but found no evidence of the flimsy wooden structures that had been tacked together before the great fire of 1868 had resulted in a city ordinance that all structures in the business district be built of stone.

— Iron Pioneers

Marquette's Old City Hall with its enormous red roof may well be the most distinctive looking building in Marquette. Built by the architectural firm of Demar and Lovejoy, its mix of Romanesque, classical, and French and Italian Renaissance architecture makes it stand out with heavy but fanciful charm. The Mansard roof of red tile is enlivened with a dome topped by a cupola. The building's sandstone and pressed red brick nicely contrast and add flavor to the Romanesque arched entrance. Inside the woodwork is rich carved oak of impeccable taste and style.

When the City Hall was dedicated in 1895, Mayor Nathan Kaufman declared it was "a city hall built to last forever." Besides its many important civic functions, the building for a short time at the turn into the twentieth century also served as home to the first classes for the Northern Normal School (today Northern Michigan University) until

City Hall

the first campus buildings were completed.

Then in the early 1970s, it was decided the city needed new offices so a new city hall was built on the corner of Baraga and Fourth Streets across from the cathedral where the original Bishop Baraga School had stood. Marquette residents feared a new city hall would mean the destruction of the old one. Had Nathan Kaufman's prediction been wrong that the building would last forever? The people rallied and in 1974 the Marquette Heritage Committee achieved recognition for the building as a Michigan Historic Landmark. The following year, Peter O'Dovero purchased the building and began its extensive renovation, bringing it up to modern heating, plumbing, and electrical standards while restoring the interior to its original grandeur wherever possible.

City Hall at Night ~ c. 1998

Interior Woodwork

Today, filled with business offices rather than city workers, and presiding over Washington Street like the grand old dame on the hill, Old City Hall does seem like it will last forever. Until recently Marquette promoted itself in winter as the City of Lights, from Christmas until the dogsled races in February, and with all of Marquette's downtown buildings lit up, the old City Hall was the most impressive with lights encircling its many arched windows. No longer lit up, on a cold winter evening, its warm sandstone walls can still bring warmth to many Marquette residents' hearts.

THE POST OFFICE

He crossed Washington Street, gazing up at the tall Post Office and Federal Building. He remembered seeing a photograph of his grandfather peering out of one of those upper windows. John's novel had started out from an idea based on his grandfather's life; he missed his grandpa so much he had wanted to immortalize his memory, but the story had gotten away from him, creating a character only loosely based on Henry Whitman; nevertheless, John knew it was the best piece he had ever written. He thought it might bring luck that he was mailing his novel at the post office his grandfather had helped to build.

Inside, three people waited in line before him. John stared at the painting of Father Marquette standing up in a canoe while Indians paddled it; everyone in Upper Michigan knows you cannot stand in a canoe, and the Indians looked crabby, as if irritated that Father Marquette was not helping to paddle. But since John had set the novel in the city named for this Jesuit priest, he thought seeing the picture might bring him good luck.

— Superior Heritage

Old Post Office ~ c. 1900

Marquette has had a post office since its very founding. Initially, Amos Harlow ran a post office out of his own home, and there was also a Carp River post office. Since the bulk of the mail was addressed to the Carp River post office, it eventually became predominant.

Delivery of mail to Marquette was not easy in the first years, and especially once winter set in, residents could go for months without receiving letters. The mail route over land was from Green Bay, Wisconsin, about a 180-mile journey. In 1850, the city fathers decided something had to be done to get the mail delivered more regularly, so they sent Peter White to Green Bay to collect the mail, hauling it by sleigh back to Marquette.

The situation did not improve, however, until in 1854, Peter White took matters into his own hands, as related in *Iron Pioneers*:

In January 1854, Marquette had received no mail for three months, so Peter had been elected to go to Green Bay to fetch it. With Indian companions and dog sleds, he set out on the one hundred eighty mile journey. Halfway, he met sleighs coming north with the village's mail. Eight tons of Marquette's mail had accumulated in Green Bay, and it took three months for the postmaster to find someone willing to carry it north. Peter sent his companions and the mail back to Marquette, but intent to resolve the situation, he continued on to Green Bay.

Upon his arrival, he discovered Marquette's mail was accumulating at the rate of six bushels a day. Frustrated, Peter traveled another fifty miles to Fond du Lac so he could telegraph Senator Cass about the situation. Determined to receive a response, he bombarded the senator with telegrams until a special agent came to Green Bay to investigate. The postmaster in Green Bay, as upset about the situation as Peter, agreed to act as accomplice. Together the two men filled all the post office's empty sacks, claiming, when the agent arrived, that every bag contained mail for Marquette. Thirty bags of actual mail now appeared to be four times as much. The agent, overwhelmed by the sight, quickly authorized weekly mail delivery to Marquette from Green Bay. Marquette had not lacked for its mail since, and Peter had been hailed as a town hero.

As Marquette grew, the mail soon surpassed even the fake amount Peter White had created to remedy the delivery issues. The need for a larger post office resulted in the 1886 construction of the Federal Building on the corner of Washington and Third Street where today the current post office stands. Construction of the building cost $100,000 but was several times delayed, among other reasons, because a stonemason who was fired from his job for being drunk decided to shoot the general

Post Office Mural of Father Marquette

contractor and then commit suicide (perhaps the earliest example of someone going "postal"). Despite the setbacks, when the Federal Building, the first U.S. Government building in Upper Michigan, was completed it was highly impressive and worthy of the beautiful city hall soon to stand beside it. The Federal Building's high tower and its arched doorways and windows make one regret it was ever replaced.

In the 1930s, the U.S. Government decided a new United States Post Office and Court House was needed, and the old Federal Building was soon no more. The new building would be built of Bedford limestone and completed in 1937. Its style is typical of 1930s Art Deco. My grandfather, Lester White, was among those employed in its construction, so I feel a fondness for it whenever I go inside. I have mailed many of my manuscripts to various publishers inside this building, hopeful, since my grandpa helped to construct it, that the post office would bring me some luck.

Inside the main lobby is a mural that was commissioned by the Works Progress Administration (WPA) soon after the building was opened. Artist Dewey Albinson depicted Father Marquette with two French voyageurs and two Indians in a canoe. Most likely to lend significance to the Jesuit

Building New Post Office ~ 1937
Lester White in center window, top right

priest, Albinson depicted Father Marquette as standing up. When I was a student at Northern Michigan University, my American literature professor, David Mitchell, told the students to go down to the post office and write a description of what they thought this painting represented about America. After reading the papers, Professor Mitchell remarked that he could tell

"New" Post Office

he was in Upper Michigan because every student had commented on how Father Marquette would have known that to stand up in a canoe would tip it over.

Mail delivery in Marquette has vastly improved since Peter White's days, but it remains difficult. The postal workers of Upper Michigan embody the saying "neither rain, nor sleet, nor snow" will stop the U.S. mail. In the worst of blizzards, I have come home to find my mailman has climbed over snowbanks to put my letters in my mailbox. The cost of stamps is small for such dedication.

SUPERIOR VIEW

Saddest of all was an old cigar box filled with photographs, faded black and white pictures of ladies in long dresses, men with turn of the century mustaches, people sitting in carriages. Forgotten faces. Ellen and John searched for family resemblances. They guessed who might be Grandma's parents or brothers, but they did not know for sure. Aunt Eleanor came over to identify multitudes of deceased Whitmans and Dalrymples, but the camera's attempt to preserve McCareys and Bergmanns had failed because names had not been written on the backs of photographs.

— Superior Heritage

If any business owner in Marquette is interested in preserving Marquette history, it is Jack Deo of Superior View. Whether they are photographs of historic buildings or forgotten faces, he has a place for them in his heart and his store.

Jack has been a photographer for over forty years. In 1978 his passion for old photographs led to the establishment of Superior View in Marquette. At the time of the store's opening, first located above Donckers and later moved to its current location at the corner of Washington and Third Streets, Jack had long been collecting old negatives from early Upper Michigan photographers, notably Brainard F. Childs, who founded the Childs Art Gallery in the 1860s. Childs was the premier photo artist of Upper Michigan, and his stereoscopic series "The Gems of Lake Superior" captured the Lake Superior region's beauty and history. For three generations, the Childs Art Gallery operated. Jack's acquisition of the Childs' negatives led to more negatives from such studios as J.W. Nara of Calumet, Peterson Brothers of Gwinn and Menominee, Nickolai Olli of Mohawk, Adolph Isler of Houghton, and G.A. Werner of Marquette and Ishpeming.

Superior View

Today Jack Deo's archive includes over 100,000 historic images. The store itself sells various sizes of historic photographs from postcard size up, as well as numerous other nostalgic and historical mementos of Upper Michigan. Jack also restores old photographs, and he has given numerous presentations on Marquette history and photography, including presentations with Marquette historian Fred Rydholm, and presentations of Marquette in 3-D.

Jack is a great enthusiast for history and a true supporter of local historians seeking photographs for their books. I purchased from Jack the rights to use the photographs for the covers of several of my books—*Iron Pioneers*, *The Queen City*, *Narrow Lives*, and *The Only Thing That Lasts*, as well as numerous photographs within the covers of this book. He also touched up the only photograph I have of my great-great-great-grandmother, Jemima Remington. Jack can improve a photograph and get it colorized or resized efficiently with unmatched expertise. Photographs from his collection frequently appear in books and publications including *The Mining Journal*. His contribution to preserving Marquette's history cannot be underplayed. For more of his historical photographs, visit www.ViewsofthePast.com

THE MARQUETTE OPERA HOUSE

The Marquette Opera House was a stately edifice, the grandest in the Queen City's downtown. The building had been constructed in 1892 at the instigation of the city's greatest benefactors, Peter White and John Long-year. The foundation was built of Anna River brick and native Marquette brownstone. The front entrance had a Romanesque arch through which the city's residents passed in their most elegant habiliments. While the building also housed a storefront and a Masonic Hall, the theatre was the building's gem. The interior reflected the height of the Italian Renaissance, while the proscenium arch served as gateway to the grandest scenes ever played on a Marquette stage. Ornate boxes filled the walls, and in one such princely

Opera House Interior ~ 1895

seat, Beth found herself seated between her lover and her annoying cousin.

First Thelma commented about the comfortable seat. Then she fretted over how well she could see the stage. Next she listed the names of everyone in the theatre whom she knew, and since the theatre could hold up to one thousand people, and almost everyone in Marquette knew everyone else, this recital lasted until the lights dimmed and the orchestra began to play.

Beth hoped Thelma would keep her mouth shut during the performance. She vowed she would never forgive her mother for sending Thelma as her chaperone. But what did it matter? Henry clearly had no intentions tonight of asking her to—

He reached over to take her hand. Beth hoped Thelma would not notice.

— The Queen City

Of all Marquette's grand old buildings that were gone before my time, the Marquette Opera House is the one I wish I had seen and the one for which I feel most fond because of its role in my family's history as well as its sensationally tragic end.

My grandparents' courtship was as intriguing a story as any to me. Their religious differences inspired two marriage problems in my novels, first when I wrote *The Only Thing That Lasts* where Robert's Grandma and Mr. Carter do not marry in their youth because she is Catholic and he a Southern Baptist, and later in *The Queen City* when Henry and Beth, based loosely on my grandparents, have a long engagement.

Despite the religion issue, my grandpa decided to propose to my grandmother. The event occurred at the Marquette Opera House sometime in the late 1920s. My grandmother, her parents being overprotective, had a friend with her as chaperone, although hopefully the friend was not as annoying as Beth's talkative cousin, Thelma. Although the religious differences would keep my grandparents from getting married until 1934, the Marquette Opera House was the place where their courtship and pending nuptials were confirmed. I doubt a more romantic place existed in Marquette for my grandparents to pledge their love since by all accounts the opera house was a truly elegant structure.

The Marquette Opera House was built in 1890 with Peter White and John M. Longyear forming a corporation to sell stock to fund its construction. When completed, the building would contain three floors, including not only the theatre but four shops on the first floor, office suites on the second, and a third floor leased to the

Masonic order.

Designed by local architect Carl F. Struck, the building's exterior was of native brownstone and brick with a Romanesque entrance of Portage Entry sandstone. The interior, however, was the most stunning. A stairway led to the ticket office. Hallways led to the dress balcony and the Masonic Hall. The style inside was Italian Renaissance with ornate boxes, frescoes depicting comedy and tragedy, and of course, an impressive proscenium arch with an Italian landscape painted on the drop curtain. The plush chairs—enough to hold 900—were the same as those in New York's Madison Square Garden. Popular plays and operas were performed including the Victorian favorite, *Uncle Tom's Cabin.*

In 1927, the building was bought by the Masons and became known as the Masonic Building. By that time, movies had come to Marquette and the Delft Theatre had been operating a dozen years, so to compete, a variety of performances transplanted some of the more traditional plays and operas. Nevertheless, many performances were played here to great success, and it was not uncommon for national celebrities to visit, including Lillian Russell, Lon Chaney, John Philip Sousa, and W.C. Fields. I only wish I knew what performance my grandparents watched the night of their engagement.

Opera House After Fire

Like many an opera heroine, the Marquette Opera House would meet a tragic ending. In the early morning hours of January 24, 1938, and during perhaps the worst blizzard in Upper Michigan's history, the employees at *The Mining Journal*, working desperately to finish the newspaper, had the electricity go out. In the blackness, they looked down the street and saw fire aglow in the Masonic Building. Here are some passages from the retelling of the story in *The Queen City*:

Residents near downtown Marquette were rudely woken by the fire brigade's sirens. People peered out their windows to see an eerie conglomeration of smoke, bright red flames, and hurling white snow. The fire had begun in the Masonic Building. How it began or how long it had already raged would not be determined until much later. For now, the fire must be stopped before the entire downtown crumbled to cinders, before history repeated itself—several residents recalled their grandparents' stories of another great downtown fire seventy years earlier. By the time the firetrucks arrived, the Masonic Building was counted as lost, including inside it, the Peter White Insurance Agency and the much-loved Opera House. Already the fire had spread along the street, engulfing Jean's Jewelry, the Nightingale Cafe, the Scott and Woolworth stores, De Hass Builder's Supply, and the Marquette County law library.

Had electricity been required to pump water, the fire's destruction would have been inestimable. Fortunately, the waterworks was powered by gas engines run on batteries. Hoses were quickly unrolled along Washington Street to fight the formidable fire. The bravest men struggled with feelings of panic and loss to see buildings that had stood since before their childhood, where they had spent countless joyful hours—the Opera House, the theatres, the stores—all at the mercy of the raging flames. No one had ever seen such a firestorm, much less been asked to fight it. Firemen dug their footholds into snowbanks and aimed their hoses at the flames, only to have the wind whip the waterstreams straight back into their faces, where ice formed on their noses while smoke choked their lungs. Yet they dared not back down.

....

Bill, although large and strong for his seventeen years, had to use all his might to brace against the frigid winds and direct the hoses so the water struck the flames. Much of the water froze on powerlines and building fronts just seconds after it spurted from hoses. Heroic efforts appeared ineffective against the blazing furnace that had once been Washington Street. At times, the slush in the street was up to Bill's hips, making him feel more like he was fishing in the Dead River than fighting a blazing fire. A firetruck froze in the slush and could not be moved. Henry waded through the watery mess to help dig out the truck so it could hose down the bank buildings on the corner of Washington and Front before the fire spread downhill toward the lake.

As morning broke, Mr. Donckers opened his cafe to provide hot coffee for the firemen and volunteers. Bill and Henry took a quick, welcomed breakfast break after learning the Kresge store was no longer in danger. They emerged from breakfast, refreshed and ready to fight again, just as the west wall of the Masonic building tumbled down. Even though the wall fell inward, glass shot out from its windows, injuring a traffic officer and three firemen, while bricks struck two other men. None were seriously injured, but even the witnesses felt shaken. The accident made everyone fight with greater determination to prevent worse accidents. Curses and prayers were muttered in hopes the blizzard would end so only the fire had to be fought. There would be many more hours of frustrating toil.

My only family member that I know actually witnessed the fire that day was my grandpa's cousin, Myles McCombie. In 1999, *The Mining Journal* featured a story about the fire and interviewed residents who recalled it. Myles McCombie was just a teenager at the time; upon hearing about the fire, he and a friend walked downtown to see it. When they reached Washington Street, a fireman asked Myles to help for twenty-five cents an hour, so Myles picked up a hose. He told *The Mining Journal*, "We stood in slush up to our hips and we were pouring water on that side [of Washington] street." Myles was also one of the volunteers who was served a quick breakfast at Donckers store when it was opened to serve the firemen.

To lose a major section of downtown Marquette had to be devastating to the residents, and I can only imagine how my grandparents felt to know a place so important to them was gone forever. I doubt the ensuing scandal that explained the cause for the fire made anyone feel better. The story was broadcast nationwide as described in *The Queen City*:

> True *magazine revealed Marquette's Episcopalian Diocese had been having financial problems. Mr. Miller, responsible for the church funds, had embezzled church money, then lost it in the stock market. He went to the bishop for help, threatening that if the bishop exposed him, he would commit suicide. In desperation, Bishop Ablewhite sought out an investment counselor named Lyons to help rebuild the church's lost savings. Mr. Lyons suggested nightclubs would be a good investment, he being a frequent visitor to them since he had quite the eye for showgirls. Soon, Bishop Ablewhite had decided to buy his own little nightclub, the income from which would be used to replace the missing church funds. Gradually, the secret leaked out to the bishop's congregation.*
>
> *Mr. Miller's office had been in the Masonic building, which also housed the Marquette Opera House. Speculations would never be confirmed regarding whether Mr. Miller had started the fire while burning the incriminating*

Bishop Ablewhite

documents of his embezzlement, or whether the fire had just serendipitously destroyed them. People became suspicious when after the fire, Mr. Miller's safe was found open and everything burned inside it. Within a year, the congregation realized money was missing from several church funds until a legal investigation was deemed necessary. John Voelker, Marquette County's prosecuting attorney, ordered a grand-jury investigation into the case. By October, Bishop Ablewhite was found guilty as an accessory to the embezzlement of church funds and sentenced to ten years in prison, although he got off after nine months in the Jackson state prison. Upon the bishop's release, his friend Henry Ford gave him a position as director of personnel in his River Rouge plant. Mr. Miller got off far more easily; he died of a heart attack before the embezzlement was discovered.

Time magazine and the *Chicago Tribune* would also announce the Bishop's resignation in 1939, noting that the money embezzled equaled $99,000 and that Ablewhite's name was stricken from the Protestant Episcopal Church's rolls.

The Opera House itself was never rebuilt although a new Masonic Temple was constructed and today is upstairs in the Washington Street Mall. Operas are rarely performed in Marquette today and no recordings of those early Marquette entertainments remain. Only memories and photographs testify to the grandeur that once was.

THE NORDIC THEATER & BOOK WORLD

Remember that murder a few years ago in Big Bay? Well, John Voelker has written a book about it called Anatomy of a Murder. *It was just in the papers a day or two after you left. He wrote it under another name, Robert Traver, I think it is, but everyone knows who really wrote it. After all, he was the lieutenant's lawyer. There's talk around town that he's even sold the movie rights to the book. Imagine that. A movie about something that happened right here in our neck of the woods.*

— Superior Heritage

The Nordic Theater, built in 1936, was directly across the street from the Delft Theatre for nearly six decades. While the Delft tended to play more children and family-oriented films, the Nordic often played the PG and R films. The first film I remember seeing at the Nordic was *Tootsie* starring Dustin Hoffman in 1982, and the theater was so packed that night that my brother and I had to scrunch into one seat together.

Nordic Theater/Book World

Duke Ellington at Mt. Shasta while filming *Anatomy of a Murder*

While I don't feel as nostalgic for the Nordic as for the Delft, the theater is historic because in 1959 *Anatomy of a Murder* premiered there and at Ishpeming's Butler Theater simultaneously. When the film was made, the movie stars all had their hands cast in cement, and in the 1980s, after Marquette's downtown was revitalized and the red bricks that today mark the sidewalks put in, the handprints were placed in front of the theater with their signatures in cement. These handprints remained until 1995 when the Nordic Theater closed; by then the cement had become so worn down by the weather—rain and snow and the salt used to fight the winter ice—that the handprints were barely recognizable. The blocks were removed but remain safely stored.

The Nordic's marquee was removed with the closing of the theater, but rather than tear the building down, it was renovated and became home to Marquette's Book World. While I hate to see any old Marquette landmark go, if it must be replaced, a bookstore is a good successor. Book World's staff has been great at selling my books and manager Lee Laforge was the person who first told me I should write a history of Marquette, which ultimately inspired me to write *My Marquette*.

Jimmy Stewart & John Voelker at Roosevelt Bar, Ishpeming

CLIFTON HOTEL & HOTEL MARQUETTE

Unlike most of Upper Michigan's clannish Finnish immigrants, Aino realized that to get ahead in this foreign land, she must assimilate into American culture. She thought working in one of Marquette's finest hotels was a fine start compared to the jobs in the mining towns of Ishpeming and Negaunee; Marquette seemed practically a cosmopolitan city compared to the nearby little mining towns, and the Clifton Hotel was frequently visited by shipping and railroad magnates.

— The Queen City

In *The Queen City*, Aino Nordmaki's employment at the Clifton Hotel results in her meeting her future husband, Karl Bergmann. Aino enters his room to clean it, not realizing he is still in it—they are immediately smitten with each other, and although she knows she should not court one of the hotel's guests, she gives in when he asks her to supper:

The Second Clifton Hotel ~ c. 1910

Finally, he found Aino Nordmaki in a stairwell and asked her to have supper with him. She tried to explain she could not be involved with the hotel's male clients. He persisted when her eyes betrayed her pleasure at being asked. He took her to the Hotel Marquette—known for its splendid cuisine—where no one from the Clifton would see them. Aino had never eaten in a restaurant before—she had certainly never dined alone with a man. That he was a giant of a man made her feel both nervous and safe, as if even losing her position at the hotel could not happen if he were with her. They did not talk much; neither knew what to say, but in the end, she thanked him for the meal.

The Mesnard House was built in 1883 and renamed the Hotel Marquette in 1891. It had one hundred rooms and was renowned for its fine dining. But like so many other downtown buildings, it would be destroyed by fire in 1930.

The Clifton Hotel would be even more ill-fated. The original hotel was first named the Clifton Hostelry, then Cole's Lake View Hotel, then Cozzen's Hotel, and finally the Clifton

Hotel Marquette Fire ~ 1930

House. It stood four stories high on the corner of Washington and Front Streets, and its top floor and an observation tower provided an excellent view of Lake Superior. A barbershop, billiard parlor, and parlors for entertainment were among its many amenities. A Christmas Day fire in 1886 would destroy it.

The Volks, owners of the Clifton, decided to rebuild a block farther up the hill on the corners of Front and Bluff Streets. This second Clifton Hotel would be where Karl and Aino met; they would walk from there down a block to the corner of Washington and Front Streets to the Hotel Marquette for dinner. Meanwhile, Amos Harlow purchased the property where the old Clifton Hotel had stood and built the Harlow Block building in 1887, constructed by Marquette architect Hampson Gregory. It remains home to numerous downtown businesses and offices today.

The second Clifton Hotel would ultimately meet the fate of its predecessor. In October 1965, fire again broke out as the result of an electric problem. Despite efforts to put it out, the fire quickly spread through the building. The hotel was never rebuilt. By that time, the US 41 bypass had been built to detour traffic from passing through downtown Marquette. Hotels were being replaced by motels springing up along US 41 as the city grew westward. Today, only the Landmark Inn survives of Marquette's downtown hotels.

FIRST PRESBYTERIAN CHURCH

The supplies to build the new Presbyterian church had been reduced to ashes.

— Iron Pioneers

The current First Presbyterian Church on the corner of Front and Bluff Streets was built in 1935, but its congregation goes back to Marquette's beginnings. Amos and Olive Harlow first held Presbyterian services in their home. In 1860, services moved to the Session House built on property belonging to Martha Bacon, Olive's mother, at the corner of Washington and Third Streets. This building, after seeing numerous businesses in it over the years, would eventually be torn down in 1975. Today, the property is a parking lot across from the Post Office.

First Presbyterian Church

The Presbyterian congregation erected its first church in 1868. The building's materials began arriving in Marquette in May of that year, but the devastating June 11th fire destroyed them. Eager still to build, the congregation ordered new supplies and the church was completed December 30th of the same year.

This first church served the congregation until 1931, when, not surprisingly, it was destroyed by fire. In its place was built the current church, one of the most impressive looking buildings in Marquette, faced with Wisconsin lannon stone and accented with Indiana limestone giving it an English flavor. The church's interior contains medieval Gothic elements including oak beams and rafters, ten pairs of stained glass windows, and handmade floor tiles.

Although the Presbyterian Church receives little mention in my novels, I attended pre-school here from 1974-1976 when I was three to five years old. My preschool teachers were Sally Hruska and Carolyn McDonald. Years later, when I was invited to talk at a local book club about *Iron Pioneers*, Carolyn, a member of the group, was able to say she had known me longer than anyone else in the room.

My preschool memories are vivid—the order of the rooms, the animal costumes, the little indoor sandbox, the large room where we would have our snacks and where stories were read to us, and the pet guinea pigs we would stick up our shirts to see whether they'd crawl out our necklines. To this day, when I read books, I find myself somehow substituting the preschool rooms as the visual locations for the stories.

In the years following preschool, I attended many used book sales in the church's basement, but not until 1994, when I went to the church to try and find Great-Grandpa Molby's funeral record, did I again see those upstairs rooms, and boy, was I surprised—how small they seemed! Since then I have attended weddings in the church, and in 1999, my great-great-aunt Mildred McCombie's ninetieth birthday was held in the parlors where I once attended preschool. But the preschool memories remain my favorite.

LANDMARK INN

"I could take all of you out," said Thelma. "We were thinking of going to the Northland."

"I've never been there," Beth replied, "but it's probably too expensive for us."

— Superior Heritage

Today's Landmark Inn was originally the Northland Hotel, built in 1930. The passage above from *Superior Heritage* takes place in the 1950s, and Beth has never set foot inside the building, but then, locals rarely visit hotels in their own cities.

The Northland Hotel was designed to be a first rate structure, proposed by George Shiras III who approached the Rotary Club to raise money with sale of stock. In 1917, the foundation was started, but then the money ran out and not until 1930 would the hotel open for business. From the start, the hotel was elegant with first-class service, but its difficulties would continue.

In 1950, Frank Russell, owner of *The Mining Journal,* purchased the Northland, but he sold it after only a decade. From that point, the hotel changed hands half a dozen times, including being owned briefly by John Voelker, author of *Anatomy of a Murder.* By the time I was a child, only the Crow's Nest restaurant on the top floor remained popular while the rest of the hotel was becoming unusable and decaying. It closed in 1982.

After years of being empty and continuing to fall into ruin, the hotel was purchased by the Pesolas in 1995.

Landmark Inn

Their hard work in renovating and restoring the building, and their vision of making it a premier hotel resulted in the newly named Landmark Inn once again achieving the stature George Shiras III originally intended.

The Landmark Inn has preserved its history with special rooms to the memory of various famous guests who stayed there in its Northland Hotel days, including Amelia Earhart, as well as having several themed rooms such as the Lilac room and rooms named for local famous people including John Voelker, Peter White, and Bishop Baraga. Famous guests during its Northland Hotel days included Louis Armstrong, Abbot and Costello, the cast of *Anatomy of a Murder,* and musical group Peter, Paul, and Mary. Under the Landmark Inn's name, guests have included authors Maya Angelou and Jim Harrison, as well as feminist Gloria Steinem, and actor Bill Cosby.

The Sky Room, Capers Restaurant, the Northland Pub, and specialty cakes by Joe the Cake Guy have made the Landmark a primary culinary center in Marquette as well as the host for special dinners and numerous community events.

For me, one of the most entertaining events held at the Landmark was the Marquette Crossings weekend in 2007 and 2008, an event that featured Marquette's haunted side, including walking tours that left from the Landmark and also secret midnight paranormal investigations at undisclosed locations. The Landmark was perfect to host the event since it is rumored to be haunted itself—notably, the Lilac Room, where a ghost named Mary Eleanor has appeared to guests, placed screws in the sheets, caused problems for men with their keys, and called the front desk phone when the employees knew the room was empty. Additional haunting tales can be read at the hotel's website www.thelandmarkinn.com.

The Landmark Inn also holds a special place in my heart because I've been asked to speak at breakfasts and dinners there about my books and Marquette's history. In the summer of 2008, the Munising Library Book Club chose *Iron Pioneers* as its book of the month and the members asked me to give them a tour of Marquette which began with a period dinner in the Landmark's Sky Room. The success of that event and especially the enthusiasm of those on the tour inspired me to give more tours, and it also encouraged me to write *My Marquette* for readers who might not be able to go on a private city tour with me.

PETER WHITE PUBLIC LIBRARY

Helen and I started up the library's high front steps.

"Isn't it beautiful?" asked Helen, stopping after a couple seconds to admire the building. "It looks just like a Greek Temple."

"Yeah," I said, "or a Southern plantation house made of stone."

"We have bigger libraries than this downstate," said Helen, "but I haven't seen one so graceful."

— The Only Thing That Lasts

Although the current impressive and beloved library building was built in 1903 and opened its doors the following year, Marquette's first library began not long after the town's founding.

In *Iron Pioneers*, several of the female characters early on form the Ladies' Literary Society, an early book club as well as a sign of social distinction in some of its members' eyes. Although this group was fictional, reading clubs, especially among

Peter White Public Library

women, were common in the nineteenth century, and such groups often were the proponents of building libraries. Marquette did have a literary society as early as 1856, and a lending library existed soon after on Baraga Avenue. This lending library was destroyed by the 1868 fire. In the 1870s the library, which belonged to the Marquette school system, was downtown in the Coles Block. At the time, Peter White also had his own personal library collection that he loaned out, so when he built the new First National Bank on Front and Spring Streets, he allowed the library to relocate there in 1878 and merge its collection with his own. Later, in need of more space, the library moved to a room in the City Hall. By 1891, the library's collection had grown to the point of needing a new home, which it found on the Thurber Block, where Book World is currently located. Because Peter White donated this building, the library was named in his honor.

Library Interior ~ c. 1950

This new building was also soon found to be too small. Peter White then tried to convince Andrew Carnegie to fund a new library in Marquette—Carnegie would do so for nearby Ishpeming—but Carnegie replied that Marquette was Peter White's city, so Peter White once again took up the challenge to play benefactor to Marquette and fundraising efforts began. John M. Longyear donated the land for the new building and Peter White and Samuel Kaufman donated most of the money.

In 1904, the new library was officially dedicated and opened on the same day as the new courthouse. The impressive limestone structure, with its large pillars and situated on top of Front Street's hill, resembled a Greek Temple of Knowledge. Complete with a downstairs smoking room for men, the new library had three floors and seemed plenty spacious for the book collection.

But within fifty years, the collection again outgrew its space. Increased use by patrons and 70,000 volumes led to building an annex on the back of the library in 1957, which included the Children's Room and storage for most of the adult fiction and the phonograph record collection as well as a large downstairs room for films, puppet shows, and book sales. This version of the library is the one I would know throughout my childhood.

But the people of Marquette soon wanted still more from the library. Far beyond just being a place to check out books, Peter White Public Library was becoming the cultural center of Marquette and a new library was needed to reflect this change. Residents' affection for the original building was too great to destroy it, so instead, in the late 1990s, the annex was removed and a new addition created which would gracefully blend in with the architecture of the original building. The remodeling would result in the library building being closed for two years and its collection being housed in dormitories at Northern Michigan University where patrons could still access it.

Then in 2001, the new library was opened. The public could not have been happier. The original building was completely retained, and it includes two large reading rooms upstairs, two more reading rooms downstairs, and an art gallery. The new addition, besides containing a collection well surpassing 100,000 volumes, also houses an enormous children's room, a café, a community room, a gift shop, and the Marquette Arts and Culture Center's exhibits and space for its art and other cultural classes. In addition, the library's film and music collection had ample room, and the Rachel Spear bell collection was given prominent display.

The Peter White Public Library is hands down my favorite place in Marquette. I began visiting it first with my preschool class—we would go on "field trips" there just across the street from the First Presbyterian Church to see movies and puppet shows.

After preschool, my library visits were rare because until about 1980, the library's bookmobile would bring books to the outlying townships. The bookmobile arrived in my neighborhood of Stonegate at the Crossroads about 3:30pm every other week just as the school bus brought us home. We would quickly leave the bus and rush to the bookmobile where Ruth Lee, the driver-librarian, would patiently let us kids dig through the books while she chatted with our parents. I brought home many, many books from the bookmobile including *Where the Wild Things Are* and numerous of the Bible story rhyming Arch books. But my absolute favorite, which I checked out countless times, was *George and Martha*, about two hippopotamuses whose friendship usually results in Martha teaching George a lesson, such as just to tell her he doesn't like split pea soup rather than hiding it in his loafers, or not to be a Peeping Tom by whacking him over the head with the bathtub. As an adult, I still find *George and Martha* hilarious as well as a wonderful way to teach children basic manners.

About the time I was in fourth grade, funding for the bookmobile was cut so my mom started taking my brother and me to the library. We were only allowed in the children's room where we would get to visit with our cousin, Merrie Johnson, who worked there. Always a favorite with the kids, Merrie retired in 2005 after more than thirty years at the library; a huge retirement party was held for her in the community room.

As a child, my favorite books to check out included Andrew Lang's colored fairy tale books and copies of the Wizard of Oz series. As I got older, I discovered the Rainbow Classics, published mostly in the 1940s and edited by May Lamberton Becker—I think I loved them mainly because they were old and they had wonderful colored illustrations, but they also infused a love of literature in me as I graduated from *Andersen's Fairy Tales* to *Little Men* to *Jane Eyre* and *Wuthering Heights*. After reading one Rainbow Classic, I would scan the list on its back cover to pick out another until I had read them all, and then I sought out more classics. By the time I was fourteen and allowed into the library's adult section, I was ready to gobble up Agatha Christie mysteries, and more classics—Charles Dickens, the Bronte sisters, Mark Twain, and Jane Austen.

Of course, it would have been impossible not to mention the library in my novels. In *Iron Pioneers,* Edna Whitman is an early librarian and mourns the library's loss in the 1868 fire. In *The Only Thing That Lasts*, Robert O'Neill is enthusiastic about his first visit to the library and impressed by its classic architecture. In *The Queen City*, Kathy McCarey is at the library when she hears Peter White has died.

As for me, today at least once a week I can be found at the library, checking out a book, CD, or video, attending a film—the annual Bollywood film night is a highlight of the winter season—or just admiring

Bust of Peter White at the Library's 25th Anniversary

the latest art exhibit. As an author, I'm pleased that my books are in the library's collection, and I've gotten to know many of the librarians over the years as I've participated in different library events and helped to plan the Upper Peninsula Publishers and Authors Association's conferences that have been held there. The library staff is wonderful, enthusiastic, and ever ready to support the arts and the community.

The building and people have made Peter White Public Library the true cultural center of Marquette. Every library patron knows how lucky Marquette is to have such a wonderful library that far outshines those in most metropolitan communities, and visitors to our city never cease to rave about it.

A large bust of Peter White sits across from the circulation desk. At Christmas, he dons a festive holiday hat or Santa's cap. Knowing Peter White's sense of humor, I'm sure he enjoys all the festivities and the people who pass him each day. His generosity in funding the library has truly been the gift that keeps on giving to the community.

FIRST BAPTIST CHURCH

*A week later, Margaret and El-
eanor were leaving to attend a luncheon at the Baptist Church. Eleanor
was fourteen this year, so Margaret
thought a church luncheon would be
good training to teach Eleanor how
to be a young lady.*

— The Queen City

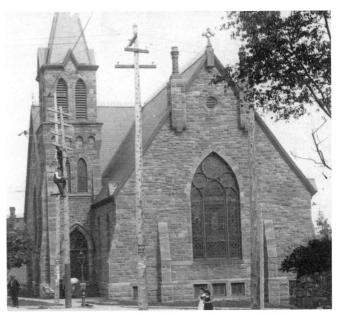

First Baptist Church ~ c. 1900

Marquette's first Baptist Church was established in 1863. It was a small wooden church on Front Street where the Marquette County History Museum was later located beside the current library. My ancestors, the McCombies and the Zryds, first came to Marquette in the 1870s and this church would have been the one they attended. My great-great grandparents, William Forrest McCombie and Elizabeth May Zryd, were probably married inside it in 1882.

When the congregation outgrew this small church, in 1886, a new church was built across the street where today is the Landmark Inn's parking lot. This church was well-known in the community especially for its fabulous organ, a Hook and Haster, for a long time one of the best organs in the state. My great-grandmother and her children would know this church intimately, and although a Catholic, my mother occasionally attended services here with her grandmother.

As with many downtown buildings, fire destroyed the First Baptist Church in 1965. Rather than rebuild downtown, the congregation erected a new church in North Marquette on Kaye Avenue, behind the music and theatre buildings of Northern Michigan University.

In *Superior Heritage*, Margaret Dalrymple writes in her diary in 1962 about what it meant to her to be a member of the First Baptist Church. The passage is based on a similar one in the diary of my great-grandmother, Barbara McCombie White:

*This Sunday the eldest Baptist members now attending church were
honored. There were 9 of us but only 5 were there. Sadie Johnson, as church*

clerk, pinned corsages on all of us and then we had pictures taken for The Mining Journal. *We all were requested to get up on the platform and give a little talk of days gone by. I was afraid I'd be stage struck, but this is what I said. "Many years ago when my parents came to Marquette they joined the Baptist church and I was raised in it. When I was 11 years old I went to a revival meeting & was converted. Shortly after I was baptized in this church. Since then, some of my happiest moments have been spent in Sabbath school and church. I had good Christian parents who taught me the right way to live and guided me through the years. I have tried to follow their example and am proud to say that I have good children, all of whom act like Christians even if they don't go to church regularly. I think God loves everyone no matter who we are and we each have different tasks to do. I think this church has helped lots of people, and I am proud to have been a member all these years."*

My great-grandmother lived long enough to celebrate her 75th anniversary as a member of the Baptist church. After her death, her children Barbara, Roland, Kit, Frank, and Sadie (the real church clerk mentioned in the passage above) would continue attending. Barbara would become a deaconess of the church, and my great-aunt Sadie at age ninety-two remains very active in the church. My grandfather, Lester White, before marrying, taught Sunday school at the church as did his cousin, Marjorie Woodbridge Johnson. As for my Uncle Kit, as a boy he did his part by passing the collection basket and taking a chunk of the money home with him, which his parents immediately made him return.

New First Baptist Church

My experiences with the Baptist Church have largely been limited to attending family funerals. I'm always struck during these occasions by the wonderful old Baptist hymns, including one of my great-grandmother's favorites, "In The Garden." The church ladies always outdo themselves with the funeral luncheons and their other church activities. I am sure my great-grandmother would be happy to know her church's good work continues well into the twenty-first century.

FIRST METHODIST CHURCH

The Methodists had undergone several disasters in the last few years while they tried to build their new church. First, their minister had humiliated the congregation by disappearing with their money from the building fund. Then when new funds were gathered and the building finally erected, a dedication ceremony was held, but during the service, the crowd in the church was so great it had caused the basement pillars to sink into the foundation. Nevertheless, the Methodists had succeeded in completing their sandstone church, complete with stained glass windows and steeples at the corner of Ridge and Front Streets. Now it was only fitting that two grandchildren of Rebecca Brookfield should wed in the church that stood as a testament to the Methodists' perseverance in Marquette for a quarter century.

— Iron Pioneers

First Methodist Church

Methodism flourished in Marquette from the city's founding. In 1851, the congregation numbered forty members with fifteen probationers, and a significant number of those early members were my relatives. Besides the Bishops, the Eddy, King, Bignall, Remington, Quarters, and White families were all church members and all interrelated. Basil Bishops' daughters married an Eddy, a Bignall, and a White. His granddaughter married a King, his grandson married a Remington, and his son-in-law's sister married a Quarters. Few members of the early congregation, consequently, were not my relatives.

My readers will remember that in *Iron Pioneers* Rebecca Brookfield is a staunch Methodist and a firm believer in the two great causes the Methodists took upon themselves in those days—tolerance and abolition. In my own family, Basil Bishop and his son Delivan were the founders of Marquette's first temperance society. Their descendants would remain firm believers in temperance throughout the rest of the nineteenth century. Basil's grandson Jerome White reputedly locked one of his sons outside of the house in the rain as punishment for coming home drunk. While I don't know that anyone in the family lobbied for abolition, Basil's grandsons Francis Marion Bishop and Jerome White willingly joined the Union Army during the Civil War, as well as Jerome's father-in-law Edmond Remington.

Delivan's wife, Pamelia Bishop, was known as the "Mother of Methodism" in Marquette. In *Iron Pioneers*, Rebecca Brookfield badgers some of the other townspeople to join her Methodist causes, but the next year, Pamelia Bishop arrives in Marquette, and then Rebecca has a friend who can relate to her causes. Delivan and Pamelia also notably named one of their sons, Charles Wesley Bishop, for the founder of Methodism's brother, the great writer of Methodist hymns. Another son, Francis Marion Bishop, would attend Illinois Wesleyan University in Illinois where

Bishop Window

he would meet Major John Wesley Powell, who was obviously named for Methodism's founder, and go with Major Powell on his second Colorado River expedition. Francis Marion would then settle in Utah and marry the daughter of one of the Mormon leaders in Salt Lake City.

In the early 1870s, Marquette's Methodist congregation was scandalized when its minister, Reverend Haukinson, left town because he didn't want to pay the suppliers for the new building. The congregation was reduced to paying the huge debt and settled for putting a roof on the basement and having services there for two years. Meanwhile, the new minister, Reverend J. Milton Johnson, solicited subscriptions to pay the debt and fund the church's completion.

When in 1873, a happy congregation gathered inside the new church for the first services, the weight of the congregation's presence caused the support pillars in the basement to sink into the foundation. Nevertheless, repairs were made, and since then, the building has remained structurally sound.

Besides its impressive sandstone exterior, the First Methodist Church has brilliant stained glass windows, including one to the memory of my ancestral aunt and uncle, Delivan and Pamelia Bishop. I don't believe any Bishop descendants remain members of the church today, however. Delivan and Pamelia Bishop's children ended up moving away, and my own branch of the family quit attending the church when my great-grandfather, Jay Earle White, married my great-grandmother who was a Baptist, so their children were raised as Baptists.

My own most memorable experience in the church was when I attended the wedding of our longtime family friends, Nick and Frances Ilnicky. When the wedding was over, one of the guests stood up to leave, but her skirt fell down. For a moment she stood there in her slip until she realized what had happened. She quickly sat back down to make herself decent, then scurried out a side door clutching the skirt against her waist while the rest of the guests went out the front door. You have to love church humor.

In 2001, the First Methodist Church celebrated its 150th anniversary and a thorough history of the church, *Sculptured in Sandstone*, was published by Rowena Jones. While Dr. Jones was writing the book, I contacted her and she provided me a great deal of information about my ancestors and I shared some information I had with her, resulting in my being quoted in the book's footnotes.

That summer, Rowena Jones also organized a Park Cemetery Tour of many of the church's significant members including local architect Hampson Gregory, lighthouse keeper William Wheatley, Marquette mayor Frank Moore, and my ancestral aunt, Pamelia Bishop as "the Mother of Methodism" in Marquette. Children dressed up to play the roles and stood beside the gravestones giving their stories. I found the tour an excellent history lesson, and it was a thrill to see one of my ancestors speaking, even in an imaginary way. If only I could hear their real voices—I have so many questions I would love to ask them—especially to find out what Pamelia Bishop thought about her son, Francis Marion, marrying a Mormon.

Girl Playing Pamelia Bishop

FIRST CHURCH OF CHRIST, SCIENTIST (MARQUETTE CITADEL)

The Christian Science community in Marquette was never large, but several of Marquette's prominent families were members. The church's history in Marquette is largely tied to the Longyear family.

In 1884, the Longyears lost their infant son, John. Mary Longyear was devastated and after seven years of grieving, she turned to Christian Science and found comfort. Her husband, John M. Longyear, remained skeptical of the religion until, as he recorded in his memoirs, he consented to a Christian Science treatment for his bad rheumatism which resulted in his being successfully cured.

Although the Longyears would leave Marquette in 1903, Mrs. Longyear would inspire several other residents to believe in Christian Science, and the Longyears would sell a portion of their property to Charles Schaffer, whose new home would be the meeting place for Marquette's Christian Scientists for many years, starting in 1908. In 1912, the Christian Science congregation began to make plans to build a church and raise funds, but when World War I broke out in 1914, all building was prohibited in the United States. By the time the war was over, the cost of the elaborate structure intended was more than the congregation could afford. After many more years trying to raise money, the congregation consented to a smaller building, which nevertheless would be impressive.

First Church of Christ

The neo-Greek revival church was constructed in 1925 of gray brick with limestone trim. The main floor auditorium seated 250 people, while downstairs was a Christian Science reading room and the Sunday school. For nearly eighty years, the building would be the congregation's home, but membership dwindled as time went on, and in 2004, the congregation felt the need to sell the church.

Today, the building is known as the "Marquette Citadel" and it functions as a bed and breakfast as well as a place for various functions including wedding receptions and corporate events. The auditorium has been converted into an elegant Victorian style ball room and the downstairs serves as a bed and breakfast with tastefully furnished rooms. While the building no longer serves its original purpose, it has become an elegant place where Mary Beecher Longyear would have felt most comfortable.

ST. PAUL'S EPISCOPAL CHURCH

St. Paul's Episcopal Church

Farther down the street stood the Episcopal Church, where Gerald and Clara had gone before Gerald had married Sophia and converted to Methodism. A new church had just been built the year before he moved away, but since then attached to it had been a chapel, built by Peter White in memory of his son, Morgan, who had died.

— Iron Pioneers

Marquette's Episcopal Congregation has held steadfast as a faith community since its founding in 1856. Like the Methodists, the first congregation met in the Washington Street schoolhouse. Then a wooden structure was built on Ridge Street where the current church stands. By 1875, St. Paul's had outgrown its wooden building, and in keeping with the rest of the surrounding churches, a new church was designed by local architect C.F. Struck and constructed of brownstone with a Lake Superior slate roof.

In 1887, Peter White, a member of the congregation, funded building of the Morgan Chapel addition in memory of his deceased son Morgan White. The chapel is notable for its brilliant inspirational stained glass Tiffany window. The main church also contains beautiful stained glass windows, including the Christian Family Window, which depicts eleven children surrounding Jesus—the children represent those of Samuel and Juliet Graveraet Kaufman. The magnificent rose window was donated in 1952 by Imogene Miller in memory of her husband Stuart Miller and mother Caroll Watson Rankin. In 1900, the church's front tower was added, the last major addition to the church as it stands today.

For many years, attached to the church was a Guild Hall which provided a place for young boys to keep them off the street. Built in 1907, it contained a gymnasium and swimming pool and provided exercise classes. Its opening ceremonies that year included fifteen young ladies doing a dumbbell routine. In 1929, structural problems resulted in the closing of the swimming pool. By the 1930s, the Guild Hall was no longer able to serve its intended purpose but it still found various uses, including being an early home for the Alger-Marquette Community Action Board and for the Women's Center. The Guild Hall was demolished in 1987.

The Guild Hall was constructed while Bates Burt was minister of the church. (Reverend Burt was no relation to the other Burt family in the area that included surveyor William Austin Burt, his son John, or grandson Hiram.) Although Reverend Burt would later move his family downstate, his children, born in Marquette, would make their hometown proud. Alfred Burt would become a famous composer of Christmas Carols. The tradition began with his father, who composed a carol every year

**Morgan Chapel
Tiffany Window**

for his Christmas card, but Alfred was the one who made the family tradition famous nationally. Although Alfred Burt's life was cut short in 1954, he would write at least fifteen well known carols, including "Caroling, Caroling." His carols have been recorded by such famous artists as Tennessee Ernie Ford, Julie Andrews, and Nat King Cole. Bates Burt's daughter, Deborah, was also very musical. She moved to Milwaukee where she taught music for many years using the Suzuki method. Another of Rev. Burt's sons, John H. Burt, followed in his father's footsteps, becoming first a minister and then eighth Episcopal Bishop of Ohio. As a leading voice for social justice, Bishop John Burt worked with Dr. Martin Luther King Jr. at the Rally for Freedom in Los Angeles, California, even having a bomb threat made on his home for his efforts for civil rights. Later, he would stand up for the right of women to become priests in the Episcopal Church, declaring he would resign if the Episcopal General Convention failed to

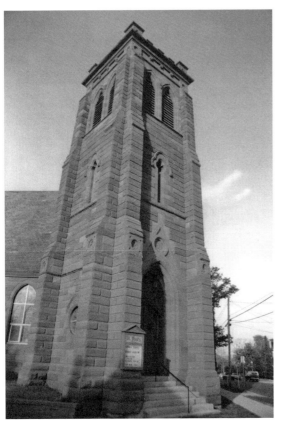

St. Paul's Tower

Burt Christmas Card

approve it in 1976. Once women's ordination was approved, Burt ordained eight women as priests during his years as Bishop of Ohio. Both Burt brothers are buried in the family plot in Park Cemetery.

The Burt brothers' descendants, although they don't reside in Marquette, remain closely linked to the town and the family's Christmas Carol tradition. Alfred Burt's daughter, Diane Bates Burt, founded "The Caroling Company" in California, and with her husband Nick D'Amico, they released the CD "A Christmas Present from the Caroling Company" which contains eight carols by her father. Bishop John Burt's granddaughter, Abbie Betinis, today carries on the family tradition by composing an annual original Christmas Carol and her mother, Emily Burt Betinis, illustrates the Christmas cards. Abbie has been featured on Minnesota Public Radio, has received several awards, and has been commissioned by numerous music organizations to compose works for them to perform. Her music is featured on six commercially available recordings. More information about this former Marquette musical family can be found at www.abbiebetinis.com and www.alfredburtcarols.com.

Every Christmas season, St. Paul's holds its annual International Craft Fair and Alternative Gift Market to sell Third World goods to benefit the artisans. For many years, the church also operated the Page Retreat Center in Little Lake, named for one of the Northern Michigan Episcopal Diocese's previous bishops.

Faith and charity have long marked St. Paul's Episcopal Church. Peter White, regardless of denomination, donated money to put the roofs on other Marquette churches, but it was grief more than generosity that made him fund the Morgan Chapel. Little could White foresee how his loss created a place of healing for many people for many years—people pray in the Morgan Chapel and Twelve-Step groups meet there for recovery—who knows how many lives have been changed because of this special chapel. Open-hearted, the Episcopal Church allows other faith communities to use its space. Its faith will fuel this congregation for years to come.

PART IV:
MARQUETTE'S HISTORICAL HOMES

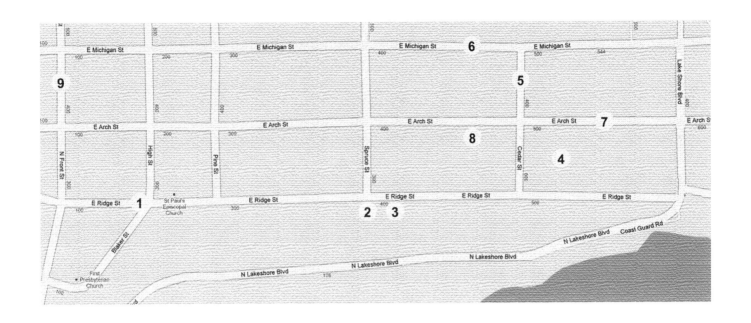

1. East Ridge Street
2. The Hundred Steps
3. The Merritt House
4. The Longyear Mansion
5. Cedar Street

6. Michigan Street
7. East Arch Street
8. Dandelion Cottage
9. Front Street

RIDGE & ARCH STREET RESIDENTIAL HISTORICAL DISTRICT

Lazarus had often walked past the grand homes on Ridge Street. He had often wondered what kind of people could afford such miniature palaces. Never had he dreamt he would meet these people, much less enter even one of their kitchens.

— Iron Pioneers

Marquette is filled with grand old homes and smaller cozy-looking ones built in the late nineteenth and early twentieth century. I am probably more fascinated by these houses than by anything else in Marquette because of all the stories that could be told about the people who lived in them. As I walk or drive around Marquette, I always ponder who the people must be in all of the houses and wonder whom I know that they might know or whether my ancestors knew theirs since ours has always been a close-knit community.

View of Ridge Street from Blaker Street

When I write my novels, although I'm usually intentionally vague, and even if I have a specific house in mind, so as not to interfere with actual history, I never name it, yet I always have a good idea of where my characters live and roughly how many blocks they must walk somewhere. For example, when I wrote *The Only Thing That Lasts*, I imagined that Kathleen O'Neill's house was probably somewhere on East Michigan Street from the directions I give:

The streetcar ran despite the snow—another surprise to me. Aunt Louisa May and I rode it up Front Street hill—quite a large hill—in fact larger than any I remembered near my home in South Carolina; with relief, I saw Marquette was not flat as I had feared—in fact, I thought the hill rather steep, but my aunt remarked, "Usually I just walk up Front Street, but it would be kind of hard while carrying our luggage." At the top of the hill, the streetcar turned onto what I would later learn was Arch Street. We disembarked and walked the couple extra blocks to Grandma and Aunt Louisa May's house.

Of all Marquette's many fine homes, the historical residential district of Ridge and Arch Streets is filled with the most impressive and interesting collection. My readers will remember how in *Iron Pioneers* Sophia Henning insists on building her large mansion on Ridge Street in 1868 because Peter White has just built the first grand house there. Although other fine homes are built around hers, Sophia continues to insist hers is the finest—a matter open to personal opinion.

It is not uncommon to see people, as they drive down Ridge or Arch Streets, slow down their cars to gawk at the sandstone mansions and brightly painted Victorian homes. Tall old trees and green lawns along the streets create an idyllic sense of the "Good Old Days." In reality, early pictures of Ridge Street show the land was largely razed when the homes were built and only fledgling trees were in the yards; those trees have long since grown into solid towering oaks and maples that provide shade and beauty to Marquette's most prestigious old neighborhood.

It would be impossible to describe in detail each old home and the families who lived in it since most of the homes are over a century old and have had numerous owners. Furthermore, the early families—the Whites, Reynolds, Spears, Calls, Joplings, Shirases, Pickandses, and Mathers among others—were closely related through marriage and blood and the relationships can be quite dizzying to try to sort out. I offer here the most thorough listing to date of this historical residential area in hopes it will inspire someone to write a yet more complete history of the homes and families of East Ridge and Arch Streets.

If you are doing a walking tour of the residential district, please remember that all the homes listed are private property and the owners' privacy should be respected.

Homes without photographs are no longer standing. Family tree charts are at the back of the book for many of the homes' former owners.

EAST RIDGE STREET

200 E. Ridge ~ Burt & Adams Home

200 E. Ridge ~ Burt & Adams Home

Directly across from St. Paul's Episcopal Church is the Burt house, more commonly known as the Adams Home. The Burt family is one of the most significant in Upper Michigan history beginning with William Austin Burt who discovered iron ore in Marquette County, thus leading to the building of the mines and Marquette as a harbor town. This home was built by William Austin Burt's grandson, Hiram Burt. Hiram and his wife fell in love with a house in France while traveling there in the 1870s, and they decided to build a replica in Marquette. Hiram owned the Burt Freestone Quarry and used its own brownstone to build his home. It included a Mansard roof with Gothic gables, and a gabled tower. Behind the house, on the sloping hill down to the lake, numerous terraces were built for gardens and a place to hold parties. Hiram Burt decided to sell the house to Sidney Adams, and then he moved to 351 E. Ridge Street.

Sidney Adams, the house's second owner, arrived in Marquette in 1850 with only a dollar to his name, but he bought an ax for fifty cents and set out to become a woodsman. He soon could afford to buy a wagon and oxen to deliver wood to his customers. Besides starting a side business as a potato farmer, he received a contract to haul iron ore in his wagons from the mines to Marquette in the years before the first railroad arrived. He also went on to own a sawmill and to invest significantly in land.

When he bought the Burt house, Adams indulged in designing terraces on the hill behind the house and filling them with fruit and vegetables, as well as bridges for people to walk on. He extended the terraces not only behind his property but behind many more houses extending eastward along Ridge Street. Adams also reputedly built an underground tunnel that ran from his house across the street to the Episcopal Church so his invalid adopted son, William Sidney Adams, could attend church without going outside.

Will Adams, the adopted son, was born in 1878 to Detroit parents who died while he was an infant. In his youth, Will was a soloist in the boys choir at school and church and enjoyed athletic pursuits, but a baseball injury resulted in soft tissue becoming hard until eventually he ossified into a living statue. By his mid-teens he was confined to a portable couch and only his face remained mobile. By sheer willpower, Will survived to the age of thirty-two. No longer able to perform athletics, he became one of Marquette's first literary figures, starting his own magazine business. His family hired him an at-

Sidney Adams' Terraced Gardens ~ c. 1900

tendant to whom he could dictate his magazine. He named his magazine *CHIPS*. Besides his own text, he included political cartoons and even caricatures of such town leaders as Peter White, Nathan Kaufman, and John M. Longyear. The paper was largely supported by advertising, so a phone was installed in the Adams home, and his attendant would hold the phone to Will's mouth so he could talk up his bi-monthly magazine to prospective advertisers.

Will also composed an opera with his childhood friend, Norma Ross, then the directress of the Marquette schools' music program. Will hummed melodies and Ross wrote them down. Their end result was the production of *Miss D. Q. Pons* an opera which premiered at the Marquette Opera House on July 3, 1905 with Ross in the title role. Will viewed the opera from the wing in his portable bed, and when its success led to the troupe traveling for sellout performances in Ishpeming, Hancock, Calumet, and Sault Ste. Marie, Will traveled with them by train. In 1906, Will also founded another newspaper, the *Marquette Chronicle* to which he contributed an original article each day. He died on August 10, 1909, preceded by his adopted father, Sidney Adams in 1906. Will once joked about his literary efforts, "Every specimen of writ is a silent story of how the author was saved from cerrebrius combustion."

After her parents and adopted brother's death, Bertha Adams remained in the house for many years, but as time went on, her father's terraces fell into disrepair and the gardens became overgrown. When the house was sold in 1946, only slight vestiges of the gardens and terraces remained. After the house was sold, the gabled tower was removed, and the house broken up into the aptly named Terrace Apartments, which it remains today.

219 E. Ridge ~ Rankin Home

Local author Carroll Watson Rankin wrote her many novels, beginning with *Dandelion Cottage* (1904), in this home. Born Caroline Watson in Marquette in 1864, she would later use the male spelling of her name, Carroll, to help her career as an author; she would alternately use other pen names to disguise her gender, but always retained the initials C.W.R.

The Rankin home was built in 1877 by Rankin's grandmother, Emily Watson, following the death of her husband Jonas Watson. Carroll Watson Rankin would inherit the

219 E. Ridge ~ Rankin Home

property and live there with her husband and children. Later, the home would be inherited by her daughter, Phyllis Rankin, long-time librarian at Peter White Public Library.

Born in 1864, Carroll Watson Rankin began writing in childhood and published her first short story at age eleven. At sixteen, she became a reporter for the *Daily Mining Journal*, a job she kept until her marriage in 1886 to Ernest Rankin. The Rankins would have four children, Imogene, Eleanor, Ernest Jr., and Phyllis. While raising her family, Rankin would continue to write and be published in major national magazines including *Harpers*, *Ladies' Home Journal*, *Gardening Magazine*, *Century*, *Youth's Companion*, and *Mother's Magazine*. She was inspired to write her first children's book, *Dandelion Cottage*, after her daughter Eleanor complained that she had read all the books ever written for children. The book would be based on a real cottage in Marquette and the antics of Rankin's daughters and their friends. (More information about the book and cottage is under the section for 440 E. Arch Street).

Dandelion Cottage quickly found a publisher and was successful enough that Rankin went on to write many more children's books. Altogether, three sequels to *Dandelion Cottage* would be written (*The Adopting of Rosa Marie*, *The Castaways of Pete's Patch, and The Girls of Highland Hall*), as well as the boy's book *Wolf's Rock* and six other novels

Carroll Watson Rankin

for children. Today the books are out of print except *Dandelion Cottage* (published by the Marquette County History Museum) but copies can still be found at the Peter White Public Library.

Carroll Watson Rankin and her son Ernest Jr. also recorded their memories of early Marquette, which are available as an unpublished manuscript at Peter White Public Library. I am sure Rankin would appreciate that her own memory lives on in Marquette as does the small cottage she made famous. Copies of *Dandelion Cottage* continue to sell as generation after generation falls in love with the charming story.

Like their mother, the Rankin children would contribute a great deal to Marquette. Phyllis Rankin would be the head librarian at Peter White Public Library for over forty years and be well known for promoting reading in the community, especially to children. Ernest Rankin Jr., as a member of the Marquette County Historical Society, would do much to preserve the area's history. Imogene would marry and move away but return later to Marquette. (For more information about Imogene, see the section on 209 E. Arch Street).

225 E. Ridge ~ Murray Home

225 E. Ridge ~ Murray Home

This home was built by David Murray, owner of the David Murray Grocery on Front Street. The family lost its store in the 1868 fire, after which time, Mr. Murray partnered with Byron Robbins to rebuild the storefront. Today the building is divided into apartments. In the 1990s, NMU professor, author and host of High School Bowl, David Goldsmith lived here. I was in his Major Authors course when he invited the class over at the end of the semester to watch the film of *Ulysses* at his apartment.

316 Pine Street (corner of Pine and Ridge) ~ Pine Ridge Apartments

Why the City of Marquette thought it a good idea to permit a high rise to be built in the middle of the historical residential district I'll never understand, but the Pine Ridge Apartments, named for its location on the corner of Ridge and Pine Streets, stands on a historical piece of property. It sticks out amid the Victorian homes, but when it was built in the late 1960s, Victorian style was out of fashion and Ridge and

Arch Streets did not yet have a historical designation. The property had also always been public land, so the City did what it felt was for the public good at the time by building apartments.

Originally, the land was the site of the Ridge Street School built in 1859. Dr. Morgan Hewitt, Peter White's father-in-law, donated the land. At the time, residents opposed the property as being the site of the first high school because it was "on the edge of the wilderness"—it would be an-

316 Pine Street ~ Pine Ridge Apartments

other nine years before Peter White would build the first of the fashionable Ridge Street homes. Nevertheless, a school was built. The initial building would include separate doors for boys and girls and be used until 1875 when it was replaced by a larger building that opened in 1878. This second school burnt down in 1900, an event which doubtless inspired Carroll Watson Rankin to write the scene in *The Adopting of Rosa Marie* where Mabel Bennett escapes from a schoolhouse that has burst into flames by sliding down a dust chute.

When rebuilt, three structures would replace the earlier schools. Commonly known as the Howard-Froebel School, the new complex consisted of the Howard Junior High School on Ridge Street and the Froebel Elementary School on Arch Street with the Industrial Arts building between the two. The elementary school was named for Frederick Froebel, the famous German educator who introduced the idea

of kindergarten, while the high school was named for Howard Longyear, son of John and Mary Longyear, who had drowned in 1900.

The school would serve Marquette for many decades until the city saw the need to build newer schools such as Graveraet in 1927 and the current Marquette Senior High School. In 1961, the Howard-Froebel School was torn down, and in 1969 replaced with the current Pine Ridge Apartments—a

Howard-Froebel School

towering nine-story high rise, Marquette's tallest building to date, decidedly out of place with the historical buildings surrounding it, but after more than four decades and thousands of people living inside it, the apartment building has become a part of Marquette history itself. Built initially to be a high rise for senior citizens, it quickly filled and by 1979 Snowberry Heights would open for Marquette's growing senior population.

314 E. Ridge ~ Wetmore Home

The home that stood here belonged to William L. Wetmore. He was one of the co-founders, along with M.H. Maynard, Peter White, William Burt, and his grocer brother F.P. Wetmore, of the Huron Bay Slate and Iron Company, which owned the company town of Arvon as well as a 200 yard wooden dock built on Huron Bay, which was never to have any ore deposited or shipped from it.

In 1871, William Wetmore cut hardwood and built kilns to make charcoal in Alger County as well as founding a general store there. When he retired in 1894, the small community was renamed Wetmore in his honor.

Wetmore Landing, also named for him, is today a popular beach on Lake Superior off the road to Big Bay, but it was initially a clearing along shore where lumbermen could bring logs out of the forest to the lake from where they could be rafted down to Marquette.

316 East Ridge ~ Boswell Home

Arthur E. Boswell, the advertising manager for *The Mining Journal*, built this home in 1906. It represents the popular early twentieth century Prairie school design, and was designed and constructed by Chicago architect J.D. Chubb.

In the 1940s, Young Kaufman, son of Louis G. Kaufman and brother to Joan Kaufman, bought the house. Later, Young

316 E. Ridge ~ Boswell Home

Kaufman would build a new unique home at 450 E. Ohio Street, which because it was built on the rock bluff appears to be only one floor but has two additional floors that stick out of the bluff.

322 E. Ridge ~ Pendill Home

This home belonged to James Pendill and his wife Flavia. James Pendill was born in New York in 1812, and after living in Niles, Michigan and Sault Ste. Marie, he came to Marquette in 1855. He was the representative for Marquette County in 1863-1864 and after moving to Negaunee in 1867, he became its mayor from 1872-1873. He is credited with being the father of Negaunee because he was responsible for laying out a plan for the city. He then moved back to Marquette where he was mayor from 1879-1882. He also was city supervisor for many years and a school board trustee. Mr. Pendill opened the Pendill and

322 E. Ridge ~ Pendill Home

McComber mines, and he was also in the mercantile business and built many storefronts and homes and also operated a sawmill. Mr. Pendill died in 1885. Several of his adult children later lived at 401 N. Front Street (see entry below).

328 E. Ridge ~ Longyear and Fraser Home

Mary Beecher Longyear boarded here in the mid-1870s as a young teacher. Later, John M. Longyear owned the property and sold it in 1886 to Edward Fraser, who owned a mill in the Marquette area.

328 E. Ridge ~ Longyear and Fraser Home ~ c. 1991

329 E. Ridge ~ Von Zellan Home

Marquette architect Carl F. Struck built this house in 1875 for Samuel Shock, the Duluth, South Shore and Atlantic Railroad Superintendent. In the 1890s, the house belonged to the Kaufman family—Samuel Sr. and his son Samuel Jr. Kaufman, then vice-president of the Savings Bank, lived here along with Daniel Kaufman.

The house today is commonly known as the Von Zellan Home for Dr. Von Zellan and his five unmarried children who owned the house from 1912 to 1972. The good doctor, as doctors

329 E. Ridge ~ Von Zellan Home

in those days were known to do, often accepted items besides money for payment. One such payment was said to be a bear cub which became a family pet and could often be seen chained in the yard. Claw marks on the interior woodwork attest to the bear's presence. Dr. Von Zellan's five children, who became lawyers, doctors, and teachers in Marquette, never married but lived together in the home for decades.

The house was later owned by John and Pat Raunch who in 1991 then sold it to Robert and Julie Schorr.

334 E. Ridge Street ~ Breitung & Kaufman Home

The Breitung home is no longer standing, but its history provides an interesting look into the lives of its owners. The house was built by Edward Breitung and his wife, Mary. Breitung, the son of a Lutheran minister, was born in 1831 in the Duchy of Saxe-Meiningen in Germany. He attended the College of Mining in Meiningen, and then in 1849, immigrated to the United States and settled in Kalamazoo County, Michigan. He moved to Detroit in 1851 and became a clerk in a mercantile house. His mining and mercantile background led him to Marquette and later Negaunee where he continued his mercantile business. By 1864, he completely transitioned into iron mining. He located several profitable mines in Marquette and Menominee Counties, and later became involved with gold and silver mining in Colorado. Breitung Township in Marquette County is named for him. Breitung Township in Minnesota is also named after him for his work in developing its Soudan Mine in the 1880s.

Edward Breitung became involved in politics and was elected to the Michigan State House of Representatives in 1873 and 1874. He served as a Michigan State Senator in 1877 and 1878. He was Negaunee's mayor in 1879, 1880, and 1882, and from 1883-1885, he was in the United States House of Representatives for Michigan's 11th congressional district.

Mr. Breitung met his wife, Mary, in a boarding house in Republic, Michigan where he often ate when in town on business and where she worked as a chambermaid. They would have two children, William, who died young, and Edward N. Breitung who was fifteen at the time of his father's death in 1887.

334 E. Ridge ~ Breitung/Kaufman Home

Breitung built this home just before his death.

Six years after Mr. Breitung's death, Mary Breitung married Nathan Kaufman, whom her husband had relied on to handle many business details for him. The marriage created gossip that Mary and Nathan had been seeing each other before Mr. Breitung's death, but considering they waited six years to marry, that seems unlikely. The gossip was more due to people disliking Nathan Kaufman and being jealous of how the Kaufman family's social position rose as a result of this marriage. In the 1890s, Nathan Kaufman would serve as mayor, be responsible for building the city hall, be involved in starting the Marquette Street Railway, and would help to establish and become president of the Savings Bank.

Nathan Kaufman

Meanwhile, Edward N. Breitung reached adulthood and married his stepfather's younger sister Charlotte Graveraet Kaufman. Nathan Kaufman would continue to oversee operation of the Breitung money and businesses until his death in 1918.

When Nathan Kaufman died, his will left everything to the Kaufman rather than Breitung side of the family. When his wife, Mary Breitung Kaufman, went to court to break the will it resulted in a trial where so many unsavory details came out about Nathan that Mary decided to divorce him posthumously.

About the same time, Nathan's younger brother, Louis Kaufman, built the impressive Kaufman Mausoleum in Park Cemetery—a scaled-down replica of the Parthenon in Greece and said to cost about three million dollars. To be buried in the marvelous marble mausoleum was not good enough reason for Mary to stay married to her deceased second husband. Today she is buried in the smaller Breitung mausoleum built of sandstone. (More about the Breitung family can be read under 350 E. Ridge).

343 E. Ridge ~ Dorothy Maywood Bird Residence

For about two decades, author Dorothy Maywood Bird had an apartment here on the second floor which she fondly referred to as "The Bird's Nest."

Dorothy M. Bird

343 E. Ridge ~ Dorothy Maywood Bird Residence

Dorothy was born in Crystal Falls, Michigan in 1899, but when she was five, her father became the minister at the First Methodist Church in Marquette, and for the next six years, she grew up at 427 N. Front Street. Chances are that the young Dorothy knew the Rankin children, although several years older than her, since they lived just a few blocks away, and she very possibly read Rankin's novels set in a fictionalized version of Marquette. Later, she would set her own novel, *Granite Harbor* (1944), in a fictionalized town based on Marquette with a Hillcrest Street very similar to Ridge Street. During the summers, the Maywood family spent their summers at Middle Island Point, as do the characters in *Granite Harbor*.

In 1910, Dorothy's father was transferred to another church and the Maywood family moved downstate. The young Dorothy was heartsick over the move and had to be taken out of school because she was so ill. She recalled of this time, "I used to go to the window on winter nights and cry for the snow, the wind, the northern lights and the roar of Lake Superior."

Dorothy would attend the University of Michigan, during which time she sold her first manuscript. She worked as a children's librarian at the Detroit Public Library before marrying John Wendell Bird. The couple would have four children. From 1930 on, the Birds spent their summers in Marquette, and in 1940, they built a camp at Middle Island Point. Bird would write three children's novels, *Granite Harbor* (1944), *Mystery at Laughing Water* (1946), and *The Black Opal* (1949). The first novel tells of Terrill Blake, who moves to Granite Harbor from Texas for a year while her father teaches at the local college. Terrill is at first homesick for Texas until she meets her next-door neighbor, Shannon O'Keefe. Bird clearly imagines Terrill and Shannon living on Ridge Street, disguising Terrill's home as 211 Hillcrest, which overlooks the lake with a view of the lighthouse, breakwater, and marina.

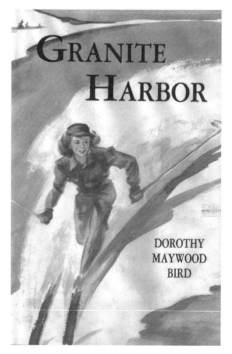

GRANITE HARBOR

DOROTHY MAYWOOD BIRD

The book reads like a tourist advertisement for all of Upper Michigan's outdoor recreational activities, especially winter sports.

Bird would go on to be Dean of Women and Librarian at Lansing Business University. After her husband's death in 1965, she moved permanently to Marquette where she started a writer's group. During that time, Lynn and Lon Emerick, local authors in their own right of such books as *Lumberjack—the End of an Era* and *The Superior Peninsula*, became friends with Dorothy. I have asked the Emericks to share some of their memories of one of Marquette's first authors:

> *When Dorothy moved back to Marquette after her husband's death, she lived in the upstairs apartment at 343 E. Ridge. We visited her there on many occasions and were honored to become part of her circle of friends. She lived elegantly, not in terms of rich possessions or money, but in her approach to life. Dining alone most days, she set out her good china and silver, along with a book of poetry on her table.*
>
> *In later years, she had quite severe arthritis and told us if she were to sit down in the rocking chair, she might never get up again, so she walked...to the Peter White Library, to church, and on other errands around town, for as long as she could.*
>
> *Upon return to Marquette, she started a writers' group, which met in her living room on E. Ridge Street.*
>
> *She was the impetus behind the formation of the Marquette Beautification Committee, at a time when the "looks" of downtown Marquette and the lakeshore were not forefront in most citizens' minds. She visited merchants personally and suggested that of course they wanted their storefronts and surroundings to be as beautiful as Marquette's setting. Who could be rude or even say no to this patrician lady with the lovely carriage and upswept white hair?*
>
> *In the 1970s, the late Dave Rood, editor of the* Escanaba Daily Press, *alerted the community to plans for Little Presque Isle, which would include blasting of a deep water harbor, a large coal fired power plant, slurry pipes inland to Harlow Lake and a chain link fence along the beaches. Horrified at this prospect, Dorothy became the local catalyst for a group Citizens to Save the Superior Shoreline (CSSS), which formed to fight the plans. We met Dorothy about this time when we became involved in the effort. Many, many meetings were held in her living room on Ridge Street as the group*

formed; her letters to The Mining Journal *alerted others to join the cause. It took two years, but the plans were dropped and the land eventually became part of the Escanaba State Forest.*

In the heat of those years, while we were driving her one evening out to Little Presque Isle, she had a proposal for saving the area: "Just boost me up in one of those Norway pines, go back to town, and tell everyone you've found a rare bird there!"

Each summer, Dorothy moved to the log cabin at Middle Island Point, which was named Laughing Water. After she moved from Marquette to Menominee for milder winters, she continued to spend some part of her summers at Laughing Water. It was such a delight each summer to come through that screen door and hear her signature greetings: "There you are! Sit down and tell me ALL about what you have been doing." Dorothy was always a "There you are" kind of person, as opposed to a "Here I Am" person.

She loved to tell the story of how she saw Halley's Comet when she lived in Marquette as a girl, and saw it again when she returned, as it did in her later life.

She also remembered, as a child, the Powder Mill explosion at Tourist Park Location, and how it shook houses and people even in Marquette.

Later, as she became increasingly frail, she moved from Menominee to South Carolina to live with her son Richard, his wife Sue, and grandson Adam. Adam and his grandmother became very close and had many late afternoon conversations after he returned from school each day.

Dorothy died there in 1989 and a memorial service was held at the Methodist Church on Ridge Street. A more informal remembrance was held by many of her fellow CSSS members on the beach at Little Presque Isle.

In her last years, Dorothy gave the rights to Granite Harbor *to the Peter White Public Library and it is my understanding that they have a number of copies available for sale.*

Remembrance of her friendship still lights our lives these many years later. She was a wonderful example of "Bloom where you are planted." She not only immortalized Marquette in her books, but she made it a better place to live through her community involvement, her fervent love of Marquette and Lake Superior, and her infectious enthusiasm for life, place, and friends.

347 E. Ridge ~ Allen Home

347 E. Ridge ~ Allen Home

This home was built in 1887 for Ephraim W. Allen, the treasurer of the DSS&A Railroad. The son of a Salem, Massachusetts preacher, Mr. Allen came to Marquette in 1880 as a bookkeeper for the Detroit, Mackinac and Marquette Railroad while the railroad was still being built. Before the railroad was complete, Senator McMillan, its prime builder, appointed Allen as its cashier and paymaster. Mr. Allen would be one of the charter members of the Huron Mountain Shooting and Fishing Club. His son, Hugh, was great friends with Howard Longyear; both boys would drown in Lake Superior in 1900 while canoeing together between Marquette and the Huron Mountain Club. Upon his son's death, Mr. Allen retired from the Club, but in sympathy, the other members granted him a lifelong membership until his death in 1916.

350 E. Ridge ~ Maynard & Breitung Home

Matthew H. Maynard, receiver for the U.S. Land Office and Peter White's law partner, built this home in 1887. Mr. Maynard came to Marquette in 1855 from Indiana. He was a lawyer and besides being Peter White's law partner, also served as county treasurer, District Attorney for the Upper Peninsula, Prosecuting Attorney for Marquette, and several other positions. Mr. Maynard's brother, Darius G. Maynard, was the only person who drowned when the *Jay Morse* sank in 1867 while taking forty-one of Marquette's most prominent citizens on a pleasure cruise. Matthew Maynard and his wife Mary Foote were the parents of three children, including Alfred Foote Maynard, who married Helen Goodwin, daughter of William Goodwin and Anna Pickands. Anna was the sister of Colonel James Pickands who built the home at 455 E. Ridge. Alfred and Helen Maynard's son James Pickands Maynard never married.

Mr. Matthew H. Maynard reputedly placed

350 E. Ridge ~ Maynard & Breitung Home

the iron fence around the property to keep out wandering livestock in the neighborhood. The fence is a rarity because most ornamental iron fences from that time period were contributed to the war effort during World War I. The veranda was a later addition to the home.

The Maynards sold the home to Dr. Edward J. Hudson and his wife, Marion Kaufman, daughter of Sam Kaufman Sr. Dr. Hudson was a chemist who worked at Cliff Dow Chemical Company in Marquette. In 1892, the Hudsons sold the house to Marion's sister and her husband, Edward N. Breitung and Charlotte Kaufman Breitung.

Edward and Charlotte lived here until they moved to New York. In 1913, they returned to Marquette to visit, which ultimately resulted in a huge family scandal. By that time, their daughter, Juliet, had grown into a woman. During the visit, Juliet became interested in a gardener named Max Kleist who worked for one of the Ridge Street families. Kleist would later

Edward N. Breitung

claim Juliet made the first moves on him, asking him to meet her at the corner of Spruce and Ridge Streets for secret liaisons. When the Breitungs returned to New York City, Kleist followed them. There Juliet and Max Kleist were secretly married, although Juliet continued to live with her parents. The Breitungs were not happy when they found out about their daughter's secret marriage, and at first, they denied it publicly, but eventually, Juliet's parents accepted it, and Mr. Breitung tried to find suitable employment for his new son-in-law within his mining operations.

The marriage did not go well and resulted in not only an annulment but a sensational hearing in 1915 that was covered by the *New York Times*. Kleist brought suit against the Breitungs for a quarter million dollars, charging that they had alienated his wife's affections from him. Besides revealing details of his courtship with Juliet, Kleist claimed that Mr. Breitung had plotted to have him killed by sending him to work in mines in New Mexico; while Kleist was working in a mine shaft, dynamite exploded over his head and rocks fell into the shaft, which Kleist interpreted as a murder attempt. In retaliation, Mr. Breitung accused Kleist of stealing his socks, which Kleist claimed Juliet gave him as a gift, making Mr. Breitung's daughter the sock thief. At one point during the trial, the judge asked Mr. Breitung whether he had ever struck Kleist, to which he replied, "I did not, but I'm sorry now I didn't."

The judge dismissed the case, and Kleist disappeared from public notice. Juliet remarried in 1918 to Herbert Richter of Long Island, whose family had made its money in the hotel business. The couple met during the First World War when Juliet was involved in doing canteen work and Richter was in the naval reserves.

That would not be the end to the Breitung family's troubles. In 1921, Edward N. Breitung

Breitung Mausoleum

was charged in New York with vagrancy when police arrested him as a customer in a house of prostitution. The *People vs. Edward N. Breitung* became a landmark case because New York laws had just changed so that men as well as women could be charged for earning money immorally. The case was dismissed because the judge interpreted the law as referring to people who engaged in immoral business but not to people who were "simply immoral."

Edward N. Breitung died in 1924, at which time his business was in a state of insolvency, mainly as a result of shipping losses during World War I. His widow, who had never been involved in business, was able to turn everything around in two years and make the family worth more than what they had been prior. Despite her lack of being in business, Mrs. Breitung had already been a primary fundraiser for the war effort, as well as a working volunteer for the Red Cross. As a society leader, she financed several events to raise money for the troops, as well as various causes such as the care of animals. In a letter to the Marquette Historical Society describing his grandmother, William Richter later said she was a great friend to him "enjoyed a dirty joke as much as I do" and despite her frame of 5'9" was strong enough to pick him off the ground when he was a grown man of 6'4". By all accounts, she was a remarkable woman in many ways. Mrs. Breitung died in 1936.

As for Juliet, by the time of her mother's death, she was married to her third husband, Howard Merritt of Bronxville, New York. Her only children were William and Charlotte Richter.

The Breitung house would change hands several times after the Breitungs left Marquette for New York. Since the 1980s, it has belonged to John and Mary Argeropoulos. Their son, Mike, went to preschool with me and later we were both Teaching

Assistants in the English Department at Northern Michigan University while earning our Master's degrees.

351 E. Ridge ~ Burt Home

After selling his home at 200 E. Ridge to Sidney Adams, Hiram Burt moved to the home that once stood here. Hiram Burt had initially come to Marquette in 1862 and began working for the Lake Superior Iron Company. In 1863 with his brother, he founded Burt Brothers, a mercantile business that did extensive trade until it was destroyed in the 1868 fire, to a loss of $158,000, the highest individual loss of the fire. They quickly recovered their losses, built the first city block following the fire, bought the Jackson Dock, and built many other city blocks. Mr. Burt would also be Director of the Peninsula Iron Company of Detroit, general manager of the Carp River Iron Company, manager of the Union Fuel Company, manager of the Union Mining Company, and President of the Marquette Manufacturing Company.

401 E. Ridge ~ Kaufman Home

401 E. Ridge ~ Kaufman Home

This house belonged to Samuel and Juliet Kaufman in the 1870s. It has since exchanged hands several times over the years. In 1993 it was bought by Cameron Howes, the head of Northern Michigan University's Health, Physical Education, and Recreation Department. During restoration work, the Howes family found letters encased in the walls dating back to the 1870s and written to and from members of the Samuel and Juliet Kaufman family.

THE HUNDRED STEPS

Spruce Street ends between the 300 and 400 blocks of Ridge Street. Because of the cliff, the street could not continue. People who wanted to go down to Lake Street below either had to walk all the length of Ridge Street and circle back, or they could descend down "The Hundred Steps." The Hundred Steps were built about the time the first houses were erected on Ridge Street. An early photo of the steps dates to 1870. At the end of Spruce Street a fairly wide boardwalk with

The Hundred Steps ~ c. 1870

high board fences at the sides extended to the steps between the Merritt house on the east and the Breitung home on the west. Occasionally they were referred to as the 101 Steps, but no one is certain exactly how many steps there were.

The steps were built about the same time as the Grace Furnace was built in 1870 on cinder fill between the sand beach and the Jackson Iron Company's dock. Their purpose was to allow the workers who lived above on the Ridge to walk down to the lake. The Cinder Pond below was named because it was the dumping place for cinders. The Grace Furnace, which produced pig iron, was destroyed in the early 1900s by fire. The Cinder Pond remained for many years. My great-uncle, Clifton White, used to talk frequently about visiting it as a boy.

Besides the Hundred Steps, which were open to the public, other stairs went from the Ridge to the lakeshore. According to Ernest Rankin in an April 4, 1977 *Mining Journal* article, steps behind Peter White's house led down to a small pond fed by a cold spring. White kept the pond stocked with speckled trout for his breakfast. The J.W. Spear house, across from the Rankin home during Ernest Rankin's childhood, also had a pair of steps that led down to the Spear stable on Lake Street. Ernest Rankin recalled that not only were the Spears' stairs difficult to reach, but "if you were caught at the top by Mr. Spear, his greetings were far from warm and cordial."

The Hundred Steps inspired local novelist Holly Wilson to write her young adult novel *The Hundred Steps* (1958). Wilson grew up on nearby Arch Street and knew the steps well. Her novel takes place in the 1950s but the steps are those Wilson remembers from her childhood. In the novel, Wilson depicts the steps as dividing the upper class on the hill from the working class living along the lakeshore in the fictional town of Clifton, based on Marquette. The main character, Marcy McKay, represents both classes of townspeople. Marcy's father is first mate on a ship and her family lives along the lakeshore, but her mother is from the hill people. Mrs. McKay encourages her daughter to befriend those who live up on the hill. Marcy, however, finds those who live up on the hill to be shallow. When she befriends the wealthy Gwen, she discovers Gwen is only using her to be near Bill, a young boy from the lower town, in whom Marcy is herself interested. Marcy and Bill go on a double date with Gwen and Walt, a rather reckless and dangerous wealthy young man. But in the end, Walt shows he has some redeeming qualities. The novel culminates when a fierce storm places Marcy's father and his ship in danger; during the storm, the true nature of the townsfolk, both from the harbor and the hill, is revealed.

Wilson's readers will easily recognize Marquette in the fictional town of Clifton, not only for the Hundred Steps but also in references to Pine and Spruce Streets and the Clifton Hotel. By the time Wilson wrote her novel, the original steps were decayed, and today they are no more. Other staircases from Ridge Street down to Lake Street have been built but they are private property, whereas the Hundred Steps were regularly used by Marquette residents. The advent of automobiles and bicycles also made the trip up and down from Ridge to Lake Street less strenuous so the Hundred Steps eventually became less necessary. (For more information about Holly Wilson, see the section on 328 E. Arch Street).

410 E. RIDGE ~ MERRITT HOME

**Marquette's Merritt House,
Montana's Moss Mansion,
Mark Twain, William Morris
&
The Madeleine Henning Mystery:
How Four Historical Homes Inspired *The Marquette Trilogy***

Many people have asked me which house in Marquette I am referring to when I write about the Henning Mansion, which later becomes the Robert O'Neill Historical Home in *The Marquette Trilogy*. Of course, the Hennings and O'Neills are purely fictional characters so the house is fictional as well. However, the idea of the house was inspired by an actual home in Marquette—the Merritt House at 410 E. Ridge Street. The cover of my third novel, *Superior Heritage*, contains a photograph of the Merritt House.

I have always thought the Merritt House the most dominant and impressive home on Ridge Street. Consequently, it had to be the model for the Henning and O'Neill homes in my novels. At the time I wrote *The Marquette Trilogy*, I had never been inside the Merritt House, only viewed it from the outside. However, when I requested permission from the present owner, Dennis McCowen, to have a

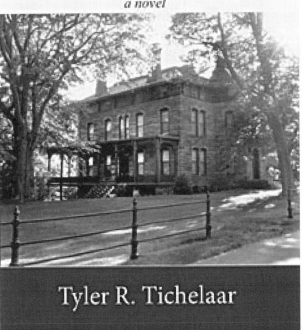

photograph of the house on the cover of *Superior Heritage*, he was kind enough to give me a tour of the home. Although the Merritt House was broken into apartments in the 1940s, it still retains much of its original elegance. Because I had never been in the home at the time I wrote my novels, I completely imagined the house's interior with some little basis upon historical books that contained descriptions of it, notably

Marquette Then and Now by Sonny Longtine and Laverne Chappell and *The Sandstone Architecture of the Lake Superior Region* by Kathryn Bishop Eckert.

The Merritt family's history is not quite as dramatic as that of the Hennings in my novels. In *Iron Pioneers*, when Gerald and Sophia Henning move into their mansion in 1868, only Peter White has a house on the prestigious Ridge Street. Daniel Merritt, by comparison, built his home in 1880. Local architect Hampson Gregory was commissioned for the task. Later, Gregory's daughter would marry Mr. Merritt's son Charles.

In *Iron Pioneers*, once the house is completed, Gerald Henning gives his wife's sister and brother-in-law, Cordelia and Nathaniel Whitman and their daughter, Edna, a tour of the house, as described below:

> *The house truly was the grandest Marquette had ever seen. The entire structure was built of sandstone and rose two stories with a central tower to serve as a third floor. Its Victorian Gothic style dominated the landscape with its emphasis on vertical lines in its tower and elongated windows. The windows were embellished with stained glass patterns along their edges. The front porch curved around the side with intricate carvings and trefoil arches. The house's interior was composed of the finest black walnut woodwork. Several tall chimneys rose from the roof, providing warmth and comfort to each of the major rooms. Compared to Marquette's early pioneer cabins, the Henning mansion seemed to have countless rooms. Downstairs was an east and a west parlor, a dining room, a kitchen, a dayroom for Sophia, a smoking room that Gerald would also use as an office, and a small room with an upright piano for Madeleine to practice upon while a grand piano graced the east parlor for social occasions. Upstairs was the master bedroom, individual bedrooms for Caleb, Agnes, and Madeleine, a guest room and two bathrooms. The tower and attic provided two servants rooms, plus a large linen closet and storage space.*
>
> *Gerald gave Nathaniel and Cordelia the downstairs tour. Edna obstinately remained in the east parlor; she was disillusioned by all the splendor when she learned there was no library.*

By comparison, the actual Merritt House contained on the first floor a reception room, billiard room, laundry, pantry, kitchen, and bathrooms. The second floor included a library, parlor, dining room, bath, and bedroom, and the third floor had ten sleeping apartments and a bath. The fawn-colored, swirled sandstone of its exterior was quarried in South Marquette while the interior was designed using walnut and cherry woodwork finished in Marquette shops. Elongated Romanesque windows were placed symmetrically. Decorative wrought-iron cresting tops the truncated hip roof with several tall chimneys. An impressive wooden porch stretches along the house's east side and behind it overlooking the lake. The tall central tower entrance gives the house a prominent and dominant look.

Doubtless, Edna Whitman would have preferred the Merritt House with its library to the home of her aunt and uncle. However, my readers will remember that in *The Queen City* and in *Superior Heritage* the library was the great showcase of the house. After the Hennings sell the house in 1876 to Robert and

Merritt House ~ front tower

Carolina Smith, Carolina has the library built, more for show than an interest in literature. At the end of the library she also builds a small conservatory.

In *The Marquette Trilogy*, the Henning and O'Neill home survives with few changes to its historical structure, but the Merritt House was not so fortunate. The Merritt family only remained in their splendid home a few years before leaving Marquette, despite Mr. Merritt's prominent role as a director of the Iron Bay Foundry and his interest in Upper Michigan's railroads. The Merritts moved to Duluth in 1886 and became dock, bridge, and marine contractors. Their descendants became partial owners of Merritt, Chapman & Scott Co., which with the American Bridge Division of the U.S. Steel Company, built the Mackinac Bridge from 1954 to 1957.

The Merritt House passed through

Merritt House ~ side view

several hands until the 1940s when it was broken into apartments. In 1974, Alfred and Edith McCowen purchased the house and have since maintained it as an apartment building. They have added to the number of apartments in the house by converting the third floor into useable space and adding new windows to that level. Much of the original woodwork remains, although sadly both the statue at the bottom of the staircase in the entry hall, which held up a lamp, and the original vintage front doorknobs have been stolen in recent years. During my tour of the house, I was able to climb up the tower, from which the view of Ridge Street was spectacular, especially during that day's April blizzard. In the walls surrounding the staircase, the original Victorian stenciling can still be seen. I imagine the residents of the house find it interesting to live in such a historical home. The house has been well preserved, and I am sure it will stand for many more generations to view on their walks along Ridge Street.

But what about that library Edna was disappointed not to find and which Carolina Smith later adds to the house, and which is so enjoyed by Robert and Eliza O'Neill and later by John and Wendy Vandelaare? The Merritt House did not contain such a library. Nor is it solely my invention, although it is the closest thing to heaven I could imagine. Here it is described in *Superior Heritage* when John Vandelaare first enters it:

> *John was unprepared for the library. He dreamt of having his own book-room someday, but he was stunned to discover a library could be a room of incomparable beauty. The woodwork on the bookshelves was astounding. The shelves themselves rose halfway up the wall, every inch of them stuffed with books. Above the shelves was delicate blue and green Victorian wallpaper which John would one day recognize as a William Morris pattern. Arranged on the wall were large paintings in vibrant colors by the Pre-Raphaelite school, depicting famous literary scenes. Arranged in the center of the room were little escritoires and high backed chairs designed for hours of comfortable reading. At the room's far end were several Boston ferns leading into a little sunroom complete with a fountain that even on a late autumn day brought a sense of springtime to the room.*

I admit even my imagination could not quite have created such a splendid retreat. The idea came from my visit in 1997 to the Mark Twain Home in Hartford, Connecticut, where I saw the most beautiful room I have ever seen. I still think the way the bookshelves were built low enough to provide space for pictures to be hung above them was ingenious. However, there is no William Morris wallpaper in the Mark Twain Home. The wallpaper was inspired by my 1999 visit to the Hixon House in La-Crosse, Wisconsin, which is said to have the best-preserved original William Morris wallpaper in the United States.

Readers of *Iron Pioneers* have to wonder, despite how difficult

Mark Twain House

Hixon House Wallpaper

her mother was, how Madeleine Henning could have faked her drowning and left Marquette, and especially such a beautiful home. The truth of the matter is that Madeleine was homesick for Marquette the rest of her life. In July 1999 while I was still in the early planning stages of writing *The Marquette Trilogy*, I knew Madeleine would fake her death and disappear, but I did not

know where she would go. Then on a drive home from Seattle, my family and I happened to stop in Billings, Montana and visit the Moss Mansion. I've visited many historical homes, but the Moss Mansion made a deep impression upon me because of all things, it was made of Lake Superior Sandstone.

I knew nothing about the Moss family or why they chose to build their home of

Moss Mansion

sandstone. And I did not inquire into the family's history beyond what the tour guide told us. But as an author, I decided anyone who would build a house in Montana of Lake Superior Sandstone must have an Upper Michigan connection; consequently, I envisioned Madeleine being so homesick for Marquette and the beautiful sandstone mansion of her parents that she decided to build her own house of Lake Superior Sandstone. In *Superior Heritage*, Madeleine and Lazarus' great-great-granddaughter Wendy explains her ancestors' decision to build their own house:

> *They were so rich by the time they were middle-aged that they built a large mansion near the Yellowstone River. Believe it or not, they built it out of Lake Superior sandstone which they had shipped from Marquette to Montana. Now that I've seen this house, I imagine Madeleine must have wanted it that way because it would remind her of her childhood home.*

After *Superior Heritage* was published, I began to think again about Madeleine and her building a similar sandstone house in Montana, and so I contacted the Moss Mansion director to find out if the Moss family did have an Upper Michigan connection. I was disappointed to find out Mr. Moss was actually from Missouri, and even the architect, H.J. Hardenburgh, was not from the Great Lakes area, although he must have been familiar with the use of sandstone and seen other structures built of it. Neither the Mosses nor Mr. Hardenburgh were homesick for Upper Michigan, but they nevertheless had good taste in their building materials.

Preston B. Moss was certainly as prominent as I envisioned Lazarus and Madeleine had become in Montana. Mr. Moss first visited Billings in 1891, and impressed by the town's activity, he moved there the following year and soon had his hand in numerous business activities. He bought into the First National Bank of Billings, built the Northern Hotel (1902-1904), was instrumental in building the BL&I Canal that irrigated the 40,000-acre Billings Bench (1908), was an incorporator of the $1 million Billings Sugar Factory (1906), founded the *Billings Evening Journal* and merged it with the *Billings Gazette* (1908), operated the central steam heating plant (1907), organized the first automatic dial system in Montana (1907), built the city's first meat-packing plant, helped start Rocky Mountain College (1906), and in 1941, he rebuilt the Northern Hotel following the 1940 fire. He also owned, in partnership with his neighbors, 80,000 head of sheep and several thousand head of cattle.

Amid all his hard work, in 1901-1903, Mr. Moss built his Lake Superior Sandstone mansion next to a wheat field. The residence of twenty-eight rooms was home to Mr. and Mrs. Moss, their six children, Mrs. Moss' parents, and a staff of three. The home was designed by New York architect H.J. Hardenburgh, constructed by the local firm E.H. Gagnon, and decorated by W.P. Nelson Company of Chicago. Mahogany, birch, oak, ash, and white pine woodwork, an onyx fireplace, rose silk and gold leaf wall coverings, stained glass windows, and a Moorish entry are among the luxurious finishing touches.

According to Joyce L. Mayer, former director of the Moss Mansion, it was the choice of sandstone that made the house unique and resulted in its preservation as a museum today. She told me that the house took nearly two years to finish and cost $105,000. By comparison, the local hospital cost only $40,000 to build in 1905.

The architect's importance also makes the Moss Mansion significant. Mr. Hardenburgh also designed such important buildings as the Willard Hotel in Washington D.C. (1901), the Plaza Hotel in New York (1905), and the Copley Plaza in Boston (1912). For the Moss Mansion, he would have decided what materials were to be used, probably with Mr. Moss' approval. Although Hardenburgh had such a high level of involvement, he never saw the Moss Mansion in person.

The Moss Mansion's sandstone was transported to Billings by railroad. The shipping of the materials for the house was probably the largest single cost in its construction. A few years ago, the Moss Mansion ordered a manmade material that resembles sandstone in color and texture. Having the fake stone shipped from Quebec cost the Moss Mansion $1,200 for forty square feet of stone.

Daniel Merritt and Preston Moss probably never met each other or saw each other's fabulous homes, but the homes are part of the same architectural sandstone family. Equally, both houses are impressive enough that they inspired a family saga, of a young girl who chose to elope with the man she loved when her mother refused to let her see him. After faking her death and running away with Lazarus, Madeleine Henning went to Montana, where homesick, but unable to bring herself to reconciling with her parents, she comforted herself by building an elaborate Lake Superior Sandstone mansion.

And so, in the end, it is sandstone and homesickness upon which I built my fictional house.

411 E. Ridge ~ Ball Home

Daniel Ball lived in this fine home with his wife, Emma. Mrs. Ball was the daughter of Philo Everett who started the first Jackson mine in Negaunee. She had come to Marquette in 1850 with her parents. Mr. Ball had attended seminary in Albion, Michigan and then attended the University of Michigan, but he had interrupted his law studies to move to Marquette in 1861 and

411 E. Ridge ~ Ball Home

assume the business duties of his deceased brother. The Balls married in 1863 and Dan Ball went on to practice law, become dean of the entire U.P. law profession, and serve as register for the U.S. Land Office as well as be publisher from 1862-1864 of the *Lake Superior News and Journal*. He was later involved in helping to organize the historical society.

420 E. Ridge ~ Burrall, Tibbitts, & Rushton Home

This home was built in the 1920s by Frederick and Margaret (Conklin) Burrall. Mr. Burrall was the nephew of Mary Beecher Longyear. His mother was Fannie Beecher, sister to Mrs. Longyear. Fannie Beecher's husband, George Burrall, abandoned his family, so the Longyears took her and her three children in, and for several years, Mrs. Burrall and her children lived in the Longyear Mansion (see the Longyear Mansion section below). Frederick Burrall would serve as general manager of the Arctic Coal Company, manager of

420 E. Ridge ~ Burrall, Tibbitts, & Rushton Home

mining for the United States and Mexico Trust Company and mining manager for the Consolidated Gold Fields in Alaska's Yukon. Then in 1922, he joined the Longyear companies and in 1931 became president.

The Burralls had no children, so the house was inherited by Mr. Burrall's nephew and his wife, Munro Longyear Tibbitts and Julia "Dee Dee" Koch Tibbitts. Julia, a granddaughter of Marquette's Schaffer family (see 509 E. Ridge), grew up on the Longyear property after the Longyears had departed.

The Tibbitts decided to trade houses in 1962 with Carroll and Louise Rushton.

The Rushtons' granddaughter is my second cousin, Nanette Rushton, so I asked her to write about the house's history and her memories of it:

The house was built on property subdivided from the large brownstone next door. The old barn with a stable in the basement was on the edge of the hill of this lot, and the yard was the grazing area for the horses. The driveway was a Y shape so the horses could go straight past what is now a garage, and curve down the hill behind the row of French lilacs to the barn. The row of lilacs was to hide the mess the horses would make on the trail. This house had two bedrooms connected by a sun porch and a maid's quarters, or in modern terms, three bedrooms with three-and-a-half bathrooms. Each bedroom has its own full bathroom.

The Burralls built the house with southern exposure which passively heats it in the winter, and with the breeze off the lake in the summer, it rarely needed air conditioning. Mr. Burrall was a master gardener who terraced the property, hauling in tons of the right kinds of dirt and clay for optimum growing and drainage. The slate patio off the dining room, sunporch upstairs, the picture window in the living room or the dining room windows and of course, the lawn were all perfect places to watch fireworks on the Fourth of July in the harbor.

My grandparents owned 505 E. Ridge Street, but when my grandpa, Carroll Rushton, was dying of cancer, he did not want my grandmother to have to care for such a large house, so they traded their house with the Tibbitts in 1962 when I was only three, so 420 E. Ridge is the house I knew growing up as my grandparents' home.

Childhood memories....In the summer, Grandma would give my brother, Daniel, and me watermelon slices and have us compete to see who could spit the seeds the farthest over the patio's edge. For many years, a baby grand piano was at the west end of the living room until it came to my parents' house so I could take piano lessons.

The Christmas tree was usually in the bay window at the east end of the living room, sometimes in front of the picture window.

In the winter, my brother and I would sled down the slope from the lilac bush level to the bottom where raspberries grew against the barn wall. We would climb back to the top of the slope by digging out the steps next to the stone wall which acted as an arbor for grape vines. The terrace directly above it had a large sour Bing cherry tree, perfect for cherry pies. The edge had yellow roses. Above that, off the patio was a rock garden under a horse chestnut tree. The west edge of the yard had yellow roses growing against a shallow rock wall, adjacent to another ledge with Tiger Lilies. The landscaping was designed to have something in bloom year-round. Gardening could be a full-time occupation there.

I moved into Grandma's house at 420 E. Ridge in 1979 to take care of the house as I attended college. I had a couple of housemates all the time. The stories that could be told…but best not told here.

Upon graduation from NMU, I had a sewing studio in the basement room with the south window. I painted the walls a soft gray, the built in cabinets in two shades of gray with white cove molding. Light gray carpet, drop ceiling. In 1987, as a single parent, when my son was a year old, I decided to move to Minnesota to be near my parents for support. It took months to empty out the house and hold an estate sale. That year it was sold to the Ameens. Bobby Ameen was an artist. My sewing studio became her art studio.

The house was originally lapboard siding on the top with the brick on the bottom. The roof was slate which grew moss on the north side. In the 1960s Grandma put aluminum siding over the wood. The Ameens added the cedar shingles on the top half making it look very "cottage." I love it that way.

431 E. Ridge ~ Reynolds Home

431 E. Ridge ~ Reynolds Home

This home was built in 1888 by Josiah G. Reynolds, the superintendent of the Lake Superior Powder Company, which made powder for blasting rock at the mines. Josiah had learned the business from his father at the Bennington Power Mills in Vermont. Mrs. Reynolds had been born Jean Kennedy, and she was one of the four Kennedy sisters who came to Marquette and who would all marry well. Lillie Kennedy married George Shiras II, Bessie married Charles Call, and Sara married Frank Spear. They would all live in homes on Ridge Street and frequently visit each other.

Josiah and Jean Reynolds' son Maxwell Kennedy Reynolds would marry Frances Jopling, the daughter of A.O. Jopling and Mary White (Peter White's daughter). Maxwell Kennedy Reynolds would be famous for bringing the wooden respirator (iron lung) to Marquette. His son, Maxwell Reynolds Jr. and wife Phyllis established the Max and Phyllis Reynolds Foundation and were notable philanthropists to Marquette.

Emma Forsyth, Bessie Call, Lillie Shiras, Jean Reynolds, Margaretta Kane, & Sara Spear at Call House

433 E. Ridge ~ Phelps Home

Built in 1892, the Phelps Home was the wedding gift of William Fitch, president of the DSS&A Railroad, to his only daughter, Mary, and her husband Peter White Phelps. Designed by Marquette architect D. Fred Charlton, the house is built of sandstone with a rounded porch and represents Richardson Romanesque architecture.

Peter White Phelps was no relation to Peter White, but he acquired his name in an interesting way. According to local historian Fred Rydholm, a well-known rumor in Marquette at the time was that Peter White had sold a bad deed to Sam Kaufman Sr. In revenge, one of Mrs. Kaufman's sisters, a Graveraet, put an Indian curse on Peter. When his children contracted diphtheria, Peter went down on bended knee to beg her to lift the curse, but all his male children died, leaving no one to carry on his family name. Only his two daughters Frances and Mary survived. They would marry George Shiras III and A.O. Jopling. Nevertheless Peter White was saddened not to have a son.

At that time, Peter White was influential in organizing St. Paul's Episcopal Church, and the wife of the minister, Joshua Phelps, gave birth to a baby boy. Peter White wrote to Mr. Phelps and

433 E. Ridge ~ Phelps Home

requested that he name his son Peter White Phelps, and he gave the child a bond for $2,000 which would bear interest until the boy came of age. Peter and Ellen White became the child's godparents. As a young man, Phelps worked as a bookkeeper in Peter White's bank. Upon White's death, Phelps inherited the Peter White Insurance Agency, the oldest insurance agency in Michigan. Phelps remained a lifelong resident of Marquette.

450 E. Ridge ~ Call Home

> *"I bet it would suit me fine," said Cordelia, "though I think the Calls' house looks more charming."*
>
> *The Call house, owned by the President of the Lake Superior Powder Company, was a Carpenter Gothic and extremely original in style. Sophia equally admired it, although she would never have acknowledged doing so. She always insisted, and not without reason, that her home was the finest in Marquette.*
>
> *"It's hard to believe how many beautiful homes are being built here now," said Cordelia. "Everyone has become so prosperous in recent years."*
>
> — Iron Pioneers

450 E. Ridge ~ Call Home

Architect C.F. Struck built this home in 1868 for Henry Mather, brother-in-law to Peter White—their wives were both daughters of Dr. Hewitt. In 1878, the house was sold to Charles Henry Call. Even so, the house was kept in the family since Call was the nephew of Peter White. Peter White's sister, Mary, had married Thomas Call of Green Bay, and the young Charles H. Call was then lured to Marquette by his uncle. The home's distinctive Carpenter Gothic architecture makes it one of the most noticeable houses on Ridge Street and has resulted in it being listed on the National Register of Historic Places.

Charles H. Call was at various times President of the First National Bank, the Marquette County Savings Bank, and the Lake Superior Powder Company. He also served on the Board of Directors as Secretary Treasurer for the Hotel Superior. His marriage to Bessie Kennedy linked the Calls by blood to many of the other families on Ridge Street. Charles and Bessie had four children, including daughter Jennie, who married Henry Pickands, a member of another prominent early Marquette family.

By the late nineteenth century, the house was sold or at least rented by the Calls to George Shiras II, who used it as a summer home. His wife was sister to Mrs. Call.

In the 1930s, the property was sold to Dr. E. Drevdahl, who converted it to apartments. By the end of the twentieth century it exchanged hands a few times, but today the house is once again a private residence.

455 E. Ridge ~ Pickands, Thurber, & Spear Home

Known today as Harbor Ridge, this home was built in 1881 by James Pickands, a colonel during the Civil War who had become the head of a large ore and shipping firm on the Great Lakes and Marquette's fourth mayor in 1876. Pickands was married to Caroline Martha Outhwaite, daughter of John Outhwaite, a director of the Cleveland Iron Mining Company, who spent his summers in Marquette. Outhwaite's other daughter, Mary (Caroline's half-sister), married Jay Morse, who had been an agent for the Cleveland Iron Mining Company. Morse and Pickands as brother-in-laws would be good friends all their lives.

455 E. Ridge ~ Pickands, Thurber, & Spear Home

John Outhwaite was one of the first residents in Marquette, actually arriving the year before the town was founded. After sleeping his first night on the sand along the lakeshore, the next day he went with his Indian guides to prospect for iron ore. He located the claims for what would become the Cleveland Iron Mining Company. Although other investors such as Dr. Morgan Hewitt and Samuel Mather played more public roles, John Outhwaite was the largest

John Outhwaite

investor in the company when it was incorporated in 1850.

Outhwaite's many other business interests included retail and wholesale groceries, provisioning, lamp (lard) oil manufacturing, investment in Cleveland's first iron mill (which was supplied with ore by Cleveland Iron Mining's mines), brewing, and land development. (His son John Peet Outhwaite of Ishpeming would follow his father's lead in the grocery and provisioning business). Outhwaite backed his two sons-in-law and Colonel Pickands' brother Henry in iron production ventures such as the Bay Furnace as well as several of his nephews in the Blackwell family. While John Outhwaite is predominantly credited with being a Cleveland resident, he was actively involved in the Marquette area and according to his descendant, James Pickands Cass, may well be counted as Marquette's first millionaire.

Colonel Pickands did well for himself with help from his father-in-law. This beautiful Victorian home he built would contain seven fireplaces, beautiful doors of cherry and walnut, and eighteen rooms, but it would not be home to the Pickands for long. Within a week of moving into the home, Mrs. Pickands died. Rumor said the family had moved into the house before the plaster was dry, which resulted in Mrs. Pickands coming down with pneumonia. Unable to live in the home where his wife had died, Pickands sold the house to Henry C. Thurber, and moved with his children to Cleveland. Despite the move, the Pickands family would remain connected to their former Marquette neighbors. Colonel Pickands' son Henry S. Pickands, would later marry Jennie Call, daughter of Charles and Bessie Call of Marquette (see 450 E. Ridge). In addition, Colonel Pickands' sister Anna married William Goodwin and in turn the Goodwin's daughter Helen married Alfred Maynard, son of Matthew H. Maynard (see 350 E. Ridge). Another of his sisters, Caroline, operated an early school in Marquette which became the inspiration for Carroll Watson Rankin's novel *Stump Village* (1935).

Colonel Pickands remarried to Seville Hanna, whose brother, Cleveland industrialist Mark Hanna, would be President McKinley's 1896 campaign manager. After Colonel Pickands died in 1896, his brother-in-law Jay Morse married his widow Seville. Pickands, who had named one of his sons for Jay Morse, probably would have given them his blessing. We can only speculate on what a friendship must have existed between these brother-in-laws. When Morse died in 1906, Matthew H. Maynard of Marquette said of him, "Jay C. Morse was the most upright and honest man I ever knew. He was thoroughly straight and I don't believe he ever told a lie in his life. His word was always as good as his bond, and he was well liked by all with whom he came in contact."

Henry C. Thurber, this home's second owner, was the co-owner of the Hebard-Thurber Lumber Company. As Marquette's tenth mayor, he would also help Peter White raise money to build the road to Presque Isle. Thurber did not live in the house for long before selling it to Frank Bennett Spear, Marquette's ninth mayor.

Frank Spear was married to Sara Kennedy, which linked him to most of the Ridge Street families by marriage. Spear had come to Marquette in 1864. He founded F. B. Spear & Co., later known as Spear & Sons; the dock he built in the harbor early on was the only one to survive the 1868 fire. Spear began his company by dealing in wholesale and retail grain and feed, and in time, the company would also handle coal, wood, lime, brick, cement, fuel oil, sand, gravel, lumber, and other building materials. After Frank Spear's death in 1924, his sons and grandchildren would carry on the business until the company closed its doors in 1993. I remember going to the Spears building on West Washington Street many times in the 1970s and 1980s with my grandfather, Lester White, so he could pick up wood to do his carpentry work.

Spear's son, Frank B. Spear II, inherited the home. His wife, Rachel, was a huge collector of bells and her collection was featured in numerous collector magazines. The collection included more than 600 bells from forty countries, one of Bishop Baraga's altar bells from the Indian Mission on Keweenaw Bay, a silver bell from a lady's garter, a Chinese costume bell, and the bell to Engine 26 from the Lake Superior & Ishpeming Railroad. Today, the famous Rachel Spear bell collection can be seen on display at the Peter White Public Library.

As for Harbor Ridge, in the late twentieth century, it would belong to another Marquette mayor, William Birch and his wife Sally. The Birchs became the saviors of Dandelion Cottage when, rather than allow it to be torn down, they moved it to their backyard where it became 440 E. Arch Street.

460 E. Ridge ~ Peter White & Frazier Home

In 1867, Peter White was the first person to build his home on Ridge Street and he lived there until his death in 1908. The home was inherited by his daughter,

Frances Jopling, Peter White, & Alfred Kidder

460 E. Ridge ~ Peter White Home

Peter White Home Interior

Frances P. White, and her husband, George Shiras III. George Shiras III was the son of Supreme Court Justice, George Shiras II and his wife, Lillie, another of the Kennedy sisters. George Shiras III would be famous as a naturalist who engineered the ability to photograph wildlife at night. At the 1900 World's Fair in Paris, his work took first prize. Shiras Hills, Shiras Pointe Condominiums, and Shiras Pool at Presque Isle are named for him, but I think he would have been most pleased to be remembered with the Shiras Zoo at Presque Isle. George Shiras III would also become a congressman for Pennsylvania and become a friend of President Theodore Roosevelt, having a major influence on Roosevelt's conservation efforts. Roosevelt would stay at the Shiras home when he visited Marquette, most notably in 1913 during his famous trial at the Marquette County Courthouse. George Shiras III died in 1942 and was buried in Marquette. The Shirases would have two children, George Shiras IV and Ellen Shiras.

Theodore Roosevelt & Mrs. Reynolds at the George Shiras III home

Ellen would marry Frank Russell Sr., owner of *The Mining Journal.*

The historic Peter White home was torn down by the family in the late 1940s because it was considered too expensive to heat. The current home was built in 1949 by Lincoln and Ann Frazier. Ann Reynolds Frazier was a cousin of the Shiras family and the daughter of Maxwell Kennedy Reynolds and Frances Q. Jopling (Frances' mother was Mary White, Peter White's daughter). This new home was the first Ranch style home in the historical residential district of Marquette, which makes it historic in its own right despite its looking out of place among its neighbors. The house was featured in *Home and Garden* as a model modern home. The entire home is built on one level—no upstairs, no basement—and provides spectacular views of the lake from several rooms. Behind it is the original carriage house and Peter White's terraced gardens. One can imagine Peter White entertaining his guests there with his famous

460 E. Ridge Today

Peter White punch. Today, the home is owned by Lincoln and Ann Frazier's son Peter White Frazier and his wife, Peggy.

461 E. Ridge ~ Kidder Home

Another modern intrusion stands on this property, but the original home here was the first of several Marquette homes lived in by Alfred Swineford, owner of *The Mining Journal*. Swineford then sold the house to Alfred Kidder, an agent for the Champion Iron Company, the Pittsburgh and Lake Angeline Iron Company, and the

Milwaukee Iron Company. He was also director of the Iron Bay Manufacturing Company and an early member of the Huron Mountain Club. Alfred's son Alfred V. Kidder would become a famous archeologist who explored the cliff dwellings of Arizona and New Mexico. Alfred Kidder's other son, Homer Kidder, would be responsible for recording the oral narratives of Chief Charles Kawbawgam and his brother-in-law Jacques LePique. The manuscript was published posthumously as *Ojibwa Narratives* by Wayne State University

461 E. Ridge ~ Kidder Home

Press in 1994. In *Superior Heritage*, John Vandelaare is surprised to discover in *Ojibwa Narratives* that a story his great-grandfather once told him was actually based on one of Chief Kawbawgam's stories. Later, the house belonged to Phil Spear, brother of Frank B. Spear II. The original home was demolished in 1949 by his son, George Spear, and the more modern home was erected in its place. George Spear operated the Lower Harbor dock until it ceased operations in the 1970s, and then when George Spear died in 1977, he left the land to the City of Marquette, which eventually became Ellwood Mattson Park.

500 E. Ridge ~ Reynolds Home

500 E. Ridge ~ Reynolds Home

Maxwell and Frances (Jopling) Reynolds built this classic colonial home in 1909 blending the Federalist and Georgian styles. The house has a fantastic view of the harbor from a solarium porch on the house's south side. In the late twentieth century, Max Reynolds Jr. and Phyllis Reynolds sold the home to Michael and Martha Conley.

THE LONGYEAR MANSION

...She walked slightly behind her family, unwilling to speak with her obnoxious sister, whose meaningless babble would otherwise distract her from admiring the Longyear mansion as she passed it.

Not all the Waverley novels Sir Walter Scott had penned could work on Margaret's imagination as did this Marquette home. The Longyear mansion filled a block between Ridge and Arch streets, looking out over the lake and dwarfing all its neighbors. Inside were sixty-five elegant rooms and a bowling alley. The house perched on the top of the hill, like a castle whose owners could glance down upon the commoners living below.

Margaret had never met any of the Longyears, but she knew they must be genteel people. She had a notion that if she could get inside the mansion and meet the family, they would have the breeding and taste to realize she was of their kind. They would recognize her natural attributes and help her realize her dreams. If she could only get inside that house—but Margaret had never gotten further than peering through the front gate and pondering which windows were for the servants' rooms, and which were for the family's rooms, and which one belonged to the guest room where one day she would stay. Going up to the front door was something even a girl with her grandiloquent notions would not consider, but if she stood at the gate enough, one day Margaret was certain some elegant person inside would look out a window and wonder, "Who is that lovely girl?" Then a maid or footman would be sent out to fetch her, to bring her inside, to a luxurious parlor where Mrs. Longyear would receive her. The mistress of the house would recognize by Margaret's speech

Longyear Mansion

and manners that she was a fitting companion for her own daughters, and then Margaret would be adopted and given her own room in the house. Never would the Longyears consider the horror of making her return to her parents' cramped house, the dingy room she had to share with her unfastidious nine year old sister who lacked even the good taste to wash behind her ears at night, despite the number of times Margaret told her what an embarrassment she was. No, once she was inside the house, the Longyears would love her as part of the family, probably even send her to a private school with their own daughters, or better yet, take her with them to Europe, where she was certain to meet a Duke or Count.

— Iron Pioneers

The Longyear Mansion's official address was 536 E. Arch but it encompassed the entire 500 block between Ridge and Arch Streets and consisted of three acres. It would be the finest home Marquette would ever see.

John M. Longyear came to Marquette from Lansing, Michigan where his father was a congressman and judge. He arrived in 1873 and worked as a landlooker, someone looking for profitable property who

John & Mary Longyear

estimated its worth. In addition, he would become involved in developing the mineral wealth on the Gogebic Range in Upper Michigan and the Mesaba Range in Minnesota. Later, he would be involved in founding a mine in an island off Norway, resulting in the town of Longyearbyen being named for him.

Longyear's contributions to Marquette would include serving as mayor, funding the Marquette Opera House, donating the land where the Peter White Public Library was built, helping to found the Huron Mountain Club, and helping to start Northern Michigan University, resulting in Longyear Hall being named for him. Despite these many contributions, Longyear is best remembered in Marquette for his impressive sandstone mansion.

After living in a couple of different Marquette homes, none of which met with his satisfaction, John M. Longyear decided in 1890 to begin building the famous Long-year Mansion which would not be completed until 1892. D. Fred Charlton, who had already built many fine homes in Marquette, was hired as architect for what would become his masterpiece. Literally, tons of the local Jacobs quarry's raindrop sandstone would be used at a cost of $500,000. The home would have sixty-five rooms, leaded glass windows, parquet floors, an octagonal entry that rose up to a Tiffany stained glass dome, a library, music room, and a basement containing a bowling alley and billiard parlor. The elegant gardens were designed by famous landscape artist Frederick Law Olmsted, who would also design New York's Central Park, and numerous other landscaping projects across the nation. When the Longyear family moved in at Christmas 1892, the home had the distinction of being the first in Marquette to use electric Christmas lights. Marquette had never seen such a home and never would again.

The Longyear Mansion's residence in Marquette would be short-lived as the result of family tragedy. In 1900, Howard Longyear and his friend Hugh Allen drowned in Lake Superior while canoeing between Marquette and the Huron Mountain Club. The Longyears were devastated and walked the entire shoreline from the Huron Mountains to Presque Isle Park, hoping to find their son still alive.

Once they accepted Howard's death, the Longyears decided they would donate their property below the bluff to the City of Marquette to build a memorial park named for their son. When the Marquette and Southwestern Railroad announced it wanted to run a railway through the property, the Longyear family entered into a legal battle with the railroad which was settled in the railroad's favor.

When the blasting for the rail bed began, the Longyears decided to go to Europe. Mrs. Longyear was so angry at the railroad and the City of Marquette that she vowed never again to set foot in Marquette. Mr. Longyear agreed to move back East, but he did not want to leave behind their fabulous home, so while the couple was riding down the Champs Elysees in Paris, he suggested they actually bring the house with them when they moved to Massachusetts. Mrs. Longyear readily agreed.

The undertaking was massive. In January, 1903, the dismantling began and by June, the house was starting to be reassembled in Brookline, Massachusetts, three miles inland from the ocean because Mrs. Longyear did not want to hear the ocean's pounding surf, which would remind her of Lake Superior's roaring waves that had claimed her son. The move would take three years, longer than it

Howard Longyear
1897

took originally to build the house. Each stone block had to be cleaned, numbered, carefully wrapped in straw and cloth and then shipped east. In all, 190 train cars would be used to transport the house. The move was considered an engineering miracle at the time and listed in "Ripley's Believe It or Not." Before reassembly was completed, it was decided the house would not look well on its new property in its current shape, so it was laid out differently. When the newer version of the home was completed, new additions were made until it contained one hundred rooms.

My great-great grandfather, William Forrest McCombie, was among those hired to disassemble the house. My great-grandmother, Barbara McCombie White, wanted to see the house, so her father told her if she would bring him his lunch about noontime when most of the workers were on their lunch breaks, she wouldn't be in the way and could look around. Once she started walking through the house, she became lost and her father had to go find her. This family story inspired a scene in *The Queen City* where Margaret gets lost in the mansion.

The Longyears lived in their Brookline home until their deaths. John M. Longyear passed away in 1922 and Mrs. Longyear in 1931. Mrs. Longyear bequeathed the home to the Mary Baker Eddy Foundation—Mary Baker Eddy was the founder of the Christian Science religion. After the Longyear children contested the will, the home became both the headquarters for the Longyear Foundation and a museum for the Christian Science church. In 1985, an episode of the popular television show *Spenser for Hire* was filmed there. In 1996, the expense of maintaining the home as a museum became too high and it was sold for $6.5 million to a developer who turned it into luxury condominiums.

Mrs. Longyear never did set foot again in Marquette, but because Mr. Longyear needed to continue doing business there, he built a home at Ives Lake at the Huron Mountain Club where the Longyears would stay whenever they were in Upper Michigan, and Mr. Longyear would often stay overnight in Marquette as needed. Today, many of the Longyears' descendants continue to live in Upper Michigan.

501 E. Ridge ~ Burtis Home

501 E. Ridge ~ Burtis Home

Built in 1910 on the former Longyear property, this home originally belonged to George Burtis, who was the owner of the Burtis Sawmill in the Lower Harbor near the foot of Ridge Street. Mr. Longyear had actually bought the sawmill while living in his mansion because he did not like it near his home—not long after, the sawmill mysteriously burned one night. The home has nine bedrooms and includes a servants' quarters on the third floor. For a time, it was divided into a two family home. In the 1980s, the home belonged to Ed Dembowski, who would turn the Lutheran Church on West Ridge across from the Peter White Public Library into apartments. In 1989, the Lewis family purchased the home and began renovation to return it to a one family dwelling. One of the highlights of this home is a room, once a sun porch, which houses an extensive collection of Dr. Larry Lewis' hunting trophies from across the globe.

505 E. Ridge ~ Paul & Rushton Home

This home was also built on the site of the former Longyear Mansion by the second generation of the Longyear family—Helen Longyear and her husband Carroll Paul. The house was built in 1918. Mr. Paul died in 1937, and a few years later, Mrs. Paul moved into an apartment in the Longyear Building on the corner of Ridge and Bluff Streets. She sold the house in 1942 to Carroll and Louise Rushton. I wonder whether Mr. Rushton sharing Mr. Paul's first name had anything to do with Mrs. Paul's decision in selling the house to the Rushtons. Mr. Rushton was a judge and one of author John Voelker's fishing buddies. My second cousin, Nanette Rushton, is Carroll and Louise Rushton's granddaughter, so I asked her to provide her memories of the house:

My grandparents moved several times while living in Marquette. In the

505 E. Ridge ~ Paul & Rushton Home

1930s they rented on Front Street, then had a house on College across from the hospital. They were both teachers until Grandpa took a correspondence course for his law degree—one of the last lawyers to get a degree that way. He was in private practice, then Probate Judge and then Circuit Court judge. Carroll's father, Herbert, was an attorney in Escanaba and later State Senator in Lansing and then State Attorney General. Carroll was involved with some of the opinions written during Herbert's term as SAG. Carroll's portrait hangs both in the Delta County Courthouse in Escanaba and the Marquette County Courthouse's courtroom.

Carroll Rushton (left) & John Voelker

My grandparents next moved to the white house on the corner of 403 E. Arch Street until 1942 when they sold it while my father, Tom, was still in grade school, so they could move to the larger gray house at 505 E. Ridge Street. That house has eight bedrooms and a maid's quarter. My favorite room was at the top with the arched window looking toward the lake. The living room has a stage where Louise would put on marionette shows for kids in the neighborhood. They entertained many out of town guests, some in town on court business. Carroll was a Circuit Court Judge for Marquette, Baraga, and Delta Counties in the 1950s. My father Tom, after finishing college and serving in Korea, returned to Marquette and married my mother, Rose Marie Johnson, in 1957. The Groom's dinner for my parent's wedding was held at the house. My parents' wedding was at the Baptist Church that formerly stood at the corner of Ridge and Front and their wedding reception was held at the Women's Federated Clubhouse.

In 1962, when Grandpa realized he was dying of cancer, he wanted Grandma to have a smaller house to take care of so they down-sized to the house at 420 E. Ridge which belonged to their friends, the Tibbitts. The two properties were traded between the Tibbitts and the Rushtons with some money thrown in. Julia Tibbitts lived at 505 E. Ridge for a number of years. She redecorated everything but the dining room which had scenic rice paper on the upper half of the walls. Julia had one room set up for weaving with a large loom. I remember visiting her there and trying the loom in the late 1960s.

The Tibbitts would later sell the house and live elsewhere but retain their Marquette connection. Munro Tibbits would die in 1973. In 1992, Julia Tibbitts would publish a book about Presque Isle Park, *Let's Go Around the Island*. She passed away in 2008. After the Tibbitts sold the house, it passed into the hands of Dr. Robert and Becky Berube until 2009 when it was sold. The property is notable since the retaining walls from the Longyear Mansion are on its east end, along with the original stairs leading down toward the lake, which are along the sidewalk path.

509 E. Ridge ~ Schaffer Home

Also on the former Longyear Mansion property is the Schaffer home, which Charles Schaffer, an iron manufacturer, purchased from Mr. Longyear in 1918 for the price of $16,250. Schaffer made his fortune in the charcoal business in Alger County, and went on to become president of the Union National Bank of Marquette. He built his home in 1911. Although not as large as the Longyear Mansion, Schaffer's house would contain an impressive

509 E. Ridge ~ Schaffer Home

thirty-four rooms. The home is three-stories with four stories on the lake side due to the walk-out basement. The grounds are said to be landscaped by Frederick Law Olmsted, but since he died in 1903, they were either landscaped by his sons who carried on his work, or the landscaping was retained from Olmsted's original landscaping of the Longyear Mansion.

Schaffer was, like the Longyears, a member of the Christian Science congregation, and his home became the meeting place for the congregation until its church was completed in 1925. Schaffer left the home to his daughter, Onota Schaffer, and her husband Otto Koch. Their daughter, Julia, would later marry Munro Longyear Tibbitts, great-nephew of the Longyears, original owners of the property. The Kochs lived in the home until they decided to move to California. The house was then vacant until 1942 when it was leased to the Coast Guard for vacant training for the remainder of World War II, and then sat vacant again.

In 1956, Otto Koch sold the house to Franz Menze of Menze Construction who divided the home into five apartments. Since then it has been sold a few times. Today, it is owned by Dr. Craig Stien and contains ten apartments.

CEDAR & MICHIGAN STREETS

321 Cedar ~ Mather & Jopling Home

Henry Mather, the original owner of this home, was part of the prominent Mather family which has been so involved with the iron industry in Marquette County. The Mather family had already been famous since the seventeenth century in New England where their ancestors included prominent Puritan ministers Increase and Cotton Mather. The Mathers moved to Cleveland, Ohio from where the family would operate

321 Cedar ~ Mather & Jopling Home

their interests in Upper Michigan's iron mines. The Cleveland Iron Mining Company, today Cleveland-Cliffs, was begun by the Mather family.

Samuel Livingston Mather Sr. was a co-founder of the Cleveland Iron Mining Company, today known as Cleveland-Cliffs. Samuel Sr.'s first wife, Georgiana Woolson, would give him two sons, Samuel and Henry, and his second wife, Elizabeth Gwinn, would be mother to William Gwinn Mather. William Gwinn Mather would be head of Cleveland-Cliffs from 1890-1940 and would name the town of Gwinn, Michigan for his mother.

Samuel Sr.'s first wife, Georgiana Woolson, was the sister of Constance Fenimore Woolson. The sisters were great-nieces to the novelist, James Fenimore Cooper. Readers of *The Only Thing That Lasts* may remember Robert O'Neill's visit to Anne's Tablet on Mackinac Island and how it inspires his literary aspirations. Anne's Tablet is a monument to Constance Fenimore Woolson, author of *Anne* and several other novels set in the Great Lakes area. Woolson lived in Cleveland where her nephews often visited her, and Samuel Jr. would later become her financial advisor. Although no record exists that Woolson ever visited Marquette, I count her as a literary predecessor for being one of the first authors

Anne's Tablet
Mackinac Island

to depict Upper Michigan—specifically Mackinac Island—in fiction, and she certainly would have known about Marquette. She also did well picking Samuel Jr. as her financial advisor; he became not only the richest man in Ohio, but he also had Anne's Tablet built in her memory.

As for Henry Mather, he married Mary Hewitt, sister of Ellen Hewitt White, thus making him Peter White's brother-in-law. Henry Mather built his home at 321 Cedar in 1888 and had it designed by Charles VanIderstine. Mather later sold the house to James Jopling, who had married his daughter Elizabeth "Bessie" Walton Mather. James Jopling had first come to Marquette in 1881 as a civil engineer. His brother, Alfred O. Jopling, would marry Peter White's daughter Mary. Over twenty-six mining companies would employ Jopling as a mining engineer before he went to work exclusively for Cleveland-Cliffs for forty years. James Jopling would be hired by the city to build the road to Presque Isle, which included filling in the swamp that separated it from the mainland.

James and Bessie's only child, Richard Mather Jopling, was born in Marquette but attended school back East. He reputedly loved Marquette and returned home frequently to visit. His aspirations as a writer were cut short when he died in World War I while serving in the ambulance corps in France. His only book *Prose and Verse by Richard Mather Jopling* was published posthumously in 1919. His parents signed a copy they gave to Alfred O. Jopling, his uncle, which is now part of the Peter White Public Library's collection.

The Jopling home would later belong to Dr. Fred Sabin, an ophthalmologist for nearly fifty years. In 2009, it was again sold.

The home is approximately 4,000 square feet in size, contains a formal dining room, large butler's pantry, an enclosed sun porch with a south view of Lake Superior, five bedrooms and baths and several stately fireplaces. It retains its original woodwork, oak wainscoting, and French pocket doors.

419 Cedar ~ Eldredge Home

This home was built in the early 1920s by Ralph Richard Eldredge, a member of a prominent family of Marquette attorneys. Eldredge was the general solicitor for the DSS&A Railroad. Later, the home would belong to Dr. John and Mary Kublin.

419 Cedar ~ Eldredge Home

424 Cedar St. ~ Swineford Home

> *"Gigantic? It's a good size, but hardly gigantic compared to the one Mr. Swineford has put up."*
>
> *"What he built is hardly a house," said Molly. "It's more like a castle. I understand there's an elevator in that four-story tower. I'd hate to have to clean the place."*
>
> *"I'm sure they have a maid," said Jacob.*
>
> *"I've always felt," Molly replied, "that if you need someone else to clean your house, then it's just too big. Sometimes I think I was a lot happier in my parents' old dirt floor cottage than I am in this fancy house."*
>
> — Iron Pioneers

424 Cedar St. ~ Swineford Home

When first built, the Swineford Home was the largest and most impressive in Marquette and would only be surpassed when the Longyear Mansion was built. A common misconception in Marquette is that Alfred Swineford built it as a wedding gift for his daughter Nellie Flower Swineford, but the house was built in 1882 and Nellie did not marry Edward O. Stafford until 1884. Swineford lived at 430 E. Arch while building this house, and after he moved into his new home, the newlywed couple lived at his former residence.

Besides owning *The Mining Journal*, which he bought following the 1868 fire, Swineford was heavily involved in politics. He was a member of the Michigan House of Representatives from 1871 to 1872. In 1878, he was a candidate in the Democratic primary for Lieutenant Governor of Michigan but was not elected. As a friend, he campaigned for U.S. President Grover Cleveland, which resulted in his appointment as Governor of Alaska. He was the first resident governor of the Alaska territory from 1885-1889. He would remain in

Alfred Swineford

Alaska until his death in 1909.

When Swineford moved to Alaska, he sold his new home to John M. Longyear, who found it was not large enough for his family, so he kept adding rooms to it until he finally decided to build his much larger mansion.

The Swineford Home was the first to have an elevator. Supposedly, one night a guest was looking for the bathroom and instead opened the upstairs elevator door and fell down the shaft; fortunately, her hoopskirts ballooned up to cushion her fall. Another popular story among children in Marquette was that Santa Claus lived in one of the house's chimneys.

In 1935, the house was broken into five apartments by its owner, Mr. Harris. In the 1960s, the McClellan family changed four of the apartments back into a main house on the first and second

424 Cedar ~ Interior

floors, leaving only the third floor as an apartment. In the 1980s, Bob and Camilla Adams bought the home. Finally, in September 2007, Gregg Seiple and Babette Welch bought the home and began renovations. As of late 2009, they have renovated nine of its twenty-three rooms.

453 E. Michigan ~ Seymour Home

At the end of Cedar, between Michigan and Ohio Streets, is a giant house that once belonged to Horatio Seymour Jr. and included property for two blocks between Michigan and Ohio Streets where today a dozen homes fill the land. Seymour was the nephew of Horatio Seymour Sr., the Governor of New York from 1853-4 and again from 1863-1864. Horatio Seymour Sr. would also run for president as the Democratic nominee in 1868, but he lost to Republican candidate Ulysses S. Grant. In 1882, Horatio Seymour Jr. came to Marquette for his father, John Forman Seymour, to act as

453 E. Michigan ~ Seymour Home

agent for the Michigan Land and Iron Company, formed for speculation. In 1883, Seymour would lay out the first golf course in Upper Michigan just below the Prospect Street bluff, later known as "Pine Plains." He would also be involved in organizing the Huron Mountain Club.

Being from a well-to-do Eastern family, Seymour did not feel even the finest families in Marquette were good enough to associate with his children, not even the Longyear children who lived next door. Needless to say, he was traumatized when in 1901, his twenty-year old daughter, Mary, eloped with Henry St. Arnold, a man who was one quarter Indian and a guide who had worked for the Longyears and been entrusted in building a camp for Seymour. St. Arnold was also considerably older than Mary—he may not even have known his own age, but various accounts state he was anywhere from fifty to sixty-five at the time of the marriage. When Mr. Seymour found out the couple had boarded a train for L'Anse, he had the train delayed. When Mr. Seymour caught up with his daughter, Mary told him the decision was her own and she would go through with it. Both Mr. and Mrs. Seymour were so infuriated by their daughter's marriage that they completely disowned her, sold their home to Louis G. Kaufman, and moved back to New York. The home would later become known as the Kaufman Apartments.

Meanwhile, Mary and her husband went to live on Seventh Street along with their daughter, also named Mary. A few years later, Mr. Seymour died, and in 1905, Mrs. Seymour returned to Marquette to visit her daughter's family. One day when St. Arnold wasn't home, Mrs. Seymour convinced Mary to return to New York with her along with the child. The three females left without even a letter saying goodbye. When St. Arnold learned what had happened, he told his neighbors it was probably for the best. St. Arnold's daughter would grow up back East, knowing little of her Native American background.

When in his eighties, St. Arnold became ill, so his wife returned to live with him in L'Anse for the last years of his life. After St. Arnold's death, Mary lived in Marquette for a few years before returning to New York.

As for St. Arnold and Mary Seymour's daughter, she reportedly married well to an Eastern man of high social class. Her grandfather would have been proud.

Mary Seymour & Daughter Mary ~ 1914

EAST ARCH STREET

558 E. Arch ~ Menze Home

Franz Menze lived here. He was the owner of Menze Construction. He first came to Marquette to help dig the foundations for the Granite Loma farm buildings. He went on to build many of the city's finest mid-twentieth century buildings.

540 E. Arch ~ Roberts Home

This home was built by Alton T. Roberts, husband to Abby Longyear, oldest daughter of John and Mary Longyear. The house was built on the property of the former Longyear mansion, on the opposite end from where Abby's sister Helen and her husband Carroll Paul built their home at 505 E. Ridge. Mr. Roberts would be president of the Union National Bank in Marquette, and he and Abby would expand the Ives Lake property that the family owned at the Huron Mountain Club. Prior to building this home, the Roberts had lived in the Case home on East Ohio Street where they had entertained Presidents William Howard Taft and Theodore Roosevelt on their visits to Marquette. The Roberts would also later build a house, designed by Frank Lloyd Wright in 1936, on their property at the begin-

Abby Longyear Roberts 1897

ning of Whetstone Creek called "Deer Track" off County Road 492. Their daughter, Mary Roberts, would marry the famous architect John Lautner Jr. of Marquette. The Roberts would later divorce and Mr. Roberts would move away from Marquette. In the later part of the twentieth century, the home belonged to Dr. and Mrs. Daniel Powell Hornbogen, who were friends with Jack and Joan Kaufman Martin who lived across the street.

529 E. Arch ~ Russell Home

This home belonged to Frank Russell Jr., who owned *The Mining Journal* as well as the *Escanaba Daily Press* and *Iron Mountain News*. He also began the local television station, TV 6. His grandfather, James Russell,

529 E. Arch ~ Russell Home

had taken over *The Mining Journal* from Alfred Swineford. James passed it on to his son, Frank Russell Sr. whose second wife and Frank Jr.'s mother was Ellen K. Shiras, daughter of George Shiras III and granddaughter of Peter White, thus linking the Russells to most of the other wealthy old Marquette families. Frank Sr. died in 1947 and from that time Frank Jr. managed the paper. Frank Russell Jr. and his wife later moved to Iron Mountain. Today, their home is a rental property owned by Gregg Seiple and Babette Welch who also own the Swineford home at 424 Cedar Street.

515 E. Arch ~ Martin Home

In the 1950s until Mr. Martin's death, this property belonged to John "Jack" Martin and his wife Joan Kaufman. It was their "in town" house when they were not living at the family lodge Granot Loma on Lake Superior. (For more on the Martins and Kaufmans, see the Granot Loma section below).

501 E. Arch ~ Ablewhite Home

For many years, this home was the residence of the bishops of the Episcopal Diocese of Northern Michigan. Occupants included Bishop Ablewhite who resigned in 1939 due to an embezzlement scandal (see the section on the Marquette Opera House), and Bishop Page, for whom the Page Center in Little Lake, Michigan was named.

501 E. Arch ~ Ablewhite Home

477 E. Arch ~ Kaufman Home

Where today there is a vacant lot once stood the Kaufman home, owned by Samuel Kaufman, brother to Marquette mayor Nathan Kaufman and banker Louis Kaufman.

Sam Kaufman's wife, Una Libby, was a member of the wealthy Chicago canning family. The house was originally built in 1908, but in 1929 it was sold to the Theta Omicron Rho Fraternity. It changed hands among fraternities and ultimately belonged to Delta Sigma Phi when in 1982 it was torn down.

477 E. Arch ~ Kaufman Home

440 E. Arch ~ Dandelion Cottage

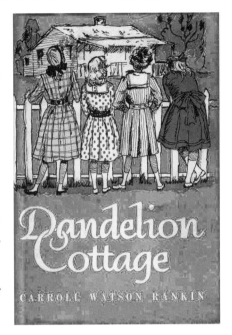

"See that house across the street?" my aunt said as we walked along Arch Street.

"That little one?" I asked.

"Yes. That's the house the famous book Dandelion Cottage *was based on. I'm sure you've read that, haven't you?"*

"No, I've never heard of it before," I replied, thinking the house didn't look like much, just a tiny little one floor square box.

"Oh!" replied my aunt. "Your mother always wrote that you were addicted to books."

"I am."

"It's strange then you never came across it, but we have the book at home. You can start reading it tonight if you like."

"All right," I said, trying to sound interested, but my fingers were really freezing. My aunt had let me pack my suitcase, and I had never thought to pack gloves—I only owned one pair and never wore them.

"I'm sure you'll love the book," she said. "It's one of the best children's books ever written, and the author lives right here in Marquette. We're very privileged to have such a famous woman in our community. The book's about four little girls who rent the house as their summer play cottage."

It didn't sound too exciting to me. After all, I was a boy, and not interested in flowers, especially not dandelions, which were really weeds. I hoped Grandma and Aunt Louisa May would have some Jack London, or even Tarzan books, but I rather doubted it.

"Mrs. Rankin has actually written several children's books, including some sequels to Dandelion Cottage," *said my aunt. I think she would have summarized all Mrs. Rankin's books for me if we had not now arrived at her and Grandma's house.*

— The Only Thing That Lasts

Dandelion Cottage was a real place, and its story is yet another example of how Marquette seeks to preserve its past.

No one knows when the cottage was initially built, but Peter White, who owned it as a rental property, donated it in 1888 to St. Paul's with the understanding that it would be moved from its original home on High Street, a couple of hundred feet north to 212 E. Arch Street, behind the church. White had it moved to make room to build the Morgan Memorial Chapel. The cottage would remain at its second location for 103 years and soon become famous.

Dandelion Cottage

In 1904, the house became known as "Dandelion Cottage" after Carroll Watson Rankin wrote her children's book of the same name with the cottage at its center. The story is a fictional account of four girls, loosely based on Mrs. Rankin's daughters and their friends. The characters, Bettie, Jeanie, Mabel, and Marjory, earn the right to use the cottage as their playhouse for the summer in exchange for picking the dandelions from the cottage's lawn.

Although the girl's antics and adventures are largely fictional, dandelions were a problem in early Marquette. John M. Longyear recalled a contest held to see which child could collect the most dandelions in Marquette, but the contest, despite its popularity, and 3,500 bushels of dandelions being collected, did not rid the city of its weeds. Another possible real-life source is the character of Mr. Black, rumored to be a fictional portrait of Peter White.

While the cottage's notoriety grew throughout the twentieth century along with the popularity of *Dandelion Cottage* and Mrs. Rankin's other books, it remained a rental property for the church. Then in 1988, St. Paul's decided it needed to expand its parking lot and Dandelion Cottage and the other small house beside it were in the way.

Thankfully, the church acknowledged the historical significance of Dandelion Cottage, so rather than simply tear it down, it sought someone to buy it for the sum of $1.00 and then move it. The church did not give up easily, and after three years, in early 1991, Mayor William Birch and his wife Sally came forward to purchase and move the cottage. On October 12, 1991, the cottage was moved to its present location, which was directly behind the Birchs' Ridge Street home.

The Mining Journal ran numerous stories about the attempts to sell the cottage and its successive move. Estimates to relocate it two blocks down Arch Street were said to be $20,000. But the Birchs went beyond just moving it. Dandelion Cottage was given a beautiful restoration. It was repainted yellow, remodeled inside with a modern kitchen, woodwork was replaced and where possible replicated to match the original hardwood; the maple floors were refinished, and dandelions stenciled on the walls. In all, the restoration cost over $60,000, but William and Sally Birch understood that if a thing is worth doing, it is worth doing well. Soon after, Phyllis Rankin, the then ninety-seven year old daughter of the author, suggested a state historical marker be sought which today appears on the cottage.

June 28, 1992 was a gala day when Dandelion Cottage was opened to the public. My brother and I were among the many who stood in a long line down Arch Street to tour the newly restored historic cottage. I doubt a single visitor was anything but pleased and grateful that this Marquette landmark was preserved. Phyllis Rankin told *The Mining Journal*, "I am glad it was saved and I know my mother would have been delighted about it. It looks lovely....It's a beautiful job."

The cottage has since been resold and continues as a residence. Visitors to Marquette make a point to seek it out, and customer reviews at Amazon reveal that *Dandelion Cottage* remains a favorite among readers, and the Marquette County History Museum sells numerous copies of the book each year. What appears as a weed can turn out to be a gift to future generations.

430 E. Arch ~ Ripka Home

C.F. Struck built this fine sandstone home in 1875 for A.A. Ripka, a mining investor. The house features an arched portico, gabled dormers with pointed arch windows, and a steeply pitched Lake Superior slate roof.

Not long after its construction, the house was sold to Alfred Swineford, owner of *The Mining Journal*. Swineford would later build the house at 424 Cedar Street, and give this Arch Street home to his daughter Nellie Flower and her husband Edward Stafford when they married in 1884. When Alfred Swineford moved to Alaska, the Staffords remained in Marquette, and in 1890, their only child, Ruth, was born. In 1917, Ruth would marry Roscoe Conkling Main, the county health officer for Marquette County. Later, the Main family would move to California.

430 E. Arch ~ Ripka Home

Today the home belongs to Dr. Peter and Barbara Kelly. Dr. Kelly was among the preservers of the Savings Bank Building downtown and Barbara Kelly is well known for over thirty years of dedication to the Marquette Beautification committee, landscaping and planting flowers throughout the city. The Barbara H. Kelly Historic Preservation Award is named in her honor and regularly given to those who preserve and restore historic architecture in Marquette.

425 E. Arch ~ Read Home

Lumber baron F.W. Read had this home built in 1883 with Upper Michigan wood finished in his own mills at Eagle Mills and Michigamme. The interior still has nine varieties of local wood, including different types of oak, birch, cherry, bird's eye maple, pine, and tamarack used for doors, paneling, staircases, and floors. The home contains seven ornate fireplaces and some

425 E. Arch ~ Read Home

of its original bath fixtures remain. The large veranda and portico were added in the 1920s. In 1951, a fire destroyed the original carriage house and it was replaced with a modern garage. In 1988, Joel and Barbara Thompson purchased the house and have since been lovingly restoring it to its original grandeur.

412 E. Arch ~ Kaufman Home

This home once belonged to Bernard Kaufman, another of the many sons of Samuel Kaufman Sr. (Pictured on next page.)

411 E. Arch ~ Sherwood Home

Built in 1905, this home has been known as the "copper house" because it is copper-plated. It was built for James Russell with profits from the Calumet-Hecla Copper mine. At the time, Mr. Russell was the warden of the Marquette Branch State Prison. The house next belonged to Myron Sherwood, attorney to John M. Longyear. The

411 E. Arch ~ Sherwood Home

third owners were the Sloan family, and the fourth owners are Dr. and Mrs. Craig Stien.

403 E. Arch ~ Rushton and Hilton Home

Carroll and Louise Rushton lived here until 1942 when they moved to 505 E. Ridge. The house was then sold to Frank Hawn and later sold to Earl and Miriam Hilton. Earl Hilton was an English professor at Northern Michigan University, and Miriam Hilton wrote the 75th anniversary history of the university. The

403 E. Arch ~ Rushton & Hilton Home

home is one of the few in the historical residential district which still has a carriage block.

344 E. Arch ~ Apostle Home

344 E. Arch ~ Apostle Home

Peter Apostle owned this home. The Apostle family was Greek and owned several restaurants in Marquette. Louie Apostle opened the Candy Land restaurant on Washington Street in 1915 and then sold it to his nephews, Peter and James Apostle, who operated it until 1938. Later the brothers owned Emmy's restaurant which when sold became The Coffee Cup. The family owned Apostles Restaurant on Washington Street which opened in 1949, later to be replaced by The Marq in the 1970s, Entre Amigos in the 1980s, and a few restaurants later, in 2009 beautifully restored as The Wild Rover. The Apostle Family was one of several Marquette Greek families in the restaurant business. Other Greek families owned the Bon Ton, the Jet Grill, Superior Shores, and Vango's.

412 E. Arch ~ Kaufman Home

343 E. Arch ~ Dollar Home

Captain Robert Dollar was a Scottish lumberman who produced timber for the English market. He came to Marquette in 1882 from Canada and soon after built this home. He only remained until 1888, however, when he moved to San Rafael, California due to ill health. In California, he became a prominent lumberman and ship-owner and pioneered trade between North America and the Orient. In 1914, he was considered one of the fifty greatest men in the United States. He died in 1932 at the age of 88, known as the "Grand Old Man of the Pacific." Dollarville, Michigan, where he once worked as the general manager of a logging camp, is named for him.

343 E. Arch ~ Dollar Home

329 E. Arch ~ Flanigan Home

329 E. Arch Street ~ Flanigan Home

Martin J. Flanigan lived here. He and his brothers, Louis and Joseph, formed the firm Flanigan Brothers, known by the locals as "The Three Twins." It was a continuation of the dray and transfer line business which their father had established in 1863. Following their acquisition of the business in 1907, the brothers expanded the company's activities to include transfer, storage, livery service, and in 1919 they began operation of the Marquette-Negaunee-Ishpeming motor line. In 1927, they built the Flanigan Bros. building in the Lower Harbor, which was renovated in 2003 as offices and condominiums.

328 E. Arch Street ~ Finnegan Home

This home has belonged to the Finnegan family for several generations. Author Holly Wilson (Helen Finnegan Wilson) grew up here. She was born in Duluth, Minnesota, but after her father died, her mother, sister, and she came to Marquette to live with her grandmother. Wilson grew up ice skating on

Holly Wilson

Lake Superior, playing on Arch Street, and devouring books at the Peter White Public Library. She stated, "I began writing as soon as I knew what a pencil and paper were for." While a college student, she wrote an adult novel *The King Pin*, which received the highest award in the Avery and Julie Hopwood Awards Contest in fiction.

Wilson married her husband, psychiatrist Frederic W. Wilson, while they were students at the University of Michigan. After her daughters Mary and Anne were born, she continued to write when they napped, and when they were older, she often took them to Marquette to visit their grandmother. While they explored the lakeshore and bluff, Holly Wilson enter-

328 E. Arch ~ Finnegan Home

tained her daughters with stories about her childhood on Arch Street which resulted in her writing her young adult novel *Deborah Todd* (1955) about the title character and her friends who make up the Arch Street gang. The novel is set in Henry's Bend, a fictional and thinly-disguised version of Marquette which also makes mention of the Hundred Steps.

Finding that she preferred to write for children and teenagers, Wilson was inspired to write several more young adult novels set throughout Michigan. Her next novel *Caroline, the Unconquered* (1956) is also set in Henry's Bend, but in 1853. Clues to its being a fictional Marquette include the village burning down, a reference to Marquette's 1868 fire. The title character travels across the Great Lakes on the *Fur Trader* and *Siskiwit*, schooners that sailed into Marquette in the 1850s. *Caroline, the Unconquered* was the first novel to depict Marquette's early years. Wilson said she wrote the novel because "I grew up in northern Michigan and all my life I have been fascinated by the courage and endurance of the pioneers who went there when that country was an unknown wilderness....The people who went there during the early days of the iron industry were so possessed by a desire to set down roots that, in spite of the almost unbelievable hardships they had to endure, they refused to be defeated."

Snowbound in Hidden Valley (1957) was written because Wilson explained, "When I was a little girl in northern Michigan, we once had a Big Blizzard that we talked about for years. The entire Upper Peninsula of Michigan was snowed under and we were cut off from civilization for more than a week." Although not a sequel, the main character, Jo Shannon, just happens to live next door to Doc Todd, father to Deborah Todd, the title character of Wilson's earlier novel. Jo befriends Onota Leroy, an Indian classmate, and while visiting her in Hidden Valley, she not only learns Chippewa customs but ends up being lost in a blizzard. The novel represents Wilson's social conscience—the female main characters are friends despite their racial and ethnic differences. Similarly, in *The Hundred Steps* (1958) Wilson breaks down social class distinctions to show the goodness of all the townspeople. Oddly, Wilson decided in *The Hundred Steps* to name the town Clifton, despite the Hundred Steps having been mentioned earlier in *Deborah Todd* where the town is Henry's Bend. Wilson would write several more novels including *Singamon* and *Always Anne*. The novels are today out-of-print, but they retain their charm and most of them are available to be checked out at the Peter White Public Library.

Wilson was honored in 1965 by attending a dinner for Michigan Artists and Writers hosted by Governor Romney. In 1967, she received the University of Michigan Sesquicentennial Award for her contributions to children's literature. By 1970, she was an assistant professor of English at Ferris State in Big Rapids, Michigan. Her last book, *Double Heritage*, was published in 1971.

Her husband's career as a psychiatrist would result in Holly Wilson living in Kansas, Pennsylvania, and New York as well as Traverse City, Michigan, but she always remained close to Marquette as did her children. Her daughter, Dr. Mary Helen Martin and her husband Willard Martin, would return to Marquette to live in the family home. Dr. Martin served as the Director of Mental Health at Marquette General Hospital for over thirty years. She died in 2009.

209 E. Arch Street ~ Miller Home

Carroll Watson Rankin's daughter, Imogene Miller, lived here. She had married Stuart Miller and moved away but returned to Marquette with her husband when he retired; they bought this property just a block from where her sister, Phyllis, lived in the Rankin family home. My second cousin, Nanette Rushton, knew Mrs. Miller so I asked her to contribute her memories of the family:

209 E. Arch ~ Miller Home

Mrs. Miller was in her early nineties when I first met her and her "little sister" Phyllis Rankin, who was then in her eighties. Phyllis would go to the Garden Room Restaurant every day for lunch. I had been waitressing at the Coachlight and later the Garden Room at this time while working for the Trust Department at Union Bank. Some mutual friends, Homer and Margaret Hilton, called me to ask whether I was available to help a friend. They knew I worked for the Trust Department at Union Bank and wondered whether I would work for the Trust Department of First National, which handled all of Mrs. Miller's business as well as that of her sister, Phyllis Rankin. Mrs. Miller had just lost her son, Berwick Rankin

Mrs. Miller

Miller, to a heart attack and was now living alone. She did not care to leave the house so needed someone to grocery shop and keep up the house. Her home was painted white, had a green mansard roof, and lace curtains in the tall windows.

Mrs. Miller's house was almost exactly a block behind her parents' house on Ridge Street where her sister Phyllis lived at that time. Across the street was a parking area for the Episcopal Church, an empty lot, and Dandelion Cottage with a couple of more houses on the block toward Pine. Mrs. Argeropoulos was then living in Dandelion Cottage. Her daughter Joyce and son-in-law Scott Matthews would eventually live next door to me. Mrs. Argeropoulos had quite a large garden and would bring beets and "greens" for Mrs. Miller that she liked.

Mrs. Miller told me about how she became engaged to her husband at this time. In the early 1900s, Mr. Stuart Berwick Miller was in town to oversee the local branch of DuPont while it was being built; he was a chemical engineer in the munitions field. According to Mrs. Miller, he originally dated her sister Eleanor, but when he asked their father for Eleanor's hand in marriage, Mr. Rankin said, "I have to have the eldest daughter married first." So Mr. Miller ended up marrying Imogene, since she was the oldest. They were married in 1910, and they moved back "out east" when Mr. Miller was finished overseeing the project. Over the years, the Millers tried many times to have children. It was heartbreaking for Mrs. Miller that only her son Berwick had survived out of her many pregnancies. Because he never married and died before her, she never had any grandchildren.

When Mr. Miller retired from DuPont, they moved back to Marquette. Besides the house on Arch Street, they had a cabin for summer and hunting not far out of town. During World War II, Mr. Miller was volunteering in the Rationing Stamp office where he died at his desk. Mrs. Miller was always a member of the Episcopal Church and in 1952 she donated the stained glass rose window above the church entrance in her husband and mother's memories.

*Besides grocery shopping, I often visited with Mrs. Miller and stayed with her for a few hours. She did not have a TV until her sister Phyllis talked her into buying one in 1981 by telling her, "Nan would really like to watch the royal wedding" (of Prince Charles to Lady Diana Spencer). I could have watched the wedding at home but played along so Mrs. Miller would buy a TV. Once she owned the TV, she rarely watched it. She preferred to do crossword puzzles, read books and magazines, (*The New Yorker, Atlantic Monthly, *etc) and read the five newspapers she subscribed to... the local* Mining Journal, Washington Post, New York Times *and a couple of others. She knew everything worth knowing without seeing anything on TV.*

Working for Mrs. Miller was like having another grandparent. She was very shy, quiet, reserved, and very humble. I enjoyed hearing about her first ride in a car (the doctor had the first car in town), antidotes about the neighbors as she grew up at the turn of the century, her experiences out east involving the DuPont mansion when Stuart worked for the family. My interest in history was developed during our conversations. One day, she mentioned something about "...when my husband was in the war." I was trying to figure out if she meant World War I or World War II, so I asked, "Which war was that?" I was totally unprepared for her answer. She sat up straight, gave me a look with a pause, and said, "The Spanish-American War, of course!"

In January of 1986, Mrs. Miller passed away at the age of ninety-nine in her home. She had fallen in November, and then had round the clock nursing care at home since she refused to go to the hospital because her son had died there. She is buried with her family in Park Cemetery.

The best word to describe Mrs. Miller is "shy." It's always the first word that comes to my mind. She was very down to earth, unassuming, yet had known unique experiences in life. A conversation with Imogene Watson Rankin Miller was equal to interaction with an encyclopedia, history text, and society column all at the same time.

203 E. Arch ~ Gillett Home

This Carpenter Gothic home belonged to John H. Gillett, a lumber manufacturer who also owned a tugboat line. The steep gable contains ornate wood work typical of the late Victorian period.

203 E. Arch ~ Gillett Home

MORE MARQUETTE HISTORICAL HOMES

Marquette has many other wonderful historical homes, but it would be difficult to discuss them in any specific order since they are scattered throughout the city. Anyone who loves older homes will find plenty to enjoy just by walking up and down Marquette's streets. Whenever I go out walking, whether in summer when Marquette is truly a green city, or in winter when Christmas lights reflect off the snow, I marvel at how beautiful the houses are, the sense of comfort they evoke in me, and how well most of them are preserved. I also wonder who lived in each of them and what all those people's lives were like—the stories that could be told are countless. Below are just a few more Marquette homes worth taking a look at if you are really an enthusiast.

220 Craig ~ Burt House (Pioneer Home)

220 Craig ~ Burt House (Pioneer Home)

This small sandstone building was probably never lived in by John Burt, son of William Austin Burt, but rather was constructed to serve as offices for the nearby Burt Freestone Company. Built in 1858, its twenty-inch thick sandstone rubble walls made it probably the first "permanent" Marquette building in the sense that it could not be destroyed by fire. It is the oldest "home" in Marquette.

In 1954, the Marquette County History Museum purchased the house and restored it under the direction of Helen Longyear Paul. It remained open for tours until well into the 1980s—one summer day when I was about nine years old, my mother took my brother and me to visit it. I don't remember much about it except it was relatively dark inside and the upstairs was reached by a ladder. In front of the building were some of the gravestones formerly at the Old Catholic Cemetery in Marquette. The building was not financially sustainable as a museum and was sold not long after. Since then it has been the home to several private owners.

104 W. Ridge ~ Women's Federated Clubhouse

In 1883, Martin Vierling bought this property for $1.00. In 1908, Lewis Bosworth purchased the property and sold it to the Marquette Federation of Women's Clubs. It has been a clubhouse ever since and has played a cultural role in the history of Marquette. My great-grandparents, Jay and Barbara White, held their fiftieth wedding anniversary here in 1953. In the 1980s, my piano teacher, William Weber, held piano recitals here, where I performed such pieces as "When Irish Eyes are Smiling" and "If Ever I Would Leave You." On Sundays, the Unity Church today meets here. The clubhouse is also rented out for numerous events from Christmas parties to book signings. When the family of my great-aunt, Barbara White Specker, outgrew her house for parties, she hosted a Christmas party here for her many children, grandchildren, great-grandchildren, siblings, nieces and nephews. For over a century now, the Women's Federated Clubhouse has been a focal point of cultural and community activities in Marquette.

104 W. Ridge ~ Women's Federated Clubhouse

316 N. Front ~ Jacobs Home

Behind the First Methodist Church sits a vacant lot where once stood the historic Jacobs home. John H. Jacobs came to Marquette in 1870. He owned the Woolf & Jacobs Quarry which produced the sandstone used to build most of Marquette's oldest downtown buildings, including the First Methodist Church and the foundation of the Jacobs home. Jacobs served twice as Marquette's mayor in 1895-1896 and 1911-1912. After Mr. Jacobs' death, his daughters, Ella and Laura, lived here. They sold the house to the First Methodist Church in the 1950s. The church used the house for offices, but by 2002, the home had been empty for several years and the cost of renovating it was more than the church could afford. Attempts were made to sell the home for $120,000 but because it was in a commercially zoned section of town, no more than half of it could be used as a residence. None of the offers the church received were close to what it hoped for so the church decided to raze the property to save itself from liabilities as the home further decayed. Bill Pesola, who won the bid for the home's demolition, took many of the wonderful antiques in the house for a modern Victorian style home he was building. Among the antiques removed were antique fireplaces, stained glass windows, ornate door hinges and beautifully preserved woodwork. Today, only an empty lot remains where once stood the home of the man whose stone built so much of Marquette.

401 N. Front ~ Pendill Home

401 N. Front ~ Pendill Home

This house was built in 1878. It belonged to Frank Pendill, son of James and Flavia Pendill (see 322 E. Ridge). Frank owned Pendill drugstore in Marquette which operated for many, many years. His brother Louis also lived here and was involved in the drugstore. Later, their sister Olive lived here after her parents had passed away. Olive was a registered nurse who served in Cuba during the Spanish-American War. She later became the first superintendent of nurses at St. Luke's Hospital, and she was the first historian of the Marquette County Historical Society when it was founded in 1918. She died in 1957 at the age of eighty-nine.

Several visitors and owners of the house in more recent years have claimed to see the ghost of a woman in white inside the home, although it is unclear who the woman is.

427 N. Front ~ Eastman & Maywood Home

Methodist minister C.S. Eastman resided here in 1894-1895. Later it was the childhood home of local author Dorothy Maywood Bird when her father, Reverend Ames Maywood, was minister at the First Methodist Church from 1904-1910.

427 N. Front ~ Eastman & Maywood Home

438 E. Ohio ~ Charlton Home

D. Fred Charlton, the architect who designed so many fine buildings in Marquette, resided here. Charlton was born in England in 1856. He migrated to Canada in 1884 and Detroit in 1886 where he joined the firm of architect John Scott. In 1887, Scott sent Charlton to Marquette to oversee the erection of the Marquette Branch Prison's buildings. Charlton decided to stay and eventually began his own firm. Among the highlights of his career

438 E. Ohio ~ Charlton Home

was in 1893 when he was chosen to design the Mining Building for the 1893 World's Fair in Chicago. The list of buildings he and his firm built across Upper Michigan is exhausting and a complete list may well be impossible, but among them were the following:

- The Peter White Phelps Home 433 E. Ridge
- Dr. O.D. Jones Home 418 E. Hewitt
- The Vierling Home 114 W. Hewitt
- Bishop Vertin's home on Superior Street (Baraga Avenue)
- The Longyear Mansion
- The Waterworks building
- The Marquette Opera House
- The Guild Hall for St. Paul's Episcopal Church
- The Delft Theatre (three total, in Marquette, Escanaba, and Munising)
- The Clubhouse at the Huron Mountain Club
- The Butler Theatre in Ishpeming
- The town hall and library in Republic, Michigan
- The Masonic Block in Crystal Falls, Michigan
- Four buildings and the original design for the Northern State Normal School (today's Northern Michigan University)
- Seven buildings for the Michigan College of Mines (today's Michigan Technological University)

D. Fred Charlton

- The Insane Asylum in Newberry, Michigan
- Three buildings and two additions for the Marquette Prison
- The Marquette, Alger, Ontonagon, and Gogebic County Courthouses
- The Escanaba, Ishpeming, and Hancock City Halls
- The Negaunee, Escanaba, and Ishpeming Fire Halls
- A hotel in the village of Birch, Michigan
- Three Carnegie libraries
- Sixteen Upper Michigan banks
- Nine Upper Michigan churches
- Three Upper Michigan YMCA's
- Approximately two hundred fifty different city blocks throughout Upper Michigan
- Approximately twenty other public structures

Charlton closed his firm in 1918, citing the lack of building as a result of World War I as the reason. He then retired and passed away in 1941.

114 W. Hewitt ~ Vierling Home

114 W. Hewitt ~ Vierling Home

This home, with its turret and rounded roof, was designed in 1890 by D. Fred Charlton for Martin Vierling, a German saloonkeeper. Rumor has it that another dome existed on the house that was removed and affixed to a house on Front Street. Louis Vierling reportedly bought the home's ornate electric light fixtures at the 1893 Chicago World's Fair. The home remained in the Vierling family for nearly a century, during which time four men named Louis Vierling would occupy it. Today, the Vierling name remains well known because of the Vierling Restaurant on Front Street.

825 N. Front ~ Vierling Home

825 N. Front ~ Vierling Home

This home was built by Louis Vierling. The tower on this home is rumored to be the "other" tower taken from the Vierling House at 114 W. Hewitt although it is highly doubtful. The towers do not closely resemble each other. The house was built in 1896.

1025 N. Front ~ Lovejoy Home

Andrew W. Lovejoy, an architect, designed this home for his own family in 1893. His architectural expertise is testified to by its stone arched front porch, curved glass, woodwork, and its upstairs bay window capped with a partial dome. Lovejoy's other architectural work included building the Old City Hall with his partner Edward Demar. The house was next occupied by the Hornstein family. In 1986, it was purchased by Russ and Judy Dees who did significant restoration to it. It has since exchanged hands again.

1025 N. Front ~ Lovejoy Home

229 N. Fourth ~ Wagner Home

This home was built by Honorable George Wagner, who was born in Prussia, Germany in 1834 and came to Marquette in 1854. He served the community in numerous capacities including justice of the peace, township treasurer, and alderman. In the early 1890s, he represented the First District of Marquette County as a member of the Michigan Legislature and introduced the Upper Peninsula Insane Asylum bill. In 1855, as a contractor, he laid the first tram road from the Jackson Mine to the Cleveland Mine. He erected sawmills in Alger County and in 1881, he discovered the Breitung Mine of which he became superintendent. Mr. Wagner was married to Gertrude Dolf in 1869, who was a relative of a relative on the Zryd side of my family. Consequently, my great-grandmother Barbara McCombie White used to visit

229 N. Fourth ~ Wagner Home

the Wagner family in the early twentieth century. The last Wagner to own the home was Nettie Wagner, who later went to live with her Dolf family relatives. My distant cousin, Dorothy Dolf Drozdiak remembers when she was a little girl in the 1930s that Nettie Wagner used to toss her pennies from the tower's windows. Today, the home is divided into apartments.

301 N. Fourth ~ Gregory Home

This home belonged to Hampson Gregory, a local architect and builder whom *The Mining Journal* said was the man more than any other who was responsible for building Marquette. Gregory was born in Devonshire, England in 1834. He and his family migrated to Canada and then arrived in Marquette in 1867. He frequently worked with sandstone, and many of his buildings reflect the style of English architecture common in his native Devonshire and neighboring Cornwall, England.

Among the buildings Gregory built were:

301 N. Fourth ~ Gregory Home

- The Adams Home 200 E. Ridge
- The Rankin Home 219 E. Ridge
- The Merritt Home 410 E. Ridge
- The Call Home 450 E. Ridge
- The Pickands Home 455 E. Ridge
- The Hornbogen Home 212 E. Arch
- The Read Home 425 E. Arch
- The Powell Home 224 E. Michigan
- The Ely Home 135 W. Bluff
- St. Mary's Hospital (the original building, no longer there)
- St. Peter's Cathedral, prior to the 1935 fire
- The first high school on Ridge Street, burnt in 1889
- The Harlow Block on Washington Street
- The Gregory Block on Washington Street (no longer there)
- Iron Bay Foundry on the corner of Lake and Washington, later to be the LS&I office
- The First Methodist Church – (the foundation only)
- The People's State Bank in Munising, Michigan

One of his finest homes, the Merritt home, introduced Gregory to the Merritt family, and later his daughter Clara would marry C.H. Merritt. The First Methodist Church has a memorial stained glass window to the Gregory family's memory. Hampson Gregory died in 1922 and is buried in Park Cemetery. Today, nearly a century after his death, Gregory's true memorial is the many homes and public buildings he built and which still stand today. *The Mining Journal* was correct—he remains one of the men most responsible for building Marquette.

1308 Presque Isle ~ Lautner Home

1308 Presque Isle ~ Lautner Home

This home was built by John Edward Lautner Sr. in 1912. He was a professor of modern languages at Northern Normal School and his wife was a budding artist. The house is a New England salt box style which looks like it belongs in Salem, Massachusetts. While an architect drew up the plans for the house, John Sr. and his son John Jr. built the house by hand. John Jr. would later become a famous architect himself who would study with Frank Lloyd Wright. John Lautner Jr. married Mary Roberts, the granddaughter of John and Mary Longyear. He would go on to design numerous buildings including the Googie Coffee Shop at the corner of Sunset Strip and Crescent Heights in Los Angeles, the Bob Hope home in Palm Springs, and the Chemosphere house, a raised octagonal home which looks like a flying saucer and was used in the film *Body Double*. Movie stars David and Courtney Cox Arquette today reside in one of his homes. Two books have been published about his work—*John Lautner, Architect* by Frank Escher and *The Architecture of John Lautner* by Alan Hess.

The Underground House ~ 1830 Altamont

This home was built in the early 1980s by the local business North Country Terra Dome, headed by Charles Sanford and David Drury. It was quickly dubbed "the Underground House" by the community. It was a new style at the time and believed to be the style for the future. Built into a hill, its roof has a lawn that can be mowed, and the garage door opens out of the hillside. When it was first built, my mom,

1830 Altamont ~ Underground House

brother and I went to the open house. We were impressed by its ingenuity but not convinced we would want to live there. Most impressive was that although the house is underground, it does not lack for light. A skylight brings natural light into the kitchen and dining room and the front of the house has solar windows. Another advantage is that following the great hailstorm of June 2008 that did so much damage to Marquette buildings and vehicles, the Underground House was the only one on its street that did not need its roof repaired due to golf ball size hail.

Nearly thirty years have passed since the Underground House was constructed, and while it has yet to catch on in popularity, the recent emphasis on conservation, alternative fuel sources, and the move toward going green may just make the Underground House still a pioneer in a future architectural style.

Today, Lorana Jinkerson, author of *Nettie Does the NTC: North Country Trail*, is the current owner of what may be Marquette's most original home.

*

Marquette's houses continually become more modern and the "fashionable places" to live have changed over the decades. A century ago, Ridge Street was the place to live. When I was a young boy, Shiras Hills in South Marquette was where the fine homes were being built. Then in the 1980s and 1990s the area known as The Summits became the desirable new subdivision. Since about 2000, the shift has been to condominiums, which are popping up all over Marquette, some new, such as those off McClellan or across from the Lakeview Arena, but others along the Lower Harbor are renovated old warehouses and offices, such as the Flanigan Bros. and Lasco buildings, thus preserving the old with the new. The needs of residents have changed over the decades, but Marquette continues to have interesting and original architecture designed by creative architects and homeowners.

HOMES BUILT BY MY GREAT-GRANDPA JAY EARLE WHITE

"Hello, my father just died. I wanted to have you announce it over the radio, please."

"Uh, okay, um, just a minute," said the girlish sounding receptionist, scrambling on the other end, presumably to find a pencil. "Okay, what's the name of the—um—dead person?"

"Mr. William Whitman."

"Occupation?"

"He was a carpenter."

"Oh," said the woman. "We only read the obituaries of prominent people."

Eleanor hesitated a moment. It was only nine in the morning. Her day had already been trying enough. She had just lost her father, and her husband wanted her to move away, and now this woman was saying her father's life had been unimportant.

"My father was prominent," she stated. "Everyone in Marquette knew him. He built some of this city's finest homes."

"I'm sorry, ma'am. If he were a doctor or a lawyer, or—"

"My father built the doctors and lawyers' houses. He built beautiful homes for them, for Dr. Fisher and many others. He helped to build the First National Bank and the Post Office on Washington Street. He helped to dismantle the Longyear Mansion when they moved it out East, and he helped to build Granot Loma for the Kaufmans, and—"

"All right," huffed the radio chit. "What year was he born?"

— The Queen City

The above conversation is based on a real one that took place when my great-aunt Viola White Lopez called the local radio station to ask that they read my great-grandfather's obituary on the radio.

While none of my ancestors were fortunate enough to live in the grand old mansions of Ridge and Arch Streets, my great-grandfather, Jay Earle White, was busily building homes for people throughout Marquette in the early 1900s. Amazingly, he learned carpentry through a correspondence course.

I don't know how many homes my great-grandfather built, but in the late 1990s, my Great-Uncle Jolly drove around Marquette with me, letting me know which houses he remembered his father building, some of which my great-uncle helped to build as a teenager in the 1920s. Most of the houses Jay Earle White built are in the residential East side of Marquette. Some of the homes he built are long gone, but those that remain, according to my great-uncle's recollections eighty years later, are listed below with approximate dates for when they were built. I have not verified the accuracy of all these dates but simply submit them as my great-uncle best remembered them.

- **South Side Pioneer Road** — a home on this street was built in 1927 for Fred Odett.
- **307, 323, and 325 College Avenue** — these houses are just a couple of blocks from Marquette General Hospital, St. Luke's at the time, and were built as homes for nurses.
- **400 Crescent Street** — built about or slightly after 1927.

710 N. Front ~ Youngquist Home

- **537 Center Street** — built for the Duquettes. It is next door to my grandparents' house at 1622 Wilkinson Avenue.
- **710 N. Front Street** — built for Dr. Youngquist in 1924.
- **714 Spruce Street** — the Huetter Flats, built in 1924, at the time a "modern" apartment building. Known today as "Spruce Manor," it is still an apartment building. A building was located here as early as 1900 which was also apartments.
- **810 N. Front Street** — built for John Robinson.
- **1041 Pine Street** — built about 1925 or 1926.
- **1111 and 1116 High Street** — built in 1927 for Charles Gustafson.
- **1119 Pine Street**
- **1222 N. Front Street** — built for Leo Tonn

714 Spruce ~ Huetter Flats

• **1820 Wilkinson Avenue** — built in 1938 by Jay Earle White for his own family.

My great-grandfather did a lot of other carpentry work including working as a cabinet maker at what was then Northern Michigan College. Great-Uncle Jolly told me his father never wanted to belong to the Carpenters Union because his work was so good people would pay him $1.00 an hour, and the union carpenters only made $0.75 an hour, so the union carpenters took up a collection to pay his carpenter dues so they wouldn't have to compete with him and he'd get what they were paid.

I wonder whether my great-grandfather ever considered that the houses he built would still be standing well into the twenty-first century. Over time, hundreds of people must have lived in these homes. His work lives on in his homes as well as in his family long after he is gone.

1820 Wilkinson ~ White Home

PART V:
LAKESHORE & PRESQUE ISLE

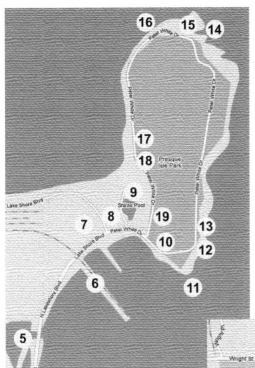

1. Maritime Museum
2. Lighthouse
3. Picnic Rocks
4. Lombardy Poplars
5. The Hot Pond & The Dead River
6. LS&I Ore Dock
7. Presque Isle Station Railway
8. Bog Walk
9. Shiras Pool
10. Presque Isle Playground &
    Picnic Area

11. Breakwall
12. Gazebo
13. Kawbawgam's Grave
14. Cove
15. Black Rocks
16. Sunset Point
17. The Pavilion
18. Shiras Zoo
19. Bandshell

MARITIME MUSEUM

The sudden lurch catapulted several passengers over the ship's rail. Sophia, having momentarily released Gerald's arm, found herself thrown overboard with several other ladies. Panic-stricken, she scrambled in the waves, fighting to keep her head above water while her skirts quickly soaked through, growing so heavy they threatened to pull her under. The lake was calm that evening, the waves nearly indistinguishable, yet Sophia was terrified. She had not swum in twenty years, and she sadly lacked for exercise. The sudden surprise and the biting cold water nearly sent her into shock. Gerald was almost as surprised as he stood clasping the rail and trying to spot his wife. After a few initial screams, the other women thrown overboard began to swim toward the ship. One man, Mr. Maynard, had also been pivoted overboard, and like Sophia, he struggled to stay afloat. Sophia's terror increased when she saw Mr. Maynard's head sink beneath the waves. She instantly feared he had drowned, and his failure to resurface made her splash and scream frantically until she began to swallow water. Hearing his wife's screams, Gerald spotted her and dove to her rescue.

— Iron Pioneers

The Marquette Maritime Museum was formed in 1980 and opened to the public in 1982. It is located in the old Marquette Waterworks building designed by D. Fred

Maritime Museum

Charlton in 1890. In 1897, the Father Marquette statue was placed on the waterworks building's property, although it was later moved to its present location. The construction of a new waterworks building resulted in the old one being converted into the Maritime Museum.

Maritime Museum Facade

In 1999, when I first conceived the idea to write *The Marquette Trilogy*, I visited the Maritime Museum to see the exhibits as research for my books. During that visit, I learned about the sinking of the *Jay Morse* which I knew would make a great dramatic scene since most of Marquette's wealthiest people were on the ship. The passage above resulted from my visit to the museum. Fittingly, my novels have since found a happy place in the Maritime Museum's gift shop. The friendly employees have read them and frequently recommend them to their customers, something for which I am always grateful.

The museum includes numerous displays about the early schooners and ore boats on Lake Superior as well as dioramas, old rowboats, and a small theatre with ongoing films. In 2002, the museum also acquired the Marquette lighthouse as part of its property.

LIGHTHOUSE & COAST GUARD STATION

1866 Marquette Lighthouse

The ship passed Marquette's new lighthouse; built three years earlier, it provided safety for all who traveled into Iron Bay on Lake Superior's rough, rolling waves.

— Iron Pioneers

Marquette was built to be a port for shipping iron ore from the mines in nearby Negaunee and Ishpeming. Every harbor town requires a lighthouse, and Marquette constructed its lighthouse in 1853, just four years after the town's founding. No building records exist for this first lighthouse, but it was reputedly thirty-four by twenty feet in size. The lantern room contained seven fourteen-inch Lewis lamps which were used until the introduction of the Fresnel lens in the later 1850s. Because the living quarters and tower were poorly constructed, they were replaced with the present lighthouse in 1866.

The 1866 lighthouse is today the oldest structure of any real historical significance in Marquette. The original structure was a one-and-a-half story brick building with an attached forty-foot square brick tower housing a fourth order Fresnel lens. An identical lens is on display today in the Marquette Maritime Museum. The original lens showed an arc of 180 degrees. In 1870, it was increased to 270 degrees.

The keeper and his family lived in the lighthouse. As long as the keeper's job was only to maintain the light, a single man was able to do the work. However, when the light at the end of the breakwater was added and a two whistle signal system installed at the end of the point, the work was too much for one person so an assistant keeper was hired and a barn behind the lighthouse was converted into living space for him. In 1909, a second story was added instead for the assistant's quarters. Additions were also made to the back of the lighthouse in the 1950s.

The Maritime Museum has available on CD the lightkeeper's log books which reflect some of their interesting experiences. In 1859, Peter White complained about the lightkeeper because "He is a habitual drunkard, frequently thrashes his wife and throws her out of doors." This lightkeeper also failed to light up until sometimes after midnight which caused great danger for ships.

During the Civil War, the lighthouse keeper was Nelson Truckey, but because he enlisted to serve in the infantry, the light was left to his wife and children's keeping. A descendant of the Truckey family, Chris Shanley Dillman, wrote the novel *Finding My Light* in 2006, a fictional account of the Truckey children and their adventures during this time. Nelson Truckey became a captain in the Michigan 27th and my great-great-grandfather, Jerome White, a corporal, and Jerome's father-in-law, Edmond Remington, a sergeant, both served under him. I have pension records for my ancestors with Nelson Truckey's signature, testifying to their service. The Truckey family's descendants still live in Marquette today.

Marquette would also have a life-saving crew, but it was separate from the lighthouse and its keeper's duties. Before Marquette's life-saving crew was established in 1891, Marquette had to send distress signals by telegraph to Portage Lake over a hundred miles away. This delay could easily result in lost vessels. At one point, tugboat skipper, Captain John Frink, rather than wait for the life-saving crew, decided to take matters into his own hands. On November 17, 1886, a fierce storm washed away the Marquette breakwater light, which later was washed up on shore. That afternoon, a schooner, the *Eliza Gerlach*, was seen about to smash into the breakwater. Captain John Frink risked the waves with the tug *Gillett* and managed to tow the schooner clear of the breakwater. As soon as the rescue was complete, Captain Frink's crew went back out to rescue the schooner *Florida* which had managed to find Iron Bay solely by listening to fog signals, but was now too close to the beach. Eight of the *Gillett*'s crew jumped aboard the *Florida* to attach a tow rope to it, but a ninth crew member miscalculated the jump and fell between the vessels, being crushed to death. Despite the casualty, the *Florida* was towed to safety. *The Mining Journal* commemorated Captain Frink by saying he deserved the government's life-saving medal.

Captain Frink came from a family not of sailors but lighthouse keepers. His father Reuben Frink was the keeper of the Grand Island North light from 1865-69 and later the Granite Island light from 1884-85. Captain Frink's brother William was the assistant keeper at Grand Island North from 1865-70 and another brother Richard was acting assistant at Granite Island under his father in 1884-85. But perhaps the most successful and fascinating member of the Frink family was Captain Frink's sister, Grace, who would end up marrying quite well—or perhaps not so well.

In 1879, Grace Frink married Michigan lumberman, Martin Pattison, who would make his fortune in mining veins of iron ore he discovered in the Vermillion Range near Ely, Minnesota. The couple met and married in Marquette and then moved to Superior, Wisconsin where they built the magnificent forty-two room Fairlawn

Mansion. The house was lavished with $150,000 worth of Guatemalan mahogany, English glazed tile, Mexican onyx fireplaces, and white-birch woodwork covered with 22-karat gold. An elegant entry hall, a fine staircase, a ball room on the third floor, and a swimming pool in the basement completed the mansion's impressive accessories. Today, the home has been beautifully restored and is open for tours.

Fairlawn Mansion

Unfortunately, Grace would eventually learn that everything that glitters is not gold. While Martin was serving as mayor of Superior, his first wife came calling. In fact, he had abandoned a wife and children in Lower Michigan before marrying Grace, who had no idea about her husband's other family or that by marrying her, her husband had become a bigamist. Things were apparently smoothed over with the first wife, and Pattison stayed with Grace, but rumor has it that after that, they slept in separate bedrooms.

Just west of the Marquette lighthouse, the U.S. Life-Saving Service established a station in 1891. Led by Captain Henry Cleary, the life-savers performed death-defying rescues on the lake. Their fame grew until they were invited in 1901 to escort President McKinley down the Niagara River during the Pan American Exposition in Buffalo, New York. (The following day the president would be assassinated by Leon Czolgosz, who for some time had worked in various lumber camps in Michigan, including in Seney. In 2009, Marquette author, John Smolens, published *The Anarchist*, a novel about the McKinley assassination.) Eventually the U.S. Life-Saving Station was absorbed into the Coast Guard, and it became the building in operation for the longest time that was owned by the Coast Guard until 2009 when a new Coast Guard station was built directly on the south side of the Maritime Museum and in front of the Lower Harbor's breakwater.

The Marquette lighthouse remains one of the city's most recognizable landmarks for its bright red walls, and it is probably photographed more than any other place in Marquette. When I worked at Superior Spectrum, a former local telephone company in Marquette, the lighthouse was used in numerous marketing pieces, some of which I helped to design. Today, the lighthouse is open for tours operated by the Maritime Museum, and it is being refurbished to reflect the lighthouse keepers' living quarters in the early twentieth century.

PICNIC ROCKS

By taking the bike path from the Maritime Museum, one can traverse Marquette's entire lakeshore in either direction. The people of Marquette know well how fortunate they are for their long stretches of sandy beach and that the lakeshore remains open to the public rather than being privately owned.

Following the beach north from the lighthouse leads within a mile to a small rocky point known as Picnic Rocks for the three small rocky islands off the shore. People have frequently waded or swam out to these islands, although the lake's depth here has increased over the years, and strong currents can make the swim dangerous; a few people have drowned here as a result. Nevertheless, many people risk the journey by swimming or by canoe or kayak to the largest and closest of the three rocks.

For decades, it has been a tradition to paint your high school class' graduation year and class colors on the largest rock's face. Typically these are Marquette High School's Redmen team colors, red and white, and the year is typically the current graduating class or that of a class having a reunion, although just a few years back I saw "23" painted—I'm not sure if a baby or a centenarian swam out to paint that one.

Although my family is from Marquette, because I attended Gwinn High School, I never expected to see my class on the rock, but in 2009, the Gwinn class of 1989 had its twentieth reunion at the Lakeview Arena and a few of my classmates decided they would paint the rock, so for a few weeks in August, the rock was claimed by the Gwinn Modeltowners with black and gold and "89" painted on it.

The park at Picnic Rocks has been the home for many years to the Outback Art Fair the last weekend in July. Each year over one hundred artists display their paintings, metal artwork, jewelry, books, and other original creations. Both locals and artists from throughout the Midwest attend, making it one of the largest arts and craft shows, in conjunction with the Art on the Rocks art show usually that same weekend, in the nation. Since 2007, I have signed and sold my books here—rain or shine—and I always enjoy meeting the many people who stop by to talk with me about Marquette, literature, history, writing, and life in Upper Michigan.

Picnic Rocks

LAKESHORE BOULEVARD

The blue and the green—that moment, as I walked home from Presque Isle, along the beach, and saw the noble lean white birches, the enormous maples, and the shimmering poplar trees, saw how their vibrant green leaves so perfectly contrasted yet enhanced the changing deep and light blues of the lake behind them, and how they were also in contrast with the sky's own lighter blue and the green drifting patches of the lake—all like an emerald mixed with a diamond, or perhaps like the lustrous Connemara marble my Irish forebears had once mined—all that priceless blending of color suddenly bolted through my eyes and dazzled my very soul until I felt so exhilarated I nearly thought my soul would leave my body, my heart leaping up with joy over such grandeur. I am tempted to belittle the experience, to make light of it by saying perhaps it was only the cold water from my swim or the heat making me almost hallucinate, but it was neither of these. It was a deep felt appreciation for Nature's wonders, for their constant reminders that if only we will look, we can be assured all is well with the world. How can it be otherwise? How can anyone doubt, when standing on the shore of Lake Superior, a magnificent lake before him, a plenitude of plant life behind him, trees, bushes, a diversity of vegetation, and the billions and billions of grains of sand on the beach, the roaring of waves capped with white, the wisps of cloud adding texture to the sky, and sunlight sparkling over it until all is so magnificent I can scarcely stand such good—how can anyone see all this and doubt that the Creation is not the greatest piece of art ever made, and that a master plan exists for all?

— The Only Thing That Lasts

Lombardy Poplars ~ c. 1990

The road along the lakeshore is named—what else? Lakeshore Boulevard. I am fortunate to live only a few blocks from the lakeshore and most days from spring through fall and even occasionally in winter, I go for a walk along the lake. It was in the summer of 2005 that I was so struck by the green leaves of the trees projected against the ever changing blues of the lake that I was inspired to write the above quoted passage. I even toyed with naming the novel *The Blue and the Green* simply because those are my two favorite colors, definitely favorites as a result of growing up in Upper Michigan and seeing those colors daily (except in winter when green is replaced by white). I never cease to be amazed by Lake Superior and the way its color can change each day from a faint gray, which blends in with a cloudy sky so you cannot see the horizon, to deep rich blues that can become almost black.

Lakeshore Boulevard leads to Presque Isle Park. In the mid-nineteenth century, Presque Isle, a peninsula whose French name means "almost island" was fairly far from Marquette—the city had yet to grow north past the point of Picnic Rocks, and a great boggy swamp as well as the Dead River divided the peninsula from the mainland so it was not easily accessible. Furthermore, the land belonged to the Coast Guard. But in 1886, Peter White decided Presque Isle should become a park, declaring once he purchased it from the government, "The park belongs to the people of Marquette and must be preserved for all who in years to come shall call Marquette 'home'." White offered the property to the city, but the city did not want the park because it was thought inaccessible and too far from Marquette for anyone to use.

Never one to take "No" for an answer, Peter White decided not only to have a road built to Presque Isle, but he lined it with beautiful Lombardy Poplars. These beautiful towering trees remained for well over a century until in 2002 the last of them had to be removed because most were dead or diseased. Nevertheless, a few Lombardy Poplars can still be seen around Marquette, seeds having made their way into the city. For years, the trees beautified the road to Presque Isle, if you weren't too busy looking at Lake Superior.

Today, even without the Lombardy Poplars, the drive along the lake to the Island can be breathtaking as ore boats appear on the horizon coming into the Upper Harbor. Bikers, joggers, and walkers fill the bike trail, and whether they know of Peter White's gift or not, everyone seems to think Presque Isle the perfect destination for a Sunday drive or picnic.

THE HOT POND & THE DEAD RIVER

Jacob and Will discovered the Dead River, despite its name, was sorely lacking in sea serpents, but its trout were abundant.

— Iron Pioneers

To reach Presque Isle requires crossing the Dead River Bridge, with Lake Superior and the beach still on the right and on the left the power plant that generates the electricity for the Tilden and Empire mines near Negaunee and Ishpeming.

When I was a kid in the early 1980s, the Hot Pond was the place to swim rather than the Shiras Pool. The Hot Pond existed for a short time because the Dead River wound its way under the bridge north toward the ore dock, cutting through the land, thereby creating a warm swimming hole between two beaches. People would often float down the Hot Pond on inflatable rafts and inner tubes, and it was perfect for swimming since it was no more than five feet deep in the middle so parents felt their children were safe swimming there. But rivers flow as they will, and soon a hard winter changed the river's flow back into a relatively straight line under the bridge into Lake Superior. The Hot Pond was no more.

Had winter not changed the river's course, doubtless the Flood of 2003 would have. In May 2003, heavy spring rain and rapidly melting snow caused water levels in the Dead River to rise, and the water pressure from the current became too strong for the Silver Basin Dam to withstand. The dam broke, releasing some 90 billion gallons of water. Not only did the river overflow its banks, but trees and boats plummeted downstream. The Dead River flows through the Silver Basin to the Hoist Dam. Fear that the Hoist would also break as water poured over its top caused the evacuation of homes from the Silver Basin and McClure Basin and all along the river. The Dead River flows just north of Marquette's Wright Street along the Holy Cross Cemetery and then under the Dead River Bridge out into Lake Superior, so that meant all of Marquette north of Wright Street was evacuated—two thousand people total.

Fortunately, the Hoist Dam withstood the flooding and no one in Marquette lost a home, but the flood did wipe out the Dead River Bridge, making Presque Isle inaccessible. The Presque Isle Power Plant was out of commission, resulting in power to the mines being shut down—it would be a month before it was operating again at full capacity. All residents north of Marquette including Big Bay lost power. Marquette's Tourist Park's dam and levee just a mile west of the river's mouth also failed. The

Dead River at Tourist Park ~ This area was a lake before the 2003 flood

Tourist Park's landscape would forever be changed—the water from the small lake where so many people swam flowed down the river, leaving behind naked land that had once been underwater. The park has never been the same.

Flooding in Upper Michigan is not uncommon in the spring due to melting snow and rain, but the 2003 Dead River Flood holds the record for being the most traumatic ever seen in Marquette County. The damage was estimated at $100 million. Hopefully, the flood's like will never be seen again.

LS&I ORE DOCK

*Then John took Wendy on a walking tour around Presque Isle. Luckily,
an ore boat was in the harbor, so they walked out on the breakwall to watch
the boat load its cargo from the pocket dock.*

— Superior Heritage

By the late nineteenth century, three ore docks operated in the Lower Harbor. Then in 1912, an ore dock was built in the Upper Harbor. Nearly a century later, it is Marquette's only operating dock and nineteen years older than its Lower Harbor sister which sits silently.

The Upper Harbor's LS&I Dock, belonging to the Lake Superior and Ishpeming Railroad, unloads ore from the mines onto ships bound for Canada and various ports in the Great Lakes. The dock stands seventy-five feet high and projects 1,200 feet into Lake Superior. Nearly 10,000 timber piles are driven twenty feet deep to support the dock's size and weight. Workers must climb 103 steps to the dock's top to help load the ore. Lucky tourists will see a ship along either side of the ore dock with the dock's chutes open to load the ore, a process that can take several hours.

Marquette's last remaining operating pocket dock is considered so important that following the September 11, 2001 terrorist attacks, the government was concerned it would be a target by terrorists to disrupt shipping on the Great Lakes.

The LS&I dock remains a testament to Marquette's *raison d'etre*—to carry ore to industrial centers like Buffalo and Cleveland so it can be made into steel. Upper Michigan's iron ore has played an integral part in the United States' modernization from its use to build cannons and ships in the Civil War to over a century of constructing automobiles. As long as the mines operate and ore boats pull up to the LS&I dock, Marquette will remain connected to its past.

***Herbert C. Jackson* at LS&I Ore Dock**

PRESQUE ISLE STREETCARS, SHIRAS POOL, & THE BOG WALK

At first, the trip there on the streetcar did not seem promising. The lakeshore in those days was full of commerce, businesses, factories and just a large mess in general. Not that the lake itself appeared polluted, though perhaps it was, but the land along the lake was rather a mess, while now it has been cleaned up. The streetcar passed all this industrial hodgepodge, however, and left it behind, and then we crossed over the Dead River Bridge, and suddenly, we were at Presque Isle Park.

— The Only Thing That Lasts

Just past the ore dock on the left side of the road is the Studio Gallery Shops, owned by several local artists. These quaint buildings were originally the Presque Isle Station for the railway that connected the train from Negaunee and Ishpeming to the Marquette streetcar railway.

Not long after Presque Isle became a park in 1891, the streetcar came to Marquette and soon one ran out to Presque Isle. In *The Only Thing That Lasts*, Robert O'Neill is forced to walk home along the lakeshore because he loses his streetcar money—it is then he is overwhelmed by the beauty of "the blue and the green" as described earlier in the section on Lakeshore Boulevard. My readers will also remember in *Iron Pioneers* when Gerald Henning returns to Marquette in 1895 and rides the streetcar with his family to Presque Isle for a picnic.

When the Shiras Pool opened in 1921, the streetcar became popular with people who wanted to visit the pool. In *It Seems Like Only Yesterday*, Clyde Steele recalled that youngsters on the streetcar would open the windows and jump out before the streetcar reached its final destination so they could avoid paying the fare. By 1935, the automobile had won out as the preferred mode of transportation so

Shiras Pool ~ c. 1925

Marquette's street railway was dismantled.

The pool would outlast the streetcar by decades but also eventually see its end. I went swimming there in the 1970s, but my family more regularly went to Tourist Park or the Hot Pond. Even though a circular water-slide was built in the late 1980s, the pool always struggled to stay open, and in 2008 it was closed permanently.

Behind the pool is the Bog Walk, a newcomer to the park, or

Shiras Pool Slide

perhaps its oldest attraction. A swamp once separated Presque Isle from the mainland. In *Iron Pioneers*, Caleb and Jacob cross this swampy marsh in 1855 so they can go camping at the Island as young boys. After the Shiras Pool opened, the marsh behind it became an unofficial dumpsite. Local schoolteachers and the Citizens to Save the Superior Shoreline were concerned that the natural habitat they used as an outdoor study resource was being destroyed, so they banded together to preserve the bog. In 1988, a 4,000 foot trail and boardwalk was completed, designed by local architect, Barry Polzin. Interpretive signboards along the trail provide information about wildlife, flora, and fauna. The property where the Shiras Pool once stood is now

Bog Walk

being allowed to return to its natural state as part of the bog and wetland. In late October each year, the area is transformed into a Haunted Bog Walk, complete with ghosts and ghouls, and hosted by the Moosewood Nature Center, located near the former pool.

PRESQUE ISLE PLAYGROUND & PICNIC AREA

> *Peter had told Gerald how he had purchased the land of Presque Isle from the federal government, then built the road to it, lining it with Lombardy poplars to make the shoreline picturesque. Presque Isle would now be preserved as a park for all those who were to call Marquette home. Forever protected would be its towering cliffs, its rich vegetation, its wandering deer, its marvelous black rocks. Gerald had been delighted by Peter's public benefaction; he only wished he had thought to make an equally grand gesture toward Marquette.*
>
> — Iron Pioneers

Presque Isle Park is indisputably the most romantic place in Marquette. If you were to ask all the people in Marquette what is their favorite place, I have no doubt the vast majority would say, "The Island," as Presque Isle Park is commonly known by the locals.

Few cities can claim such a beautiful, natural three hundred acre park within its city limits. London may have Hyde Park and Kensington Gardens, and New York its Central Park, but none are as naturally beautiful. When Frederick Law Olmsted was asked to landscape Presque Isle, he only provided a plan for laying out the roads and then recommended the rest of the park be left alone to retain its natural beauty. Fallen trees remain, wildlife runs free, and vegetation grows as it will. Presque Isle's natural beauty and geological attractions are more than sufficient to make it the greatest jewel in the Queen City's crown.

The playground here is often filled with children playing and picnics are popular, despite the seagulls. No feeding of birds or animals is allowed at Presque Isle, and the seagulls are particularly aggressive so they should not be encouraged. I have attended numerous summer picnics and birthday parties at Presque Isle, including my own birthday parties. The scene in *Superior Heritage* set in 1986 at Presque Isle for John's birthday is based on one of my birthday parties.

Driving past the marina, visitors who want to walk around the park (it takes roughly an hour) will want to park along the small circle drive or lot behind the playground to view the park's many charming features. Biking around Presque Isle is also popular, and the road is closed off three times a week so people can walk or bike ride without traffic. Except for the small hill at the beginning and a little incline, the majority of the road is downhill, creating a great coasting experience on a bicycle.

No matter the season, the park is beautiful, in summer with lush forests surrounded by sparkling Lake Superior, in winter a true wonderland with ice formations on its cliffs. Although the locals adore Presque Isle, visitors are always impressed by it. Even Helen Keller, on a brief visit to Marquette, when driven around the Island declared it was "wonderful" just from what her senses told her.

Family fun at Presque Isle Playground

BREAKWALL

He remembered a happy night with Frank and Holly when the three of them had walked to the Island at night and stood on the breakwall to watch the black waves in the moonlight.

— Superior Heritage

A good place to start after parking the car is the breakwall, built by the Lake Superior and Ishpeming Railroad to protect ships coming into the harbor from the waves. Initially built in 1896 of rock, in 1926 a more substantial wall of concrete was constructed, and in 1936 the additional 1,600 feet of rocks were added at the end. On a clear, sunny day when there are no waves, people can walk down the cement breakwall and even past the cement onto the rocks all the way out to the light at the end. But on windy days when waves are high, the breakwall is a dangerous place because waves can sweep over the breakwall, pulling anything on it into the lake. In 1988, two Northern Michigan University students drowned by going out on the breakwall in bad weather. A plaque in their memory is situated at the foot of the stairs leading down to the breakwall.

The view from the breakwall on a sunny summer day is unmatched. Visitors can see the Superior Dome across the bay, watch the ore boats being loaded at the pocket dock, see Presque Isle's towering cliffs, and even fish off the breakwater.

Presque Isle Breakwall

GAZEBO

Next they left the hot sun behind to sit in the cool gazebo and admire the sparkling lake for a few minutes before beginning their trek around the Island. John told stories about the Island, such as how Jacob Whitman had fished there with Chief Kawbawgam.

— Superior Heritage

Wedding at Presque Isle Gazebo

Walking toward the hill, you will come to the gazebo, erected in the early 1990s and a popular place for weddings and wedding photographs. My friends Daniel and Allison Alexander were married here on an unseasonably warm day in early October 2007 with their reception in the Presque Isle Pavilion on the other side of the Island.

Presque Isle Gazebo

KAWBAWGAM'S GRAVE

Climbing that hill just about did me in. I better stop for a breather. There's old Charlie Kawbawgam's gravestone. I'll just lean against it for a minute.

Pagan Indian grave—treated like some place of honor. But it is remarkable that old Kawbawgam lived in three centuries 1799-1902; his wife Charlotte lived nearly as long. Think of all the changes they saw. If it weren't for this stone, soon only us old-timers would remember the Kawbawgams ever lived at Presque Isle. I can't believe I'm an old timer already—I'll be sixty soon. I'll never see a hundred-and-three like Kawbawgam did. Won't be long now I imagine before I'm lying beneath a stone myself.

— Narrow Lives

A set of stairs will bring visitors up the hill to Chief Kawbawgam's grave.

Kawbawgam is known as the last Chief of the Chippewa Indians per the sign at his gravesite. It's hard to say when the first Native Americans visited the Island. Presque Isle was a popular place to the Chippewa who often resided in the area in the summer. Robert Hume, Presque Isle Park's first caretaker, discovered many arrowheads on the Island and speculated it may have once been the sight of a great Indian war.

In the 1840s before Marquette was founded, some silver mines were operated on the Island. They did not last long, but their remains are still slightly visible although inaccessible to the public. Some of the huts of the miners were moved to Marquette when it was first founded to serve as houses until more stable homes could be built.

Kawbawgam Grave

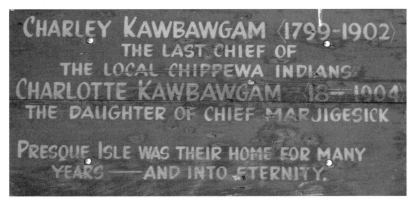

The Island was largely deserted after that although Chief Kawbawgam and his family took up residence near the entrance to Presque Isle. Peter White, after being caught in a blizzard and being given shelter by Kawbawgam, built Kawbawgam a home at Presque Isle, where the chief lived out his days.

When Chief Kawbawgam was actually born is unknown, but the sign at his gravesite says he lived in three centuries from 1799-1902. Suggestions have been made that Kawbawgam was younger than this, but he could remember his father coming back from fighting in the War of 1812, and pictures taken of him in the mid-nineteenth century when Marquette was young show him as already middle-aged.

Kawbawgam married Charlotte, the daughter of Chief Marji Gesick who had first led the white men to the "shining rocks," the iron ore that would become the Jackson mine. Marji Gesick would receive a share in the mine which was never paid to him. After his death, Charlotte took the mine to court to claim her father's share; although the case was settled in her favor, the mine had no money to give her. A highly romanticized version of the trial, depicting a historically inaccurate much younger Charlotte, is told in John Voelker's novel *Laughing Whitefish* (1965).

Chief Kawbawgam appears in my novel *Iron Pioneers* in 1855 just in time to save Caleb Rockford from plunging over a cliff at Presque Isle into the lake. This incident leads to his forming a friendship with Caleb's cousin Jacob and becoming his fishing partner. Later, in the same novel, a scene is set at the house that Peter White would have built for Kawbawgam, when in 1894 Homer Kidder visited the chief and recorded his Ojibwa tales. In my novel, Will Whitman is present to hear some of the stories told, including a story he later tells his son, Henry, replacing himself as the hero; Henry in

Chief Charles Kawbawgam

turn tells the story to his grandson John, and John in *Superior Heritage* then finds it written down a century later in the tales of Chief Kawbawgam compiled by Homer Kidder and published a century later. This coincidence is based on my Great-Uncle Jolly telling me a story about his father that I then discovered in Kidder's book, of course, without my great-grandfather as the hero. My great-grandfather, Jay Earle White, reputedly knew Chief Kawbawgam (he would have been in his early twenties and the same age as Will Whitman when Kawbawgam died) so it's very possible he heard the story directly from Kawbawgam's lips, or simply that it was a popular Ojibwa story that circulated in the Marquette area at the time. It is the kind of tall tale people would have enjoyed:

> *In the spring, Kitchi Nonan took a walk to another lake, and there he saw several swans. Wanting to catch them but not knowing how in the world to do it, he finally dove under the water and swam around till he found where the swans were; then tied all their feet together with a line and gave it a jerk. Away went the swans through the air, with Kitchi Nonan hanging on to the line. After being carried for miles, he lost his hold and fell. As luck would have it, he landed right in the top of a hollow pine just as a bear was coming out. Nonan tumbled on the bear and surprised it so it scrambled out of the tree and ran away.*

When Chief Kawbawgam died in 1902, a large funeral was held for him at St. Peter's Cathedral, as described in *The Queen City*. Two years later, his wife, Charlotte, would join him. They would be buried at Presque Isle, making the Island forever their home. A large unique stone was placed on their grave. Presque Isle caretaker Robert Hume found the granite boulder washed up on shore following a storm, and although a visiting geologist offered him $1,000 for it because of its unusual diagonal stripe of red (which has faded more to white today), Hume decided the stone was to be the marker for Kawbawgam's grave. The base of the grave is made of stones from along the beaches and park where Charley Kawbawgam would have walked.

In 1979, Kawbawgam's grave was featured in the Nancy Drew spoof novel *The Mystery of Kawbawgam's Grave* by David Goldsmith, writing under the pseudonym Clifford S. Cleveland (a play on the Cleveland-Cliffs mining company). I read the novel soon after it was published and loved it for its comical mystery. Not knowing who the author was until I was in college, when Dr. Goldsmith was one of my favorite English professors at Northern Michigan University, I reread the book in my early twenties and found far more to appreciate about its humor, including how Dr. Goldsmith wrote himself into the novel as a comical character; he was not afraid to poke fun at himself. The book again confirmed for me that Upper Michigan deserved its own literature.

Near Chief Kawbawgam's grave, in 1986, was discovered the dead body of Paul Gerard. Murder is so rare in Marquette that the entire community was shocked. Despite numerous rumors, the murderer has never been found—it is believed police know who killed Gerard but lack enough evidence to convict the culprit. The feelings of Marquette residents about the murder are related in *Superior Heritage*.

Author David Goldsmith

Chief Kawbawgam welcomed the first residents of Marquette to his home in 1849. A half-century later when he died, he must have been surprised by the changes he had witnessed in his lifetime. Now more than two centuries after his birth, his grave stands as a reminder of Marquette's past and of the past that existed here centuries before even Father Marquette stepped on these shores in 1671 to preach to Kawbawgam's ancestors.

TRAILS

> *They crossed the road and started down one of the trails that cut through the woods. John thought the trail looked like the forest scene on the cover of* Walden. *Chad chattered about the different flowers growing along the trail. Roy began to name all the trees they passed.*
>
> — Superior Heritage

Few experiences are more relaxing, more satisfying than simply walking around Presque Isle. Besides the main road, numerous trails crisscross through the Island's center. Other paths along the Island's edge can be somewhat dangerous but some great views of the lake are accessible.

One of my goals in writing *The Marquette Trilogy* was to depict how the environment of Upper Michigan influenced the characters, and how this influence changed and did not change over generations. I enjoyed creating parallel scenes for this reason in *Iron Pioneers* and *Superior Heritage* on the trails that run through Presque Isle. The two scenes—of Gerald Henning walking through the woods with his grandsons, Will and Clarence Whitman in 1895, and then of John and Chad Vandelaare with their great-uncle, Roy Whitman in 1986—are both based on a walk my brother and I took in the 1980s with our Great-Uncle Jolly. He would have been in his seventies then, and we perhaps nine and eleven. I remember Uncle Jolly telling us what each type of tree was, and we not caring a whit, yet still enjoying the walk. I wish I had listened to him more closely now—he knew a great deal about nature and vegetation—a field of study where the average person in earlier generations surpassed the current generations. I depicted that walk from a boy's viewpoint in *Superior Heritage* but from the older man's viewpoint in *Iron Pioneers*.

In *Narrow Lives*, Danielle goes for a walk on one of the trails with the intention to have a secret meeting with her lover, Gary Marshall. Her grandmother, Cecilia, spies on her and sees her kissing Gary in the woods. Woods can hide many things. Who knows how many secret rendezvous have occurred at Presque Isle Park.

What Authors Won't Do For A Good Photo

COVE

He walked off the main road and down the dirt path to the cove. For a warm summer day, the spot was strangely lonely. Yielding to a childish impulse, he walked up to the pebble filled beach between the black rocks and shoreline cliffs. He removed his shoes and socks, rolled up his pant legs, and waded into the water. For centuries, the lake had pushed pebbles up from its floor into the cove; the little rocks were Nature's tokens to the children of Marquette, who collected the neverending supply of brilliant red, white, yellow, brown, green, black, and blue stones. John leaned over to dip his arm in the lake; the cool water was refreshing as he pulled up one rock after another to look at their marvelous colors, then return them to the lake, thankful to have admired them, and wanting others to have the same pleasure. A gentle wind rustled the trees; the breeze stirred miniature waves that plunked up against the rocks on the shore. He looked straight out into the lake until he could not tell where it merged with the sky. He had admired the beauty of the cove's rocks but ignored the magnificent vista. He felt his entire life could be described as focusing on little rocks without seeing the grander view. He had limited himself to his writing and teaching until his writing had become lifeless, and his life dull. He had squelched all but the strict voices of academia, perhaps worthy voices, but not all knowing. The lake, rocks, trees, the wind—all had their voices, voices which never ceased to whisper patiently until he would listen.

"I think," he said aloud—so stunned by this sudden knowing, "that I'm going to stay in Upper Michigan. I've been so worried about getting a job, making money, and trying to prove I'm intelligent that I forgot to be happy. Until now, I don't think I've realized how unhappy I was downstate. This is my home. Here I will stay."

— Superior Heritage

The Cove is, without a doubt, my favorite place at Presque Isle, both for its beauty and because it is a true rock hunter's paradise. Every year, thousands of pebbles wash up onto the beach and allow for wading to collect rocks.

In *Iron Pioneers* when Madeleine is thought to have drowned in the lake, she actually manages to be washed up into the cove of Presque Isle, where her boyfriend,

Lazarus, finds her and they decide to run away together because her mother doesn't approve of their relationship.

It is at this same place in *Superior Heritage* in the passage quoted above that John Vandelaare comes to his decision that he will not move away from Marquette, no matter if it means giving up his career, a decision I had to make myself, having left academia to return home and write my novels rather than continuing to move from one university to another in search of a long-term teaching position. Home means more than a career, and many people have told me the novel resonates with them for that reason—many young people have left Marquette, only to return. It's a theme I know my readers can relate to—even those in faraway places who have left Upper Michigan feel the homesickness and understand this need to stay in the place where we belong, a sense of place that seems to be stronger among Upper Michigan residents than for people from many other areas of the country. I believe that sense of place comes from Upper Michigan having so much more of value—one has only to look around Presque Isle to find evidence of it.

The Cove

BLACK ROCKS

"'And look here,' I said, pointing to the ground.

"Where we had cooked ox meat all winter, the rocks had turned completely black.

"So that's how the Black Rocks came to be at Presque Isle, and they'll always stand as a monument to an animal who loved a man enough to give his life for him."

— The Queen City

In *The Queen City,* Karl Bergmann tells a Paul Bunyan story about how the Black Rocks got their name—it is a tale completely fabricated by me with no local sources, which to the clever observer, can be seen to be borrowed from a Norse myth about the god Thor. The influx of immigrants from Finland and Scandinavia in the late nineteenth century, and Karl's marriage to a Finnish woman, would have made him familiar with many of these tales, so he liberally borrowed the tale of how Thor ate his oxen and brought them back to life, by replacing it with Paul Bunyan cooking Babe the Blue Ox for dinner on the rocks, the result being the rocks turning black. Of course, Babe is also restored to life.

The Black Rocks are along the lakeshore just past the Cove, and they can be walked on clear to the lake. Nothing grows on them, and strangely, unlike the sandstone, no soil sticks to them. By jutting out into the lake, they are easily distinguishable from the rest of the forest-canopied island. They are windswept and washed by the lake, with little pools of water trapped in some of their crevices.

Although commonly known as the Black Rocks, they are actually Keweenawan Periodite and reverenced by geologists for being four billion years old. Some historians have even suggested these rocks provided black dyes for the early Native Americans, becoming the source for the name "Blackfoot Indians."

The Black Rocks

SUNSET POINT, SANDSTONE CLIFFS

At the point where the Island curves from west to south is Sunset Point, looking out over the bay and the shoreline heading north. This spot is a favorite for locals to sit and watch the sunset go down. The only time I've ever watched the sunset here, my friends and I found the antics of a raccoon in a nearby garbage can just as entertaining.

Walk Like an Egyptian

The path from Sunset Point leads toward the Pavilion, and it is the original road around the Island, parts of which have now been washed into the lake due to regular erosion. Concern about the erosion has led to debates about whether the park should naturally be allowed to erode or whether preventive measures should be taken. It has also been suggested that automobiles no longer be allowed to drive around the Island because the weight of the traffic lends to the erosion.

From the path, a better view of the sandstone cliffs can be seen. The cover of my novel *The Only Thing That Lasts* was taken in this spot in the 1890s. The last of the arched rock in the picture eroded away in the 1980s. In winter, the entire bay on this side of the Island can be seen filled with snow and ice, pushed in by currents from the lake. The best ice formations can also be seen along this side of Presque Isle in winter, making truly amazing frozen sculptures out of trees, rocks, and icicles. When waves are high, people can be seen surfing here off the beach—winter surfing has become quite popular in recent years in this sheltered bay.

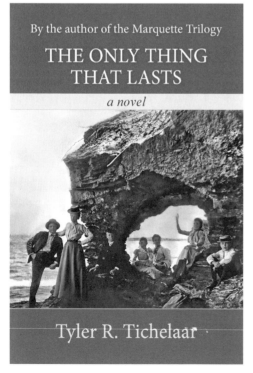

By the author of the Marquette Trilogy

THE ONLY THING THAT LASTS

a novel

Tyler R. Tichelaar

Arched Rock ~ c. 1890

THE PAVILION

They stopped to admire the new Presque Isle Pavilion, receiving its finishing touches, a gift from the people of Marquette to celebrate their city's sesquicentennial.

— Superior Heritage

The original Presque Isle Pavilion stood directly across the road from where the current one stands. This first pavilion had been built on Partridge Island by John M. Longyear in 1894. It was a private place where parties and dances were held and guests were transported there by a steam excursion boat. Rough waves often made it difficult to get to the pavilion, and the novelty of going to Partridge Island soon wore off, so in 1898, the city had the pavilion brought across the ice in winter and placed it at Presque Isle. In *The Only Thing That Lasts,* Robert and Helen hold their wedding reception in the pavilion.

Over the years, the pavilion started to show its age, and by the 1980s, discussions about repairing it or destroying it circulated. The large number of Canadian Geese in those years was a large problem because of the mess their droppings made in the park, so one suggestion was to capture all the geese and burn them inside the pavilion, thus killing two birds (or hundreds) with one stone, so to speak. While local residents would not agree to this act of animal cruelty, the pavilion was razed in 1986.

In 1999, to celebrate Marquette's sesquicentennial, residents donated money to build the new Presque Isle Pavilion as a birthday present to Marquette. Each person who donated was issued a certificate to hold shares of "goodwill to the City of Marquette on the occasion of the 150th founding in 1849" which included pictures of Peter White and Chief Kawbawgam.

The new pavilion has

New Pavilion

proudly lived up to its past and is a favorite picnic and event spot in Marquette. My friends Dano and Allison Alexander held their wedding reception here in 2007, and most summer weekends, people who drive around Presque Isle will see wedding parties celebrating and posing for pictures. In winter, the interior offers a respite from the cold and hot chocolate is served to people cross country skiing or snowshoeing around the Island. The people of Marquette can be proud of their much-loved birthday gift to the city.

The Author's Share of Goodwill to the City of Marquette

SHIRAS ZOO

As a child, John had come here with his father and brother to pick dandelion leaves to feed the deer when the Shiras Zoo existed.

— Superior Heritage

Shiras Zoo Plaque

George Shiras III was famous for his wildlife photography, and consequently, the most appropriate way to memorialize him was building the Shiras Zoo. A zoo was at Presque Isle from its first years as a park. In 1887, makeshift cages housed a small menagerie that included partridge, coyotes, wolves, and bears. In 1932, zoo cages of concrete and iron bars were built directly across from the caretaker's residence. This became the Shiras Zoo most residents today remember. The zoo was occupied throughout the summer months by animals. It was never large but had perhaps a half dozen different animals, mostly from Upper Michigan, but at various times included non-indigenous animals such as monkeys and peacocks. As a boy, I remember watching the bears and coyotes frequently, as well as peering into the smaller cages to see the ferrets and minks.

The enormous deer cage that filled the entire field next to the smaller cages always attracted the most attention. I don't know how many deer occupied this large cage, but it was probably about two dozen. Corn and feed machines were outside the cages

Remains of the Shiras Zoo

so people could buy food to feed the animals, but my dad always took my brother and me to the edge of the woods where the dandelion leaves grew. We would pick these and shove them through the chain link fence and the deer would come to inhale them. There were always young fawns to admire—I remember one in particular who liked attention and would run in circles for the crowd. Often an albino deer was also in the zoo—I always felt sorry for him because the other deer tended to ignore him.

In 1988, the smaller animal cages were removed, but the deer cage remained until 1994. When the deer cage was pulled down, the deer were not transported to the mainland but allowed to roam free about the Island. People continued to feed them and they became very tame. They tended most often to be seen on the woodland trails in the Island's center or in the area where their former cages had been. Today, it is not uncommon to turn a bend in the trail and come upon a deer in your path. One of my college friends was once jogging around the Island, and not looking where she was going, she ran into a deer, which just looked at her like she was crazy and walked off.

The freed deer population soon outgrew the Island. Studies reflected that the deer were eating too much of the vegetation, and a census found one hundred deer on the Island where fifteen was considered desirable. In the early winter of 2001, the City of Marquette outraged many local residents when it decided to hire a team of sharpshooters to go in and reduce the deer population. *The Mining Journal* was flooded with letters to the editor complaining about the City's plan to turn Presque Isle into "Blood Island" but the dastardly deed still took place.

Fortunately, or perhaps stupidly, the surviving deer have chosen to remain. It has since become illegal to feed any animals on the Island so they are encouraged to leave if resources become scarce. Perhaps this is not such a bad idea since I once saw the owner of a car with a Florida license plate stop to feed a deer an orange. The deer looked leery of the strange object and decided to walk back into the woods.

Zoo escapee near caretaker's house ~ c. 1940

BANDSHELL

Presque Isle Bandshell

Presque Isle Park's bandshell was built in 1928 and has often been the sight of band concerts. The Marquette City Band performs here regularly in the summer, and various other musical performances are given each year. Recently, local musicians have regularly performed on Friday evenings, including my friend Dano Alexander in the summer of 2009.

My earliest memory of the bandshell was as a kid of maybe eight years old. My mother was interested in Art on the Rocks, the annual art show that for many years was held at Presque Isle but in 2009 moved to the Lower Harbor. While my mom looked at the art, my brother and I were happy to watch a play at the bandshell, which I believe was based on a scene from the *Kalevala*, the great Finnish epic, a well known work locally because of the large Finnish population in Upper Michigan. The *Kalevala* also ties in with Upper Michigan because Henry Wadsworth Longfellow used its poetic meter—trochaic tetrameter—for his poem, *The Song of Hiawatha*, largely set in Upper Michigan.

The bandshell provides a wonderful outdoor musical experience—the breeze off the lake blows through the trees, creating a pleasant rustling that only adds to the musicians' melodies.

Dano Alexander Performing at Presque Isle Bandshell

OLD RAILROAD & BLUEBERRY TRAINS

"I'm coming," Kathy called. She had promised to take the girls blueberry picking. Last year a huge forest fire near Birch and Big Bay had resulted in this summer's mammoth blueberry crop. A "blueberry train" had been organized to take people to the berry fields north of Marquette so they could spend the day filling their pails. When Kathy heard reports that people were returning with tubs full of berries, she was determined to go; she just hoped the fields were not completely picked over; she longed for blueberry pie and did not want to disappoint the girls.

— The Queen City

Before leaving Presque Isle, be sure to stop at the Island Store for ice cream. Jilbert's Dairy, until a few years ago locally owned, provides the ice cream. Mackinac Island Fudge is the recommended favorite, although sadly it no longer compares with the ice cream Jilbert's made when locally owned, despite claims it is the same.

Then proceed back out of the park's entrance. Presque Isle is really the northernmost point within the city limits, but it would be a shame not to go up the lakeshore a bit farther, and Big Bay is featured in several of my novels so we'll take a small detour north before exploring the rest of Marquette.

As we pass the Presque Isle Railway station again, it should be noted that in the early part of the twentieth century, people would gather here in July and August to take the "blueberry train" to the wild blueberry patches north of Marquette up on the Yellow Dog Plains. In *The Queen City*, Kathy McCarey goes with her daughter Beth and niece Thelma. It is during their berry picking excursion that Beth first meets Henry whom she will eventually marry. Carroll Watson Rankin, in her novel *Finders Keepers*, also depicted her characters taking the train, although for huckleberries.

Since the trains no longer run, visitors will have to proceed by car, but that will allow for a couple of stops along the lakeshore.

Presque Isle Railway Station

PART VI:
ON THE WAY TO BIG BAY

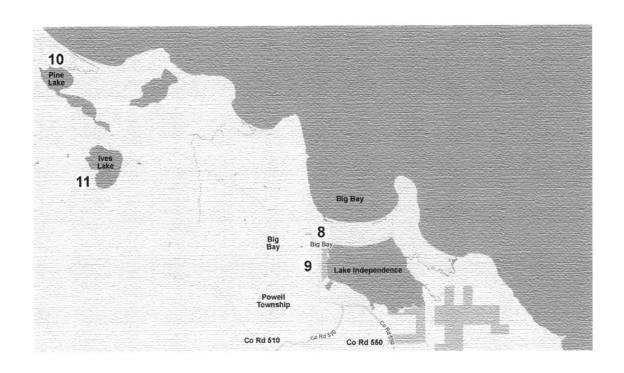

1. Sugarloaf
2. Partridge Island
3. Pickerel (Harlow) Lake
4. Wetmore Landing
5. Little Presque Isle
6. Birch
7. Granot Loma
8. The Thunder Bay Inn
9. The Lumberjack
10. The Huron Mountain Club
11. Ives Lake

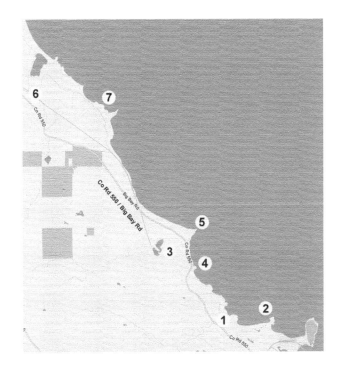

SUGARLOAF

Upon reaching the summit, Father Marquette found his efforts well re-paid. He could see several islands lying spread out along the lakeshore, and to his right was Presque Isle, the most beautiful little peninsula on Lake Superior. Out across the lake the view was spectacular as the water gradually faded into the horizon; dark indigo blended into light shades of blue revealing shallow water that in the distance appeared like clouds with little islands poking up through them. The Black Robe imagined he was viewing Heaven spread before him among the cloud-like waters. For years he had been traveling on the Great Lakes, but at such moments as this one, he never failed to experience awe as the lakes changed hourly from being bathed in rays of sunlight to being darkened by overcast skies; each lighting revealed a new wonder upon the waters. Father Marquette had never seen the lake look so placid as today's cloudy appearance. What a contrast from the rolling waves he frequently experienced while plummeting over the water in his canoe. The beach was golden and warm while the water looked refreshing as its breezes blew inland, cooling the thick forests. Behind him, the Jesuit could see the towering pines, birches, maples, and oaks that spread into the horizon. It was an uncharted region, a bountiful country reminiscent of the biblical promised land flowing with milk and honey. He saw that the bay would provide shelter and that it served as an outlet from the two nearby rivers. It would be an ideal settlement in years to come. He imagined his own French people would someday settle this land, and he hoped they would do so peacefully, sharing it with the People whom he loved.

The wind rustled through the leaves, like a whispering voice, almost like the voice of God uttering a blessing; silently, the Jesuit prayed the land would always know peace and fellowship among its inhabitants, whomever they might be.

— Iron Pioneers

The view from the top of Sugarloaf Mountain is breathtaking. The mountain is really a high cliff overlooking Lake Superior just a few miles north of Marquette. It was called Tadosh by the Indians, and it is believed Father Marquette may have visited the beaches near it, so in *Iron Pioneers*, I depicted Father Marquette climbing its heights to view, like Moses looking over the Promised Land, the place where one day would stand the city named for him.

I don't know how early Sugarloaf Mountain became popular with Marquette residents, but its first notable event was in 1920 when the local Boy Scouts carried hundreds of stones up it to build an obelisk to the memory of their fallen leader, Bartlett King, who had died in France as a soldier during World War I. My grandpa, Lester White, was among those boy scouts.

Boy Scouts at Bartlett King Memorial Dedication

Perry Hatch, an early scoutmaster, led the boys in the effort. Marquette actually had one of the first Boy Scouts organizations in the country. Nearly a century later, the Bartlett King obelisk still stands.

Sugarloaf is depicted in my books as a place where you can get a perspective on life—it is a quiet place far from the mild bustle of the city, and the perfect scene for contrasts. In *The Queen City*, while the Boy Scouts are busy erecting their monument, below on the winding Big Bay Road, Harry Cumming is being chased by the police for selling liquor during Prohibition. Sugarloaf is also where Henry Whitman brings his city bred cousin, Theo Rodman, who feels exhausted by the climb and unable to appreciate the surrounding beauty. In *Superior Heritage*, Tom Vandelaare proposes to Ellen Whitman, and a generation later, their son, John, first feels himself falling in love with Wendy Dawson while climbing Sugarloaf. If I live long enough, I envision writing a fourth novel to create *The Marquette Tetralogy,* bringing the story up to 2049 when John Vandelaare, now an old man at age seventy-eight in Marquette's bicentennial year, shall look down from Sugarloaf, like Father Marquette before him, to reflect upon the changes he has witnessed in the city he has all his life called home.

PARTRIDGE ISLAND

They would row to Partridge Island, picnic there, and return by dark.
— Iron Pioneers

Pavilion on Partridge Island

From Sugarloaf Mountain can be seen Partridge Island, where the first Presque Isle Pavilion initially stood. In *Iron Pioneers,* Partridge Island is first the site of the *Jay Morse*'s sinking and where the survivors of the wreck shiver through the night as they wait for a rescue boat from Marquette. Later in the same novel, Partridge Island is the place where Madeleine Henning celebrates the Fourth of July with her friends. During this event, Madeleine is upset about her mother's disapproval of her love for Lazarus Carew. When the party leaves Partridge Island in rowboats, Madeleine is washed overboard and takes advantage of her friends' belief she has drowned to elope with the man she loves.

PICKEREL (HARLOW) LAKE

Pickerel Lake. August. Those most precious last days of summer when the trees take on that deep forest green that forewarns they will soon turn color, that summer is almost over, and soon winter will arrive, so each remaining warm day must be lived to the fullest. The family drove to the lake that Saturday in their trucks and cars, down a dusty dirt path off the Big Bay Road to their favorite fishing hole.

— The Queen City

Harlow Lake was renamed for the Harlow family in the twentieth century, but prior to that its great fishing led to its name being Pickerel Lake. It was Pickerel Lake in my mother's childhood and she and her parents, aunts, uncles, cousins, and grandparents often went fishing here. These family fishing parties went on for many decades, although by the time I was a child, I remember my grandparents more often fishing at Ives Lake or the Dead River. Nevertheless, the large family fishing party in *The Queen City* at Pickerel Lake is based on those family events. Although the characters are all fictional, as are their actions and words, my great-grandmother Barbara White, whose middle name was Margaret and was known as Maggie by family members, did like to sing and my great-grandfather did tell her, "Shut up, Maggie; you're scaring the fish" just as Will tells Margaret in the novel.

Although not mentioned in my novels—it's impossible to include everything—across the street from the entrance to Harlow Lake is the entrance to Wetmore Landing, and just a little bit farther down the road is the entrance to Little Presque Isle.

Wetmore Landing is a popular beach for swimming, as well as surfing, and the rocks along the shore make a good spot from which

Author's Grandma Grace White at Pickerel Lake ~ c. 1950

to fish. It is named for W. L. Wetmore and was originally a clearing where lumbermen could bring their logs from the forest so they could be rafted down to Marquette.

Little Presque Isle is also "almost an island" depending on when you visit it. One can easily wade out to it and occasionally walk to it on dry land depending on the water levels. It is very picturesque and provides splendid views of the sandstone cliffs up close in the water as well as being another fine place to collect Lake Superior's many wonderful pebbles.

Little Presque Isle

THE BIG BAY ROAD

The Big Bay Road points north from Marquette, curves along Sugarloaf Mountain, skirts the shore of Lake Superior, then blazes through the forest to the little village of Big Bay and on to the Huron Mountain Club. Originally built to provide easy access to the Club for its wealthy members, the road also served as access to little mining communities like Birch, which had operated for only a few years. The rugged terrain and rocky hills had resulted in one of the most treacherous, sharp twisting roads in the country.

Harry Cumming Jr., formerly a soldier in the United States Army, was racing down the Big Bay Road in his automobile; in hot pursuit were the Michigan State Police. Harry Jr. had returned home from war, traded his uniform for civilian clothes, and gone into business as a bootlegger.

— The Queen City

The Big Bay Road does have some dangerous curves and many an accident has happened along it. It's a beautiful drive, however, from Marquette up to Big Bay, especially in autumn when the fall colors are most brilliant.

As a boy, I think the Big Bay Road was most familiar to me in summer when my brother and I would spend time with our grandpa while my mom and grandma went shopping. Grandpa frequently would take us up the Big Bay Road to go pick up Great-Uncle Kit, who liked to be dropped off to spend a few hours out in the woods to dig for worms—nightcrawlers he would later sell to fishermen. For a few years, my grandpa also was a seller of worms. Worm farms were popular at the time and people raised worms to sell to fishermen and gardeners. I remember big troughs of worms in my grandpa's woodshop which he would have to water so the soil stayed moist. I also remember him letting me play with the worms and my mom getting upset when I accidentally pulled one in half, but my grandpa said not to worry because its ends would grow back. Invariably, after picking up Uncle Kit, we would stop at the 550 Store on the Big Bay Road to pick up something like milk, but really, I think it was an excuse to stop and buy candy bars. Grandpa always bought us candy bars and he had a sweet tooth himself—it was no mistake I made mention of the "Whitman sweet tooth" in my novels.

My other great-uncles, Jolly and Jack, both at different times built houses and lived along the Big Bay Road which inspired me to have Roy Whitman in *The Marquette*

Trilogy live there, although farther back in the woods and close to the border of the Huron Mountain Club's property where in Nature he finds peace from his war memories and unrequited love. In *The Queen City*, Harry Cumming Jr. is arrested on the Big Bay Road after a high speed car chase for selling liquor during prohibition. In *Narrow Lives*, it's revealed that Harry was probably coming from the cabin of his partner in crime, Leo, who lives up on the Big Bay Road where he makes and sells liquor and is also apparently in hiding from the law after a misunderstanding he had with a fellow in Chicago.

BIRCH

"Maybe we can stop in Birch to get ice cream," he suggested.

She said that would be fine. But they had been disappointed when they reached the little town. Birch had once been a prosperous village, home to a sawmill and close to Frank Krieg's gold mine, but the sawmill had closed and the mine had long since failed to yield enough gold to make a profit. Only a few families and a street full of empty buildings remained of what was fast becoming a ghost town.

"I haven't been here in years," Henry said, "but I remember getting ice cream with my father one summer when he was working around here."

Birch's present state was a sign that the great days of logging and homesteading had passed. Beth had not thought of Uncle Karl last night, but now she realized he was like Birch, part of the old world of great lumberjacks and mining. She and Henry had driven down Birch's deserted main street. The car's headlights had lit up ghostly houses and former stores. The rumbling car engine had been the only sound. An eerie silence had settled over Beth's soul.

Then in the gathering dusk had burst out the song of a whippoorwill. The sun had disappeared; it was mid-October; most of the birds had migrated south, but this whippoorwill sang anyway.

— The Queen City

Birch ~ c. 1910

By the time Henry and Beth visit Birch in *The Queen City* in 1928, it has become a ghost town. Today, hardly a trace of it exists.

In the last decades of the nineteenth century, the area around Birch became known because of gold fever. Several pieces of gold were discovered resulting in several gold mines being established. Among the gold seekers was Frank Krieg, who was married to my great-grandpa's second cousin, Lilly Hapgood. Frank would eventually own his own mine in this area. He would also be one of the most prominent residents of the town of Birch.

Birch was a short-lived community built around the logging interests of the area. George Raish moved to the area in 1900 with his sons and established a logging camp. He would be a partial owner of the Northern Lumber Company, formed in 1905. That same year, Frank Krieg, who homesteaded nearby, would become manager of the Northern Lumber Company's store. He would also be the community's postmaster for many years. D. Fred Charlton, who had designed so many Marquette buildings, was hired to build a two-story hotel with a dining room, offices, and twenty rooms. The building became the social center of the town, hosting dances and social events.

In 1919, a big forest fire between Birch and Big Bay resulted in the blueberry crops being spectacular and the blueberry trains passing through Birch. But by that point, Birch was facing the closure of its mills. A decade before the town had boasted a population of six hundred, but now it quickly declined. By 1920, the post office closed and the remaining residents, except the Kriegs, moved elsewhere. Finally, in 1928 the Kriegs moved to Marquette and Birch became a ghost town.

Logging would continue in the area north of Marquette. Nearby off the Big Bay Road is Remington Road, named for Wallace Remington, a second cousin to my grandfather, who was a logger in the area. George Raish also continued for many years to log this area, along with his son Pete Raish. In 1954, my grandpa, Lester White, would build a house in Florida for Pete Raish, assisted by my great-uncles, Jack and Jolly. I still have the many letters my grandpa wrote at this time, almost daily for four months, home to my grandmother, which inspired the letters between Henry and Beth in *Superior Heritage*. My grandparents so disliked being apart that in the 1960s when Raish wanted the house remodeled, my grandma and mom travelled to Florida with my grandpa and Uncle Jolly while they did the work.

In 1991, Betty Waring published *Birch, Michigan: Gold'n Memories* capturing the memories of several people who recalled Birch, including descendants of the Raish and Krieg families. The memories have lasted longer than the gold or lumber.

GRANOT LOMA

Bird's Eye View of Granot Loma

"Tell us more about Granot Loma," said Kathy. She did not want to talk more about Henry's family; his connection to the Cummings reminded her that Sylvia's sons had come home from the war while Frank had been killed in France.

"Is Granot Loma as grand as everyone says?" asked Thelma. "It sounds like a castle in the wilderness."

"Sort of is, like a castle masquerading as a log cabin," laughed Henry.

He launched into a description of the Kaufman family's magnificent mansion on the shore of Lake Superior. Intended as a summer home, it far outrivaled any cabin in the great North Woods, even those at the exclusive Huron Mountain Club. The Kaufmans had named the cabin for their children by using the first two letters of each of their children's names to spell out Granot Loma. The famous architect, Marshall Fox, had been hired with several assisting architects to design the monstrous getaway. The main sitting room alone was to be a tremendous eighty feet long, forty feet wide, and thirty-six feet high. Henry did not know all the details, but he remembered those dimensions because they were so unfathomable. His parents' entire house could fit into that one room. Stonemasons, plumbers, electricians, all were working constantly, yet completion of the building, already begun a year earlier, was estimated to take another five years. Rumor said the Kaufmans would build several smaller yet ornate cabins in the surrounding woods, one for each of their children, locally known as the "million dollar babies."

"I just can't imagine anything so grand in Upper Michigan," said Thelma, jealous that despite her father's own lumberjack prosperity, he would never be able to afford anything a quarter so splendid.

— The Queen City

Granot Loma is probably the most impressive home on the Lake Superior shoreline. Rumor has it that the Kaufmans were not allowed to become members of the exclusive Huron Mountain Club, apparently because of their Jewish or Indian blood, so Louis G. Kaufman decided to build his own cottage along the lake. By the time he was done, it far

Granot Loma

outshone any cottage at the Huron Mountain Club and any home in Marquette as well. In fact, it is one of the most distinctive homes ever built.

Louis G. Kaufman made his fortune in banking, as well as marrying into money. His wife, Marie, was the daughter of Otto Young, who was worth $20,000,000 in 1900 and had made his fortune in banking, real estate, and jewelry stores. Mr. Young had agreed to give $1,000,000 to each grandchild born, resulting in the Kaufman children being known as the "million dollar babies."

The house was built in 1919 on a granite loma (a flat, broad-topped hill), but the name was spelled as Granot Loma by using the first two letters of each of the first five Kaufman children's names: Graveraet, Ann, Otto, Louis, and Marie. Louis G. Kaufman's other children would be Juliet, Mary, and Jane. Built as a summer lodge, the 20,000 square foot home contains thirty-five rooms, and sixteen additional buildings for its Loma Farms to result in a full 5,180 acres, with 3.6 miles of Lake Superior shoreline. The lodge itself was built of Idaho pine from Oregon. Nearly three hundred workers were involved in the lodge's construction.

The size of everything in the lodge is astounding. The fireplace in the Great Room is large enough to hold four foot logs. The garage was built to hold twenty-four automobiles with room above it for twenty-four male servants. Above the laundry are rooms for twenty-four female servants. Even more impressive is the décor. Rustic Northwoods and Indian motif themes are notable throughout. All the original furniture was handcrafted by imported Norse craftsmen. Beds, chairs, and tables are

Louis Kaufman & Children

made of white pine. The Great Room's chandelier is made from a large pine stump. Birchwood and bark line the bedroom walls.

The Kaufmans had no trouble attracting guests to the lodge when it was finished. George Gershwin himself picked out the grand piano (another would be chosen by Gershwin for Kaufman Auditorium in the Graveraet School). Other famous visitors included Lionel Barrymore, Mary Pickford, Fred Astaire, Cole Porter, Alma Gluck, and Irene Castle. Entire Broadway troupes would come to entertain, complete bands would be transported here so the guests could dance, and a hundred guests at a time would descend on the lodge to go hunting and fishing.

Meanwhile, the Loma Farms flourished with thirty purebred Guernsey cows, two hundred Yorkshire pigs, one hundred fifty cows and race horses, and six hundred chickens. Mr. Kaufman even had polo ponies which he took with him each winter when he went to Florida.

When Mr. Kaufman died in 1942, his son Otto Young Kaufman continued to operate the farm until 1947 when it closed. Mrs. Kaufman died in 1956 in Monte Carlo. In her will, she left bequests to all her daughters and $80,000,000 in trust until the death of her last surviving daughter. The lodge was inherited by her daughter Marie Joan Kaufman and her husband Jack Martin.

Joan Kaufman, as she was more commonly known, had several failed marriages before she married Jack Martin and inherited the lodge. The Kaufmans, being a banking family, naturally came into contact with the Biddle banking family of Philadelphia. Anthony Drexel Biddle would be known as "The Happiest Millionaire" with a film of that name based on his eccentric life. His nephew, George Drexel Biddle, son of his brother Craig Biddle, would be Joan's first husband. They were married in 1926 when George was twenty-three and Joan only nineteen. The marriage lasted several years, resulting in two daughters, Daisy Laura Biddle and Lou Ann Biddle, and a son, Drexel Biddle. Drexel would be born at Granot Loma.

For whatever reason, the Biddle marriage did not last, and Joan would go through a string of husbands, although she would have no more children. She married a man named Polk, divorced him, then married him again. She also married a man named Winterstien who was apparently a bully. Then in 1941, she embarked on her short-lived marriage to W.F. Ladd Jr. Her fifth divorce would be her last one. By 1946, she wed her sixth husband while still only thirty-nine years old.

Jack Martin had started working at Granot Loma in 1938 as a barn boy or laborer, but soon he was travelling with Mr. and Mrs. Kaufman to New York and became close with the family. Like Joan, he had a history of divorces. He divorced his first wife about the time he went to work for the Kaufmans and married his second wife, Mary Lou Ellis, a young girl who worked at the farm. After Joan Kaufman divorced Mr. Ladd, she became jealous of Mary Lou, even calling the police to have her put off the property at one point. In 1946, Jack Martin divorced his second wife and married Joan. Jack and Joan would stay together the rest of their lives—nearly thirty years.

My grandfather, Lester White, worked at Granot Loma in the 1950s and my uncle Jay White accompanied him at times. My family has several photographs which my grandpa took of the farm buildings from this time. During these visits, my Uncle Jay became friends with Joan Kaufman's son, Drexel Biddle. My mother recalls Drexel visiting my grandparents in the 1950s to see my uncle. One year my grandmother gave Drexel an Easter basket, which he really thought was splendid. I guess millionaire's children don't get Easter baskets.

After Joan Kaufman died in 1975, her husband Jack inherited the estate until his death in 1982. Then, Granot Loma was sold outside of the Kaufman family. Already in the 1970s, famed boxer Mohammed Ali had considered purchasing it, and Gerald Ford had thought about buying it to serve as his Michigan-based Western White House. The lodge was bought instead by Mr. L. Tom Baldwin, a bond trader and investor from Chicago for $4,255,000. After Baldwin made extensive repairs, he put it on the market again for $12,000,000 in 1990. When there were no takers, he continued to own the house as a vacation home to get away from the stress of the New York stock exchange. Today, he resides at Granot Loma full-time while operating his business. What better place to work from home?

BIG BAY

The gatekeeper said more, but Roy was too stunned to hear it. Mike Chenoweth was the proprietor of the Lumberjack Tavern in Big Bay. Roy had known him for years. Mike had always been so friendly that even Roy, who was no great socializer, had willingly spent an occasional evening drinking in the bar and enjoying his company. Mike was known throughout the area for having been in the Marine Corps and as a former Marquette policeman. He was widely respected as one of the best shots in Marquette County. Thanks to Mike's successful proprietorship, the Lumberjack Tavern had become a gathering place for the Big Bay locals. When the U.S. Army had recently established a firing point near the Big Bay Lighthouse, Mike's personality had caused the soldiers to flock to his tavern. Roy could not fathom why anyone would wish Mike harm, much less want to kill him.

— Superior Heritage

The little town of Big Bay became famous as a direct result of the murder of Mike Chenoweth in 1952. The ensuing trial, in which Voelker was lawyer to the defendant, inspired Voelker to write, under the pseudonym of Robert Traver, his phenomenally popular novel *Anatomy of a Murder*. The book led to the equally popular film starring Jimmy Stewart and Lee Remick.

Long before the murder, the quiet little community had been prosperous and it would still have been known for its history and famous visitors had the murder never happened.

The town grew up around Lake Independence. In my upcoming novel *Spirit of the North*, Karl Bergmann tells a Paul Bunyan tale about how Paul tried to change the route of the Yellow Dog River, but it instead circled back and formed a lake, resulting in Paul calling it an independent river, thereby giving the lake its name. However, the true story is that the lake was named for William Austin Burt's survey crew which arrived at the lake on Independence Day, July 4, 1845.

From the 1860s onward, the area was logged, and several settlers homesteaded in the surrounding vicinity. Then in 1899, a town and lumber mill were built by the McAffee brothers of Lower Michigan. A bunkhouse and cook shanty and then family homes were constructed, soon followed by a schoolhouse and company store. All the buildings were painted red, so the town became known as Red Town. By that point, the Huron Mountain Club had existed for a decade just west of where the town was built. Traveling to Marquette over land was a two day experience until the first Model-T came to town in 1910 making it a four hour drive. In 1905, the railroad came to connect Big Bay to Marquette. The company town continued its connection to logging and several different mills were built over the years. More details about the town and mills' early history can be found in Betty Waring's *The Story of Lake Independence* and Fred Rydholm's *Superior Heartland.*

In 1943, the Ford Motor Company bought the sawmill and town. The sawmill began to produce the wooden panels for the Ford station wagon, known as the "woodie." Since the Depression the mill had struggled to survive, so Henry Ford's purchase brought back hope to the town, as Ford did for many other Upper Michigan communities where he became involved. Henry Ford had been interested in Big Bay ever since he had built his cottage at the Huron Mountain Club. He did much in the 1940s to remodel the town buildings and make them flourish. He had been a community benefactor even before he bought the town when in 1937, the school burnt down and he sent the township a school bus to carry the children to school in Marquette.

Today, the Lumberjack Tavern, the site of Chenoweth's murder, still stands and is open to the public. Perkins Park is a popular visitor camping and picnic area on Lake Independence. And the Big Bay Lighthouse is a popular destination. Besides lighthouse tours,

Lumberjack Tavern

it functions as a bed and breakfast, but beware the ghosts. The first lighthouse keeper, William Prior, was an unhappy man who hung himself in the surrounding woods and his ghost has supposedly haunted the lighthouse ever since.

The small town of Big Bay is big in heart. The people know the importance of community. A few years ago I was invited to sell my books at the Presbyterian Church's Christmas bazaar and found friendly people happy to spend time together, willing to come out despite cold and bad weather. And they also liked to read. I had a wonderful time visiting with them.

THUNDER BAY INN

After looking about the Thunder Bay Inn and its gift shop, they settled down to supper in the restaurant where Wendy felt it only proper to order the Jimmy Stewart sandwich.

— Superior Heritage

Thunder Bay Inn

If you see nothing else in Big Bay, stop for lunch at the Thunder Bay Inn. This building was originally built in 1911 as a warehouse, store, office, and barbershop for the local lumber companies and their workers. Then in 1940, Henry Ford purchased the building to be a vacation spot and hotel for his executives since it was close to the sawmill as well as the Huron Mountain Club. It was then renamed the Ford Hotel.

In 1959, Otto Preminger decided to film *Anatomy of a Murder* in Marquette County, but rather than use the Lumberjack Tavern where the real murder had occurred, he had the bar and restaurant built onto the Ford Hotel. This bar is featured in numerous scenes in the film and today operates still as a restaurant and bar. The film's popularity eventually resulted in the building being renamed the Thunder Bay Inn in 1986—Thunder Bay was the fictional town in the book and film, but all the locals knew it was really Big Bay. In the 1990s, when John and Wendy visit it in *Superior Heritage,* the bar and restaurant's menu included various items named for Jimmy Stewart and the film's other actors.

Although the inn has changed hands over the years—sadly, you can't order the Jimmy Stewart sandwich any longer—a pleasant fall drive from Marquette to view the autumn colors should always end with lunch at the Thunder Bay Inn and looking at the film memorabilia displayed.

THE HURON MOUNTAIN CLUB

It was late morning when Henry and Theo arrived at the Huron Mountain Club. Henry had only visited Roy once that summer to bring his brother a care package from home, and Roy had given Henry a brief tour of the Club; since then Henry had long anticipated a return to this forbidden land, preserved like a giant garden within the Club's gate, protecting the Upper Peninsula's natural beauty from the encroachments of logging and civilization. Henry imagined the Club looked a lot like Marquette must have in its pioneer days.

— The Queen City

The Huron Mountain Club was established in 1889 by twelve men who signed its articles of association, four from Marquette, the others from the Detroit area. The four Marquette men were Peter White, John M. Longyear, Horatio Seymour, and Ephraim W. Allen. No buildings were built on the property during the first few years, but the club set about acquiring thousands of acres of property, and in 1892, John M. Longyear was elected president and would remain so until his death in 1922.

Huron Mountain Club ~ c. 1900

D. Fred Charlton was hired to design a log clubhouse on the beach at Pine River where the members could gather socially, while each member was to have his own cabin. Membership would be limited to fifty members. The Clubhouse opened in 1893 and the fishing and shooting season began. Mr. Longyear would shoot the first deer in October 1893.

The members began erecting cabins soon after and by 1895 several were completed. Many of those original buildings are still standing today. Membership has remained limited to fifty people, and most memberships have been passed down in the families. Among the Club's more famous members has been Henry Ford, who makes a brief cameo appearance in *The Queen City* when Roy Whitman goes to work at the Huron Mountain Club for the first time in 1926.

Although it is frequently reported that the Club is exclusive and it is impossible to get access inside—there is a gatekeeper—the Club has always hired summer employees from the Big Bay and Marquette area. Numerous of my friends have been employed at the Club as nannies, kitchen help, or trail guides in the summers. In 1995, I went to visit a friend who was working there and we took a rowboat out onto Pine Lake. The visit inspired the scene in *The Queen City* that Henry and Theo make to Roy while he is working at the Club.

Anyone who wants to know more about the Huron Mountain Club should consult Fred Rydholm's *Superior Heartland*. Rydholm was involved at the Huron Mountain Club for over six decades as a worker and later just as a friend to many of the owners. He has written extensively about the Club, including the dolmens found in the Huron Mountains as evidence of European visits to the Great Lakes region in prehistoric times.

Because the Huron Mountains are truly some of the most beautiful and breathtaking scenery in the Midwest, and because this region of Upper Michigan is my home, it would be remiss for me not to mention that the Huron Mountain Club has joined with other local groups to protect the beauty of the Huron Mountains in the fight against a proposed sulfide mine by Kennecott Minerals and its parent company, Rio Tinto, which has the potential, despite its claims of being environmentally friendly, to pollute the Yellow Dog Plains and even Lake Superior. The company proposes, on property it has purchased, to blast under a trout stream and through a sacred rock outcrop called Eagle Rock by the Keweenaw Bay Indian Community, outraging environmentalists, nearby landowners, nature enthusiasts, and the Native American Community. The Department of Environmental Quality and the Department of Natural Resources have been involved in determining the viability of such a mine and its potentially harmful effects despite Kennecott's insistence it provides environmentally friendly mining standards.

While the mine is supported by many as a good source of jobs to the area and mining is promoted as part of Upper Michigan's history, sulfide mining is a different process than the iron

Huron Mountain Club Members ~ c. 1910

and copper mining that has flourished here, and the mine would only operate for about fifteen years, a benefit most of the local residents deem not worth destroying the region's natural beauty or potentially polluting the water, including Lake Superior, the world's largest freshwater lake and source of eighteen-percent of the world's fresh water; should the lake be harmed it would take two centuries for contaminants to cycle through Lake Superior. The sulfide

Huron Mountain Club

mining controversy has raged since 2003, and while at the time of this writing, the downturn in the economy has resulted in Kennecott not making any recent efforts to open the mine, the threat still looms for residents, and many local groups, including the Huron Mountain Club.

In efforts to oppose the mine, Elinor McLennan, president of the Huron Mountain Club, in a letter to Michigan Governor, Jennifer Granholm, noted that Kennecott placed a culvert on the Triple A Road which in April 2005 washed out, sending ninety-eight tons of sediment into the Salmon Trout River, which flows downstream through twenty-thousand acres of the Huron Mountain Club's land. The sand suffocated fish eggs and organisms eaten by fish. McLennan told Granholm,

> *While a stream washout may be a small disaster that can, we hope, be ameliorated, it is an ominous harbinger of a much greater disaster that can not. If Kennecott and the DEQ cannot properly install and manage a simple flow diversion system, how are they to be trusted to operate and oversee a potentially dangerous sulfide mine?*

The beauty of the Huron Mountains deserves our respect. The water that flows through the mountains and the surrounding Yellow Dog Plains, as well as into Lake Superior, is our very source of life. While I know jobs are needed in Upper Michigan, jobs matter little if our water is polluted. Nothing on earth deserves protection more than our water. To learn more about the potential threat of a sulfide mine to the welfare of Upper Michigan and to help save this beautiful land and our freshwater supply for ourselves and the generations to come, visit www.SavetheWildUP.org.

IVES LAKE

Henry and Beth had spent their last few summers at Ives Lake because Henry had taken a seasonal job there as a caretaker for the Huron Mountain Club. Ives Lake had originally been the vacation home of Marquette's pioneer Longyear family. The property included a barn, a small caretaker's house where Henry and Beth stayed, a large red house, and farther along the lakeshore, a stone house where the Longyears had lived. Henry's job was to maintain the property, mow the lawns, and keep the houses prepared for any guests, who were usually college students the Club had given permission to study the geology and minerals available in the Huron Mountains. Between doing repairs, Henry and Beth had plenty of time to go fishing or to take long walks in the woods; sometimes, Roy even came over from his own little cabin just outside the Club property. Being a caretaker was the perfect summer job for a retired man and his wife, and visiting Ives Lake became nearly a summer festival for the rest of the family; there were frequent weekend picnics when Henry's brothers, sisters, nephews, and nieces came up to visit; sometimes Tom and Ellen would take a little vacation to Green Bay or Mackinac Island for a few days, leaving John and Chad at the lake with their grandparents. Whenever the snow began to melt, the entire family became impatient for another summer spent at Ives Lake.

— Superior Heritage

Longyear Family at Ives Lake ~ c. 1910

Ives Lake was named for William Ives, who was the compassman of the William Austin Burt surveying party that discovered the iron ore near present day Negaunee. The property on the south and west sides of Ives Lake would be purchased by John M. Longyear in the 1890s at the same time the Huron Mountain Club was being formed. Longyear had already built a cabin on the

Huron Mountain Club's property but also built a small log bunkhouse on his property along Ives Lake with just two rooms. His children preferred staying at Ives Lake over the Huron Mountain cabin so Longyear decided to build a summer home there for the family. In 1901, he built the Stone House at the rocky edge overlooking the lake. The house is thirty-two feet wide and eighty feet long with a veranda that runs along three sides and out over the lake. The house contains a large living room,

Longyear "Stone House" at Ives Lake

kitchen, pantry, dining room, and eleven upstairs bedrooms. On the nearby land, Longyear planted an orchard of over 150 cherry, apple, pear, and plum trees, and experimented with raising chestnut trees.

After Mrs. Longyear vowed never to set foot in Marquette again because the city and railroad interfered with her plan to build a memorial park to her drowned son Howard, the family would stay at Ives Lake while Mr. Longyear operated his business out of Marquette. In 1908, the Longyears' son-in-law, Alton Roberts, took over managing the farm. A 160 foot barn was built along with two silos and pure-bred Holstein cows were purchased. A milking house was added and the dairy became known as "Emblagaard," Swedish for "elm garden." Alton Roberts also started a chicken farm operation a mile behind the cow barns. In 1918, the Emblagaard Dairy moved operations to the Blemhuber farm. Robert Blemhuber, who had a large farm between Marquette and Big Bay, had been successful in growing remarkable crops despite the short growing season in Upper Michigan. Blemhuber was an ancestor of my Johnson cousins.

The Longyear family retained the property at Ives Lake until the 1960s when it was sold and incorporated into the Huron Mountain Club. After that, a caretaker was hired to keep up the property and open the Stone House and the nearby Guest House for the geology

Author on Stone House Porch

and wildlife students who would come to study from Michigan State University.

From 1971-1976, my grandfather, Lester White, was the caretaker at Ives Lake. He and my grandmother would go up to the lake in the spring and stay through the summer, only coming home occasionally on a week-end. I can vividly remember riding in the car with my mom and brother when we would drive up to Ives Lake to visit my grandparents. We would sing "Here Comes Peter Cottontail"

Ives Lake Guest House

and any other songs my mother cared to teach us along the way. We would come to the gate where the gatekeeper would let us in because he knew us as part of my grandpa's family.

My memories of Ives Lake are fragmented since I was only five when those years ended, but I can recall my cousins playing baseball on the large lawn, having big family picnics with all the cousins, great-aunts, and great-uncles there, swimming in the lake and my cousins collecting clams, and going fishing with my dad—I caught my first fish at Ives Lake. I remember my grandparents' dog, Tramp, swimming in the river, and I remember going in the barn with my grandpa to see the barn swallows.

Author with Grandfather Lester White (above)
Author in front of Caretaker's House

I distinctly remember my fifth birthday party was held here. I remember it mainly because I got a record player, an orange box that folded and locked up like a case. With the record player came several records made by the Peter Pan record company, including a book and record of "Little Red Riding Hood." My cousin, Kenny White, who was born on July 4th, also had his birthday party here one year.

The clearest memory I have is of walking with my grandpa and Great-Aunt Vi behind the barn to the chicken coop, and my brother and I pretending to be Peter Pan as I described in *Superior Heritage*. While I don't remember it myself, my cousins, Leanne and Jaylyn White, who are several years older than me, remember Grandpa feeding Chucky the Woodchuck, whom I also depicted in my novel.

One time, Grandpa took my brother and me into the Stone House where one of the rooms had a table with numerous rocks on it that the geologists must have been studying. Grandpa told us we could each have one of the rocks. I still have mine today, a curious two shaded brown rock like none I have ever seen since. Someday I will find a geologist who will tell me what it is.

My family has hundreds of photographs of summers spent at Ives Lake including fishing parties, picnics, and Grandpa and me on the riding lawn mower. The child's mind is highly impressionable so perhaps that is why I remember this beautiful magical place so well.

The visits to Ives Lake ended on a sad note when my mother received a phone call that her grandmother, Barbara McCombie White, had died. I remember I was coloring in a color-by-number book when the call arrived. I didn't understand, but I remember my mother crying and her telling me to go back to my coloring while she got ready to go. We had to drive up to Ives Lake where my grandpa was—he had no phone there—so my mom could tell him his mother had died. The two events may not have been related, but my great-grandmother's death seemed like the end of the Ives Lake summers to me. It was also the end of an era in another way—my great-grandmother would be the only person I would know who was born in the nineteenth century, 1885, to be exact, and being at Ives Lake was equally like being in another era.

PART VII:
NORTH MARQUETTE

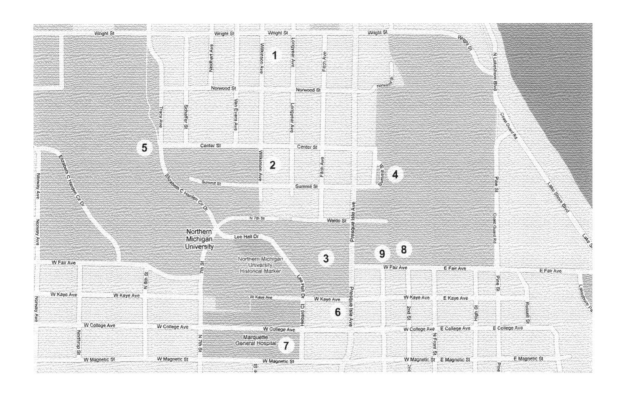

1. 1820 Wilkinson Ave. ~ Jay Earle White Home
2. 1622 Wilkinson Ave. ~ Lester White Home
3. Northern Michigan University
4. The Superior Dome
5. Olson Library
6. St. Michael's
7. Marquette General Hospital
8. Memorial Field
9. The Palestra

WILKINSON AVENUE, THE WHITE HOUSE, & MY NINE MUSES

At the beginning of this book I talked about how I fictionalized my family's history in my novels, but I ended that section with my great-grandparents, Jay Earle White and Barbara Margaret McCombie. The rest of the family story is largely a North Marquette story. My great-grandparents had nine children, born between 1905 and 1921. Jay Earle was a carpenter during that time, building houses, but the family also owned a farm in Cherry Creek until the 1930s when they moved to Wilkinson Avenue in Marquette.

My grandfather, Lester Earle White, started building a house at 1810 Wilkinson Avenue about 1932 or 1933. It would become his and my grandmother's home once they were married in 1934 and my great-grandpa, John Molby, would also live with them for the first couple of years until my grandma gave birth to my Uncle Jay. In 1938, my great-grandparents would build a home next door at 1820 Wilkinson Avenue on property my grandfather gave to them. My Great-Uncle Jolly told me in those days how many of the streets in the area were not yet paved, and how he would go down to Presque Isle Avenue, three blocks east, to catch the streetcar. After their parents died, my great-uncles, Kit, Jolly, and later Frank, all lived in this house until they had all passed on and it was sold out of the family in 2008.

Across the street from my great-grandparents at 1825 Wilkinson lived my great-grandmother's brother Wallace McCombie and his family. Around the corner on Norwood Street

Jay and Barbara White with children on 50th Wedding Anniversary 1953. Left to Right: Sadie, Roland, Barbara, Frank, Jay, Clifton, Barbara, William, Lester, Ione. Missing: Viola, who sent the bride and groom dolls in her place.

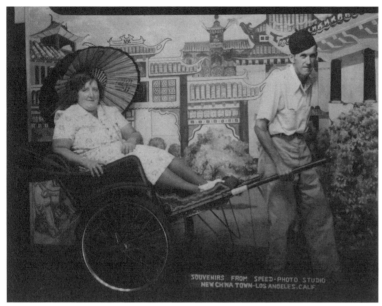

Grandma & Grandpa White in New China Town (Los Angeles, CA) ~ 1948

lived Barbara's parents, William Forrest and Elizabeth May McCombie, although not for long since they both died in 1938. At 1733 Wilkinson, my grandpa's sister, Barbara and her husband, Harold Specker, built a home.

In 1947, my grandparents sold their home and moved to California, but they were back in Marquette by 1949 and built a new home at 1622 Wilkinson Avenue. This house would be "Grandpa and Grandma's house" to me until 1993 when it was sold the year after my grandma's death.

In 2005, my Great-Aunt Sadie, who had been living in Maryland until her second husband passed away, returned to Marquette and bought a home across from her sister, Barbara, and down the block from her brothers so she would be near her siblings. Today, Aunt Sadie is the last of the White and McCombie family living on Wilkinson Avenue.

Having the last name of White has some advantages. At my great-grandparents' house, the telephone was always answered, "The White House" which always surprised several callers. My mother used to tell people she grew up in "The White House."

Everyone thinks his or her family is remarkable, and I guess I'm no different. Despite my last name being different, I was blessed to grow up as part of the White family. My grandpa and his brothers and sisters were always there, forming a large, extended, and loving family. With the exception of Great-Uncle Jack, they all lived well into their eighties and nineties

Lester White & Crew Building House at 1622 Wilkinson Ave. ~ 1949

so I had plenty of time with them, although I wish I could have had more. The love they all had for each other and extended to everyone else in the family, kept us all close—to this day I stay in touch with many of my distant cousins as a result. These nine children always spoke of their parents with great love and respect. In one of his letters, Great-Uncle Jack calls his parents the "salt of the earth." In a poem she wrote, Great-Aunt Vi said, "I won't give up 'cause I'm a White." They were all strong, all survivors. None of them ever became rich or famous, but they were all highly creative and artistic. They are like my nine muses. I cannot begin to do them all justice but will just say a few words about each one here.

Lester Earle White (1905—1987)

My grandpa, Lester Earle White, was the oldest and therefore the "big brother" to the rest. He was named for Miss Lester, the nurse my great-grandmother had in the hospital. He was born premature and about the size of a kitchen knife. Consequently, he suffered with health problems throughout his life. He was a workaholic, but when he got sick, he would be laid up in bed for days.

My grandfather, as the oldest child, helped to support his family. At fourteen, when he graduated from eighth grade, he went to work with his father. In time he would own his own salvage and scrap metal business and was known as Haywire White in the 1930s. However, most of his life he spent as a carpenter building houses, cabinets, furniture, fences, and anything else anyone needed. Many people said he was the best carpenter in Marquette and if nothing else, his work was always sturdy. He retired when he was seventy, but he never really retired. Until a couple of weeks before he died, he was daily in his workshop putting in more than an eight-hour day making tables, lazy susans, benches, mirrors, and anything else he thought he could sell. My brother and I spent many hours in his woodshop with him and to this day I have many of the little houses, wagons, and other toys he made for us.

Like Henry in *Superior Heritage*, my grandfather died as a result of his flannel shirt catching on fire one morning when he went to light his woodstove so he could start working. Although he was flown to the Milwaukee Burn Center, after two weeks his body could not

Lester and Grace White with Daughter Nancy & Son Jay ~ 1953

take the pain and his kidneys failed.

Other than his work, I remember my grand-father most for his kindness. I wanted to be with him every minute I could. I always wanted to sit next to him at the table, and I always had to go with him to help with his craft sales. He never complained about having me around, although he didn't like me getting dirty or getting crumbs on the floor. He was always giving my brother and me money or treats, as did my grandmother, and often, he would stick dollar bills between paper plates at supper so we would discover them later when we cleared the table.

The scenes in *Superior Heritage* of Henry Whit-man feeding the animals at Ives Lake are all based on my grandfather. He would have chipmunks come into his woodshop, jump into his hand, and take peanuts from him. One time he took care of a pigeon with a broken wing in his shop until it was able to fly again. He always had peanuts to feed to the squirrels and fed all the pigeons even when

Grandpa Ready for 4th of July Parade ~ c. 1930

the neighbors complained. Until late in his life he always had a dog, and after, when I had my dog, Benji, he would tell us we weren't allowed to visit unless we brought Benji with us.

Grandpa with Chipmunk ~ 1971

Grandpa did everything he could for his family, including giving his broth-ers and brother-in-laws work, and buy-ing the property for his parents where their house on Wilkinson Avenue would be built.

There isn't a day that goes by that I don't think about my grandpa and my grandma. They were the happiest married couple I ever saw. When my grandpa went to Florida to work for three months, my grandparents wrote to each other almost every single day, and my mother remembers when Grandpa came home, how he jumped out of the truck and ran into the house to see Grandma. I'm sure they are happy together in heaven. I don't think I will ever stop missing them.

Clifton "Kit" Adrian White (1906—2002)

Uncle Kit was a character if there ever was one in our family. He got the nickname "Kit" because as a youngster he was obsessed with Kit Carson. Uncle Kit had a vivid imagination to the point where he sometimes believed his own stories. He always had stories to tell me about his youth including the Indian Princess who was six feet across in the shoulders and so tall her feet dragged on the ground when she rode a horse. She was supposedly guarding my uncle's gold mine somewhere out west, which was hidden behind a waterfall.

When he got older, Uncle Kit became convinced there was a woman he had known as a young man who now lived in Fargo, North Dakota and they were having an affair.

He would sneak away from the rest of the family—he was living in his parents' house with his brother Jolly at this point—and go down to the bus station, hop the bus, ride out to Fargo, stay a few days, then come back again. One time when my Aunt Barb called the hotel where he stayed, he answered the phone. The owner said he just came and sat and played cards for a few days then went home, although he would have some amorous stories of his adventures he would tell me when he returned.

When Uncle Kit was about ninety years old, he had to go to Norlite Nursing Home. He was there for several years until his death. During that time, everyday at least one of his brothers or sisters made sure to go visit him. He received wonderful care at Norlite, and his siblings all became friends with the staff there, which was a benefit to them when they also ended up going to Norlite. Although Uncle Kit

Uncles Kit, Jolly & Frank at Norlite Nursing Home ~ 2001

was always a bit different, his family loved him and looked after him throughout his life. I remember going to visit him at Norlite with my mom and Aunt Barb. One time, we left him when it was time for his nap. Aunt Barb gave him four kisses and then reminded him, "Do you remember why you get four kisses? One from me. One from Vi. One from Ione, and one from Sadie." By that point, Aunt Vi had died, but they never told Uncle Kit so as not to upset him. I can't say enough about the love these brothers and sisters had for one another—they were a sense of security and stability to me until well into my adult years.

William "Jack" John White (1908—1977)

Uncle Jack died of lung cancer when I was only six years old. I only have one memory of him calling me "Tiger" when I came in the door at Aunt Sadie's house. In *The Marquette Trilogy*, I had to keep the number of characters manageable so Henry Whitman, based on my grandfather, only has two brothers and two sisters. Roy in the novel is mostly based on Uncle Jack. The events in the novel are fictional—especially Roy's love for Chloe (although he never did marry)—but Uncle Jack did serve in World War II, being stationed in England in the air force. More specifically, some of the "different" ideas Roy has about life and religion were inspired by my learning that Uncle Jack was a Rosicrucian—I had studied the Rosicrucians as part of my doctoral dissertation on nineteenth century British Gothic novels, so to find out my uncle was a Rosicrucian intrigued me. From some of his letters that remain, Uncle Jack clearly believed in a spiritual world as well as telepathy. My cousin, Piddy Lopez, recalls that he could lay his hands on people when they had a headache and make it go away. What a loss that I did not know him better.

Roland "Jolly" Adrian White (1910—2007)

Uncle Jolly got his nickname because he was a jolly baby. I never once heard him called Roland. In fact, Aunt Sadie told me she remembered him once telling a teacher his name was Roland and her demanding why he had said that when he knew his name was Jolly.

Uncle Jolly often worked as a carpenter with his father and my grandfather. He also served in World War II and in his later years told us stories about driving jeeps for the officers and how he had been in France and Germany. He was interested in trapping and taxidermy and also in rocks. When I was a kid, he would sell polished rocks at the craft shows while his sisters sold their crafts and my grandpa sold his carpentry work.

Uncle Jolly also was a huge source of information to me about family history and had many stories to tell me about his parents and cousins. Although he built a house on the Big Bay Road, he mostly lived at home with his parents and took good care of his mother at the end of her life. He then lived with his brother Kit and later brother Frank. In 2006 when I published *Iron Pioneers*, he insisted on buying a copy although he could not see well enough to read it. My Aunt Barb then read it out loud to him and Uncle Frank. He was in good health until just a few days before he died. He went to Norlite in November of 2006, but more to keep his younger brother Frank company than because he was sick.

Uncle Jolly inspired several scenes in my novels, most notably the scene in *Superior Heritage* where Roy walks through the forest at Presque Isle with his great-nephews. Uncle Jolly probably knew more about trees, animals, and nature in general than anyone else I've ever met. I wish I had listened to him more on those walks.

Viola "Vi" Margaret Anna White Lopez (1912—1997)

Today, I can't say I have a favorite great-aunt or great-uncle, but when I was a child, my brother and I both would have agreed that Aunt Vi was our favorite because she was the adult who most appreciated us as children. She and Grandpa were the only ones who would get down on the floor and play with the kids. Aunt Vi lived in Louisiana because she had moved there to work and eventually married and stayed there to raise her family of two daughters, Juanita (Bug) and Lolita (Piddy), a stepson Richard, and an adopted daughter, Mary. Her husband, Uncle Charles, owned a piano store that Aunt Vi helped to run, and later she operated a doll hospital store.

Every summer, Aunt Vi would come home to visit, an event to which everyone looked forward. She was a creative, artistic woman who was constantly busy making something— afghans, quilts, Christmas decorations, dolls and dollhouses, paintings, and anything else

**The Author's Mother &
Aunt Vi ~ 1953**

imaginable. One time, she had even been hired to make all the bonnets for a film *The Belles of Cajun,* although I don't believe the film ever made it to the big screen. She was always ready to share what she knew with others, and it was a treat for my brother and me to join her in making craft projects because she always knew how to entertain us. Once at Ives Lake, she made me a toy princess out of a bottle and construction paper, and when

Aunt Vi, the Author, & His Brother Danny

I said I needed a prince to go with the princess, she sent me a prince paper doll she decorated with sequins and other little fake jewels. I think the bottle princess broke, but I still have the prince, as well as a jigsaw puzzle she made me and several Christmas ornaments. For my brother, she made a wooden walking witch that he continues to treasure.

Aunt Vi had a terrific sense of humor. She loved to write humorous letters to companies about what was wrong with their products and her difficulties with them. She also liked to make crank phone calls to relatives. Once she called my second cousin Nan Rushton when Nan was operating her tailoring business and insisted she wanted Nan to sew her a horse blanket. Another time she called to ask me whether I sold potatoes.

She liked to write stories and poetry, and she encouraged me in my own writing, telling me how beautifully I put my words together.

The Whitman sisters in my novels are not based on any specific aunts, but Ada moves to Louisiana in the novels, just as Aunt Vi did. Aunt Vi also was the maid of honor for my grandparents' wedding, a role similar to Eleanor in *The Marquette Trilogy.*

Barbara Alma White Specker (1915—2007)

Aunt Barb was married to Harold Specker, who passed away before I was born. She kept herself busy, first working at St. Luke's Hospital, and then later raising her family of four sons, Ron, Terry, Bob, and Jack, and three daughters, Gail, Sandra (Pudgy), and Liz. She was a loving mother, a faithful Christian, and never one to criticize her family. She always made time for everyone in her family even when her family kept growing with grandchildren and great-grandchildren. About the year 2000, she informed me she had over fifty descendants, and the number has grown considerably since then.

My mom always took Aunt Barb, my grandma, and Aunt Sadie shopping on Wednesdays. Aunt Barb was the star shopper and we always used to joke about how she knew how to recycle her money because she would buy something, then return it the next week, buy something else, and then return that.

One of my favorite memories of her is once when I was a teenager I tagged along on one of these shopping trips primarily so I could have lunch with them at Ponderosa. I had a little problem making my ice cream sundae that day, putting more ice cream in the dish than I should have, and once the toppings were included on top, I had an overflowing mess by the time I got back to the table. For the next twenty years, Aunt Barb would tease me about the piles of napkins I used to clean up that mess.

I also distinctly remember the large family parties at Aunt Barb's house. During my childhood, Thanksgiving was always spent at her house, while Christmas was at Aunt Sadie's, and New Year's at my grandparents. Because of Aunt Barb's huge family, the house would be packed with people, but there was always room and food for everyone. She also never forgot anyone at Christmas—even though it must have meant buying a hundred Christmas presents once she included all her descendants, siblings, nephews, nieces, great-nephews, and great-nieces. Until the end she was devoted to her family and she always made time to spend with all of them.

Sadie Eleanor White Johnson Merchant (1917—present)

Aunt Sadie, soon after she graduated from Graveraet High School, married Lowell Johnson (his brother Gerald would marry her first cousin Marjorie Woodbridge) and they had one daughter Rose Marie, who then married Tom Rushton, son of Judge Carroll and Louise Rushton. Rose Marie and Tom are the parents of Nanette (who contributed information to the historical home section of this book) and Daniel Rushton.

Besides raising a family, Aunt Sadie worked for many years at the Singer store, both downtown and then later when the store was located in the Marquette Mall. I remember visiting her at work at the mall just before she retired. She sewed and did numerous crafts all her life just like her sisters. She never lacked for activities to keep her busy.

Although she would eventually divorce her first husband, Aunt Sadie remained good friends with him and cared for him when he was dying. Then in 1989, she eloped by moving to Maryland with her husband's widowed first cousin, H. Clyde Merchant. They were married on her seventy-second birthday. She then lived in Maryland, but returned home to visit each summer with Uncle Clyde for a couple of months, staying at Aunt Barb's house. After Uncle Clyde passed away, Aunt Sadie returned to Marquette and bought a house in 2005 across the street from Aunt Barb. She came home to spend time with her brothers and sister in their last years. When Uncle Jolly, Uncle Frank, and Aunt Barb were all in Norlite Nursing Home in 2007 she visited them every day.

In 2007, Aunt Sadie had an enormous ninetieth birthday party at the First Baptist Church attended by hundreds of friends and relatives from all across the country. Since then, she has continued to live on her own, staying busy doing crafts, including sewing, making afghans, and creating beaded angel Christmas decorations. She also continues to be very active in her church.

Aunt Sadie has been my greatest source of genealogy information, willingly sharing old family letters, obituaries, and family photographs with me. Her vivid memory can recall events that happened in her childhood, and historical moments such as when Amelia Earhart came to Marquette, as if these events happened just yesterday. She is a true treasure to her family, someone who has always put her family first.

Ione Margaret Hagen (1919—present)

Aunt Ione and her husband, Claude Hagen, lived in Washington State, so I did not get to know her as well as my grandfather's other siblings. Nevertheless, she is a sweet lady and I have always enjoyed her visits to Marquette and the couple of visits I made to Washington with my family. Like her sisters, she has constantly been busy making a variety of crafts, including plastic canvas Christmas decorations. When well into her eighties, she still walked several miles a day.

Aunt Ione raised five children, Marge, Perry, Steve, Lon, and Ron, and was a devoted wife to her husband, especially in his later years when he could barely get around. They were married for sixty-nine years when he passed away in 2009. Today she is enjoying her recent move to an assisted living home in East Wenatchee, Washington where she is making new friends.

Frank Byron White (1921—2007)

Uncle Frank, like his brothers, Jack and Jolly, served in World War II, but unlike them, he was stationed in the Pacific. He was proud of his war service and that he had once been able to shake General Douglas MacArthur's hand.

Uncle Frank worked as a carpenter, and although he lived in Lower Michigan for a few years, most of his life he resided in Marquette, or nearby Harvey and Deerton. He had one daughter and three stepdaughters. Among other projects, he was involved in building the Lakeview Arena and also the Presque Isle Power Plant. He told me about being let down by ladder from a helicopter to work on the power plant's smokestacks.

Uncle Frank married Hazel Wagar and was the father to Judy and stepfather to Hazel's daughter Sharon. After Frank and Hazel divorced, Frank married Midge and acquired three stepdaughters, Sharon, Beverly, and Judy. After Aunt Midge died, Uncle Frank moved in with his bachelor brothers, Kit and Jolly, and did the cooking and helped them to keep house. He suffered from several health problems in his later years but was always in a cheerful mood. Among the many stories he told me, one of the most memorable was of how he traveled to Marquette on snowshoes from the family farm in Cherry Creek as the Blizzard of '38 was letting up so he could visit his mother who was staying at her parents' house on Norwood Street, and then he snowshoed back to the farm—the distance would have been at least eight miles each way. He would have been sixteen at the time.

*

Wilkinson Avenue has been practically as much my neighborhood as any place I've actually lived. In summer, my brother and I often spent the day at our grandparents, helping Grandpa in his woodshop while Mom took Grandma shopping. When Grandpa was dying in the hospital, my brother and I stayed with Grandma for two weeks at her house and after that I stayed over many nights to keep Grandma company. My grandparents' house is the home I have known best after my parents' house. I can still hear its furnace turning on and the clocks ticking. I can smell the warm dusty air from the furnace, Grandma's soapy smelling bathroom, and the wood shavings and sawdust in grandpa's shop.

On those summer days when my brother and I would stay at Grandpa and Grandma's, Grandpa would spoil us by letting us eat cereal for lunch—but not any cereal—Rice Krispies with ice milk on top of it and plenty of sugar. Our dog, Benji, always joined us—Grandpa had him trained to sit with him in his chair and paw at his arm whenever he wanted a bite of Grandpa's bologna sandwich. Until I was nine, we only had three channels on TV, but Grandpa and Grandma had cable, so Grandma would let us sit and watch cartoons on Detroit's TV50 without complaining that she could not watch what she wanted.

Some of the best memories I have are of the large family parties. Grandma always held a party on New Year's Day for all the family. Grandpa's birthday on February 27th seemed like a bright moment in the dead of winter, and Grandma's birthday on April 1st, April Fool's Day no less, was a sure sign spring was almost here. The house was always packed on these occasions—one time Grandma had twenty-seven people for dinner. My brother and I and usually my mom and maybe Aunt Sadie, would sit in the kitchen, but I never felt left out. And I remember so well all the food—huge bowls of mashed potatoes and sweet potatoes, turnips and rutabagas, a plate of ham and little dishes of pickles and olives and cheese and rolls, and of course, birthday cake or pies depending on the occasion. After the food would be the opening of birthday presents and passing around of birthday cards, and then often a game of Rummy. I did not play cards but usually sat content in a corner reading a book. I am not doing justice to these parties—it wasn't so much what happened at them, but that everyone was there—together, the house packed, the windows steamed up from food cooking, seeing the mound of winter coats laid on the beds, the smell of car exhaust creeping in with the sharp winter cold as people departed in cheery moods, and just the general sense of warmth and companionship in the dead of winter. The best thing I can say is that I wish I could go back and experience one of those parties again.

Pictures often speak better than words so I have inserted a couple here. It was a different world then. That generation has passed away now, the generation that went from no electricity into the computer age, some say the greatest generation.

NORTHERN MICHIGAN UNIVERSITY

The old normal school was now Northern Michigan University with an enrollment of nine thousand students. Marquette had become a true college town, and with the decline of the iron ore industry, the university became a major player in Marquette's survival.

— Superior Heritage

Northern Michigan University had humble beginnings.

As early as 1875, Peter White, as a member of the Michigan legislature, proposed a Normal School be placed in Marquette. Nearly a quarter of a century later, he saw his dream come true when Northern Normal School was established in 1899. A "normal school" was a facility where teachers were trained. The original school would provide training to elementary and secondary teachers to receive two-year degrees and lifetime teaching certificates. Since teaching was one of the few professions open to women at the time, the majority of students were female.

The first buildings were erected where the Cohodas Administration Building is today. The property was donated by the Longyear family, and the original complex consisted of Longyear Hall, the Peter White Science building, and the Library Wing.

While those first buildings were being built, the first classes, beginning September 19, 1899, were held in the City Hall on Washington Street. Six teachers oversaw classes for thirty-two students. The first president, Dwight B. Waldo, would himself teach classes to save the school money.

President Waldo would only remain at Northern a short time. By 1903, he had moved to Kalamazoo, Michigan, where he became the first president of Western

Longyear Hall ~ c. 1907

Michigan University. The two schools over the years would often be thought of as sister schools. I would later attend Western to earn my Ph.D. in literature, and I knew several other students who also went to Western from Northern. Later in the 1990s and early 2000s, Judy Bailey, like Waldo, would serve as president at NMU and then later at WMU.

President Waldo was succeeded by President James H.B. Kaye. President Kaye was born in England and his family was said to have been friends with famous English authors including Alfred Tennyson and Charles Dickens; ironically, they happen to be my favorite poet and favorite novelist. During Kaye's presidency, from 1904-1923, the school grew to 600 students. In 1915, an administrative building was constructed that would connect Longyear Hall and the Peter White Science building. This structure would be named Kaye Hall for Northern's president. It was also the site of many theatrical performances at the school and is perhaps the most fondly remembered building in Northern's history. My moth-

Kaye Hall

er recalls seeing plays here when she was a student in the 1950s, and my Great-Aunt Sadie remembers a Christmas program at Kaye Hall that included live camels walking up the aisles.

In 1928, Northern Normal School became Northern State Teachers College, and the first courses for graduate education were established with a Master's Degree program. In 1940, the school's name changed to Northern Michigan College of Education, and then in 1963, another name change resulted in Northern Michigan University.

As a teaching school, Northern also had on its grounds the J.D. Pierce School where classes were taught by regular teachers from K-12 but Northern's student teachers were able to be trained there as well. My mother, uncle, and many of their cousins attended J.D. Pierce, which functioned as a school until the 1960s.

Northern's student population increased along with the campus' growth. By the time I attended Northern from 1989-1995 to earn my bachelor and master's degrees, the population was about 10,000 students. While there have been some lulls since then, notably after K.I. Sawyer Air Force Base closed, the university continues to grow and thrive. In the last decade or so, NMU's laptop initiative ensured every student have a computer and the campus has become one of the nation's most wireless—clear signs that not only can Upper Michigan keep up with but often surpass the rest of the world.

Northern may be more isolated than most schools, but its presence has helped to make Marquette arguably the most cultural and cosmopolitan city in Upper Michigan. The school's distance from the major metropolitan centers also allows many students to flourish in a more relaxed learning environment. Even so, Northern's athletes know how to compete. In 1991, NMU's hockey team won the national championship, and the school's United States Olympic Training Center has been the home to champion Olympians in speed-skating and boxing.

In 1992, the J.D. Pierce School was torn down, and in 1993, Longyear Hall, the last of the original campus buildings, was demolished to great consternation among the community. The cost to renovate Longyear Hall was considered too expensive to preserve it. In *Superior Heritage*, the letter John Vandelaare writes to protest the demolition of the historic building is an actual letter I wrote, but my letter and many others had little effect on the final decision. Ironically, within weeks after the demolition, Northern announced it would begin locating historical places on the campus to prepare for its centennial celebrations.

Northern has brought in an impressive list of commencement speakers over the years, including Lloyd C. Douglas, author of *The Robe,* in 1922, future president George H.W. Bush in 1974 while he was Chair of the Republican Committee, and in 1993, when I graduated with my bachelor's degree, the controversial novelist priest, Andrew M. Greeley, who wisely told a story rather than give a speech; it was the most memorable commencement address I've ever heard. Many famous people have visited and spoken at the university, including Vice-President Al Gore, former president Gerald Ford, controversial author Ann Coulter, and famous poet Gwendolyn Brooks. Famous alumni include Michigan State Head Football Coach Tom Izzo, San Francisco 49ers Head Football Coach Steve Mariucci, and Starbucks CEO Howard Schultz—NMU as a result had the first Starbucks store in Upper Michigan located in the University Center.

In recent years, the university has continued to grow and expand its offerings while staying up to date with the twenty-first century. Skywalks and underground tunnels now connect buildings which during my undergraduate years could only be accessed by walking outside, often during a stormy winter day. The new Seaborg Center and the fountains in front of it are truly impressive new structures, and the Hedgcock Building has been beautifully renovated.

While I cannot give the entire history of Northern Michigan University here, Miriam Hilton's *Northern Michigan University: The First Seventy-Five Years* is an excellent and detailed source for the university's early history.

What follows is based on my own memories as a student at Northern—what were probably the six happiest years of my life.

THE SUPERIOR DOME

"You're mother's right," said Eleanor. "We can't take our safety for granted anymore. Marquette isn't like when I was young and everyone knew everyone else. Why there's something like twenty-five thousand people living here now and that big sports building they're putting up—the world's largest wooden dome or whatever they claim it is, it's only going to attract more people here."

"I doubt it," said Tom. "No one's going to come all the way up here to see that dome."

"They're only building the dome," said Ellen, "because NMU is going to be an Olympic training center, and they want to impress the governor so he'll give the school more money."

"It just makes me sick to think what that dome and the Olympics will attract to this area," said Eleanor. "All those kids training for Olympic boxing will be coming up from Detroit, nothing but a bunch of undesirables from the ghettos. They'll only bring trouble with them."

— Superior Heritage

Superior Dome

The Superior Dome was controversial from its start when it was first proposed in the late 1980s.

People claimed it was built to impress the governor so the university would receive more money, including to fund the new Olympic training program. Many people felt the nearly $3,000,000 price tag was a waste of money, and people mocked the project and wanted to name it "The Yooper Dome." Nevertheless, it was built and opened in the fall of 1991. While impressive from a distance, up close one wonders about the rather messy looking grey roof. The building was supposed to have a wooden appearance, but from early on, the Dome leaked and the rubber material had to be placed over it. Despite the leak, on May 1, 1993, commencement services were held in the Dome for the first time. I was part of that first graduating class.

The Superior Dome replaced the old football field, a huge advantage since half of Northern's football season is played when snow is likely to fall, so games could now be played inside. The Dome, and later the Berry Events Center, built for hockey, also shifted community activities away from the Lakeview Arena. Today, numerous recreation and other shows are held in the Dome. Every year, I can be found there the first weekend of December at the TV6 Christmas Craft Show, the largest craft show in Upper Michigan, where I sign and sell my books as thousands of visitors stream through the Dome.

After twenty years, it's fair to say the Dome has become one of the most recognizable sites in Marquette and part of its history. Despite how people felt about it when it was first proposed, I doubt anyone would part with it now.

OLSON LIBRARY

After his class that day, John had an hour to spend at the library doing research for his paper on James Joyce's A Portrait of the Artist as a Young Man *before meeting Frank for lunch downstairs at Bookbinders. Throughout Olson Library, snuck in between bookshelves, were arrangements of rectangular shaped tables, each table with four chairs around it. John knew these study sections best by the colors of the metal bookshelves that surrounded them. His favorite section was across the aisle from the volumes of Joyce criticism, in a dark area of the library where the fluorescent lights were not too bright and the bookshelves had metal book holders the same shade of shamrock green as Ireland, where John and Joyce's ancestors had lived. Here John usually sat to study.*

— Superior Heritage

Olson Library was built in 1956 and named for longtime librarian Lydia Olson. The four story building is built into a hill so that only two levels are visible on the building's west side while three appear on the east side and another level underground where Public Radio 90 and Public TV 13 are located. The first floor used to be the academic mall while the upper two floors are actually the library.

Half of my undergraduate years must have been spent in the library, when I was not in class. Like John, my favorite section was on the top floor near the British literature section—it made most sense to sit there as I did research for my English papers. Here I first read many of the classics from British, French, American, and Arabic literature as well as studied history, sociology, geography, chemistry, and a number of other disciplines. I must have

Olson Library

read hundreds of books here. Many papers on topics ranging from Simone de Beauvoir's metaphysical novels to the Father and Son theme in James Joyce's *Ulysses*, and the use of Celtic mythology in Coleridge's poem "Christabel" were researched and drafted by hand here (then later typed up at home on my computer in the days before laptops). They were happy and exciting days since I was naturally inclined to being a scholar and chose to study literature over creative writing because I wanted to learn from the very best writers who had ever lived. In those days as I discovered great literature, I felt as stunned and speechless as the poet John Keats when he first read Homer:

> *Then felt I like some watcher of the skies*
> *When a new planet swims into his ken;*
> *Or like stout Cortez when with eagle eyes*
> *He star'd at the Pacific—and all his men*
> *Look'd at each other with a wild surmise—*
> *Silent, upon a peak in Darien.*

BOOKBINDERS

John held the table while Holly and Frank stood in line. Maggie was the manager of Bookbinders, and the students who worked there loved her. Today, she was in a grand mood fussing and joking at them. John listened to the banter. When Frank got to the register, Maggie told him he needed to eat more—maybe he and John should switch meals for once. Holly smiled, glad to be in a friendly environment. She had been lonely at U of M, but now, she hoped John would be her friend again.

Frank and Holly returned to the table. In a couple minutes, Maggie shouted, "Nachos and a chocolate shake" and John went up to gather his lunch.

—Superior Heritage

To take a break from studying in the library, I could always run downstairs to the Bookbinders coffee shop. Most days I met my friends here for lunch. Maggie Britton was the manager who oversaw a host of student employees with whom she was always joking. My friends and I seemed to live on nachos with heated cheese sauce. Most days that was lunch for us at Bookbinders, and on days when we splurged, we would add a chocolate or strawberry shake—perhaps not the most nutritious food but typical college student fare.

When I left NMU, I missed those nachos and shakes. One summer, while I was writing my doctoral dissertation and home in Marquette visiting, I went to Olson Library to do some research and planned that day to have lunch at Bookbinders. By then the restaurant had moved to another part of the academic mall and Maggie had long since retired. I went up to the counter to order nachos and a shake and was told they didn't have either in the summer. I settled for mozzarella sticks and a coke. I sat eating my solitary lunch and missing my old college friends. It was a bittersweet experience.

THE ENGLISH DEPARTMENT

Below the library in the academic mall were the offices for many of the professors, including most of the English Department until early 1995 when the department moved to Gries Hall. In 1993, as I completed my bachelor's degree in English, I did not know what to do. My plan had been to write novels while earning my bachelor's degree and end up published and famous by the time I graduated so I could begin my career as an author. While I did write and send my manuscripts out for publication, I was not successful finding a publisher. During these years, I completed writing the first draft of *The Only Thing That Lasts* which I had begun in high school as well as the original version of *Narrow Lives* and another long-winded novel that remains in a drawer.

Upon graduation, and still not a famous author, I decided I would get a Master's Degree, and when I learned that being a teaching assistant paid $4,500, I was thrilled since I had spent most of my undergraduate years working at McDonalds and NMU's Writing Center for minimum wage which over a year had averaged about the same as the teaching assistant wage. And better yet, the teaching assistants got a gigantic raise that semester, so I felt quite prosperous making $6,000 a year and living at home while I earned a Master's Degree. After a few weeks of teaching, I found I liked it and decided I would get a Ph.D. and become an English professor—again, until I became a famous author.

As a teaching assistant, I was given my own little office down a hallway off the academic mall along with about a dozen other new teaching assistants (T.A.s) who were working on their M.A. degrees. We dubbed our new office space T.A. Alley and set

The Author at His Desk in T.A. Alley

about becoming great friends. Some of my best and longest friendships began during those two years.

I have nothing but good things to say about the education I received at Northern Michigan University, and especially in the English Department. And beyond the stellar professors I had, what I most appreciated and failed to find later at other universities was a real camaraderie among the students and professors. I've been in other English departments where

Jill, Larry, & Chris in TA Alley

you walk down the hall and all the doors are closed, but at Northern, the professors' doors were always open. Most of them spent several hours a day in their offices and were always available to their students. Professors and students passed each other in the halls, we all knew each other, and we always talked to one another. Even if I did not have a class with a professor, I never felt I couldn't talk to him or her. While I was just a graduate student, nevertheless, I felt accepted as part of the department and encouraged in my teaching and academic goals. I saw none of the snobbery or competitiveness among graduate students or professors I unfortunately witnessed elsewhere in academia. I don't think I could have had a more fulfilling start to my career than being part of that supportive, learning environment, and while I have long since left academia, those years remain frequent and pleasant memories.

I did not party a lot in college. Yes, I did occasionally hang out at the Shamrock with my friends, and we had parties at friends' apartments, and the camaraderie added a great deal to the general happiness of those years, but part of what made me so happy was the learning environment. My classes at Northern fulfilled my intellectual needs without making me feel stressed about competing with others. Sitting in Dr. Maureen Andrews' Survey of British Literature class, where I was first introduced to the poetry of William Wordsworth, was like having rockets go off in my brain. Dr. Peter Goodrich was the insightful director for my master's thesis *King Arthur's Children in Fiction and Tradition.* I enjoyed working under Dr. Mark Smith at the Writing Center and also being a teaching assistant under Dr. Bill Knox. Although I eventually left teaching in an official way, today as an author and editor, I continue to teach people as well as entertain them, and I feel highly fulfilled as a result; without the education I received at NMU along with a little

creative entrepreneurship, I wouldn't have been able to start my own business Superior Book Promotions (www.SuperiorBookPromotions.com), writing, editing, reviewing books, and basically, doing what I most love to do.

Many of my college friends remain my friends today—Stephanie, Becky, Tom, Chris, Paul, Dana, Greg, Jill, and Larry. Hopefully I have not forgotten any. Larry Alexander ended up sharing an office with me when the English Department moved to Gries Hall. In those days, he and his wife, Ann, had a newborn son, Max, whom Larry would bring to school with him. I ended up volunteering to babysit Max while Larry went to teach his

Back ~ Paul, Heather, & Jeff
Front ~ Dana, Max, & Larry

class. The paternal instinct unexpectedly blossomed in me at that time. I changed many diapers, but it was all worth it whenever Max fell asleep with his head propped on my shoulder. Time goes by too fast—Max is sixteen today—but time's passing shows that friendships last a long time. And little did I know then that someday Larry would design my websites as well as the layout for this book.

Joanie, Larry, & a Very Young Max

I cannot discuss every professor and student I knew at Northern, nor all my friends I had in college. I hope it is sufficient to say that whether I was teaching a class, hanging out in T.A. Alley, having lunch at Bookbinders, attending a play at Forest Roberts Theatre, sitting in a class at Jamrich Hall, studying in the library, or walking across campus, I was happy at NMU, and everyone I knew there contributed to that beneficial experience for me. It's been said before a million times, but for me, the college years truly were the best years of my life.

When I finished my Master's Degree, I moved to Kalamazoo where for five years I worked on my Ph.D. at Western Michigan University. While I found a couple of good friends there and I appreciate the excellent education I received, the atmosphere was not as friendly as what it was at NMU. Partly I'm sure the experience was different because doctoral students have more stress than undergraduate and M.A. students, partly because I didn't know anyone in Kalamazoo when I moved there, and partly I felt displaced from my native environment, but I think the truth is ultimately that Northern Michigan University, like all the U.P., is a superior place.

ST. MICHAEL'S

St. Michael's

Until a few years ago, St. Michael's Church had been an abandoned college dormitory first built in 1900. The first president of the Normal School, Dwight D. Waldo, had lived there with his family and seventy college students. Eventually, the Diocese of Marquette had acquired the four story building, but they had only used it sporadically until World War II. The building had steadily disintegrated, so to turn it into a church during the war years, the top two floors had been removed and a church, convent, and school were established in the remainder of the building. Recently, a foundation had been laid to build a new Catholic school beside the old dormitory building. The new parish testified to the strength of religious faith in time of war and economic adversity, but to Ellen, the building was simply frightening.

— The Queen City

It is fitting after talking about Northern Michigan University that St. Michael's is next discussed because the church and its property originated as part of Northern.

As early as 1940, members of the church and the laity recognized the need for North Marquette to have a church. St. Peter's Cathedral and St. John the Baptist were both downtown, but the city's population kept spreading north.

When the Most Reverend Joseph G. Pintent, titular Bishop of Sela, donated to the Diocese of Marquette the title and deeds of what had been a dormitory and property from Northern Michigan University, he made two stipulations: one that the church had to be named St. Michael's, and secondly, that a school be built and run by the Sisters of St. Joseph of Carondelet.

In 1942, Bishop Francis J. Magner of Marquette commissioned Monsignor Joseph L. Zryd to set about organizing a new parish. Many Catholics living in North Marquette were not happy about the idea because they were parishioners of the cathedral, but the announcement that Monsignor Zryd, a Marquette native, would be their pastor helped a great deal. He was well-liked by his congregation and to this day I hear people talk about what an influence he had upon them, or how their parents loved him. His popularity was the result of his deep belief that it was the Church's responsibility to serve the people as much as it was the people's responsibility to serve the Church.

The new church was to exist in an old dormitory building built in 1900, a four-story wood frame structure with forty-four apartments as well as living quarters on the main floor for President Dwight Waldo. In Northern's early days, half of the school's 140 students resided in the dormitory. The building would later serve as the Marquette unit of the Student Army Training Corps during World War I.

Then in 1919, it was acquired by Bishop Pinten and used as a home for various sisterhoods who taught in the Marquette diocese, but by 1942, it was badly in need of remodeling. Nevertheless, renovations went quickly and on September 6, 1942, the first Masses were held. That same month, on September 15, the school opened with ninety pupils in kindergarten through third grade. By 1948, 367 students and a faculty of ten sisters with classes through eighth grade meant a new school was needed, which was completed in 1949. Reverend Joseph Dunleavy, later pastor of St. Michael's, would deliver the dedication sermon for the new school.

Monsignor Zryd would be reassigned to St. Paul's Church in Negaunee, during which time, Father Robert Cordy would be pastor, serving the parish well—as late as the 1990s when he was retired, he would often join the pastor to say Mass. When Monsignor Zryd was reassigned to St. Michael's in 1955, he dealt with overcrowded Masses and the need to build a new church which the congregation enthusiastically worked to achieve although their pastor would not be there to see the plan come to fruition.

In 1960, Monsignor Zryd was named Spiritual Director of Casa Santa Maria, the student house for post-graduate work for American priests in Rome. He would remain in Rome the rest of his life. *The Mining Journal* announced his departure on August 9, 1960 with a headline that exclaimed, "Fabulous Msgr. Zryd, In New Post In Rome, Italy, Will Boost Baraga Cause"—perhaps not the most professional journalism to include "Fabulous" but it reflects how Monsignor Zryd was so well-appreciated. Once Monsignor Zryd departed, the new pastor, Father Patrick Frankard, carried on the task of building the new church. Work on the new building began in 1962, and on Palm Sunday, April 5, 1963, it was dedicated with a symbolic procession from the old church into the new one.

The new St. Michael's church and school would be very familiar to me as I grew up attending Catholic Child Development (CCD) and accompanying my parents, brother, and Grandma White to Mass. Although the interior of the church was remodeled in 1992, with the rose window from St. John the Baptist hung inside, and a new gathering space was added to the church a few years ago, the building has really not changed much in all the years I have attended Mass there.

From its beginnings, my family has been connected to St. Michael's since Monsignor Joseph Zryd, the first pastor, was my Great-Grandma White's first cousin. Readers of *The Queen City* will recall that Margaret Whitman is a staunch Baptist but pleased when she learns her daughter-in-law's brother is a monsignor. In truth, it was my great-grandmother's cousin who was a monsignor—his father had married a Catholic so the children were raised Catholic. For consolidation's sake, I made the monsignor a bit more closely related to the main characters. Monsignor Michael McCarey is completely fictional except that, like Monsignor Zryd, he was appointed to teach in Rome.

Msgr. Joseph L. Zyrd
Pastor of St. Michael's Church
1942 – 1951

Orate fratres—"Pray, brethern, that my sacrifice and yours may be acceptable to God, the Father Almighty."

Prayer Card for Monsignor Zryd when he left St. Michael's

Despite her uncle marrying a Catholic, my great-grandmother's family stayed close to Monsignor Zryd's family. Close enough that once her cousin became a monsignor, Great-Grandma was proud to say she used to change his diapers as a baby. But having Catholic cousins was not the same as her son marrying a Catholic; so Great-Grandma was not happy when my grandpa wanted to marry my Catholic grandmother. As I mentioned earlier, my grandparents were engaged for about eight years as a result before they compromised by being married at the courthouse. From their marriage in 1934 until 1947, my grandparents and their children did not attend church to keep peace in the family.

Then in 1947, my grandparents decided to move to California for my grandpa's health. Grandma refused to make what to her must have seemed like a long and dangerous trip across the country unless their marriage was blessed by the priest and her children were baptized. This event inspired the scene in *The Queen City* where Henry and Beth take Ellen and Jim to be baptized at St. Michael's. My mother, who was six at the time, recalls that it was December so it was dark early, but she thought at the time, her parents waited until after dark so they could sneak to St. Michael's without her grandparents, who lived next door, seeing them go. I don't know how my great-grandparents initially reacted, but everyone in the family got over it. My grandparents, mom, and uncle moved to California, but by 1949, they had returned to Marquette. My grandma then took the children to Mass while Grandpa stayed home. My mom was always close to her paternal grandparents and doesn't remember any issue over religion after that. She even sometimes went to the Baptist church with her grandmother.

Like both my parents, I was raised as a Catholic. I've always been naturally interested in religion and read the Bible starting from an early age. I wanted to be a priest or missionary when I was younger but ultimately decided that as an author and teacher, I could better serve God. Like many people today, I know organized religion has its faults, and I don't always agree with everything the Church or even Christianity teaches, but I am thankful for being raised in a faith community.

In the many years I have attended St. Michael's, I can attest to the wonderful priests who have served as its pastors and associate pastors, carrying on the fine work Monsignor Zryd began. St. Michael's priests have been loyal and dedicated servants to God, the Church, and their parishioners. I cannot name them all, but a few of them deserve special mention. My parents were the first couple Monsignor Jed Patrick married on October 19, 1968. Monsignor Casanova baptized me. I made my first communion with Monsignor Joseph Dunleavy who later commented to my mother when I was in middle school that I knew more about the Bible than him. My first confession was to Father George Maki. Father Paul Nomellini said the funeral service for my Grandpa White at Swanson's Funeral Home. Father Jamie Ziminski consoled my mom at the hospital during my Grandma White's final illness while Father John Shiverski said my grandmother's funeral mass. St. Michael's priests have been involved in every aspect of the parish and the parishioners' lives, showing love, compassion, and concern as they walk with their parishioners in the footsteps of Jesus, and while I have named only a few of them here, I remember them all. Today, our pastor Father Larry Van Damme and associate pastor Father Ben Haas carry on the church's good work assisted by the many devoted members of the parish whose faces I see week after week attending Mass and living their faith.

The Spirit of Christ's Church survives at St. Michael's. G.K. Chesterton, the Catholic writer and novelist, once said, "Christianity has not been tried and found wanting; it has been found difficult and not tried." For most of the world that is probably true, but I believe the people of St. Michael's and their pastors have embodied the saying, "They'll know we are Christians by our love."

MARQUETTE GENERAL

Before him was the former St. Luke's Hospital where he had been born. Since then, it had merged with St. Mary's Hospital to form Marquette General Hospital, now the largest hospital for hundreds of miles in any direction. While yet a boy, John had seen built a towering skyscraper on the west of the hospital's property. Now, to the astonishment of even Marquette's proudest residents, another towering structure was being built on the opposite side of College Avenue. The future Neldberg building, named for the hospital's current administrator, would contain the first and only escalator in Upper Michigan, and perhaps most amazing of all, it would be connected by a skywalk to the hospital buildings across the street. John was thankful his mother had said she would meet him in the hospital lobby; otherwise, he would have been lost amid the maze of medical buildings where two thousand people were employed.

— Superior Heritage

Marquette has had some sort of hospital since its earliest days. Readers of *Iron Pioneers* will recall that typhoid struck the village the first year and that Peter White was instrumental in caring for the sick, mostly German immigrants. It was to a makeshift hospital in my first novel that Peter White took Clara Henning and where she met her great friend, Molly Bergmann.

This makeshift hospital would be followed by several others, including private homes that doctors would rent for their patients. The Sisters of St. Francis came to the aid and built a hospital on the corner of Rock and Fourth Streets, but during the 1890 typhoid epidemic, the hospital overflowed and tents were used to hold all the patients. Then in 1890, between Fourth and Fifth Streets, St. Mary's Hospital was built. An addition to it in 1905 provided a 100 bed capacity. By the time St. Mary's celebrated its

St. Mary's Hospital ~ Torn Down in 1963

**Doctor-owned Home Used as
Hospital in 1890s**

fiftieth anniversary, it had cared for 35,675 patients.

Meanwhile, nearly fifty years after Peter White first bathed sick Germans with typhoid, he sold some property he owned on Washington Street and donated the $5,000 he made from it to establish the first St. Luke's Hospital in 1897, located at 123 W. Ridge. Today the property is the Peter White Public Library's parking lot. This first hospital would hold thirty-one patients. Here in *The Queen City*,

when Molly goes to visit a sick friend, she is pleasantly surprised to learn Margaret Whitman has just given birth to her first child, Henry. Henry is the great-grandchild of Molly's old friend, Clara, and Molly herself delivered Margaret, although in the Whitman boarding house—a birthplace Margaret has always resented. In truth, my

St. Luke's Hospital ~ c. 1905

great-grandmother gave birth to my Grandpa White in St. Luke's in 1905. My great-grandmother's nurse, Miss Lester, was so nice that my grandfather ended up being named Lester as a result.

**Second St. Luke's & New
Marquette General**

The first St. Luke's was soon deemed too small, so in 1915, a new three-story hospital was built at Hebard Court between Magnetic and Specular (today College Avenue) and made possible by a memorial grant of $20,000 by Mrs. Charles Hebard from money left by her husband to build some sort of institution in Upper Michigan—again Peter White had a hand in the hospital, convincing Mrs. Hebard the new hospital would be the appropriate institution. This initial building remains part of the hospital complex today.

Soon after, my great-grandfather, Jay Earle White, built three houses for nurses on College Avenue between Third and Fourth Streets, and shortly after in 1934, the Wallace Nurses' Home was erected as a nursing school. Nurses would be trained there until 1972 when NMU would take over nurse-training and the building became the Wallace Building housing the

Wallace Building Today

administrative offices. In 1973, St. Luke's Hospital merged with St. Mary's Hospital to form Marquette General Hospital. The old St. Mary's had been torn down by this point and a new building constructed in 1955. Eventually, Marquette General Hospital decided to focus on the property at St. Luke's so St. Mary's became the Jacobetti Veterans Home.

My earliest memory of what would become Marquette General Hospital (I was born in St. Luke's but do not recall the event) is sitting in the parking lot across the street from St. Luke's Hospital when I was five years old. At that time my Grandma White, Grandma Tichelaar, and Great-Grandma White were simultaneously all patients in the hospital. I remember staring at the little round window of what is the brick Wallace Administration Building and thinking that was the room they were all in.

My mom worked in Medical Records in the Wallace Administration Building so I remember going there with her several times to pick up her check. In the years following, I saw the hospital expand to the gigantic complex it is today. In 1981, the eight story "skyscraper"—by Marquette standards—was built beside the Wallace Administration Building, and then in 1992, the Neldberg Building was built across the street along with the skywalk that connected it. The

Neldberg Building & Skywalk

Neldberg Building holds the special designation of being the first, and to this day, the only building in Upper Michigan that has an escalator. Another floor was added onto the skywalk in 2000.

In the early 1990s when I was attending NMU, I spent many hours sitting in the lobby of the new Neldberg Building where my mom's office had moved, while waiting for my mom to get off work so we could drive home together. Although my mother retired in 2006, I still walk through the lobby often to the gift shop where my books are sold.

Today, as part of Marquette General Health Systems, Marquette General Hospital is the largest hospital in Upper Michigan and a Regional Referral Center. It has 315 beds, provides care in 65 specialties and subspecialties, and has a staff of over 200 doctors and 2,200 employees who care for approximately 12,000 inpatients and over 350,000 outpatients each year.

For my family, the hospital has been a place of employment and a place for meeting future spouses. My grandma met my grandpa while working in the diet kitchen. Like Henry in *The Queen City*, my grandpa came to pick up another woman who worked there, but she couldn't go out on a date that night, so my grandma went out with him instead.

My mom worked in the diet kitchen for six years. During that time, she first met my dad, Richard Tichelaar, who was in the hospital for surgery on his flat feet, and my mom was delivering the meals; she would deliver food to him last so she would have extra time to spend talking to him. After finishing her degree at Northern, my mom returned to work at the hospital as a floating secretary and doing the payroll. Soon she was working in Medical Records as a transcriptionist. There she stayed typing dictation for patients' records until she retired in June 2006. When she retired, not only had she worked there forty-two years, but she was the longest-term employee in the hospital's history. When her years in the diet kitchen are added in, she worked at the hospital for forty-eight years.

Over her long employment at Marquette General, my mom came to know hundreds of people, so when I became a published author, people kept asking me whether I was related to Nancy Tichelaar. My books have now made me well-known in the community, but I think I'm still better known as Nancy Tichelaar's son than as Tyler Tichelaar, the author.

MEMORIAL FIELD

Margaret told Roy he had no choice but to drive her to Memorial Field for the fireworks. "It won't hurt you to take me and then stay at your mother's house another night before going back to that old cabin of yours," she insisted. Roy knew better than to argue. Henry and Beth talked Michael into piling into their car with the children. Then they followed Roy's vehicle while Eleanor and company brought up the rear. Once the three automobiles reached Memorial Field, the Whitman clan found thousands of people crowded together, eagerly awaiting the finale to the centennial celebrations.

— The Queen City

Ice Sculpture, USS Marquette ~ 1941

Memorial Field, located off the aptly named Fair Avenue, was the site of many fairs and other festivities in the early and mid-twentieth century. Marquette would hold winter carnivals here, most notably one during World War II that featured a giant snow sculpture of a navy ship—the sculpture was so large that when it began melting, it was blown up to prevent people from being trapped in its melting slush.

Memorial Field was also the sight of the NMU Wildcats football stadium for many years—games that were often played in the snow until the Superior Dome was built.

Perhaps the most memorable event in Memorial Field's history, however, was the 1949 Marquette Centennial Celebrations which included the prize for the beard growing contest going to Mike Chenoweth (whose murder three years later would inspire *Anatomy of a Murder*). I think my favorite moment in all my novels takes place here at the end of *The Queen City* as the characters watch the Fourth of July fireworks during the centennial celebrations:

Beard Growing Contestants ~ Left to Right: Roland, Jack, Jay Earle, & Frank White, Claude Hagen

At that moment, the first loud cracking thunder broke. Memorial Field was packed with thousands of city residents and visitors who lifted their eyes to the glorious explosions in the night sky. Pink blazing sparks spread in every direction. Then a burst of blue, an explosion of green, a shot of white, a spray of orange, then yellow, then blue again, and red, and green, and blue, and orange, and yellow, and pink, and white. Burst after burst, straight firing white lines, kaleidoscopic green, pink, purple, all at once. One separate firework to mark each year of Marquette's history. Up into the sky they shot in shimmering streaks like a hundred candles blazing on a bombastic birthday cake. Ellen covered her ears; the fireworks were so delightfully loud.

Henry leaned over to kiss his wife's cheek.

"Ouch, that tickles," Beth giggled. "When will you shave off that silly beard?"

"First thing tomorrow morning," he promised, "but you have to admit it looks pretty good for having been grown so quickly."

"Shh, Daddy, you're missing the fireworks," Ellen scolded.

Henry and Beth both chuckled, glad to see their daughter happy. They were happy themselves. They were back where they belonged, in their hometown for its centennial, which they would not have missed for anything. Henry thought back on all of Marquette's remarkable history, the raising of the courthouse, the library, the banks, the houses, the bravery of its people, the struggles through fires and blizzards, economic woes and wars. He thought of the ore docks, those formidable giants of the iron industry, stretching out into the world's greatest lake as emissaries to distant lands. For a hundred years, from Iron Bay, the Upper Peninsula's riches had been shipped out to bolster a nation, yet Marquette had scarcely received mention in a history book. Many people could not even pronounce its name, much less find it on a map. But its Northern sons and daughters knew the great privilege they shared in living here. They knew Nature had blessed them by giving them this land of pristine beauty, mighty forests, fresh air, and remarkable weather. Henry and Beth were grateful to have been born here, and thankful they had been wise enough to return. Thousands that night felt in their hearts what Henry spoke as he turned to Beth.

"We truly do live in THE QUEEN CITY OF THE NORTH."

THE PALESTRA

"Palestra" is Greek for "a place of recreation for young people". The building had already served as the favorite gathering place to generations of Marquette's youth. Although first built in 1904 in the town of Laurium, in 1921, the Palestra had been moved to Marquette. Since then, it had hosted countless hockey games, ice skating competitions, and dances in its upstairs ballroom. Originally, the Palestra had had a floor of real ice that needed to be scraped, but in 1950, an artificial floor had been laid, making the skating better and the Palestra all the more popular. On this snowy Saturday, a couple hundred people were skating, from senior citizens to children, but teenagers and college students made up the overwhelming majority.

— Superior Heritage

On Fair Avenue at the end of Third Street once stood one of Marquette's all time most loved places—the Palestra.

Before the Palestra opened, Marquette had several ice-skating rinks, including one at the bottom of Ridge Street, but they were all outdoors and short lived. Then in 1921, the Palestra, a building built in 1904 and located in Laurium, was purchased by a group of Marquette businessmen and moved to Marquette. On December 26th of that same year, the building opened to the public for hockey games and recreational ice skating. The building would be home to the Marquette Rangers hockey team for many years, as well as the site of numerous public events. For the next half century, it may be said the Palestra was the cultural and social heart of Marquette.

In the 1950s, my Uncle Jay was one of the broomers there—young men hired to care for the ice. My mother recalls that she went skating there about four days a week in winter. The Palestra would open for skating on Halloween with a special

The Palestra

costume party and contest. One year, as a young girl, my mother dressed up as a clown for the opening night costume party. Between her oversized costume and her tight skates, she had difficulty keeping her balance and kept falling over on the ice. The judges, because they thought she was intentionally "clowning" around, awarded her the prize for best costume. When she had to go up to claim her prize, she fell over right in front of them. She was very embarrassed but everyone still thought she was just acting. Her prize for all that pain and embarrassment was a half-gallon of ice cream.

Beyond ice skating and hockey, the Palestra hosted the second largest dance floor in the county. The bands that played there were broadcast on the local radio stations. In 1925, one of the greatest athletic attractions ever staged in Upper Michigan took place at the Palestra when Harry Greg, middleweight champion, fought Jimmy Nuss of Newberry. Greg took home the $4,500 prize when he knocked out Nuss in the fourth round. Gus Sonnerberg, heavyweight wrestling champion would also make an appearance at the Palestra. In 1925, Amos and Andy, before they became famous on radio, hosted a traveling circus at the Palestra, and later Tex Ritter came with his horse Wonder. The Palestra was also hired out for various functions, including St. Michael's holding its annual bazaars there.

In 2009, the Marquette County History Museum hosted a special event to remember the Palestra. The room was packed with people who grew up skating and playing hockey there. Several former hockey players for the Marquette Rangers attended, including Ronnie Johnson, and many present spoke fondly of coach Leonard "Oakie" Brumm. All were in agreement that the Palestra was a special place and when it was torn down in 1974 after the opening of the new Lakeview Arena, skating in Marquette just never was the same. The Lakeview Arena never had the same magic as the Palestra—nor did it have the same quality facilities such as separate changing rooms for men and women—it did not even have changing rooms.

Hockey lives on in Marquette. The NMU Wildcats play in the Berry Events Center and junior hockey is played in the Lakeview Arena. But by the time I was a kid, ice-skating's popularity in Marquette had passed. Roller skating was the craze then, and my brother, friends, and I spent many Sunday afternoons at the Peninsula Roller Rink, which has since become home to the Salvation Army after rollerblading replaced roller skating.

Its bleachers no longer ring with screaming hockey fans, but the Palestra continues to hold a place in the hearts and memories of many of Marquette's sons and daughters who today still tell their children and grandchildren of its glory.

PART VIII:
THIRD STREET (THE VILLAGE)

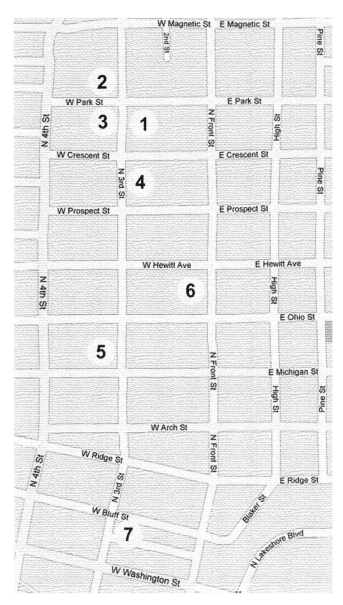

1. Swanson-Lundquist Funeral Home
2. White's Party Store
3. Vango's
4. Marquette Monthly Cottage
5. The Tip Top Café
6. Graveraet High School & Kaufman Auditorium
7. Snowbound Books

SWANSON-LUNDQUIST FUNERAL HOME

Ellen asked the priest from St. Michael's to say the funeral service at the Swanson Funeral Home. Then the Baptist minister said a prayer at the Catholic cemetery, and the funeral luncheon was held at the Baptist church.

— Superior Heritage

With the exception of one funeral at the Tonella-Canale funeral home, every funeral I have ever attended in Marquette has been at the Swanson Funeral Home. The Tonella Funeral Home, farther down Third Street, was typically the Catholic funeral home; it was established in 1893 and moved to its current location in 1929. My Great-Grandma Molby's funeral visitation was held there in 1933. In 1986, Mark Canale purchased the funeral home and renamed it Tonella-Canale.

But because most of my relatives were Baptists, family funerals—or at least the visitations—were held at Swanson's Funeral Home.

The Swanson Funeral Home is an almost Gothic looking building with its brick front. It was built in 1927 by Albert E. Swanson, who had previously operated a funeral parlor on Washington Street. Mr. Swanson eventually sold the funeral home to Jack L. McCracken, who in turn sold it in 1977 to David Lundquist and the name was changed to Swanson-Lundquist. David Lundquist still assists at the funeral home, but he semi-retired in 2006 and sold the funeral home to Jeremy Hansen. Just prior to the change in ownership, Swanson-Lundquist also acquired the Fassbender Funeral Home down the street.

The owners and employees of Swanson-Lundquist Funeral Home, especially Dave Lundquist, Gordie Peterson, and Jeremy Hansen, have always been good to our family over the years and over the course of many funerals when you consider my great-grandparents, grandparents, great-aunts and uncles, and numerous cousins.

Swanson-Lundquist Funeral Home

318 ~ MY MARQUETTE

I have always found it interesting to go to a funeral and find other people there I know but whom I did not know also knew the deceased. Marquette is small enough that we are all just a couple of degrees apart, so if I don't know someone, most likely he or she still knows people I know. I continually tried to express this small town feel in my novels; such a situation leads to family wounds being healed in *The Queen City* when at the Tonella Funeral Home, Will Whitman attends the funeral of Patrick Mc-Carey, his daughter-in-law's father. Will is surprised to see his nephew, Harry Cumming, at the funeral home, but Harry knew Patrick because Harry was incarcerated in the prison, and as a guard, Patrick was kind to him. Harry comes to pay his respects to Patrick, little thinking he will meet his uncle there and they will reunite after their branches of the family have been estranged more than thirty years.

The quote at the beginning of this chapter describes Henry Whitman's funeral in *Superior Heritage*. The funeral description is similar to my grandfather's funeral which was held at Swanson's. Such events are never pleasant to attend, but Swanson's has always been excellent at accommodating our family and taking good care of its clients. Its parlor has been a place of family gatherings nearly as much as our homes. Operating a funeral home has to require a special patience, compassion, and professionalism, qualities the Swanson-Lundquist Funeral Home has embodied with grace for decades.

WHITE'S PARTY STORE

Plenty of places around Marquette have been named after Peter White, and I'm sure he would be happy to have his famous Peter White punch for sale with the rest of the liquor in White's Party Store, but White's Party Store has nothing to do with Peter White. Instead, it was named for my grandpa's cousin Almet Jerome White, the original owner.

Several stores have existed on this site since the early 1900s. It became White's Party Store in 1946, and prior to that had been Bittner's. Almet J. White would operate the store until 1965. It would then pass out of the family, but while the store has since had a few different owners, the White's Party Store name has been retained because of its familiarity to everyone for so many decades now.

While the store carries a variety of products, it has become well-known in Marquette as the best store to find quality vintage beer, wine, and liquor. I wonder what my great-great grandfather, Jerome White, the descendant of

White's Party Store

Marquette's first temperance movement founders, and a man who reputedly locked his son out of the house for getting drunk, would think of his name attached to a liquor store. Yet the store is a mainstay of Third Street, and after the Peter White Public Library, probably the place in Marquette that most comes to mind when the name White is mentioned.

VANGO'S

I can't imagine how I managed in my novels not to have a scene set at Vango's. Although not mentioned, doubtless John Vandelaare went here to eat many times during his college years.

Most of my favorite Marquette restaurants—Entre Amigos, Los Tres Amigos, Taco

Vango's Restaurant

John's (I'm sensing a pattern here that Vango's doesn't fit into)—have long since closed, but Vango's has remained open for decades. I frequently went here during my college years and still do today. When I was a graduate student at NMU, the other teaching assistants and I would frequently get together here on Fridays for lunch.

Vango's is the oldest pizza parlor in Marquette. In fact, it started out in 1957 at its current location under the name Bimbo's Pizza Parlor. Then in 1975, when it got its liquor license, owner Clark Lambros changed its name to Vango's Restaurant in honor of his father Vangos Lambros. Vango's retains its pizza parlor origins in the fantastic pizza it serves, but it is as well known for its Greek food; after all, the Lambros family itself is Greek.

When I moved to Kalamazoo, I often had insomnia—due to homesickness I think—and then I would lay awake craving a Rudolfi Gyro from Vango's. None of the Greek restaurants around Kalamazoo could make a decent gyro sandwich—they all were more like salads, so eating at Vango's was always a top priority whenever I came home. If you want a gyro done right, Vango's is definitely the place to go. The Chicken Avgolemono soup and Spanakopeta are also delicious. Remember to save room for Baklava.

MARQUETTE MONTHLY COTTAGE

For now, he was cataloging memories. He began reading historical articles whenever they appeared in the Mining Journal, Marquette Monthly, *and* Marquette Magazine. *He cut out articles and filed them, realizing the potential source of fiction in Marquette's history, in the environment, the buildings, lake, trees, all of this land that had helped to form him.* — Superior Heritage

When people ask me where I did the research for my books, *Marquette Monthly* is a large part of that answer. Since I wrote a good part of *The Marquette Trilogy* while living in Kalamazoo and South Carolina, I had to rely largely on what I could bring with me. I had been clipping historical articles and collecting historical books since the early 1980s, and *Marquette Monthly*'s "Back Then" column made up a fair portion of my research collection.

At that time, I had no idea I would eventually work at *Marquette Monthly*. When I decided I was going to become self-employed and was working toward that goal, I applied for a part-time job there as a proofreader. I was hired first to work on the June 2007 issue and have proofread every issue since as well as writing occasional articles and monthly book reviews.

Marquette Monthly began in 1987 with its first issue in October, produced from the home of editor and publisher Mary Kinnunen, with seventeen ads, and work from Leonard Heldreth, Sylvia Kinnunen, and a photo spread by Tom Buchkoe. Both Buchkoe and Heldreth continue to be involved with the publication today. In 1988 the publication moved to Washington Street, and for the next few years, Don Curto served as the editor. In 1992, Pat Ryan O'Day became the monthly paper's owner and editor. Several more editors have followed but Pat has remained the owner and been heavily involved in overseeing production of each issue since. In June 1999, *Marquette Monthly* moved to its current location at 810 N. Third Street in the Marquette Monthly Cottage.

Marquette Monthly Cottage

Few people are better to work for than Pat Ryan O'Day. She has a real knack for finding excellent writers and a variety of interesting topics as well as hiring a staff that does amazing work. Kathy Jeske Casteel continually impresses me with her talents as a graphic artist and ad designer. Carrie Usher keeps track of a dizzying number of events for the calendar and lays out the pages each month. Kristy Basolo can edit a story perfectly to get it to fit just right on the page while never losing the story's flavor or marring the author's style. They are all talented and great to work with, and they even trust me with the hot wax when it comes time to paste up the pages on deadline day.

Besides the "Back Then" columns, often written by Larry Chabot, I greatly appreciate the regularly recurring film reviews by Leonard Heldreth, "Notes from the North Country" by Lynn and Lon Emerick, and perhaps most of all, Don Curto's column "Food and Other Important Things"—I'm not too interested in cooking, but his columns are always full of common sense and his memories of Marquette make the past come alive in a way I only wish I could do so well in my novels.

Despite a few long nights right before deadline, I enjoy working for *Marquette Monthly*, and I and all the staff appreciate the positive responses we receive from the community, although we are unlikely any time soon to fulfill our readers' desire to make it a daily paper.

THE TIP TOP CAFÉ

By that time, she knew the library was closed, yet Ron still did not come home. She suspected he was down at the Tip Top Café, hanging out with his idolizing students. He was always seeking to be worshiped for his mind.
— The Queen City

For forty-five years, from 1938 to 1983, the Tip Top Café was a popular college hangout, owned by Nick Arger and operated by Gert Johnson. In *The Queen City*, Ronald Goldman is a professor at Northern who hangs out there with his students. Since the Tip Top closed before I ever entered college, my memories of it are limited to one visit made there about 1980.

Tip Top Cafe Staff ~ Nick Arger & Gert Johnson in back ~ c. 1940

That evening, my brother Danny, our friend Ronnie, and I were to be taken by Ronnie's mom out to supper and to the movie. The plan was to go to Taco John's for supper, but Ronnie's mother said her stomach couldn't handle eating there, so she suggested we go to the Tip Top. When I asked, "What's the Tip Top?" she replied, "It's a place I think everyone should experience at least once."

I don't know what I expected when she said that, but I did not expect what it turned out to be—a bar! My brother and Ronnie ran off to play the pinball machines (this was in the days before video games). Meanwhile, I sat in the booth with Ronnie's mother, refusing to go play. College students were there and I'm sure they were drinking beer. I knew my mother would not want me in such a place. Besides, everything smelled of smoke—a clear sign it was an unsavory bar. We had fish which I barely ate—it tasted like smoke. I was embarrassed and ashamed because I felt I was doing something very bad by being there.

I was much relieved when we left for the movies—we saw *Mary Poppins*—nothing I could complain about there, and Ronnie's mom let us sit by ourselves right in the front row and buy gigantic sodas.

When we got home, I felt I had to confess to my mom that we had gone to a bar, but strangely, she was a lot less concerned about it than me.

In 1983, the Tip Top Café closed. The building was sold and became Ten O'Clock Charlie's for the next several years before becoming Mainely Wood. Today, the building is home to Casualties Skate & Snow, a retailer of brand name snowboards and skateboards, both very popular in Marquette.

Ronnie's mom had said the Tip Top Café was a place everyone should experience at least once. I had my once, but if I'd had a second, I'm sure I would have liked it better.

GRAVERAET HIGH SCHOOL & KAUFMAN AUDITORIUM

And for the first time since colonial days, Upper Michigan feared an attack upon its very own soil. The importance of the region's mineral and timber resources caused concern that the Germans might bomb the Soo Locks to destroy shipping on the Upper Great Lakes. The enemy might even attack Marquette County as a

Graveraet High School

major harbor and outlet for the iron mines. The Marquette County Aircraft Warning Service was formed by volunteers who would watch the skies and send up the alarm in case of attack. Inmates of the Marquette Prison watched from the prison's spotting tower while in Ishpeming, a watchtower was established on the roof of the Road Commission's offices. In Marquette, Graveraet High School's roof became a lookout. Over the course of the war, two hundred sixty-two local men and women would watch the skies to ensure the community's protection from foreign planes.

— The Queen City

Graveraet High School is a block from Third Street off Hewitt Avenue on Front Street. It is not technically part of "The Village" but it is an integral part of Marquette's social life so this seems the best place to include it.

Built in 1927 at the cost of half a million dollars, the school was named for the Graveraet family, specifically Juliet Graveraet, sister of Marquette founder Robert Graveraet, and mother to Louis Kaufman. Kaufman had reimbursed the school district for the $26,000 spent to purchase the property, so the board unanimously chose to name the school in honor of his mother. When the building was near completion, the board decided to name the auditorium after Kaufman and the gymnasium after Sidney Adams because his wife, Mrs. Harriet Adams, had originally donated some of the school property as well as the money to build the gymnasium.

My great-aunts attended school here, and my Great-Aunt Sadie remembers seeing Amelia Earhart when she came twice to speak at Kaufman Auditorium in the 1930s. The school's central tower was the highest point in the center of Marquette at the time of World War II so it became a watch tower and was manned twenty-four hours a day to keep an eye out for enemy aircraft. In 1965, when the current Marquette Senior High School was built, Graveraet became a middle school. A few years ago, a fundraising drive began to raise money to restore the courtyard fountain, but in 2009, the student population in Marquette had dropped off so much that the school no longer was needed to hold classes. While the halls may not be flocked with students any longer, the school continues to be used, primarily, Kaufman Auditorium.

Since I did not go to school in Marquette, my memories of Graveraet High School are centered around Kaufman Auditorium. I have seen everything here from exotic performances by Yothu Yindi in 1994 to concerts and local plays. The Marquette Senior High School has held impressive performances here in recent years including *Thoroughly Modern Millie* and *Fiddler on the Roof*. I've seen the Pine Mountain Music Festival perform *Carmen*, attended spelling bees here when in grade school, and seen the Marquette Arts and Culture Center's performances by children of such plays as Rodgers & Hammerstein's *Cinderella*. Perhaps the most enjoyable events I've been to at Kaufman Auditorium were the Marquette General Hospital *Follies*, a humorous variety show put on by the locals to raise money for the hospital in the 1980s and early 1990s. More recently, Fred Rydholm and Jack Deo provided a celebration of Kaufman Auditorium and photographs of early Marquette, including Bob Buchkoe playing the song "Old Marquette" on the grand piano that George Gershwin himself picked out for the auditorium. In October 2009, Jack Deo also presented an impressive slide show of Marquette history in 3-D.

Kaufman is not the largest auditorium in Marquette, but it is definitely the most historical. Whatever the school's future, I trust Graveraet High School will continue to be a significant landmark in Marquette.

Kaufman Auditorium ~ c. 1940

SNOWBOUND BOOKS

During his lunch break, he popped into Snowbound Books, thinking he might like a British novel, something by Galsworthy or Waugh, but when he entered the store, the local history section caught his eye.

— Superior Heritage

Marquette has had several bookstores over the years, most of which have not lasted long. B. Dalton's, formerly in the Marquette Mall and then the Westwood Mall, after more than thirty years, closed in January 2010, and the Book Rack or Book Shoppe on Division Street that survived under various managements for about thirty years is also now closed. Other shops like Sandpiper Books and the Iron City Bookstore only lasted a few years before they also went out of business. Today, Marquette is left with the small chain store, Book World, and a true independent bookstore, Snowbound, which since 1984 has been a favorite among Marquette residents.

From the day it opened its doors, Snowbound was the primary place I went to buy my books, especially because I loved that it had a good used book collection. I always had an affinity for reading the classics, and while I could find *David Copperfield* and *Wuthering Heights* at B. Dalton, at Snowbound I could find all of Dickens' lesser known books plus more obscure novels by classic writers.

When I bought my house, I chose it for the large room downstairs that could serve as my library. I thought it would provide me with plenty of space, but within a few years, it has become packed wall to wall. I have far too many books for me to try to count them anymore, but a fair number of them came from Snowbound— I wouldn't be surprised if it were five hundred or more.

In the passage above, John Vandelaare goes into Snowbound and buys a copy of *Ojibwa Narratives*, a collection of stories told by Chief Kawbawgam which leads to his revelation that

Snowbound Books

one of Chief Kawbawgam's stories has been handed down in his family.

Many of the books I've bought at Snowbound have had a significant impact on me. To this day, I think Marion Zimmer Bradley's *The Mists of Avalon* remains my favorite novel. I also have an attraction to old and ornate books. In 1993, after returning from a trip to Great Britain where I had climbed the Sir Walter Scott

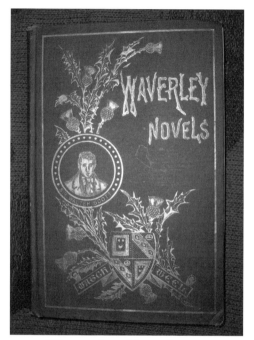

Waverley Novels By Sir Walter Scott

Monument in Edinburgh, I decided to read Scott's novels, and at Snowbound I purchased a complete set of the *Waverley Novels* in nine volumes, which were published in the late 1800s. The ornate and old look of these novels, as much as their contents, inspired me to write the scenes in *Iron Pioneers* and *The Queen City* where Margaret Dalrymple, and later her son, Roy Whitman, read Scott's novels—Margaret later blames the novels for her many delusions of grandeur.

In recent years, I've gotten to know the staff at Snowbound well because they have been kind enough to sell my books and to host several book signings for me. As an independent bookstore, Snowbound had to compete with the chains like B. Dalton in its early days, and in the twenty-first century it competes with Amazon, but it has also gone online to sell with surprising results and orders from all over. When I interviewed owner Ray Nurmi in 2008 for a *Marquette Monthly* article, he told me, "The sultan of Brunei bought a book on making biscuits from us—really. I shipped a book on Al Gore's father to the *Washington Post* and a book on Edward R. Murrow to NBC." Another reason for Snowbound's success is that the staff knows books well. Manager Dianne Patrick serves on the board for the Peter White Public Library and was also on the U.P. committee with me to help choose the Great Michigan Read for 2009-2010. Dana Schulz creates a wonderful newsletter for the store including reviews by customers and staff. Hosting book clubs, book signings, and readings by local and famous authors has also made Snowbound successful.

As an author, I appreciate how Snowbound has worked to keep reading and local books a major part of Marquette's cultural life. And I can't think of a bookstore with a better name—what is more satisfying on a snowy day in Upper Michigan than to cuddle up with a good book?

PART IX:
WEST MARQUETTE

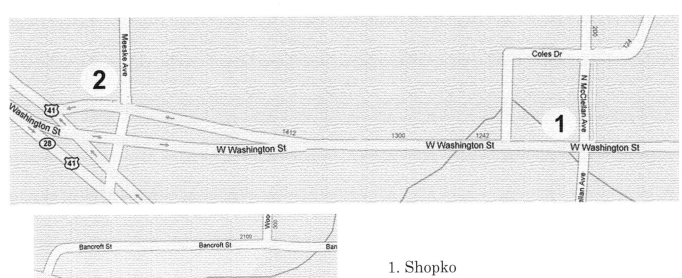

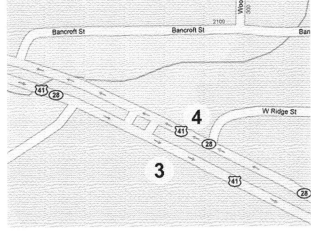

1. Shopko
2. Castle Brewery
3. The Marquette Mall
4. Hamburger Heaven & The Villa Capri
5. Bonanza
6. The Bavarian Inn
7. The Northwoods

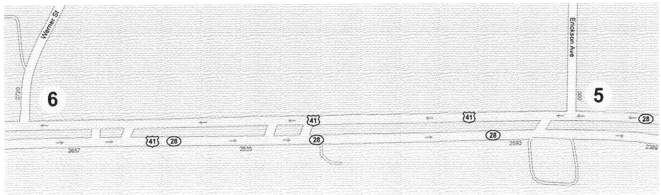

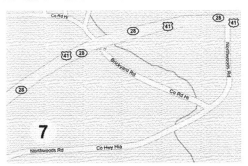

WEST MARQUETTE

Once the City of Marquette had ended at Lincoln Avenue. Now McDonalds, Shopko, motels and the Marquette Mall sprang up until a bypass was built so vehicles would not have to travel through downtown Marquette at all; new businesses grew along the bypass until US 41 West became the focus of the city's commercial interests. Acres that for the city's first century had lain empty save for a farm or brewery were paved into parking lots, used car dealerships, and fast food restaurants. Old timers, grumbling that Shopko and the Marquette Mall were too far away, vowed they would continue to shop downtown, but automobiles carried most residents to the new shopping areas within ten minutes.

— Superior Heritage

As the mid-twentieth century came to Marquette, the city started growing westward along Washington Street and US Highway 41. When the bypass was built in the 1960s, automobiles coming from south of Marquette no longer had to drive through the downtown to head toward Negaunee and Ishpeming. The bypass led to the decline of downtown Marquette for a couple of decades while new restaurants, motels, and department stores sprung up along US 41. When I was a child, the city stretched as far as Kmart, which was located where Kohl's is today—the Westwood Mall was not built until several years later. Since then, the city has stretched a mile or two farther west.

This modern part of Marquette is largely in Marquette Township—the city limit is just west of the Marquette Mall. Most of this territory is not of great historical interest yet, but in my lifetime I have seen a lot of changes take place here. Again, I could not possibly mention every place in West Marquette, but a few that have special memories for me deserve recognition.

SHOPKO

It was the summer of "...And Ladies of the Club" and Shopko was determined to sell every copy of Helen Hooven Santmyer's blockbuster novel.

— Superior Heritage

Shopko was the primary place to go shopping when I was a kid. In the 1970s, there were only three places to shop—Shopko, the Marquette Mall, and Kmart. We never shopped downtown—the downtown didn't really revive until the mid-1980s when all the shops became popular again. Today, Kmart is gone and Kohl's is in its place, but in those days Kmart stood by itself without even a Westwood Mall attached to it. The Marquette Mall is far from what it was as a shopping destination, but Shopko remains basically the same with a few things inside rearranged.

Well, maybe a lot of things rearranged—at least according to my grandmother. As I mentioned earlier, my mom always took my grandma and great-aunts shopping on Wednesdays and occasionally I would tag along. As Grandma entered her eighties, she had a harder time walking, and for a long time, she was too proud to use a cane, so she would hang onto her shopping cart for support. Then she would go up and down the aisles, looking for the Little Debbie snacks that filled the kitchen drawer at home. She was convinced Shopko moved things around every week, probably just to confuse senior citizens. I didn't really like Little Debbie snacks, except the Dutch Apple Treats, but Grandma kept buying them for us, and it made her happy, so I would always help her track them down wherever Shopko had hid them.

It was on one of those summer shopping trips that my mom bought a copy of *"...And Ladies of the Club"* by Helen Hooven Santmyer at Shopko. And because its 1,433 pages made it the biggest novel I had ever seen, I decided to read it.

Shopko

That novel had a huge impact on how I learned to write historical novels, and I borrowed Santmyer's method of simply naming each chapter by a year when I wrote *The Marquette Trilogy*. Santmyer took her small hometown in Ohio and made it into a world full of interest, showing how the daily events of life could be fascinating, and I have tried to do the same with my own books.

To this day, Shopko is where I go first to shop. Since it is based in Green Bay, it's the closest thing to a "local" department store. It's also the store closest to my house and perhaps has a bit more sentimental value to me than the newer Walmart and Target.

CASTLE BREWERY

George Rublein, one of Marquette's first residents, built the Castle Brewery. Although it does not feature in any of my novels, I had initially planned to set a scene in *Iron Pioneers* there but later cut it out. Nevertheless, the building has struck a chord with me from early childhood because of my love for castles.

Castle Brewery

Today I find the brewery's history interesting because Rublein, like Fritz Bergmann in *Iron Pioneers*, was one of the German immigrants who came to Marquette in 1849 from Milwaukee. He and his wife Catherine were probably among those who suffered from the initial typhoid outbreak that summer and later in December started walking back to Milwaukee so villagers in Worcester (later Marquette) would not starve to death without their winter supplies. Fortunately, the supply ship arrived on Christmas Day and the Germans were called back to the village.

Rublein bought 160 acres of land for $1.00 on what became County Road 492. There he built his home, farm, and his beer brewery. He later would expand his business to the west end of Washington Street, building the Castle Brewery, of which a small sandstone portion remains today. Quite far from town at that time, the brewery's beer gardens would have been a fun excursion out of town for residents.

In *Iron Pioneers*, the scene I did not include in the novel was to center around Karl Bergmann visiting the Castle Brewery as a young man. The visit would make him feel sentimental over his deceased father and inspire him to make his trip to Germany. Although I left out the Castle Brewery, in *The Queen City*, Karl did go to Germany, and when he returns, he brings home the German pickle Christmas ornament he gives to his sister Kathy. Decades later, John Vandelaare sees the ornament on his grandmother's Christmas tree and wonders how such a strange ornament came into the family's possession. Although no one in the family remembers how the pickle was acquired, it serves as a symbol that the past is always with us.

My grandmother never really had a pickle ornament—I just thought it an interesting German tradition, and I do have my own Christmas pickle ornament today. But Grandma always had pickles on the table at parties—bread and butter pickles. I buy them all the time—they remind me of her; we all have our comfort foods.

THE MARQUETTE MALL

The Marquette Mall, with its fountain of sparkling multicolored lights would delight John's eyes...

— Superior Heritage

On the day I was born, May 26, 1971, *The Mining Journal*'s headline announced the building of the largest mall in Upper Michigan, soon to be known as the Marquette Mall. It may just be a coincidence that we shared the same birthday, but the Marquette Mall was always my favorite place to go shopping in the 1970s and 1980s. It had a wider

The Marquette Mall ~ c. 1975

variety of shops and was far more attractive inside than the later Westwood Mall. The Westwood Mall was not built until a good decade later, and even in the 1980s, it was just a few shops between Kmart and Prange's, where today are Kohl's and Younkers. Only in the late 1980s when the Westwood Mall expanded by building the long hallway that ends at J.C. Penney did it become a major shopping center and lead to the near-death of the Marquette Mall. It may be a little bigger, but it badly lacks the Marquette Mall's style.

For two decades, the Marquette Mall was the best place in Marquette to shop. At the east end was Angeli's grocery store, complete with a rolling beltway and a drive-up window to pick up groceries, and on the west end was Woolworth's, including its little restaurant. The mall's Cinema was Marquette's third movie theater, where as a boy I was thrilled to watch *Star Wars, The Empire Strikes Back, Superman,* and *E.T.* Of course, B. Dalton Bookseller was my favorite store, but I also liked the Natural Habitat, Hallmark, and Bressler's ice cream shop—33 flavors. Clothing and shoe stores, the Onion Crock Restaurant, one of Marquette's two Big Boy restaurants, a jewelry store, a video arcade, and Gordie's Patio were just a few of its many other businesses. At the start of Piper's Alley was a flower shop, followed by the pipe and tobacco store, and then down the hall a T-shirt printing shop, a record shop, and

Loretta's Craft Corner. Aunt Vi always had to go to Loretta's when she visited—she thought it the best craft store she had ever seen.

Most memorable of all, in the Marquette Mall's center was a large pool with a bridge over it; eight fountains with colored lights shot up sprays of blue, pink, and yellow water. When I included mention of this fountain in *Superior Heritage*, several people told me, "Thank you for mentioning it. I loved that fountain." The bridge was usually roped off, but sometimes it was used for events—I especially remember that Willy Wonka visited and gave a performance here, although I don't think he handed out golden tickets to his chocolate factory—I wouldn't have wanted one anyway; I thought the film rather scary back then.

At Christmas, the Marquette Mall was always decorated wonderfully—I remember giant storybooks with fairy tale stories in them and little trains going around in circles in the center of the hallways. Mom would take us to see Santa Claus arrive at the mall in a fire truck and then we would wait in line to sit on his lap. I don't remember what I asked for, but I remember he gave my brother and me plastic rings with Mickey Mouse and Donald Duck on them. Years later, I was part of the Gwinn High School Choir that performed Christmas Carols in the mall the Friday after Thanksgiving.

For many years, the Marquette Mall also featured craft shows, so Grandpa would go there to sell his tables, mirrors, lazy susans, and stools. Aunt Sadie and Aunt Barb sold their crafts—dolls, plastic canvas Kleenex boxes, hot pads, and towels—and Uncle Jolly would sell his polished rocks. I frequently went along to help.

Today, Riverside Auto has taken over where Angeli's once was, and the Dollar Tree and Big Lots take up the location of the former Woolworth's. I believe only Wells Fargo is still in the place it originally occupied back when it was still First National Bank. The Marquette Mall has changed, the fountain is gone, but memories remain of dozens of shopping adventures, books and Christmas gifts bought, movies attended, and ice cream cones eaten.

Boy Scouts at Marquette Mall Fountain ~ 1973

HAMBURGER HEAVEN & THE VILLA CAPRI

"Hey, are you hungry? I haven't had any lunch yet. We could go to Hamburger Heaven."

— Narrow Lives

Hamburger Heaven

Today where the Villa Capri stands, and long before the fast-food chains came to town, was Marquette's first hamburger place, Hamburger Heaven. It was a popular restaurant from the time it opened in the 1950s, mostly with the teenagers and college students who had cars to drive that far to visit it. Hamburgers, French fries, and milkshakes were of course menu favorites, and one could eat at its drive-in without leaving the car, or go inside to dine. Here in *Narrow Lives*, Scofield Blackmore tries to comfort Carol Ann, after her stepfather mistreats her, by taking her out to eat, an event that will lead to a long and rocky relationship between them.

But Hamburger Heaven was short-lived, and from my earliest memories, the Villa Capri occupied the spot. The first Villa Capri actually opened on N. Third Street in 1967, but it burned down just two months after it opened. Its current location opened in 1968.

When I was a child, the Villa Capri was the fancy place to go. Yes, there was Clark's

Villa Capri

Landing and the Northwoods, but those were reserved only for really special events like anniversary parties so we rarely went to either. Many nights I remember we went to the Villa and did not even mind the forty-five minute wait to get seated. Today there is rarely a wait, but only because Marquette has more restaurants.

Since I was a boy, the Villa has been one of my favorite restaurants. Like John Vandelaare, who takes Wendy there for supper when she is visiting in *Superior Heritage*, it is the restaurant where I most often take visitors to eat. They always seem impressed by the food portions and the flavor. You can't go wrong with the steak or the lasagna, and that's just the beginning. For great Italian food, the Villa Capri remains the best place in Marquette.

BONANZA

Bonanza

Grandpa and Grandma were regulars at Bonanza, which ensured that Chad and John got extra suckers with their little wrangler meals. They all overstuffed their stomachs with steak, chili con carne, salad, french fries, and ice cream.

— Superior Heritage

When Bonanza opened in 1977, it was one of those new restaurants, springing up along U.S. 41 leading out of town and actually in Marquette Township, but today, it is a mainstay as one of Marquette's longest operating restaurants.

Soon after it opened, my mom and grandma went there for lunch. At that time, Grandma thought Grandpa wouldn't like it because it wasn't a "sit down and be waited on" kind of restaurant. Boy, was she wrong!

Grandpa loved Bonanza. Soon my grandparents were going there for supper at least twice a week. They became good friends with Mitch Lazaren, the owner, and all the Bonanza staff. My grandpa made some frames for different maps and posters for the restaurant, and for Christmas one year, my grandparents were given Bonanza jackets with their names embroidered on them.

For years, my grandparents, parents, brother and I could regularly be found at Bonanza on Saturday nights. It was my favorite restaurant as much as Grandpa's. The Chili Con Carne alone was enough to keep me going back.

How special was Bonanza to my grandparents? So special that during winter blizzards, my mom had to argue on the phone with Grandpa to get him to stay home rather than go there for supper. So special that in 1983, my grandparents celebrated their forty-ninth wedding anniversary there.

Other steakhouses have come and gone in Marquette, but Bonanza has outlived all its competition. The service remains impeccable, the food fantastic, and the atmosphere friendly, if a bit overwhelmed by hungry people crowding around the salad bar—but that's the sign of a truly good restaurant.

**Grandparents
49th Anniversary**

THE BAVARIAN INN

Bonanza was John's favorite place to eat supper, but the Bavarian Inn was the best place in Marquette for breakfast. Even if there were a wait to be seated, it was well worth it. John would have waited an hour for those pancakes, just a bit thicker than crepes and topped with whipping cream and a choice of apples, peaches, or blueberries. He and Chad never had anything else. Let the grownups settle for eggs and coffee. Pancakes with whipping cream and fruit and hot chocolate with more whipping cream was his idea of a German cultural experience.

Bavarian Inn ~ c. 1980

The Bavarian Inn itself was very German. Four dining rooms were darkly paneled as if the wood itself had come from the Black Forest, while red trim, Alpine decorations, and pictures of Bavarian villages decorated the rooms. The dining rooms were separated by walls containing shadow boxes made to resemble windows looking out upon German landscapes; the windows had ornate red shutters with hearts carved into them for an Alpine flavor. Arranged along the windowsills of the boxes were several little Hummel figures for added effect.

Presiding over this Bavarian world transplanted to Marquette was Ernestine LaTour. She had immigrated to the United States from Germany, and now that her husband, who had helped found the restaurant and its motel, was deceased, she had rented out the restaurant for others to manage, but a day never passed that she was not there, making sure all was well. Her husband had hired Henry to do some carpentry work when the hotel was first built, and since then, the families had been friendly. Many times she had been included in family parties at the Whitmans' house when John was younger, but now he was at an age when her friendliness embarrassed him.

After saying hello to everyone, Mrs. LaTour asked, "John, do you remember that time you wanted to play hairdresser and I let you comb my hair?"

John smiled and nodded his head politely. He had not played hairdresser since he was five, and he could not imagine what had possessed him then.

The adults laughed, while Mrs. LaTour pulled up a chair, lit a cigarette, and visited with the family. Henry and Beth invited her for a Sunday drive that afternoon. Then she went to ensure her other guests were content while the waitress brought those delicious pancakes.

— Superior Heritage

What I wouldn't do to go back one more time to the Bavarian Inn to have the pancakes, rolled up almost like crepes, complete with loads of whipping cream and fruit topping!

But far more than the food made the Bavarian Inn special.

This German looking restaurant and motel was owned by Sherman and Ernestine LaTour. The Bavarian Inn was built in 1965, and while I don't know all the details, my Great-Uncle Jolly was among those who helped to build it, and the LaTours were so happy with his work that on the front of the building when they painted the German boy and girl in traditional costume, Uncle Jolly (without a drop of German blood in him) was the model for the boy.

Mr. LaTour at Bavarian Inn

Then in 1976, the Bavarian Inn Restaurant was built in front of the motel. My grandfather was hired to do much of the restaurant's fancy interior woodwork. The

Mrs. LaTour & Uncle Kit at a Family Birthday

restaurant had shadow boxes in the walls separating the four different dining rooms, and these boxes contained pictures of Bavaria; to make the boxes look like windows with views of Germany, Grandpa made shutters with hearts carved into them. He would use the same heart pattern to make the shutters for my parents' house. Grandpa also designed the wooden porch awning that ran inside the restaurant. The result was one of the most distinctive and beautiful restaurants in Marquette.

The Bavarian Inn Restaurant featured such German foods when it opened as *weinerschnitzel*, *sauerbraten*, and *rostbraten*. Eventually, however, the restaurant made a shift and became instead famous for its breakfasts and was renamed the Alpine Pancake House until 1986 when management changed and it became The Chalet Restaurant. In either case, throughout the 1980s it was always packed on Sundays for breakfast and remained open through the 1990s.

Because my grandparents became good friends with the LaTours, they always attended our family parties. Mr. LaTour was a short little man who was content to sit on a stool that was almost like a high chair at the kitchen table. He died in 1981 when I was only ten, so I barely remember him, but Mrs. LaTour I knew well. She had been born in Germany and retained her German accent. My grandparents would take her for Sunday drives after her husband died, and she was frequently at their house. One day when I wasn't much more than five, she came over and let me play hairdresser with her hair. That was a mistake on my part. She never let me forget it. For years after that, she would always ask me whether I wanted to play hairdresser.

After my grandparents died, we did not see Mrs. LaTour very often. In the summer of 1998, when I came home from downstate to visit, I went with a friend to the Bavarian Inn for lunch. Mrs. LaTour was in a wheelchair by then and sitting on the other end of the restaurant. I was too embarrassed to go over and say hello to her from fear she would embarrass me in front of my friend by asking the usual hairdresser question.

Later, I felt guilty that I had not made a point of speaking to her. She died only about a month later. Her daughter who lived in Germany—we had no idea she had a daughter—came for the funeral, but since she lived in Germany, the Bavarian Inn was sold. It was soon after torn down. Today a Citgo gas station occupies where once it stood on the other side of Werner Street across from the Westwood Mall's parking lot.

But I can still taste those pancakes with whipped cream and peaches on them—they really were that good.

THE NORTHWOODS

The Northwoods Supper Club opened in 1935 a few miles west of Marquette back in the days when Marquette basically ended at Lincoln Avenue. The Great Depression meant few people could afford to drive out of town to eat,

The Northwoods Supper Club ~ c. 1998

but nevertheless, Fred and Emma Klumb built an impressive restaurant on an eight acre piece of land that became so popular it would stay open for over seventy years.

The Northwoods saw numerous expansions during its long life. A beer and wine bar was added in 1937, followed by the Fireside Room in 1961 with a seating capacity of one hundred, and in 1965, the 240 seat Theatre Room was built where community theatre productions were occasionally held. Later the Embers Room would provide space for another 250 people to eat. Some tourist cabins were also erected, but they were all torn down in 1967. In 1983, a fire destroyed the center of the restaurant but the building was soon reconstructed. Wedding receptions, birthday and graduation parties, and business meetings would continue to be held for many more years until in 2007 when the restaurant finally closed. At that point, it was discussed whether the building should be demolished or remodeled as condominiums. It currently sits empty.

My family rarely went to the Northwoods to eat, but in 1984, my grandparents' fiftieth wedding anniversary was held there. It would be one of the largest parties

Grandparents 50th Anniversary

I would ever attend, with both sides of my grandparents' families as well as numerous friends coming from near and far. My grandma's nephews came from across the U.P. and as far away as Washington D.C. My grandpa's sisters came from Washington and Louisiana. My aunt and uncle and my cousins came from Seattle. Both my Aunt Vi and Ed Barkow, who had been maid of honor and best man for my grandparents, attended.

It was a big day for my grandparents, and one they well deserved for all the years they were married and the love they always showed each other.

*

I did not know it at the time, but my grandparents would only have three more years together. To that point, my childhood had been wonderful, surrounded by a loving family. But my grandfather's loss seemed to mark the end of innocence to me, and in the years that followed, more and more people I had known as a child would pass away.

Part of why I started writing was because as I reached my teenage years, I came to realize how fortunate I had been to be raised in such an extended, loving family and in such a wonderful place as Marquette. On June 4, 1987, three months before Grandpa died, I began writing my first novel which would eventually become *The Only Thing That Lasts*. The original plan was to write a book about my grandpa's childhood, but somehow Robert O'Neill, the main character, ended up being a year older than my grandpa and born in South Carolina. Nothing about the book had anything to do with Grandpa, but I kept writing, and after some other false attempts and fragments set in Marquette, I eventually sat down in Marquette's sesquicentennial year of 1999 and began writing *The Marquette Trilogy*, not knowing it would be a trilogy at all, or that more books would follow. I wrote from my heart and tried to find interesting historical events to build scenes around. Deep inside, I sensed that the history of Marquette was as important to thousands of other people as it was to me—that we all knew it was a special place. Each of my novels has a quote at the beginning, but the one that best fits my reason for writing is the one at the beginning of *Superior Heritage* from Helen Hooven Santmyer's *Farewell to Summer*:

> *Solitary women like me, old men like Cousin Tune: in every day and time there have been many of us, clinging with all the strength of our memories to the old ways—old men and old maids who eye each other on meeting, and in that silent interchange promise to hold fast, by their futile stubbornness, in their own minds—who when they see the life they know not only doomed, but dead and very nearly forgotten, sit down alone to write the elegies.*

When I started writing *The Marquette Trilogy*, I lived in Kalamazoo and then in South Carolina. I was very homesick and almost despairing that I would never return home. I enjoyed teaching, but somehow my heart and intuition knew I was meant to be in Marquette—trying to follow an academic career only made me feel miserable. I felt old, like my best days were past. I had no idea then how many good days were before me if I only followed my heart rather than what I thought was the responsible, financially secure thing to do. Life was not easy when I returned home, but I came back to Marquette in 2001 determined to write and publish my novels, even if it meant starving. I never came close to starving. Instead, I found a job at Superior Spectrum and worked my way up in the company while I wrote every evening and weekend. Eventually, I had money to buy a house and then as my novels were finished, to publish them. In time, I used my books as a platform to build my own business as an editor, book reviewer, and author, and ultimately, I created the life I had initially dreamed of having when I first started writing. Everything has worked out for the best, and I trust it always will.

I have learned how amazing life can be just by having a positive attitude and doing what you love and believe in. Rather than live one of the "narrow lives" some of my characters live, I have chosen otherwise. When I started writing *The Marquette Trilogy,* I was mourning the past to some degree. Today I see my books as a celebration of the past, and as an inspiration for the future—if the generations before us could persevere despite all the odds, we who live in such better times have no excuse not to do the same. I refuse to believe the world is not a better place than it was in the past or that it will not continue to evolve into being a better place. I have no time for naysayers and those who bemoan the current political or financial problems of the world or who claim our best years are behind us. That kind of thinking would have kept us living in caves. If my readers gather nothing else from my novels, I hope they will take up the call to be Iron Pioneers in their own lives. Our ancestors, all those who struggled and followed their dreams, in Marquette or anywhere else, I trust would tell us the same. Don't give in to the darkness. The world is filled with shining light. Add to it!

Marquette has changed a great deal since my childhood, but I also recognize the wonderful efforts to keep the city beautiful, to use the lakeshore for the greatest good—certainly, our nineteenth and twentieth century ancestors, with their coal and iron ore and chemical plants, would scarcely recognize our beautiful city today. While some grand old buildings are gone, for the most part Marquette has preserved what was the very best of its past, and what was good that is now gone still lives forever in memories.

PART X: STONEGATE

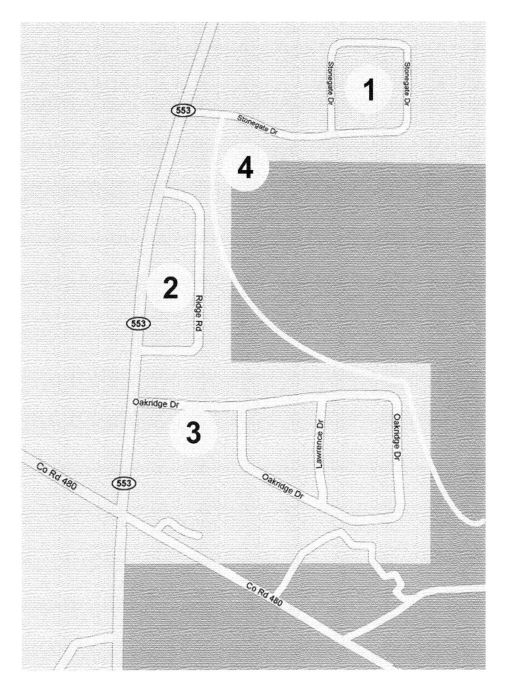

1. Stonegate
2. Ridge Road
3. Oakridge
4. The Oakridge Trail

NATURE & THE IMAGINATION: MY WORDSWORTHIAN CHILDHOOD

Soon the boys and Dickens were outside. They quickly discovered the wind was still strong, so seeking protection, they set Dickens up on the high snowbank, then climbed up themselves. They trudged on top of the snow, at times six feet above the buried grass, until they reached the shelter of the neighboring woods. They found a giant pine tree whose lowest branches, usually eight feet above the ground, were now heavily weighed down with snow, until they curved down three feet to touch the top of the frozen banks. The boys were forced to bend down to enter beneath the tree whose branches were too high for them to reach on summer days. Beneath the tree's bent limbs, they felt sheltered in their own little lodge house. A small depression around the tree formed snow walls to provide further insulation from the bitter chill wind, while leaving room for John, Chad, and Dickens to sit and watch the dying storm. Exhausted from the heavy trudge into the woods, the boys and Dickens were content to listen to the storm's fury. The dazzling whiteness of everything was breathtaking—snow was clustered against the brown and gray tree trunks, turning them into giant white poles, while tree branches had glazed over with frozen ice and snow that perched precariously until the morning sun would come to melt it away.

Neither brother was eloquent enough to express his awe over the beauty of the scene, but neither could fail to notice it. Now free from the stifling, still air inside the house, the boys gratefully opened their mouths and breathed in the fresh coolness, enjoying the pleasure of it biting down their throats. They pulled off their gloves to coil their fingers into fists, then replaced their gloves with their fingers curled together to ward off the numbness a short while longer. They took turns petting Dickens with their fisted gloves, while Dickens huddled against them to stay warm.

Serenity filled the moment, yet in this serenity was an exhilaration surpassing yesterday's anticipation of the storm. As the wind slowly died down with less frequent gusts, the boys felt proud to have survived the storm. Nature's fury had left behind three feet of snow, broken tree branches, enormous snow drifts, hundreds of hours of snow removal work, and downed power lines, but it had also revived the courage of its witnesses; they were survivors like their pioneer ancestors who had fought similar storms a century before when snowblowers and electricity had not been imagined; the pioneers' survivor spirit had resurrected itself, making the Vandelaare boys respectful admirers of Nature's sublime power.

Tichelaar Backyard After a Snowfall ~ c. 1985

John's spirits had been especially stirred by the wind, now no longer a screeching banshee voice wreaking havoc, but a simple whisper carrying the last twinkling fall of snowflakes that resembled confetti more than ice bullets. John recalled the Bible story of God's appearance to the prophet Elijah. There had been a wind, an earthquake, and a fire, but God had not been in any of them. God had been found in a gentle whisper. Now John felt he understood that passage. The wind had subsided to a whisper, a promise of peace and renewal as the snow cleansed the earth to create a new landscape. John felt a deepened sense of contentment, as if he had learned a secret about Nature's incredible power, yet sheltered beneath the pine tree, he felt he would always be safe in the northern wilderness, no matter how fierce the blizzards might blow.

"We better go in," Chad broke into his brother's thoughts. "Mom'll be worried if we're not in by dark."

— Superior Heritage

Most people in Upper Michigan share my deep love for Nature, for none of us are ever more than a few minutes away from the forests and lakes, and all of Upper Michigan is really just a gigantic forest with a few small towns carved into it. For me, that love was fostered by growing up in Stonegate Heights near the Crossroads about five miles south of Marquette. As a result I would go to school in Gwinn rather than Marquette, but I always felt more attached to Marquette since it was closer, it was my mother's family's home, and we went "to town" numerous times every week to shop, go to church, and visit my grandparents.

My parents built a house in Stonegate in 1974, just about a year after the subdivision was created. I was three years old. I am forever grateful that no developers came in and cut all the trees down to create the subdivision. Instead, wooded half-acre lots were sold. My parents bought one right on the top of the hill. We had neighbors on the right but not on our left where throughout my childhood would be two empty wooded lots and another two diagonally across the street.

My bedroom was in the back of the house, and one window looked out into the large shaded backyard and woods that followed behind our property for many, many acres, while my other window looked directly into the empty wooded lots. Through these woods ran many old snowmobile trails from the Hiawathaland Snowmobile Club just a half-mile or so away on County Road 553. The trail that ran from the edge of our yard and connected with a larger trail wound its way through the woods and behind all the houses on one end of Stonegate. Across the street the Oakridge Trail—so named because it ran behind the neighboring Oakridge subdivision—could actually be followed five miles all the way to Harvey; as children, my brother, our friends, and I would many times ride our bikes back through the woods that far.

My earliest memories of living in Stonegate were playing in the woods by my house, building forts out of sticks and picking ferns to make roofs for the forts. As kids, we were always in the woods. We even named some of the trees, and we were constantly found climbing in them. It was nothing for us to climb up thirty feet in a tree, although we tried not to tell our parents we did so. "Frederick" was the biggest, strongest tree and the one in which we could climb the highest, but we also loved "Bernard" which had fallen over long before but wedged itself in between two other trees so that it slanted. We could actually walk up this tree to sit between the two trees that held it in place about seven feet above the ground. That tree survived in that position for about ten years before it finally weakened and we destroyed it from fear someone would actually be hurt if it fell. It was perfect for playing *The Poseidon Adventure* on since we could grab the little birches growing up around it and jump onto them to swing off Bernard, and since Bernard was not that high, we could easily jump off him as well, pretending the *Poseidon* had been flipped by a tidal wave and we were being plummeted to the ceiling that now made up the floor.

Years later, a high school substitute teacher, who must have been from Lower

Michigan, had us read Robert Frost's poem "Birches" in class. She asked us whether a person could really "swing" on a birch tree. She was convinced it was a metaphor and did not believe it was really possible. Even when a friend and I tried to describe to her how to swing on a birch tree, she thought we were joking. Later in English classes at Northern Michigan University, I would be introduced to the wonderful Nature poetry of William Wordsworth. I immediately knew exactly how he felt, loving every tree, every little hill, every fern, every fallen log, every little knoll and copse in the woods. In graduate school at Western Michigan University, one of my professors commented how wonderful it must have been to have had a Wordsworthian childhood and asked whether any of us had—I was the only one who raised my hand. I cannot begin to express how grateful I am to say that I knew what it was to feel at one with Nature as a child because I grew up in Upper Michigan.

Wordsworth wrote, "Nature never did betray/The heart that loved her." I have never forgotten that quote and I instantly felt upon first reading it that it was true. It is that feeling more than any other that I sought to express about Nature in my novels. Yes, hurricanes and even Lake Superior can cause destruction, but I feel a deep-seated belief nevertheless in the sanctity of Nature and that it ultimately is a blessing that refreshes our souls. In *Superior Heritage*, I expressed this belief in the scene quoted above when during the end of a blizzard, John, Chad, and their dog Dickens go outside to play. If you love Nature, it will not harm you—only if you expect it to (positive thinking again).

But most importantly, I loved to walk through the woods, whether it was summer or fall. My dog, Benji, and I daily went for walks. I would jump in the puddles, admire the changing leaves, pick the blueberries, relieve my frustrations with life and restore my soul. No matter how bad a day I might have had, a walk down the Oakridge Trail would find me returning home refreshed and at peace. Often once out of sight of the houses, Benji would good-naturedly tolerate my singing—I couldn't help singing—it felt so good to be in the woods.

The forest was also one of my first pages upon which to write my stories and books. One of the first stories I wrote was "The Ghost of Stonegate Woods" based on my fantasizing about what it would have been like to be a pioneer in the Upper Michigan forest in the early 1800s. I later reworked the story so that the main character, Annabella Stonegate, was mentioned in the background of *Iron Pioneers* and a ghost story was told about her in *The Queen City*. But I am still not done with Annabella as my next novel, *Spirit of the North*, will soon reveal. Becoming reacquainted with her made writing that novel perhaps my most exciting and enjoyable writing experience, and I think it may be the best book I've ever written, but that's up to my readers to decide.

My first, albeit unpublished because never written down novel, was written daily in my mind as I walked the trail beside our house that made a circular path through the woods. Here at about twelve and thirteen years of age, I imagined myself as all of the characters in *Gone With the Wind*, a book that had a tremendous impact on my desire to write historical fiction. In the forest, I lived on the Tara plantation and soon along that circular trail through the woods, I imagined a village was built, and I created an entire new cast of characters as I imagined Scarlett and Rhett's marriage developing as well as their relationships with new characters. Ultimately, Rhett went on a business journey to England and his ship was reported sunk. Scarlett grieved, but she then married Ashley, only to learn Rhett had not drowned. She was in quite a pickle when he returned. I quit creating the story then, not sure how to resolve the situation, and instead turned, just a week after my sixteenth birthday, to writing the first draft of what would eventually become *The Only Thing That Lasts*. But that Robert O'Neill in that novel is from the South is a sure sign that *Gone With the Wind* was still heavily influencing me as I wrote.

Looking back today, I find it a great blessing to have had all that time in the forest, both with my childhood friends, and on solitary walks with only my dog for company. It gave me time to think, to dream about life, to use my imagination, and it gave me a connection with the world beyond concrete streets and television. I was also fortunate to have been born in a time before electronics and television could distract me. We only had three channels on television until about 1982 when I was eleven, so we had to play outside to entertain ourselves. There were no video games then—I don't remember anyone owning an Atari until I was in fifth grade. I am not surprised that I grew up to love Victorian novels. I feel I had quite a Victorian childhood in this sense. My world was more akin to the lives of the country families in Jane Austen's novels or the Ingalls' family in *Little House on the Prairie*. My grandparents were all born between 1900-1912, children of pioneers and Victorians. Growing up in the 1970s and 1980s and spending so much time with my grandparents, I felt more part of the world of their early years than I do to this modern world of email and electronic gadgets.

By the late 1990s, the Stonegate I knew had changed. A retired couple from downstate bought the property behind us and stuck up "No Trespassing" signs so we could no longer walk on the trails. Another person bought the property that gave access to the "Oakridge Trail" and blocked it off with a log pile. The empty lot next to us was bought and a house erected there. My parents still live in the house where I grew up, but my childhood world of Nature is largely gone. Nevertheless, like Wordsworth, I cherish those days as "spots of time" that renew my soul. I have found myself since in stressful jobs, times when I did not know how I would survive, and have literally found myself reverting to visions of the woods, of walking with my dog down the Oakridge Trail, of recalling comforting scenes.

Author & Benji ~ 1985

As I come to the end of this book, I feel much of it, and all of my books, have been an attempt to recapture the scenes and experiences of my childhood. Even when I was a boy, I was always saying "Remember when..." and my mom would say, "Tyler lives in the past." I guess that's true. I seem to remember vividly little things no one else in the family can recollect. I've felt at times like Mary, who "pondered all these things in her heart." I am grateful God has blessed me with such a memory because it has led to my ability to recreate and imagine scenes for my novels.

Would I have become a novelist had I not grown up in Marquette and experienced its beautiful natural scenery, its history, its diverse people? I do not know, but I do know that I could not have written the specific books I have, had it been otherwise. It is these many layers of experiences and this deep-seated connection to the places and the feelings they engender in me that allows me to feel proud to write about "My Marquette."

There are in our existence spots of time,
That with distinct pre-eminence retain
A renovating virtue, whence—depressed
By false opinion and contentious thought,
Or aught of heavier or more deadly weight,
In trivial occupations, and the round
Of ordinary intercourse—our minds
Are nourished and invisibly repaired;
A virtue, by which pleasure is enhanced,
That penetrates, enables us to mount,
When high, more high, and lifts us up when fallen.
          — William Wordsworth, The Prelude

MARQUETTE'S TIMELINE

1637 — Jacques Marquette is born in Laon, France.

1671 — Father Jacques Marquette, Jesuit missionary, holds a large Mass on the shore of Lake Superior, reputedly close to where the city of Marquette will one day be built.

1673 — Father Marquette and Joliet leave Mackinac in two bark canoes to explore lands to the west, including the Mississippi River.

1675 — Father Marquette dies.

1797 — Frederic Baraga is born in Slovenia, then part of the Austro-Hungarian Empire.

1836 — Michigan territory representatives vote not to accept the Upper Peninsula as part of the state boundary. Then Democrats at the "Frost-Bit Convention" accept the U.P. as part of the Michigan statehood bill.

1837 — Michigan becomes the 26th state, upon acceptance of the U.P. instead of the Toledo Strip, following the Toledo "War."

1840 — William Austin Burt hired by Surveyor General to survey U.P.

1843 — U.P. divided into six counties: Chippewa, Houghton, Mackinac, Marquette, Ontonagon, and Schoolcraft.

1844 — Iron ore is discovered in Upper Michigan by William Austin Burt when his compass goes crazy while surveying due to magnetic iron ore rocks.

1845 — Philo Everett, having heard of William Austin Burt's discovery, travels to Upper Michigan. He meets Marji Gesick, a Chippewa Chief, who leads him to the site of iron ore where Negaunee is located today. The discovery begins the iron ore industry, resulting in more mineral wealth being mined than during the California Gold Rush.

Spear Coal Dock

1846 — Chief Marji Gesick is promised a stake in the Jackson Mining Company.

1849 — The village of Worcester is founded by Amos Harlow, Robert Graveraet, Waterman Fisher, and Edward Clarke. Peter White comes to Marquette with Graveraet. The first school is in the Harlow home, as well as the first post office, and first church meetings. First teachers are Mrs. Dan Ball and Mrs. Samuel Barney. First students are the Harlow and Bignall girls. The first winter the inhabitants nearly starve to death until a supply ship arrives on Christmas Day.

1850 — Worcester is renamed Marquette. When the ship *Manhattan* docks in Marquette, Dr. Livermore eulogizes it and Marquette's future glory as an industrial mecca.

1851 — Bishop Frederic Baraga becomes the Bishop of the Diocese of Amyzonia, later named Marianopolita, and then finally, the Diocese of Marquette, consisting of the entire Upper Peninsula. — Peter White becomes county clerk. — The first white child, Elbert Joseph Bignall, is born in Marquette. — The First Methodist Church is founded.

1852 — Peter White named postmaster of Carp River post office, which puts Amos Harlow's early post office out of business. — The Marquette School District is established.

1853 — Charles Harvey arrives at Sault Sainte Marie to begin construction of a shipping canal — Dr. Morgan Hewitt and family come to Marquette. — Lake Superior (Cleveland) Iron Company organized — On October 12th, Bishop Baraga first visits Marquette and selects the site for its first church, eventually to become St. Peter's Cathedral.

1854 — Peter White tricks the U.S. Government about the amount of Marquette mail so the government will make regular mail deliveries to Marquette from Green Bay, Wisconsin.

1855 — The Sault Locks open in Sault Sainte Marie, making shipping on the Great Lakes expand, especially for shipment of iron ore from Marquette's harbor. Charles Harvey, later the founder of neighboring Harvey, Michigan, is the designing engineer. — Marquette celebrates its first Independence Day on July 4th with a lavish party at Samuel Ely's home. — Peter White and M.H. Maynard open a law firm specializing in real estate. — The first two permanent docks are built in Marquette's harbor in Iron Bay. — The first locomotive, the *Sebastopol*, arrives in Marquette. A railroad line is built from Marquette to Negaunee.

1856 — The first Catholic priest arrives in Marquette. — Amos Harlow and Charles Harvey found the First Presbyterian congregation out of the Harlow home. — St. Paul's Episcopal Church is established.

1857 — Peter White marries Ellen Hewitt, daughter of Dr. Morgan Hewitt. White becomes a land agent in Marquette. White also wins a land grant in the Michigan legislature for a railroad to be built in Marquette. The city honors him by referring to him as The Honorable Peter White. — The first U.P. state road links Marquette to L'Anse. Regular stagecoaches begin between the cities until railroad lines are built. — Robert Graveraet becomes the first state senator from Marquette County.

1857-1858 — The first pocket dock is erected in Marquette by the Cleveland Company with 100 pockets. It is believed Marquette will now become the greatest port on Lake Superior and be capable of handling all iron ore shipped for many years to come.

1859 — A state road is built to link Marquette to Bay de Noc. — On February 18th, Marquette is officially incorporated as a village. — Property for the first high school is donated.

1860 — Marquette's population reaches 1,000.

1861 — The Civil War begins. Upper Michigan sends a company for the Michigan 27th, including many Marquette men. Upper Michigan's iron ore is a major resource for the Union to win the war.

1863 — The neighboring town of Harvey is founded after the original Chocolay settlement is destroyed by fire.

1864 — Completion of the Bay de Nocquet and Marquette Railroad's pocket dock, thirty feet high. — Peter White opens the First National Bank on May 10th. Samuel Ely is president. — Cornerstone laid for St. Peter's Cathedral. The diocese now officially becomes the Diocese of Marquette and Sault Sainte Marie.

1866 — Bishop Baraga dedicates the cathedral to St. Peter.

1867 — Peter White builds for himself the first house on Ridge Street. — Ursuline nuns found Marquette's first Catholic school.

1868 — Bishop Frederic Baraga dies. He is succeeded by Bishop Mrak. — The Marquette and Pacific Rolling Mill begins operations. — Marquette burns. Nearly 75 percent of the city is destroyed, including the entire business district and two of three docks. The residents are determined to rebuild. All business buildings must be built of stone from that time on, resulting in many fine examples of Lake Superior Sandstone architecture. — Alfred Swineford starts *The Mining Journal.* — The Fisher Street School is built. — Peter White is a delegate for U.P. Statehood efforts, which fail.

1869 — Peter White is named president of the First National Bank of Marquette for the rest of his life.

1870 — Jacobs takes over sandstone quarry.

1871 — Compulsory school attendance begins in Michigan.

1872 — Samuel Ely becomes Marquette's mayor. To celebrate his friend's success, Peter White begins the first city library. — Marquette becomes connected to national railroads via Escanaba, Menominee, and Chicago.

1873 — A financial panic causes many prominent Marquette citizens to move back East. — John Longyear comes to Upper Michigan as a landlooker. — The First Methodist Church, Marquette's first sandstone structure built by Jacobs, is erected on the corner of Ridge and Front Streets.

1874 — Charles Harvey builds the elevated railroad in New York City. — Harlow's Wooden Man is built. — The first telegraph lines connect Marquette to Western Union. — Alfred Swineford becomes mayor of Marquette. He makes new efforts for U.P. Statehood. — St. Paul's Episcopal Church on Ridge Street begins construction.

1875 — Peter White receives a legislative grant to build a railroad from Sault Sainte Marie to Marquette. — Zachariah Chandler runs as U.S. Senator with the goal to make the U.P. a separate state.

1877 — Bishop Mrak digs up what is believed to be Father Marquette's grave at St. Ignace Mission Chapel. — Marquette's Park Cemetery opens—the property had already been a graveyard since Marquette's early years.

1878 — The Marquette schools' library books get a home in the First National Bank Building.

1879 — John Longyear marries Mary Beecher. — Bishop Mrak resigns his office because of ill health and is succeeded by Bishop John Vertin, the first Catholic bishop consecrated in the Marquette diocese. On October 2nd, St. Peter's Cathedral burns down. Rumors say it was done by parishioners angry at Bishop Vertin for transferring their priest to another parish.

1881 — The Detroit Mackinac Railroad begins providing service over the Mackinac Straits to Lower Michigan. — On June 19th, the cornerstone is laid for the new St. Peter's Cathedral.

1882 — Alfred Swineford builds a home on Cedar Street, which includes several chimneys and an elevator.

1883 — The Messiah Lutheran Church is built on Ridge Street.

1884 — Peter White builds a camp along the Laughing Whitefish River. The Marquette Pacific and Rolling Mill ends operations.

1885 — U.S. President Grover Cleveland appoints Alfred Swineford as Governor of Alaska.

1886 — Peter White presents Presque Isle Park as a gift to the City of Marquette. He states: "The park belongs to the people of Marquette and must be preserved for all who in years to come shall call Marquette 'home'."

1887 — Peter White donates money to build the Morgan Chapel on St. Paul's Episcopal Church in memory of his son Morgan who died young. — The Clifton Hotel burns down.

1888 — The Soo Line Railroad begins providing service from Sault Sainte Marie to Minneapolis with a stop in Marquette.

1889-1892 — The Longyear Mansion is built. It covers the entire city block between Ridge and Cedar Streets, contains sixty-five rooms, and has a bowling alley in the basement.

1889 — The Marquette Post Office is built at the corner of Washington and Third Streets. — The first train to St. Ignace, on the Detroit, Mackinac & Marquette Line, leaves Marquette — The Marquette Branch State Prison is built.

1890 — St. Peter's Cathedral is consecrated for use. — The Ely Elementary School is built on Bluff Street. It will later serve as the elementary school for St. John the Baptist's Catholic Church. — Streetcars first begin use in Marquette.

1891 — Harlow's Wooden Man is featured in a mock marriage ceremony. — The Cleveland Iron Mining Company and Iron Cliffs Company merge to form the Cleveland-Cliffs Company. — Ishpeming and Negaunee celebrate July

Northern State Normal School ~ c. 1920

4th with Marquette; 5,000 visitors make it Marquette's biggest celebration to date. — The Hotel Superior is built. — The Huron Mountain Club, an exclusive hunting and fishing club north of Marquette, is established. Members will include the Longyears, Peter White, and Henry Ford.

1892 — New efforts for U.P. Statehood. The U.P. now has 180,000 residents, more than five other states currently in the Union. — Peter White gives the city library the Thurber Block, later the site of the Nordic Theater on Washington Street. — St. Mary's Hospital opens in South Marquette. — The Marquette Opera House is opened, following funding efforts by Peter White and John M. Longyear.

1895 — Homer Kidder records Ojibwa tales of Chief Charles Kawbawgam.

1897 — The Father Marquette statue is dedicated. It is placed beside the new city waterworks building. The statue is said suspiciously to resemble Peter White who commissioned it. — St. Luke's Hospital opens on Ridge Street. It will later become Marquette General Hospital.

1899 — Northern State Normal School is founded. In the dedication speech, Peter White declares Marquette will become an "Athens" of the North.

1900 — Howard Longyear drowns. His parents John and Mary Longyear wish to dedicate a park along the lakeshore for him, but the city instead allows a railroad to be built. Angered, Mrs. Longyear vows never to return to Marquette. — The Howard-Froebel School's connected elementary, high, and manual training building begins construction.

1901 — Captain Cleary's lifesaving crew from Marquette gives demonstrations at the Pan-American exhibition in New York where U.S. President McKinley is assassinated. — Louis G. Kaufman of Marquette gains majority control of First National Bank stock, but Peter White remains its president. — The Citizen's Home (the Marquette Poor Farm, later the Brookridge estate) is built in South Marquette. — July 15th is Marquette's record hottest day at 108 degrees. Men take off their coats and walk around in just shirtsleeves!

1902 — Buffalo Bill's Wild West Show comes to Marquette. — The Hotel Superior closes. — Charles Kawbawgam, last Chief of the Chippewa, dies and is buried at Presque Isle. His wife Charlotte, daughter of Chief Marji Gesick, is buried be-

Chief Kawbawgam & Family at Presque Isle Home

side him upon her death in 1904.

1903 — Still angry at the City of Marquette, the Longyears have their enormous mansion dismantled and shipped on railroad car to Brookline, Massachusetts.

1904 — The Peter White Public Library is built at its present location on Front and Ridge Streets. It originally includes a "men only" smoking room in the basement. — The Marquette County Courthouse is built. — September 17th is a day of great Civic Pride for Marquette when both buildings are officially opened. — The old County Courthouse is dismantled and the lumber sold to the Catholic Diocese for building the Bishop Baraga School. — Local author, Carroll Watson Rankin, publishes her popular children's novel *Dandelion Cottage*.

1905 — Peter White organizes the 50th anniversary celebrations of the Sault Locks. — Marquette's first movie theatre, the Bijou, opens.

1908 — Peter White dies while climbing the steps of the Detroit City Hall. *The Mining Journal* runs a special edition in his memory. — The ship *Clemson* sinks in Lake Superior.

1910 — The new St. John the Baptist Catholic Church is built on the corner of Washington and Fourth Streets.

1911 — William Taft is the first U.S. President to visit Marquette while in office.

1913 — The ship *Henry Smith* sinks in Lake Superior. — On May 26th, the famous Theodore Roosevelt trial takes place at the Marquette County Courthouse when an Ishpeming reporter slanders the former U.S. president in print by calling him a drunkard. Roosevelt wins the trial.

1914 — The Delft Theatre opens; for many years, it will have the largest movie screen in Upper Michigan.

1915 — The Holy Family Orphanage opens. It will be the Catholic children's

Theodore Roosevelt With Civil War Veterans

orphanage until 1965. — A new St. Luke's Hospital is built in North Marquette.

1916 — Prohibition begins in Marquette County. The entire nation will be under prohibition from 1920-1933.

1917 — Five ships are trapped in the ice on Lake Superior in the month of May near Marquette. — Marquette sends its young men as enlisted soldiers to train at Fort Custer for World War I.

1918 — The Marquette County Historical Society is founded.

1919 — The country of Norway purchases the island of Spitzbergen from John Longyear for $40 million.

1920 — Ferry service begins at the Mackinac Straits to transport vehicles between Upper and Lower Michigan.

1921 — Marquette Branch Prison Riot. Warden Catlin and Deputy Warden Menhennett are killed.

1922 — The City of Marquette buys Laurium's Palestra building and moves it to Marquette for ice-skating and hockey. — John M. Longyear dies.

1924 — Marquette's worst murder spree. Oscar Lampinen kills three men before Officer Walter Tippet shoots him.

1927 — The new First National Bank is built on the corner of Washington and Front Streets, the world's most expensive building per square foot built to date.

1928 — Northern Normal School becomes Northern State Teachers College.

1929 — The Great Depression begins across the nation.

1930 — Marquette's Northland Hotel (later the Landmark Inn) is completed.

1931 — On July 2nd, WBEO, *The Mining Journal*'s radio station, begins broadcasting as the first radio station in Upper Michigan. — Dr. Albert Hornbogen and a prisoner are killed in a Marquette Branch Prison riot.

1935 — St. Peter's Cathedral burns again. — The First Presbyterian Church on Front Street opens. — Marquette's last streetcar quits running. — The Northwoods Supper Club opens.

1936 — The Nordic Theatre opens.

1937 — The second Marquette Post Office at the corner of Washington and Third Streets opens.

1938 — During a blizzard, Marquette's downtown catches fire. Rumor suggests a scandal in the Episcopal Church resulted in the burning of documents in a downtown office, which caused the fire. The Episcopal bishop had apparently been investing in Chicago nightclubs. Among other buildings, Marquette's

Opera House is destroyed.

1941 — Northern State Teacher's College becomes Northern Michigan College of Education. — The U.S. enters World War II. Local volunteers watch the city skies from fear of Nazi air raids to bomb the ore docks.

1942 — Louis G. Kaufman, president of the First National Bank, dies. — George Shiras III, famous local photographer and Peter White's son-in-law dies. — St. Michael's Catholic Church is established in a former dormitory bought from Northern Michigan College of Education.

1945 — World War II ends.

1949 — Marquette's Centennial. Celebrations include a beard growing contest and a best historical costume contest. Marquette holds its biggest parade to date.

1952 — Mike Chenoweth, winner of the centennial beard-growing contest, is shot in Big Bay by Lieutenant Coleman Peterson. The murder will become the source of local writer John Voelker's *Anatomy of a Murder*.

Front Street ~ 1949

1954 — The Mackinac Bridge, the world's longest suspension bridge, begins construction to link Upper and Lower Michigan. It opens to traffic in 1957.

1955 — Northern Michigan Teachers College becomes Northern Michigan College.

1956 — Marquette's first television station, WLUC TV 6, begins programming.

1957 — The Peter White Public Library adds its annex.

1958 — *Anatomy of a Murder* by Robert Traver (pseudonym of John Voelker) is published.

1959 — *Anatomy of a Murder*, based on John Voelker's novel, is filmed in Marquette County by Otto Preminger and stars James Stewart, Lee Remick, Eve Arden, Arthur O'Connell, George C. Scott, Kathryn Crosby, and Ben Gazzara. Marquette County is "starstruck."

1960s — The U.S. 41 bypass is built, resulting in a decline of downtown Marquette, and the city's growth westward.

1960 — The new Messiah Lutheran Church opens on Fourth and Magnetic Streets.

1962 — The nation's first snowmobile race takes place in Marquette.

1963 — Northern Michigan College becomes Northern Michigan University.

1965 — The Marquette Senior High School opens. — The First Baptist Church on Front St. burns down. A new church is built near Northern Michigan University. — The old Messiah Lutheran Church is destroyed. — The second Clifton Hotel burns down.

1967 — Official "Pasty Day" is first celebrated in the U.P.

1972 — Efforts begin for the canonization to sainthood of Bishop Frederic Baraga. — Public TV 13 (PBS) begins broadcasting at Northern Michigan University. — The Marquette Mall opens, the largest mall in Upper Michigan.

1973 — St. Luke's Hospital and St. Mary's Hospital merge to become Marquette General Hospital.

1974 — The Palestra Ice Rink is torn down and replaced by the Lakeview Arena.

1975 — U.P statehood appears on ballots in Marquette and Iron Mountain, but is defeated with 37.1% FOR, 62.9% AGAINST.

1978 — State Representative Dominic Jacobetti introduces a bill for U.P. separation from Michigan and Upper Michigan statehood, but the bill is never brought to vote in the State House of Representatives. — NMU students bake the world's largest pasty, wrapped in 250 lbs of dough.

1985 — The historic Delft Theatre becomes a two-screen movie house. Formerly, it had the largest movie screen in Upper Michigan.

1986 — St. John the Baptist's Catholic Church is demolished to become a parking lot. The bell tower is preserved. The rose window now hangs in St. Michael's Church.

1989 — Northern Michigan University begins constructing the Superior Dome, the world's largest wooden dome. It is affectionately nicknamed "The Yooper Dome."

1992 — The Brookridge estate (Marquette's Poor Farm) is destroyed. It will be replaced by the Brookridge Assisted Living Facility. — The John D. Pierce School, Northern Michigan University's original teaching school, is demolished.

1993 — Northern Michigan University's historic Longyear Hall, the last of its original buildings, is demolished despite public controversy. Ironically, NMU then begins preparing for its 100th anniversary by locating historical sites on campus.

LS&I Dock in Winter

1994 — U.S. Vice President Al Gore visits Marquette; he had previously visited in 1992 while campaigning. — The Historic Delft Theatre becomes five screens, and the GKC Royal Cinema opens with ten screens. — Dominic Jacobetti dies after being elected to the Michigan House twenty-one times.

1995 — The Nordic Theatre, site of the world premiere of *Anatomy of a Murder,* closes. The building is turned into Book World. — K.I. Sawyer Air Force Base closes.

1999 — Marquette's Sesquicentennial. The Presque Isle Pavilion is completed as a gift to the City from the people of Marquette. — Northern Michigan University constructs its Seaborg Center and Berry Events Center.

2000 — Removal of the Soo Line trestle in downtown Marquette. — Upfront & Co., a restaurant and nightclub, opens in the old Rosewood Inn. — The Peter White Public Library holds its grand opening of its renovated building. — The First National Bank merges to become part of Wells Fargo.

2001 — Controversy erupts over deer being shot at Presque Isle Park, resulting in angry citizens referring to the event as Blood Island. — Marquette's Frida Waara joins eleven others to become the first women to ski to the North Pole. — A Stand Up for Iron Ore rally against steel imports is held at the Superior Dome. — On September 11th, a plane of Japanese tourists makes an emergency landing in Marquette during the 9/11 terrorist attacks. The Great Lakes, Sault Locks, and Marquette harbors are under security watch.

2002 — Peter White's original Lombardy Poplars along Lakeshore Avenue are removed because they are dead or diseased.

2003 — The historical Jacobs House is torn down on Front Street. — The Great Flood: May 11-12 heavy rains cause flooding. May 14-15, the dam at the Silver Lake Basin breaks. The Dead River overflows several feet above regular levels. All of Marquette north of Wright Street, 2,000 people total, is evacuated from fear it will be underwater if the Hoist Dam also breaks. The bridge over the Dead River to Presque Isle Park is wiped out, prohibiting access to the Presque Isle Power Plant, resulting in the Empire and Tilden mines being shut down and people in Big Bay being without power. Tourist Park's beach is destroyed and the former lake becomes a river.

2004 — Marquette is named an All-America City, one of only ten in the U.S. — On July 13th, President George W. Bush campaigns at the Superior Dome. He is only the second U.S. president to visit Marquette while in office.

2005 — International Finn Fest is held. Marquette's all time largest celebration.

2006 — Tyler R. Tichelaar begins publishing his series of historical Marquette novels. — Alexander Sample becomes Bishop of Marquette, the world's youngest bishop at age forty-five when he is ordained bishop. — Quiznos, Papa Murphy's, and Starbucks open. (Starbucks' founder is a graduate of Northern Michigan University).

2007 — The Northwoods Supper Club closes after more than seventy years in business. — On June 20, the great hailstorm hits Marquette, damaging automobiles and homes. The streets are flooded, leaves and brush are left behind, and it is several days before the golf-ball size hail melts. — On June 23rd, the Shamrock Bar, after a hundred years in business, closes in Downtown Marquette. It is bought by the Wahlstrom family and becomes Elizabeth's Chop House. — The Donckers family sells Donckers store after its being in the family more than a century; the new owners restore the old soda fountain and retain the name.

2009 — Fred Rydholm, former Marquette mayor, local historian, and author of *Superior Heartland* dies. — May 18th is officially established as Founders Day, the date in 1849 when Peter White and Robert Graveraet arrived in Iron Bay and were greeted by Chief Charles Kawbawgam. The first commemorative reenactment of the event is held at Founders Landing at 6 a.m. — Marquette County celebrates the 50th anniversary of the filming of *Anatomy of a Murder*.

2010 — The National Trust for Historic Preservation announces that Marquette is the winner of the 2010 Dozen Distinctive Destinations "Fan Favorite" award chosen by the public via an online vote. — The Front St./US 41 Roundabout opens. — The Marquette County History Museum moves to its new location on Third and Spring Streets.

TYLER R. TICHELAAR'S FAMILY TREES

The Buschell and Molby Families

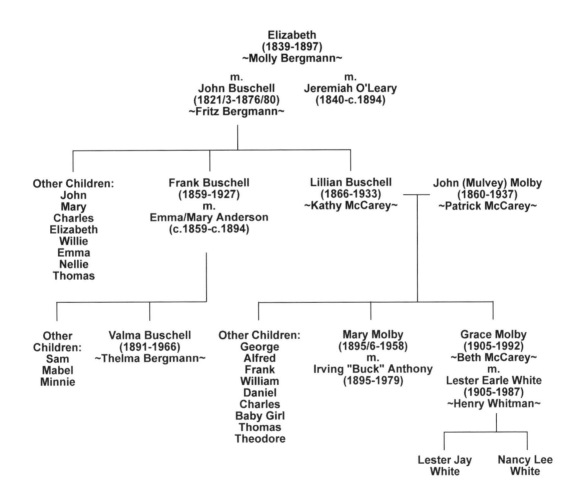

Elizabeth
(1839-1897)
~Molly Bergmann~

m.
John Buschell
(1821/3-1876/80)
~Fritz Bergmann~

m.
Jeremiah O'Leary
(1840-c.1894)

Other Children:
John
Mary
Charles
Elizabeth
Willie
Emma
Nellie
Thomas

Frank Buschell
(1859-1927)
m.
Emma/Mary Anderson
(c.1859-c.1894)

Lillian Buschell
(1866-1933)
~Kathy McCarey~

John (Mulvey) Molby
(1860-1937)
~Patrick McCarey~

Other
Children:
Sam
Mabel
Minnie

Valma Buschell
(1891-1966)
~Thelma Bergmann~

Other Children:
George
Alfred
Frank
William
Daniel
Charles
Baby Girl
Thomas
Theodore

Mary Molby
(1895/6-1958)
m.
Irving "Buck" Anthony
(1895-1979)

Grace Molby
(1905-1992)
~Beth McCarey~
m.
Lester Earle White
(1905-1987)
~Henry Whitman~

Lester Jay
White

Nancy Lee
White

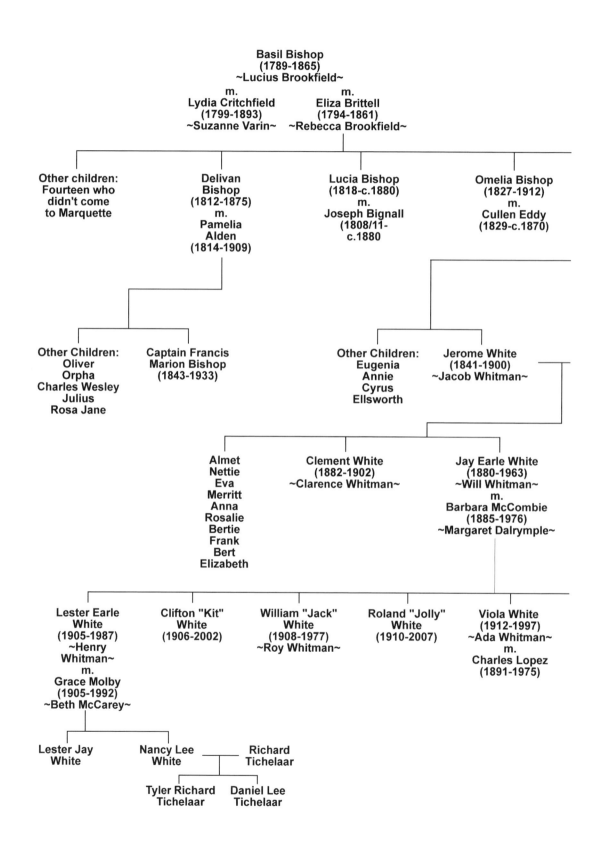

The Bishop, White, and Remington Families

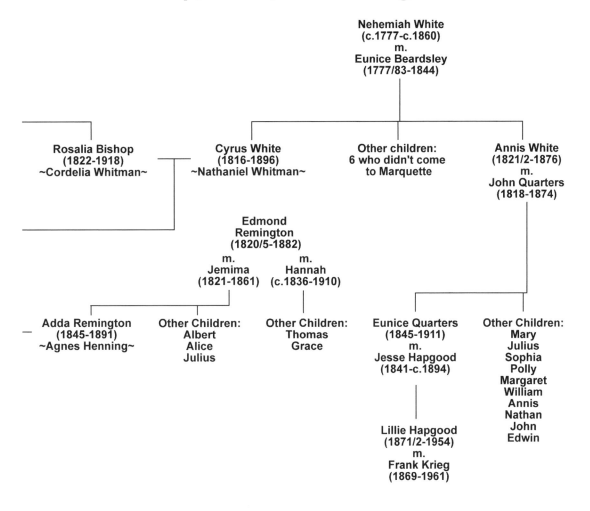

Nehemiah White
(c.1777-c.1860)
m.
Eunice Beardsley
(1777/83-1844)

Rosalia Bishop
(1822-1918)
~Cordelia Whitman~

Cyrus White
(1816-1896)
~Nathaniel Whitman~

Other children:
6 who didn't come
to Marquette

Annis White
(1821/2-1876)
m.
John Quarters
(1818-1874)

Edmond
Remington
(1820/5-1882)
m.   m.
Jemima   Hannah
(1821-1861)   (c.1836-1910)

Adda Remington
(1845-1891)
~Agnes Henning~

Other Children:
Albert
Alice
Julius

Other Children:
Thomas
Grace

Eunice Quarters
(1845-1911)
m.
Jesse Hapgood
(1841-c.1894)

Other Children:
Mary
Julius
Sophia
Polly
Margaret
William
Annis
Nathan
John
Edwin

Lillie Hapgood
(1871/2-1954)
m.
Frank Krieg
(1869-1961)

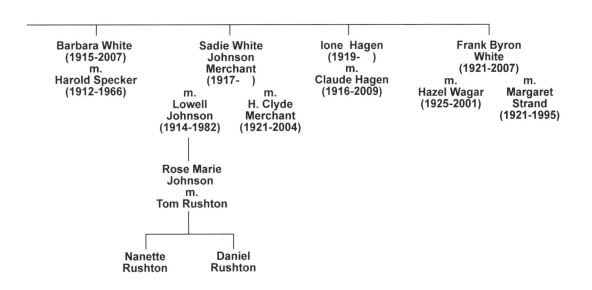

Barbara White
(1915-2007)
m.
Harold Specker
(1912-1966)

Sadie White
Johnson
Merchant
(1917-   )
m.   m.
Lowell   H. Clyde
Johnson   Merchant
(1914-1982)   (1921-2004)

Ione Hagen
(1919-   )
m.
Claude Hagen
(1916-2009)

Frank Byron
White
(1921-2007)
m.   m.
Hazel Wagar   Margaret
(1925-2001)   Strand
                       (1921-1995)

Rose Marie
Johnson
m.
Tom Rushton

Nanette
Rushton

Daniel
Rushton

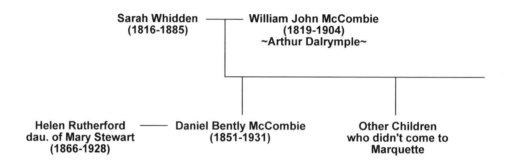

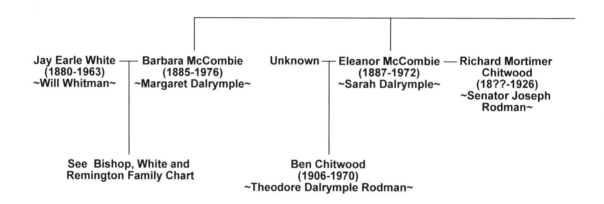

The McCombie, Stewart, and Zryd Families

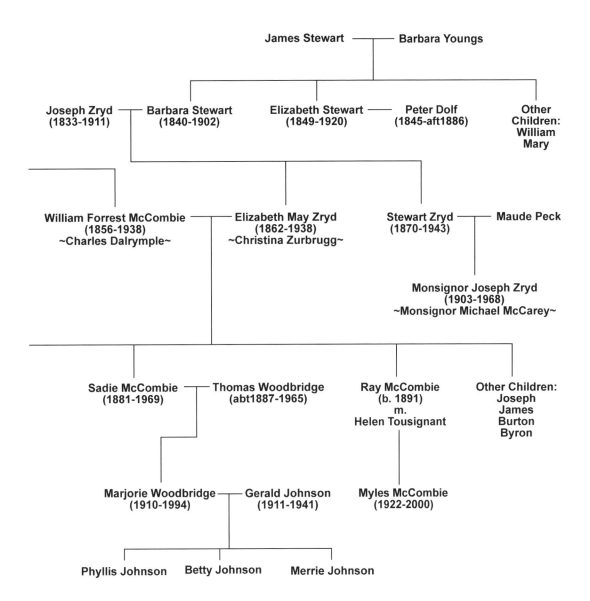

MARQUETTE PIONEER FAMILY TREES

Family Trees only include people mentioned in the text

THE PETER WHITE FAMILY

Dr. Stephen White
m. Harriete Tubbs
    Mary White
    m. Thomas Call of Green Bay
        Charles H. Call
        m. Bessie Kennedy (see Kennedy tree below)
    Peter White
    m. Ellen Hewitt
        Frances White
        m. George Shiras III
            Ellen K. Shiras
            m. Frank Russell Sr.
                Frank Russell Jr.
            George Shiras IV
        Mary White
        m. A.O. Jopling
            Frances Q. Jopling
            m. Maxwell Kennedy Reynolds
                Max Reynolds Jr.
                m. Phyllis Miller
                Alfred Owen Reynolds
                m. Anne Rauch
                Ann Maxwell Reynolds
                m. Lincoln Frazier
                    Peter White Frazier
                    m. Peggy Kalus

THE KENNEDY FAMILY

Robert Kennedy
m. Charlotte Hambright
    Lillie Kennedy
    m. George Shiras II
        George Shiras III (see Peter White family)
        Winfield Shiras
    Bessie Kennedy
    m. Charles H. Call
        Jennie Call
        m. Henry S. Pickands (see Pickands family)
    Sarah Kennedy
    m. Frank B. Spear
        Frank B. Spear II
        m. Rachel Reeve
        Phil Spear
        m. Mary Northrup
            George Spear
    Jean Maxwell Kennedy
    m. Josiah G. Reynolds
        Maxwell Kennedy Reynolds
        m. Frances Q. Jopling (see Peter White Family)
        Alice Reynolds
        m. Jay M. Pickands (see Outhwaite, Pickands, and Morse Families)

THE BREITUNG FAMILY

Edward Breitung
m. Mary
    Edward N. Breitung
    m. Charlotte Graveraet Kaufman (see Graveraet/Kaufman Family)
        Juliet Breitung
        m. Max Kleist
        m. Herbert Richter
        m. Howard Merritt

THE GRAVERAET/KAUFMAN FAMILY

Henry Graveraet
m. Charlotte Livingstone
Robert Graveraet
m. Lucretia
Juliet Graveraet
m. Samuel Kaufman Sr.
> Samuel Kaufman Jr.
> Nathaniel Kaufman
> m. Mrs. Mary Breitung
> Marion Kaufman
> m. Dr. Edward Hudson
> Charlotte Graveraet Kaufman
> m. Edward N. Breitung (see Breitung Family)
> Bernard Kaufman
> Daniel Kaufman
> Louis G. Kaufman
> m. Marie Young
>> Otto Young Kaufman
>> Joan Kaufman
>> m. George Drexel Biddle
>>> Daisy Laura Biddle
>>> Lou Ann Biddle
>>> Drexel Biddle
>> m. Mr. Polk (Joan divorced then remarried him)
>> m. Mr. Winterstien
>> m. W.F. Ladd Jr.
>> m. Jack Martin

THE PICKANDS & MAYNARD FAMILY

Anna Pickands (sister of Colonel James A. Pickands)
m. William Goodwin
> Helen Goodwin
> m. Alfred Foote Maynard (son of Matthew and Mary Maynard)
>> James Pickands Maynard

THE LONGYEAR FAMILY

John Munro Longyear
m. Mary Beecher
    John Longyear
    Howard Longyear
    Abby Beecher Longyear
    m. Alton T. Roberts
        Mary Roberts
        m. John Lautner Jr.
    Helen Longyear
    m. Carroll Paul

THE SCHAFFER FAMILY

Charles Schaffer
m. Julia Belknap
    Onota Schaffer
    m. Otto Koch
        Charles Koch
        Mary Koch
        m. Mr. Paull
        Julia Koch
        m. Munro Longyear Tibbitts (see Burrall Family)

THE BURRALL FAMILY

Fannie Beecher (sister of Mary Beecher Longyear)
m. George Burrall
    Harrison Dewitt Burrall
    Fred Burrall
    Grace Burrall
        m. Mr. Tibbitts
            Munro Longyear Tibbitts
            m. Julia Koch (see Schaffer family)

THE OUTHWAITE, PICKANDS, & MORSE FAMILIES

John Outhwaite
m. Anne Hodgson
    Mary Outhwaite
    m. Jay Morse
m. Martha Williams Peet
    John Peet Outhwaite
    Joseph Husband Outhwaite
    Caroline Martha Outhwaite
    m. Colonel James Pickands
        Joseph Pickands
        Jay M. Pickands
        m. Alice Reynolds (see Kennedy family)
        Henry S. Pickands
        m. Jennie Call (see Kennedy Family)

Note: Colonel James Pickands' second wife, Seville Hanna, would upon his death become Jay Morse's second wife. Pickands and Morse then were not only brother-in-laws but later married to the same woman.

THE MATHER FAMILY

Samuel Livingston Mather
m. Georgiana Woolson (sister of Constance Fenimore Woolson)
    Samuel Mather
    Henry Mather
    m. Mary Hewitt (sister of Ellen Hewitt, wife of Peter White)
        Elizabeth Mather
        m. James Jopling (brother of A.O. Jopling – see White family)
            Richard Mather Jopling
m. Elizabeth Gwinn
    William Gwinn Mather

ADDITIONAL READING

Baraga, Frederic. *The Diary of Bishop Frederic Baraga*. Detroit, MI: Wayne State University Press, 2001.

Bird, Dorothy Maywood. *Granite Harbor*. 1944. Marquette, MI: Peter White Public Library, 1987.

Bohnak, Karl. *So Cold a Sky: Upper Michigan Weather Stories*. Negaunee, MI: Cold Sky Publishing, 2006.

Bowman, James Cloyd. *Mystery Mountain*. Park Ridge, IL: Albert Whitman & Co., 1945.

Bradley-Holliday, Valerie. *Northern Roots: African Descended Pioneers in the Upper Peninsula of Michigan*. Bloomington, IN: Xlibris, 2009.

Case, John. *The Longyear Legacy: Land, Timber, Minerals*. Marquette: J.M. Longyear Heirs, 1998.

Cleveland, Clifford S. (David Goldsmith). *The Mystery of Kawbawgam's Grave*. Marquette, MI: Clifford S. Cleveland, 1979.

Dillman, Chris Shanley. *Finding My Light*. Baltimore, MD: PublishAmerica, 2004.

Dobson, Robert D. *The Plank Road and the First Railroad: From Marquette, Michigan to Negaunee & Ishpeming*. Negaunee, MI: Dobson Publications, 2007.

Downs, Gabriel N. and Michael C. Downs. *Marquette: Images of America*. Charleston, SC: Arcadia, 1999.

Eckert, Kathryn Bishop. *The Sandstone Architecture of the Lake Superior Region*. Detroit, MI: Wayne State University Press, 2000.

Hansen, Joan. *Anatomy of "Anatomy": The Making of a Movie*. Marquette, MI: Joan Hansen, 1997.

Havighurst, Walter. *Vein of Iron: The Pickands Mather Story*. Cleveland, OH: The World Publishing Co., 1958.

Henry, Ragene. *An Enduring Christmas (Marquette, Michigan, 1850)*. Marquette, MI: Chickadee Press, 1999.

Henry, Ragene. *The Time of the Shining Rocks*. Marquette, MI: Chickadee Press, 1999.

Hilton, Miriam. *Northern Michigan University: The First 75 Years*. Marquette, MI: Northern Michigan University Press, 1975.

Johnson, Angela. *Seasons of Faith: A Walk Through the History of the Roman Catholic Diocese of Marquette 1900-2000*. Marquette, MI: The Roman Catholic Diocese of Marquette, 2006.

Jones, Rowena. *Sculptured in Stone: The History of the First United Methodist Church 1851-1951 Marquette, Michigan.* Marquette, MI: Lake Superior Press, 2001.

Jopling, Richard Mather. *Prose and Verse by Richard Mather Jopling.* New York: The Knickerbocker Press, 1919.

Kidder, Homer. *Ojibwa Narratives of Charles and Charlotte Kawbawgam and Jacques LePique, 1893-1895.* Detroit, MI: Wayne State University Press, 1994.

Lambert, Bernard J. *Shepherd of the Wilderness: A Biography of Bishop Frederic Baraga.* 1967. L'Anse, MI: Bernard Lambert, 1974.

Lill, Ruth Alden Clark. *Twenties that Didn't Roar: Growing Up in Marquette.* Ishpeming, MI: Globe Printing, 1985.

Longtine, Sonny. *Courage Burning.* Marquette, MI: Sunnyside Publications, 2006.

Longtine, Sonny and Laverne Chappell. *Marquette Then & Now.* Marquette, MI: North Shore Publications, 1999.

Newton, Stanley D. *Paul Bunyan of the Great Lakes.* AuTrain, MI: Avery Color Studios, 1992.

Rankin, Carroll Watson. *Dandelion Cottage.* 1904. Marquette, MI: John M. Longyear Research Library, 1982.

Rezek, Rev. Antoine Ivan. *History of the Diocese of Sault Ste. Marie and Marquette.* 2 Vols. 1907. Marquette, MI: The Roman Catholic Diocese of Marquette, 2006.

Rydholm, C. Fred. *Superior Heartland: A Backwoods History.* 2 vols. 1989. Marquette, MI: C. Fred Rydholm, 1999.

Saint Michael's Church, Marquette, Michigan. South Hackensack, N.J.: Custombook, 1968.

Smolens, John. *Cold.* New York: Three Rivers Press, 2003.

Steele, Clyde. *It Seems Like Yesterday.* Marquette, MI: Clyde Steele, 1985.

Stone, Frank. *Philo Marshall Everett: Father of Michigan's Iron Industry and the Founder of the City of Marquette.* Gateway Press, 1997.

Tibbits, Julia K. *Let's Go Around the Island.* J.K. Tibbits, 1992.

Touring Marquette. Avery Studios, 2004.

Traver, Robert (John Voelker). *Anatomy of a Murder.* New York: Dell, 1958.

Traver, Robert (John Voelker). *Laughing Whitefish.* New York: McGraw-Hill, 1965.

Waring, Betty A. *Birch, Michigan: Gold'n Memories.* Marquette, MI: Johnson Printing, 1991.

Waring, Betty A. *The Story of Lake Independence: Big Bay, Michigan.* Marquette, MI: Johnson Printing, 1984.

Williams, Ralph D. *The Honorable Peter White: A Biographical Sketch of the Lake Superior Iron Country*. 1905. Cleveland, OH: Freshwater Press, 1986.

Wilson, Holly. *Caroline, the Unconquered*. New York, NY: Julian Messner, 1956.

Wilson, Holly. *Deborah Todd*. New York, NY: Julian Messner, 1955.

Wilson, Holly. *The Hundred Steps*. New York, NY: Julian Messner, 1958.

Wilson, Holly. *Snowbound in Hidden Valley*. New York, NY: Julian Messner, 1957.

Wood, Ike. *One Hundred Years at Hard Labor: A History of Marquette State Prison*. Au Train, MI: KA-Ed Publishing, 1985.

Woolson, Constance Fenimore. *Anne*. 1882. Whitefish, MT: Kessinger Publishing, 2007.

PHOTO CREDITS

All photographs are used or were taken courtesy of the following individuals or organizations. They are used by permission, all rights reserved.

Where more than one photograph appears on a page, photographs are designated by location (top, bottom, center, or corner). If more than one photograph is on a page without location designation, then all photographs on that page are credited to that individual or organization.

Betinis, Emily—140

Cass, James Pickands—175 (bottom)

Ferris State University Archives—200 (bottom)

Goldsmith, Rachel—241

Gonyea, Ann—99 (top), 163, 165, 231, 235 (four corners), 237 (top), 251 (bottom)

Ishpeming Historical Society—64, 119

Longtine, Sonny—3, 14, 16 (bottom), 21, 39, 40, 42, 43 (top), 44, 48, 50, 53, 60, 62, 71, 73, 79, 81, 83, 85, 91, 98, 105, 118 (top), 132, 133, 136, 139, 151 (center & bottom), 180, 187, 196, 213, 221, 223, 296, 303, 317, 319, 320, 334, 343 (top), 367

Mark Twain House and Museum—167 (top)

Marquette County History Museum—37 (top), 51, 52, 61, 69, 112, 117, 131, 147 (bottom), 153, 158, 173 (top), 177, 178, 179 (bottom), 182, 183, 190 (bottom), 192, 193 (top), 195, 209 (bottom), 250, 256, 257, 262, 266, 273, 274, 293, 307, 313, 323, 335, 336, 361

Merchant, Sadie E. (White Family Collection)—xxxii, 43 (bottom), 258, 287, 340, 341

Michigamme Historical Society—118 (bottom)

Peter White Public Library—129, 154 (bottom)

Rushton, Nanette—186, 203

Shusta, Rebecca—242

Superior View (Jack Deo)—9, 16 (top), 17, 27, 31, 55, 63, 66, 70, 77, 80, 100, 106, 120, 121, 127, 143, 146, 149 (bottom), 152, 161, 181, 194 (bottom), 208 (top), 227, 232, 239 (bottom), 246 (bottom left & right), 264, 265, 271, 272, 294, 308 (center), 311 (top), 326, 337 (top), 357, 362, 363, 365

Tichelaar, Nancy (White Family Collection)—xxxiv, xxxviii, 108 (bottom), 114, 275 (bottom), 276 (center), 281, 282, 283, 284, 288, 292, 305, 311 (bottom), 343 (bottom), 354

Tichelaar, Richard—89

Tichelaar, Tyler—xxv, xxvi, xxxi, xxxiii, xl, 5, 7, 23, 24, 26, 29, 30, 37 (bottom), 57, 59, 74, 75, 78, 88, 94, 95, 96, 97, 99 (bottom), 102, 103, 104, 108 (top), 109, 110, 122, 124, 126, 134, 135, 138, 145, 147 (top), 148, 149 (top), 150, 151 (top), 154 (top), 157, 159, 160, 167 (center & bottom), 170, 172, 173 (bottom), 174, 175 (top), 179 (top), 185, 188, 189, 190 (top), 191, 193 (bottom), 194 (top), 197, 198, 199, 200 (top & center), 201, 202, 205, 206, 207, 208 (bottom), 209 (top), 210, 211, 212, 214, 216, 217, 222, 225, 226, 230, 233, 235 (center), 236, 237 (bottom), 238, 239 (top), 244, 245, 246 (top), 247, 248, 249, 251 (top), 252, 259, 269, 270, 275 (top), 276 (top & bottom), 285, 298, 300, 301, 302, 308 (top & bottom), 309, 321, 325, 327, 328, 332, 337 (bottom), 339, 350

Utah State Historical Society—xxx

INDEX

Characters from my novels are indicated with the titles of the books in which they appear as follows:

A

A&P, 68
Abbot and Costello, 125
Ablewhite, Bishop, 116-17, 194
Abolition, xxviii, 134
Adams, Bertha, 146
Adams, Bob, 191
Adams, Camilla, 191
Adams, Harriet, 325
Adams, Sidney, 145-46, 160, 212, 325
Adams, Will, 145-46
African Americans, xxxviii, xlii, 18
Alaska, 170, 190-91, 197, 361
Albinson, Dewey, 108-9
Alcott, Louisa May, 27
Alexander, Allison, 237, 248
Alexander, Daniel, (Dano) 237, 248, 251
Alexander, Larry, xvii, 300-302
Alexander, Max, 301-2
Alger County, 150, 187, 210, 211
Ali, Mohammed, 267
Alibi, The, 75
Allen, EphraimW., 157, 271
Allen, Hugh, 157, 183
Alpine Pancake House, 342
Altamont Street, 48, 213-14
Ameen, Bobby, 172
Amos and Andy, 314
Anatomy of "Anatomy", 64
Anatomy of a Murder (book), 63, 118, 124, 125, 311, 365
Anatomy of a Murder (film), 63, 66, 118, 268, 270, 365, 367, 368
"...And Ladies of the Club", 332
Andrews, Julie, 139
Andrews, Maureen, 301
Angeli's, 56, 335, 336
Angelou, Maya, 125
Anne's Tablet, 188-89
Anthony, Mary (Molby), xl, 369

Apostle, James, 199
Apostle, Louie, 199
Apostle, Peter, 199
Apostles Restaurant, 199
April Fool's Day, 292
Arch Street, 141, 144, 149, 162, 177, 181, 182, 186, 190, 193-205, 212, 215
Arden, Eve, 63, 365
Arger, Nick, 323
Argeropoulos, John, 159
Argeropoulos, Joyce, see Matthews, Joyce (Argeropoulos)
Argeropoulos, Mary, 159
Argeropoulos, Mike, 159
Argeropoulos, Mrs., 203
Armstrong, Louis, 125
Arquette, Courtney Cox, 213
Arquette, David, 213
Art on the Rocks, 226, 251
Astaire, Fred, 266
Austen, Jane, 129, 353

B

Bacon, Martha, 51, 52, 122
Bailey, Judy, 294
Baldwin, Tom, 267
Ball, Daniel, 170
Ball, Emma (Everett), 358
Banks, xx, 35, 73, 77-82, 115, 127, 151, 153, 168, 174, 187, 193, 198, 203, 210, 215, 336, 312, 359, 360, 362, 364, 365, 367
Baptists, xxxv, 30, 35, 65, 102, 113, 131-32, 135, 186, 290, 305, 306, 317, 366
Baraga Avenue, 67, 69, 105, 127, 209
Baraga, Bishop Frederic, 35, 37-38, 41-46, 125, 177, 304, 357, 358, 359, 366
Barkow, Ed, 343
Barney Exchange Hotel, 17
Barney, Mrs. Samuel, 358
Barnes-Hecker Mining Disaster, xl

TYLER R. TICHELAAR'S NOVELS

The following novels by Tyler R. Tichelaar are referenced in *My Marquette* and are available in local and online bookstores and at:

IRON PIONEERS:
THE MARQUETTE TRILOGY: BOOK ONE

When iron ore is discovered in Michigan's Upper Peninsula in the 1840s, newlyweds Gerald Henning and his beautiful socialite wife Clara travel from Boston to the little village of Marquette on the shores of Lake Superior. They and their companions, Irish and German immigrants, French Canadians, and fellow New Englanders face blizzards and near starvation, devastating fires and financial hardships. Yet these iron pioneers persevere until their wilderness village becomes integral to the Union cause in the Civil War and then a prosperous modern city. Meticulously researched, warmly written, and spanning half a century, *Iron Pioneers* is a testament to the spirit that forged America.

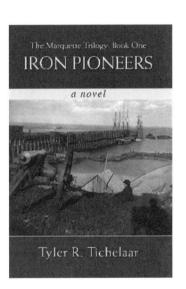

THE QUEEN CITY
THE MARQUETTE TRILOGY: BOOK TWO

During the first half of the twentieth century, Marquette grows into the Queen City of the North. Here is the tale of a small town undergoing change as its horses are replaced by streetcars and automobiles, and its pioneers are replaced by new generations who prosper despite two World Wars and the Great Depression. Margaret Dalrymple finds her Scottish prince, though he is neither Scottish nor a prince. Molly Bergmann becomes an inspiration to her grandchildren. Jacob Whitman's children engage in a family feud. The Queen City's residents marry, divorce, have children, die, break their hearts, go to war, gossip, blackmail, raise families, move away, and then return to Marquette. And always, always they are in love with the haunting land that is their home.

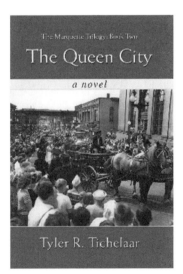

SUPERIOR HERITAGE
THE MARQUETTE TRILOGY: BOOK THREE

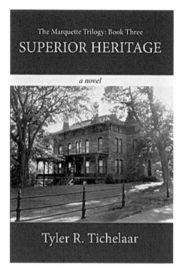

The Marquette Trilogy comes to a satisfying conclusion as it brings together characters and plots from the earlier novels and culminates with Marquette's sesquicentennial celebrations in 1999. What happened to Madeleine Henning is finally revealed as secrets from the past shed light upon the present. Marquette's residents struggle with a difficult local economy, yet remain optimistic for the future. The novel's main character, John Vandelaare, is descended from all the early Marquette families in *Iron Pioneers* and *The Queen City*. While he cherishes his family's past, he questions whether he should remain in his hometown. Then an event happens that will change his life forever.

NARROW LIVES

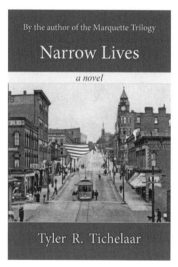

Narrow Lives is the story of those whose lives were affected by Lysander Blackmore, the sinister banker first introduced to readers in *The Queen City*. It is a novel that stands alone, yet readers of *The Marquette Trilogy* will be reacquainted with some familiar characters. Written as a collection of connected short stories, each told in first person by a different character, *Narrow Lives* depicts the influence one person has, even in death, upon others, and it explores the prisons of grief, loneliness, and fear self-created when people doubt their own worthiness.

THE ONLY THING THAT LASTS

The story of Robert O'Neill, the famous novelist introduced in *The Marquette Trilogy*. As a young boy during World War I, Robert is forced to leave his South Carolina home to live in Marquette with his grandmother and aunt. He finds there a cold climate, but many warmhearted friends. An old-fashioned story that follows Robert's growth from childhood to successful writer and husband, the novel is written as Robert O'Neill's autobiography, his final gift to Marquette by memorializing the town of his youth.

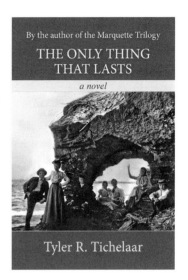

SPIRIT OF THE NORTH
(Coming soon!)

Perhaps Tyler R. Tichelaar's finest novel. Readers of *The Marquette Trilogy* will find out more about the past of *Iron Pioneers* lumberjack Ben and the truth behind the ghost story of Annabella Stonegate told by Will Whitman in *The Queen City*. The novel's heroines, Barbara and Adele Traugott, travel to Marquette in 1873 to live with their uncle, only to find he is deceased. Penniless, they are forced to survive a terrible winter in their uncle's remote wilderness cabin. Through their difficulties they find love, heartache, and ultimately, the miracle of their own being.

For more information, visit:
www.MarquetteFiction.com.